MICHELIN

500 Charming Hotels and Inns in Germany

CONTENTS

THE REGIONS OF GERMANY

HOW TO USE THIS GUIDE

Introduction

Michelin Charming Hotels and Inns features a selection of 500 establishments from around Germany, all with a certain special something. Our inspectors made their usual on-the-spot visits and picked out the best of what they found: hotels and inns with real individual charm which won't break the bank. None of the double rooms cost more than 150 € per night, and most of the establishments offer double rooms for 100 € or less. To make it even easier to choose, we've marked each hotel or inn with a symbol, to highlight the memorable little extra that we really enjoyed: it could be anything from a particularly beautiful garden or a stunning view of the countryside to the smell of home-made cakes and pastries for breakfast.

How to use the Guide

This guide is divided into twelve chapters, each of which covers one or more of the regions – or Bundesländer – of Germany. Each chapter is divided into towns and where there is more than one hotel or inn listed in the town, the establishments are set out in alphabetical order.

Within the chapters, the establishments are numbered in ascending order. The establishment's entry number relates to the map at the beginning of the chapter: the numbered dots on this map show the position of the establishment

At the front of this Guide, on the preceding page, you'll find a map of Germany, divided into twelve regions which correspond to the twelve chapters of the Guide.

And each of the twelve sections begins with a photo and a short introduction to the region, focusing on some of the local highlights to give you a feeling for the area.

Accommodation

The addresses in this guide all have one thing in common: a touch of charm in their character, warmth, authenticity or picturesque setting. But that's where the similarities end. Each establishment has a unique character of its own: you could find yourself in a medieval castle, within the venerable walls of a converted monastery, down on the farm or in a little manor house in the depths of the countryside.

Many of the hotels have a restaurant and some offer half-board rates. We indicate this in the details for the establishment.

If you're going to arrive late, don't forget to let your hosts know in good time, so that they know to hold your reservation.

The information provided by the hotels is reproduced in good faith should be considered as an indication only. Despite our best efforts, it is always possible that some of the information is not complete or accurate. Michelin Travel Publications cannot be held responsible for any such changes.

Gastronomy

If a hotel or inn has its own restaurant or dining room, we always indicate this in our entry. At the end of this Guide is a special index for "Wining and Dining breaks", listing all of the establishments whose cooking we found particularly good.

Prices

The prices listed in this Guide include taxes and service and refer to high-season rates. They were supplied to us by the proprietors of the hotels in 2004 for the year 2005 and may thus be liable to change during the year. Such prices are not contractual and Michelin Travel Publications may under no circumstances be held responsible for any possible changes or inconsistencies.

Rooms: The prices given are the highest and lowest rates for a double room in high season. Always make sure you have written confirmation of the price of your room when you make your reservation.

Out of season, many establishments offer special deals; again, it's best to ask when making the reservation. If weekend or short break packages are regularly on offer, we indicate this in the text.

Breakfast: As a rule, breakfast is included in the price of the room. Whenever this is not the case, we have indicated the price of breakfast per person.

Reservations

In a few cases you may be required to give a deposit to confirm your reservation.

Credit Cards

AE ⓓ American Express, Diner's Club
MC VISA Mastercard, Visa,
JCB Japan Credit Bureau

Access and Facilities

For each establishment we give details of:

- How to get there from the nearest town
- Facilities including swimming pool, sauna, tennis court, children's games and an indication of whether dogs are allowed.
- Handicapped access where special adaptations or arrangements have been made.
- A few tips on things to see and do nearby: tourist sites, cultural highlights and exploring the countryside and the natural environment.

Special addresses

Low-priced addresses offering rooms for under 70 € are indicated with a symbol. See index p. 538.

Wining and dining breaks lists all the establishments offering particularly good cuisine. See index p. 541.

Activity breaks offer at least one sporting activity (for example, a gym, a tennis court, a nearby golf course, facilities for horse-riding or guided hikes). See index p. 544.

Index

Two listings, both in alphabetical order, give:

- All of the selected addresses
- All of the towns with at least one establishment

Write to us!

We have aimed to make this Guide practical and readable and hope that it will accompany you on your holidays and short breaks: it's written for you and you can help to make the next edition even better. Please send us any comments or criticisms you may have, as well as any recommendations for places that you think should be in the Guide. At the end of the Guide, you'll find a questionnaire: we would be very grateful if you would take the time to complete it and return it to us.

We look forward to hearing from you!

Key to the symbols used in this Guide:

2 The number of the hotel or inn: this appears in the entry and on the map of the region

€€: Hotels and inns offering a double room for under 70 €.

We most liked What we particularly liked about the hotel or inn: the highlight that's not to be missed!

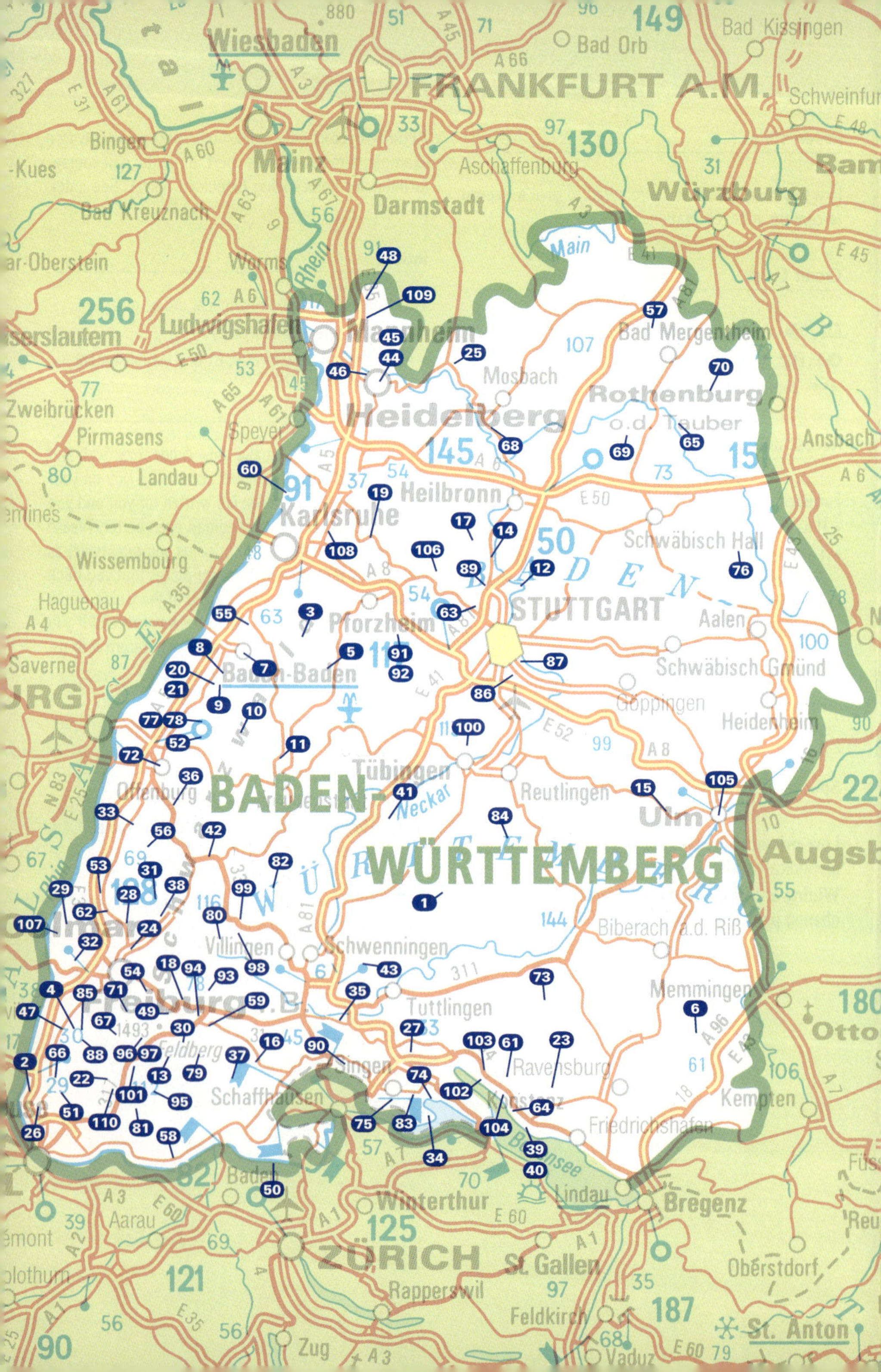

BADEN-WÜRTTEMBERG
STUTTGART
FRANKFURT A.M.
Wiesbaden
Mainz
Darmstadt
Aschaffenburg
Würzburg
Bad Kissingen
Bad Orb
Schweinfurt
Bingen
Bad Kreuznach
Worms
Ludwigshafen
Mannheim
Heidelberg
Mosbach
Bad Mergentheim
Rothenburg o.d. Tauber
Ansbach
Speyer
Zweibrücken
Pirmasens
Landau
Heilbronn
Karlsruhe
Schwäbisch Hall
Wissembourg
Haguenau
Saverne
Pforzheim
Baden-Baden
Aalen
Schwäbisch Gmünd
Göppingen
Heidenheim
Tübingen
Reutlingen
Ulm
Offenburg
Neckar
Biberach a.d. Riß
Villingen
Schwenningen
Tuttlingen
Memmingen
Freiburg i.B.
Feldberg
Singen
Schaffhausen
Ravensburg
Konstanz
Kempten
Friedrichshafen
Bodensee
Lindau
Bregenz
Winterthur
Aarau
ZÜRICH
St. Gallen
Oberstdorf
Rapperswil
Feldkirch
Vaduz
Zug
St. Anton
Main
Rhein

Baden-Württemberg

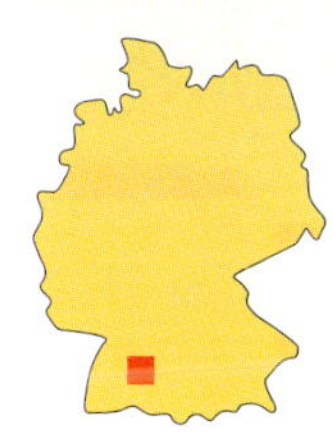

Historic roots run deep in the sunny southwest, which borders France and Switzerland, but has kept rich traditions of culture and dialect which are all its own. Right up to 1918, busy Stuttgart was a royal capital, and neighbouring Baden was once ruled from the palace in Karlsruhe: both cities now display their treasures in an array of fine museums. Badeners and Swabians, as Württembergers are known, get along fine, but while Swabians are always said to be thrifty and industrious, Badeners are considered a laid-back lot. Could it be something to do with the almost Mediterranean climate of the Rhine Valley and Lake Constance? Or is it the vineyards along the lower slopes of the Black Forest? Whatever the reason, the whole region delights in its fine wines and a reputation for some of Germany's best cuisine. The woods and valleys of the Black Forest are world-famous, but the area also boasts the uplands of the Swabian Alb. Castles there are aplenty, from robber barons' ruins to Baroque chateaux, the greatest of them all enthroned above the student city of Heidelberg.

1 LINDE

Mathias Michels

Untere Vorstadt 1
72458 Albstadt-Ebingen
Tel. (07431) 13 41 40
Fax (07431) 13414300
info@hotel-linde-albstadt.de – www.hotel-linde-albstadt.de

Open all year • 39 rooms, one with disabled access and 30 non-smoking • Restaurant with terrace (closed Sun): Gourmet restauarant menu 42-62€, Lindenstüble menu 11.50-15€; half board 26€ • Car park dogs allowed

135/160 €, Breakfast included (WE: 99/135 €)

AE VISA MC

The slippers provided to help you feel completely at home

Who would believe that this imposing timber-framed house on the edge of the traffic-free centre is a creation of the 21st century? The reason is that its shapes and features mirror the style of its predecessor on this site. Inside you'll find every contemporary comfort. The bedrooms are smartly furnished, the bathrooms lavishly appointed. The elegant restaurant with its floor of bog oak makes a splendid impression, thanks to its sophisticated decor as well as its silver plate. By contrast, the "Lindenstüble" is more rustic in style. A nightcap in the relaxed atmosphere of the hotel bar is a good way of ending your day.

Sights nearby: Raichberg (10km north); eco-friendly open-air baths in Albstadt-Tailfingen (5km north)

Access: From Albstadt-Ebingen follow signs to Albstadt-Tailfingen and turn left into the restricted traffic zone on the Bleichestraße

2 LANDGASTHOF SCHWANEN

Peter Fräulin

Rheinstr. 50
79415 Bad Bellingen
Tel. (07635) 81 18 11
Fax (07635) 811888
hotel@schwanen-bad-bellingen.de – www.schwanen-bad-bellingen.de

Closed 8-31 Jan • 26 rooms, including 18 with balcony, 2 with disabled access • Restaurant with terrace (closed Tue, midday Wed): set meals 12.50-33€; half board 14.50€ • Parking; dogs allowed • Gym, solarium, table tennis

79/91 €, Breakfast included

VISA MC

A visit to the spa in Bad Bellingen

The original building by the castle park dates from 1717, and the wine served in the inn is still kept here in the original vaulted cellars. The guesthouse is above the town, its name "Rhine View" an accurate description; to the west is a vast panorama extending over the Rhine plain to the distant blue line of the Vosges mountains. Accommodation is in country-style holiday apartments with kitchenettes - they can also be used by hotel residents. On the slopes above, there are strolls or longer walks to be enjoyed among the vineyards.

Sights nearby: Upper Rhine regional museum, Holzen stork sanctuary (7km southeast), Schloss Bürgeln (15km east)

Access: By Rathaus in town centre

3 **LAMM**
Karl Schwemmle

Mönchstr. 31
76332 Bad Herrenalb-Rotensol
Tel. (07083) 9 24 40
Fax (07083) 924444 – www.lamm-rotensol.de

Closed 7-11 February • 28 rooms, 25 with balcony, 3 with air-conditioning, 2 with disabled access and 4 non-smoking rooms • Café-restaurant with terrace (closed Mon but open to residents): lunch menu 18-28.80€, evening menu 28.80-52€; half board 16.50€ • Garden, car park; dogs allowed • Bicycle hire, organised hikes, cooking courses, wine courses and wine and schnapps tastings

82/115 €, Breakfast included
AE JCB VISA MC

The home-made fruit brandies - delicious!

Run for many years by the same family, this well-established hotel is located in Rotensol, just beneath the spa town of Bad Herrenalb. It welcomes its guests with stylishly furnished rooms, most of them with a small sitting area and balcony. Nature lovers will want to make tracks - on one of the extensive walks in the nearby countryside, while for some invigorating cultural life, Baden-Baden and Karlsruhe are within easy reach. And if it's culinary delights you're after, look no further than the rustic "Bauernstube" for solid cuisine with real local character.

Sights nearby: Frauenalb Monastery ruins (8km north); Gersbach Old Town (16km southwest)

Access: North of Bad Herrenalb; turn off towards Rotensol/Neusatz just as you enter the town

4 ZUM STORCHEN

Fritz Helfesrieder

Felix- und Nabor-Str. 2
79189 Bad Krozingen-Schmidhofen
Tel. (07633) 53 29
Fax (07633) 7019

Closed 2 weeks late Feb, 2 weeks early Sep • 3 rooms, all with balcony • Restaurant with terrace (closed Mon, Tue): set lunch from 28€, set dinner 44-54€ • Garden, parking; dogs allowed

70 €, Breakfast included
Credit cards not accepted

Friendly, personal service

You can tell just by looking at this dear little building with its hipped roof and projecting oriel window that you are going to get a warm welcome. A vine clambers all over the façade, cladding it in different colours with the changing of the seasons. The immaculately kept rooms furnished in natural wood have all the necessary facilities, but the place's great attraction is its sophisticated cuisine, served to you in elegant and intimate dining rooms with wood floors and panelling and a cosy countrified atmosphere.

Sights nearby: Vita Classica thermal spa in Bad Krozingen (3.5km northwest), St.Trudpert Abbey (10km southeast)

Access: 3.5km southwest of Bad Krozingen towards Staufen

5 BÄREN

Familie Mokni

Kurplatz 4
75323 Bad Wildbad im Schwarzwald
Tel. (07081) 30 10
Fax (07081) 301166 – www.hotelbaeren-badwildbad.de

Open all year • 44 rooms, including 1 with disabled access and 20 non-smoking • Cafe-restaurant with terrace: set meals 29-36€; half board 24€ • Dogs allowed in hotel, not in restaurant

108/144 €, Breakfast included
Credit cards not accepted

The mountain railway opposite, which whisks you up from the town into a hill-walker's paradise in only a few minutes

In 1856, when Bad Wildbad was at the peak of its international fame as a spa town, none other than the composer Rossini was a guest at the "Bear". Times have changed and Wildbad with them, but there are plenty of reminders of a glorious past, among them this traditional establishment in the pedestrianised town centre. The elegant rooms have individual decor, some of them featuring period furnishings and plaster ceilings. Guests eat well too, either in the Rossini Salon or on the terrace cafe which serves home-made cakes.

Sights nearby: Palais Thermal, Schloss Neuenbürg (12km north)

Access: Exit 43 on A 8, then by B 294

6 ADLER

Bernd Gut

Schlossstr. 8
88410 Bad Wurzach
Tel. (07564) 9 30 30
Fax (07564) 930340 – www.hotel-adler-bad-wurzach.de

Closed 1st week Jan, 3rd and 4th week Aug • 18 rooms, including 16 non-smoking, 2 with balcony • Restaurant with terrace (closed Mon): set meal 15-24.50€; half board 15€ • Parking; dogs allowed

68/75 €, Breakfast included
AE VISA MC

Experiencing the moorland, woods and tarns of the Wurzacher Ried

There's nothing spectacular about this establishment in the middle of Bad Wurzach, the oldest mud-cure spa in Baden-Württemberg. Guests are received politely without any fuss. The building with its unobtrusive façade is centrally located close to the town hall but enjoys peace and quiet. The rooms have pale oak furnishings and the restaurant in contemporary country-house style is almost plain in appearance. Nevertheless, you will be well looked after by the owners, who provide good service and tasty cooking, their success perhaps due to concentration on essentials.

Sights nearby: Wolfegg Automobile Museum (14km southwest), Illerbeuern Farm Museum (20km east)

Access: Exit 9 or 11 on A 96

7 AM MARKT

Doris Jung, Andrea Bogner-Schindler

€€ Marktplatz 18
76530 Baden-Baden
Tel. (07221) 2 70 40
Fax (07221) 270444 – www.hotel-am-markt-baden.de

Open all year • 23 rooms, including 9 with showers on landing • Parking; dogs allowed

62/80 €, Breakfast included
AE D VISA MC

Breakfast outside overlooking the market square

This is the place for an enjoyable and tranquil stay in Baden-Baden's Old Town. Once a hostel for Jesuit monks, the old townhouse of 1716 stands in the shadow of the collegiate church, in an area where traffic is kept well in check. The bedrooms are bright and cheerful, though some have showers on the landing. A holiday apartment is available for stays of five days or more. It's only a few minutes on foot to the Friedrich Spa and Caracalla Baths, or you can stroll through the crooked lanes to the main town centre and on to the Kurpark.

Sights nearby: Collegiate church, "Im Baldreit" municipal museum, Festspielhaus

Access: In Baden-Baden follow blue hotel route signs indicating "Thermen-Gaggenau"

8 **REBENHOF**
Martin Ziegler

Weinstr. 58
76534 Baden-Baden-Neuweier
Tel. (07223) 9 63 10
Fax (07223) 963131 – www.hotel-rebenhof.de

Open all year • 18 rooms, 12 with balcony, 4 non-smoking • Restaurant with terrace (closed Sun, midday Mon): set lunch 16-25€, set dinner 20-27.50€; half board 19€ • Garden, parking; dogs allowed

88/118 €, Breakfast included
AE VISA MC

A stroll through the vineyards

A room with a view - and what a view! The grand panorama extends in one direction over the Rhine plain, in the other over the vineyards all around. The splendid prospect can also be enjoyed from the restaurant and from the terrace. The establishment makes much of its ecological credentials, and so its gastronomic offerings mostly feature local produce. Bedrooms are furnished in country style or in dark oak.

Sights nearby: Yburg castle ruins (3km north), Black Forest High Road (from Baden-Baden to Freudenstadt)

Access: From B3 via Steinach to Neuweier; in Neuweier turn right by the church towards Eisental

9 ZUM WEINBERG

Anneliese Graf

Umwegerstr. 68
76534 Baden-Baden-Umweg
Tel. (07223) 9 69 70
Fax (07223) 969730 – www.weinberg-umweg.de

Open all year • 11 rooms • Restaurant with terrace (closed Tue and Wed lunchtime): menu 19.80-26€ • Garden, car park; dogs allowed • Sauna

72/85 €, Breakfast included

VISA

The establishment's very own "Stich den Buben" Riesling

On the edge of town where the vineyards begin, this property has been in the ownership of the same family for more than 170 years. The combination of family atmosphere and well-kept rooms may well make you want to extend your stay. The daily newspaper provided at breakfast-time is a nice touch. Between the restaurant and the guesthouse there is an attractive garden. In summer, the outdoor chairs and tables in this leafy setting invite you not only to dine well but also to soak up the peace and tranquillity of the lovely landscape of the surrounding vineyards.

Sights nearby: Yburg castle ruins (5km east), Lichtentaler Allee Baden-Baden (6km northeast)

Access: From B 3 Follow signs to Sinzheim or Steinbach

10 FORSTHAUS AUERHAHN

Familie Zepf

72270 Baiersbronn-Hinterlangenbach
Tel. (07447) 93 40
Fax (07447) 934199 – www.forsthaus-auerhahn.de

Closed mid-Nov to mid-Dec • 30 rooms, including 29 with balcony • Cafe; restaurant with terrace (closed Tue): set lunch 20-30€, set dinner 23-35€; half board 13€ • Children's play room, garden, parking; dogs allowed • Sauna, swimming pool, jacuzzi, wellness facilities, bicycle hire, guided walks and cycle rides, wine tasting

104/146 €, Breakfast included (WE: 136/146 €)
Credit cards not accepted

The dawn chorus

On the edge of the woods, this old forestry building is just the place to immerse yourself in rural life and really relax. After working out with a vigorous walk, cross-country ski run or bike ride, you can recover in the lavishly equipped spa-area, which offers a sauna, massages, and a range of beauty treatments. Anglers may feel the lure of the hotel's own trout stream, while children will adore the red deer in their enclosure. With furnishings in pale natural wood, nearly all the rooms have a balcony, from which your gaze can soar over the enchanting panorama of the Black Forest.

Sights nearby: Mummelsee (6km west, 11/2 hrs on foot), Hauffs Fairytale Museum in Baiersbronn (25km southeast)

Access: In Schönmünzach turn off B 462 towards Hinterlangenbach

11 AILWALDHOF

Dorothea Haist

Ailwald 1
72270 Baiersbronn-Klosterreichenbach
Tel. (07442) 83 60
Fax (07442) 836200
info@ailwaldhof.de – www.ailwaldhof.de

Open all year • 20 rooms, all non-smoking and with balcony • Cafe, restaurant with terrace: set lunch 16-24€, set dinner 24-45€; half board 17€ • Garden, parking; dogs not allowed • Gym, indoor pool, sauna, wellness area, massages, therapeutic exercise, bicycle hire, cookery courses, archery, volleyball, tennis

140/220 €, Breakfast included
Credit cards not accepted

The indoor pool with its fine views

Reached along its own approach road, this property stands amid 12 hectares of woods and meadows. It is a place where guests can enjoy peace and quiet and relax surrounded by unspoiled landscape. But this is no retreat into the desert! Quite the contrary; the stylish rooms furnished in local firwood offer every comfort, and the bathrooms are partly in marble. Named after the original owner of the estate, the "Jakob-Friedrich" restaurant will see you well looked after with a changing menu featuring a variety of international dishes. As well as a carefully chosen wine list, there's a shot or two of home-made Schnapps to sample

Sights nearby: Hauffs Fairytale Museum in Baiersbronn (3km southwest), Freudenstadt (13km south), Hallwangen "Barefoot Park" (12km southeast)

Access: 3km north of Baiersbronn by B 462

12 MÜHLE

Irene Haag

Ostlandstr. 2 (Access via Neckargasse)
71726 Benningen
Tel. (07144) 50 21
Fax (07144) 4166 – www.hotel-muehle-benningen.de

Open all year • 12 rooms, including 1 with balcony • Parking; dogs allowed • Bicycle hire

80/85 €, Breakfast included
AE VISA MC

Stuttgart is in easy reach thanks to the S-Bahn

This building close to the River Neckar dates from before the Thirty Years War, when it was used to house sheep. Its long history is reflected in the venerable timber-framing and stonework of its façade. In 1954 it was converted into a grain mill, but this chapter closed after only 30 years, and today it is a hotel that carries on the old name. The rooms mostly have furnishings in natural wood, though two of them feature brass bedsteads, and one even has a water-bed. The cosily rustic breakfast room with its exposed timbers is also used as a wine-cellar, so you can end your day here as well as starting it.

Sights nearby: Neckarparadies nature reserve, National Schiller Museum in Marbach (2km east), Fairytale garden in park of Schloss Ludwigsburg (7km southwest)

Access: From Exit 14 on A 81 towards Marbach

13 SCHWARZWALDHAUS

Norbert Goos

€€ Am Kurpark 26
79872 Bernau-Innerlehen
Tel. (07675) 3 65
Fax (07675) 1371 – www.sbo.de/schwarzwaldhaus

Closed 11-21 Apr, 24 Oct to 24 Nov • 15 rooms, including 10 with balcony • Restaurant with terrace (closed Thu): set meal 10-15€, main course 6.50-19€; half board 11€ • Children's play room, garden, parking; dogs allowed • Gym, table tennis, table football, bicycle hire, organised walks and longer hikes

56/68 €, Breakfast included

AE VISA MC

The friendly reception by the Goos family

This old farmstead beneath its typical Black Forest roof contains well-kept and comfortably appointed rooms whose rustic character harmonises nicely with the building's location in this delightful landscape. Some of the rooms feature furnishings in natural wood, others have hand-painted country furniture. You dine in the thoroughly authentic ambience of the old stables, where a tiled stove adds to the rustic atmosphere. Outside, the superb countryside offers something to do in every season, from wandering through the upland meadows in summer or breathing in the pure winter air on a cross-country ski run.

Sights nearby: St Blasien monastery church (7km southeast), Schluchsee (20km east)

Access: Turn off B 500 in Häusern towards St Blasien

14 AM MARKT

Dirk Schultz

Kirchstr. 43
74354 Besigheim
Tel. (07143) 80 30 60
Fax (07143) 8030620 – www.besigheim-hotel.de

Closed Easter and Christmas • 18 rooms • Parking; dogs not allowed

70/120 €, Breakfast included

AE DC VISA MC

A stroll through the picturesque lanes and alleyways of Besigheim's Old Town

Tucked away between the rivers Enz and Neckar, the Old Town of Besigheim boasts many an architectural gem. And this hotel, close to the historic town hall and 16th century fountain, is one of them, a delightful timber-framed edifice whose every detail seems to speak of the good old days. Exposed beams and stonework are attractive features in the bedrooms which are furnished in dark wood. A building to the rear houses apartments with kitchenettes.

Sights nearby: Ludwigsburg Baroque palace (14km south), Tripsdrill theme park (14km northwest)

Access: On B 27 between Heilbronn and Bietigheim-Bissingen

15 OCHSEN

Hermann Unsöld

Marktstr. 4
89143 Blaubeuren
Tel. (07344) 96 98 90
Fax (07344) 8430 – www.ochsen-blaubeuren.de

Closed 1-6 Jan • 34 rooms, including 5 with balcony, 2 with air-conditioning and 15 non-smoking • Restaurant (closed Sun eve): set lunch 15-24€, set dinner 18-30€; half board 18€ • Garden, parking; dogs allowed • Solarium, bicycle hire

75/95 €, Breakfast included (WE: 69/81 €)
AE VISA MC

A visit to the Blautopf, the deepest spring in Germany, and the lovely old town of Blaubeuren

Hospitality has been dispensed here since the 16th century, and the lovely timber-framed façade of 1740 gives an indication of the establishment's long past. The bedrooms have solid wood furnishings, and the ones beneath the roof feature exposed beams for extra atmosphere. The "Taubenschlag" - or "Dovecote" - comes complete with bunk beds and is ideal for families. The dining rooms in elegant country style have wood panelling and harmonious decor, which, together with the friendly service, make mealtimes a real pleasure.

Sights nearby: Benedictine monastery, German Bread Museum in Ulm (18km east)

Access: At intersection of B 28 and B492

16 SOMMERAU

Karl-Thomas Hegar

€€ Im Steinatal
79848 Bonndorf
Tel. (07703) 6 70
Fax (07703) 1541
gasthofsommerau@t-online.de – www.sommerau.de

Closed 3 weeks Mar, 1 week Jan • 12 rooms, all with balcony, all with showers on landing, 10 non-smoking • Restaurant with terrace (closed Mon, Tue): set meal 23-38€; half board 23€ • Garden, parking; dogs allowed • Sauna, bicycle hire, horses

70 €, Breakfast included
Credit cards not accepted

The seclusion of the Stein valley

In a tranquil side-valley high above the lowland mists, this 100% timber-built inn is designed in the typical style of the region, with a hipped roof reminiscent of a Black Forest farmstead. However, there's nothing folksy about the place, which invites its guests to relax and feel in touch with nature. The rooms have furnishings in untreated wood and are equipped with the minimum of facilities. Forget TV, and experience the landscape from the glazed-in balconies or by taking off for an invigorating hike. Local ingredients are used in the establishment's kitchens, including some home-grown produce.

Sights nearby: Wutach Gorge (9km east), Schluchsee (10km west)

Access: 9km west of Bonndorf; follow signs initially towards Grafenhausen

17 **ADLER**

Erich Rembold

Hindenburgstr. 4
74336 Brackenheim-Botenheim
Tel. (07135) 9 81 10
Fax (07135) 981120 – www.adlerbotenheim.de

Closed 3 weeks early Aug • 16 rooms, including 5 non-smoking, 1 with balcony • Restaurant with terrace (closed Tue): set meal 30.50-42€; half board available • Garden, parking; dogs allowed • Bicycle hire, organised walks and wine tastings

75/85 €, Breakfast included

VISA MC

The underfloor heating which means you never get cold feet

At first glance you would hardly credit that this is the oldest inn in the place. But in order to shake off the dust of the past, only the ground floor walls were preserved when the building was redeveloped and an upper floor added in contemporary style. This accounts for the traditional feel of the panelled restaurant which still exudes the charm of yesteryear, while the bright and cheerful, individually styled bedrooms are timeless in character, nicely set off by carefully chosen decorative details.

Sights nearby: Tripsdrill theme park (6km south), Kilianskirche in Heilbronn (16km northeast)

Access: 1.5km south of Brackenheim

18 **KAISERS TANNE**

Edgar Kienzler

Am Wirbstein 27
79874 Breitnau
Tel. (07652) 1 20 10
Fax (07652) 120159 – www.kaisers-tanne.de

Open all year • 35 rooms, all with balcony, 1 with disabled access • Restaurant with terrace (open from 1.30pm): set dinner 20-40€; half board 16€ • Garden, parking; dogs allowed • Indoor pool, sauna, solarium, golf course, bicycle hire

122/180 €, Breakfast included

VISA MC

Live music several times a week

The peace and quiet of this typical Black Forest inn - some of the bedrooms have a view of the Feldberg - will tempt you to put your feet up and just take it easy. However, you're bound to be tempted sooner or later by a vast range of leisure facilities nearby; there's an indoor pool, a ski lift, a cross-country ski trail, a toboggan-run and a 3-hole golf course and driving range, to say nothing of endless hiking possibilities and bikes to be hired. And you can always reward yourself for your efforts with coffee and cakes from the establishment's own patisserie!

Sights nearby: Hinterzarten ski museum (4km south), Titisee (10km southeast)

Access: On B 500, 2km south of Breitnau

19 EULENSPIEGEL

Ingo Jäger

Marktplatz 8
75015 Bretten
Tel. (07252) 9 49 80
Fax (07252) 949830 – www.hotel-eulenspiegel.de

Open all year • 8 rooms, including 3 with terrace • Cafe-restaurant with terrace; main courses from 4.90€ • Parking; dogs not allowed

85/100 €, Breakfast included (WE: 75 €)

VISA MC

The hand-crafted guest book

This establishment faces the Melanchthonhaus, and honours the town's most famous son by naming one of its eight rooms after him. Other rooms are called "Luther" and "Eulenspiegel", and together with "Melanchthon" benefit from their own outside terrace. All the rooms have an individual character, with stylish antique pieces, and are as comfortable and tasteful as one could wish in such a traditional setting. Breakfast is taken on the gallery of the establishment's own café-bistro, with its attractive old darkwood furnishings.

Sights nearby: Melanchthon House, Schloss Bruchsal (14km northwest)

Access: By B 293 between Karlsruhe and Heilbron or by B 35 from Bruchsal

20 BURG WINDECK

Rolf Fischer

Kappelwindeckstr. 104
77815 Bühl
Tel. (07223) 9 49 20
Fax (07223) 949290 – www.burg-windeck.de

Closed 7-31 Jan • 21 rooms, including 6 non-smoking • Restaurant with terrace (closed Wed, Sun eve): set meal 32-82€ • Garden, parking; dogs allowed • Gym, sauna, solarium, castle tours, wine tastings

93/138 €, Breakfast included (WE: 103/123 €)

AE JCB VISA

A snack in the novel setting of one of the horse-boxes in the old stables

An old song asks "Why is it so lovely down by the Rhine?", and perhaps the answer is to be found here, where the remains of a castle with two keeps stand out on a cone-shaped rise among the vineyards. The view westwards over the Rhine plain towards the Vosges mountains in France is literally boundless, and is especially glorious when the setting sun bathes everything in golden light. Take dinner on the splendid terrace, then retire to your room in one of the castle's outbuildings, where country-style furnishings and lovely wood floors create a comfortable ambience.

Sights nearby: September plum festival in Bühl, Friedrichsbad in Baden-Baden (20km northeast)

Access: 4km southeast of Bühl via Kappelwindeck

21 GRÜNE BETTLAD

Sabine und Peter Günthner

Blumenstr. 4
77815 Bühl
Tel. (07223) 9 31 30
Fax (07223) 931310
info@gruenebettlad.de – www.gruenebettlad.de

Closed 1-10 Jan, 2 weeks in summer and Christmas to New Year • 6 rooms • Restaurant with terrace (closed Sun, Mon): lunch menu 23-32€, evening menu 32-50€ • Parking; dogs allowed

100/120 €, Breakfast included

VISA MC

Sitting outside in the idyllic courtyard

This 400-year-old timber-framed building offers bedrooms in which great care has been paid to every detail: four-poster beds, the hand-painted country furniture and the lavish use of delightful fabrics will bring out the romantic in everyone. As trim and pretty as you could wish, the restaurant with its tiled stove once also had a famous bedstead - the "Grüne Bettlad" which gave the establishment its present name -in which a past landlord is said to have surprised his wife in the arms of their neighbour. After that, the inn's previous name - "Eintracht", or "Harmony" - no longer seemed to fit.

Sights nearby: Yburg castle ruins (9km northeast); Collegiate church Baden-Baden (16km northeast)

Access: Exit 52 from A 5

22 BERGGASTHOF SONNHALDE

Bernd Roser

Untere Sonnhalde 37
79683 Bürchau
Tel. (07629) 2 60
Fax (07629) 1737 – www.sonnhalde-buerchau.de

Closed 21 Feb to 10 Mar, 21 Nov to 16 Dec • 20 rooms, including 18 with balcony and 5 non-smoking • Restaurant with terrace: (closed Mon, Tue, but open for residents) set lunch 13-39€, set dinner 39-52€; half board 10€ • Children's playground, garden, parking; dogs allowed • Indoor pool, sauna, solarium, gym, exhibitions, organised walks

76/86 €, Breakfast included

MC

Tucked away in their leafy setting, the two holiday dwellings called "Beehive" and "Swallows Nest"

Up above the village, this mountain inn with its guesthouse offers its clients peace and quiet far removed from the noise of traffic, as well as wonderful views over the swelling uplands of the High Black Forest. Enjoy the unspoiled landscape and let yourself be pampered by the friendly hosts of "Sunny Slope", for example in the parlour, where you can treat yourself to home-made cakes and pastries. The bedrooms, some of them with balcony, are prettily decorated in country style, even with hand-painted furniture. If you find it impossible to tear yourself away from the view, you can take your meal in the front part of the restaurant or in fine weather on the panoramic garden terrace.

Sights nearby: Teufelsgrund silver mine, (13km north), Badenweiler Cassiopeia thermal spa (20km west)

Access: 3km south of Neuenweg by Wiesental road

23 LANDHOTEL ADLER

Hans-Jürgen Steuer

Roggenbeurer Str. 2
88693 Deggenhausertal-Wittenhofen
Tel. (07555) 2 02
Fax (07555) 5273 – www.landhotel-adler.de

Closed Feb • 18 rooms, including 3 non-smoking • Restaurant with terrace: (closd Wed and midday Thur) main course 7.50-19.50€; half board 10€ • Garden, parking; dogs allowed • 2 skittle alleys, solarium

66 €, Breakfast included

VISA

Scattering the skittles in the bowling alley

Conveniently located for Lake Constance, this establishment is easily identified from far away by its welcoming array of red and white striped shutters. Guests have been coming here for over a hundred years. The rooms are well-kept and have individual decor and furnishings. To the rear of the building, the attractive terrace overlooking the tranquil waters of a little river invites you to dine outside or simply relax in the sun. How to spend your time here is no problem at all, given that you are in one of Germany's favourite holiday areas.

Sights nearby: Schloss Salem (12km west), Ravensburg Old Town (20km east)

Access: By B 33 via Markdorf

24 **REBSTOCK-STUBE**
Gabi und Adolf Frey

Hauptstr. 74
79211 Denzlingen
Tel. (07666) 90 09 90
Fax (07666) 7942
www.rebstock-stube.de

Open all year • 10 rooms • Restaurant (closed Sun, Mon): set lunch 20-40€, set dinner 35-55€ • Parking; dogs allowed

65/85 €, Breakfast included
AE VISA MC

A day trip to nearby historic Freiburg

Between the Kaiserstuhl and the Black Forest, this old establishment on the outskirts of Freiburg is an ideal place to stay or simply to dine in on the way through. Its origins go back to the Middle Ages, and if you revel in a sense of the past you will not be disappointed here. The luxuriantly overgrown exterior is quite enchanting, while inside, the rustic restaurant has all the atmosphere of Germany in centuries past. In the immaculately kept rooms, light wood furnishings create an attractively cosy ambience. Friendly, attentive service completes an inviting picture.

Sights nearby: Black Forest zoo in Waldkirch (8km east), St Peter's Benedictine monastery (15km southeast)

Access: Exit 61 on A 5, or by B 3 or B 294

25 KARPFEN

Alix und Günter Jung

Alter Markt 1
69412 Eberbach am Neckar
Tel. (06271) 7 10 15
Fax (06271) 71010 – www.hotel-karpfen.com

Open all year • 50 rooms, including 5 with balcony • Restaurant with terrace (closed Tue): set meal 13.80-19.80€; half board 14.80€ • Parking; dogs allowed

75/99 €, Breakfast included
AE VISA MC

Wandering through the picturesque lanes and alleyways of old Eberbach

In the heart of the old town, this hotel consists of two buildings next to each other that could hardly be more different. There is the stately main building, its façade graced with scenes from the history of the town, then, linked to it by a first floor corridor, an almost insignificant looking little timber-framed house. The bedrooms are comfortably furnished either with period pieces or in dark cherrywood, some have delightful floral wallpaper and others feature wood flooring. In summer, it's fun to sit on the terrace in front of the building and watch the world go by - at a leisurely stroll, of course...

Sights nearby: Hirschhorn am Neckar castle (8km west), Erbach German Ivory Museum (26km north)

Access: In pedestrianised town centre; access by Uferstrasse (B 37), then Friedrichstrasse and Kellereistrasse

26 TRAUBE

Georg Albrecht

Alemannenstr. 19
79588 Efringen-Kirchen-Blansingen
Tel. (07628) 82 90
Fax (07628) 8736 – www.traube-blansingen.de

Closed 2 weeks late Jan, 2 weeks late Jul • 7 rooms • Restaurant with terrace (closed Tue, Wed): set lunch 27€, set dinner 46-71€ • Garden, parking; dogs allowed • Exhibitions, cookery courses, wine seminars

93/113 €, Breakfast included

VISA MC

The cosy corner by the tiled stove in the restaurant

By the village fountain in the middle of Blansingen, the "Grape" cannot be missed. It is an old farmhouse of 1811, with rooms that have been decorated and furnished with great attention to detail. Country-style furnishings are nicely set off by well-chosen modern works of art. Attentive service and an excellent restaurant ensure that your stay is an enjoyable one: dine in a rustically elegant ambience beneath old beams or, weather permitting, in the idyllic garden to the rear of the building.

Sights nearby: Rötteln castle (10km east), Beyeler Foundation in Basel-Riehen (18km south)

Access: Turn off B 3 between Efringen-Kirchen and Welmlingen towards Blansingen

27 ZUR LOCHMÜHLE

Anton Bihler

Hinterdorfstr. 44
78253 Eigeltingen
Tel. (07774) 9 39 30
Fax (07774) 939393 – www.lochmuehle-eigeltingen.de

Open all year • 40 rooms, including 5 with balcony • Restaurant with terrace: set meal 12-15€, main course 9-12€; half board 15€ • Garden, parking; dogs allowed • Outdoor pool, sauna, bicycle hire

80/110 €, Breakfast included
VISA MC

Rolling through the countryside in style in the establishment's own post-coach

You're not likely to suffer from boredom here, in what can be described as a "farmyard experience". There are animals aplenty - many roaming free - plus an array of activities ranging from conventional pleasures such as angling and horse-riding to more challenging pursuits like moto-cross and vintage tractor racing. If you don't fancy one of the cosy country-style bedrooms, you can always sleep in the barn or beneath the stars in a tepee.

Sights nearby: Schloss Langenstein Fasnacht museum (5km west), Engen Old Town (12km west)

Access: From Exit 39 on A 81 via Aach

28 PARK-HOTEL KRONE

Dorothea Will

Brandelweg 1
79312 Emmendingen-Maleck
Tel. (07641) 9 30 96 90
Fax (07641) 52576 – www.krone-maleck.de

Closed Fastnacht fortnight in Feb • 26 rooms, including 12 with balcony • Restaurant (closed Mon) with terrace: set lunch 17-58€, set dinner 23-58€; half board 20€ • Garden, parking; dogs allowed

75/82 €, Breakfast included

VISA MC

The stately flamingoes in the park

This establishment fully deserves its name, thanks to the well-manicured gardens with their idyllic duck-pond. The colourful building with its striped shutters is impressive enough when seen from the road through Maleck, but looks even better from inside, as you walk into a delightfully decorated foyer where every detail has been carefully thought out. The spacious and comfortable rooms are in a more straightforward style, mostly with furnishings in natural wood.

Sights nearby: Emmendingen castle (4km southwest), Hochburg ruined castle (5km southeast)

Access: Leave Emmendingen to east by Tennenbacher Strasse

29 DUTTERS STUBE

Arthur Dutter

Winterstr. 28
79346 Endingen-Kiechlinsbergen
Tel. (07642) 17 86
Fax (07642) 4286 – www.dutters-stube.de

Closed 3 weeks late Jul/early Aug • 4 rooms • Restaurant (closed Mon, Tue; but open Tue eve Apr, May, Sep, Oct): set lunch 23€, set dinner 36-46€ • Parking; dogs allowed

60 €, Breakfast included

VISA MC

Enjoying a glass of wine in the historic vaulted wine-cellar

This establishment stands in the middle of a picturesque wine village among the vineyards on the northern slopes of the majestic Kaiserstuhl. Four generations of the Dutter family have made their guests welcome in their delightful half-timbered hostelry. They offer simple but very attractively furnished rooms in pleasant pastel shades, and provide local and international specialities in the panelled dining rooms, to which a glass of full-bodied Kaiserstuhl wine is an essential accompaniment.

Sights nearby: Kaiserstuhl wine museum in Vogtsburg-Achkarren (10km south), Breisach Minster (18km south)

Access: From Riegel Exit on A 5 via Endingen and Königsschaffhausen

30 ADLER

Walter Wimmer

Feldbergstr. 4 (B 317)
79868 Feldberg-Bärental
Tel. (07655) 93 39 33
Fax (07655) 930521 – www.adler-feldberg.de

Open all year • 16 rooms, including 9 with balcony and 2 non-smoking • Restaurant with terrace: set lunch 12-18€, set dinner 28-35€; half board 23€ • Garden, parking; dogs allowed • Wine and whisky evenings

85/120 €, Breakfast included

VISA MC

The maisonettes with their bedrooms in the gable

This 19th century Black Forest inn offers ideal accommodation for active holiday-makers. Motorcylists set out from here on tours of the area, there are endless opportunities for hikers and cross-country skiers, while waters-sports enthusiasts have the Titisee and Schluchsee and downhill skiers the Feldberg. For the more romantically inclined, the rooms feature hand-painted country furnishings and most of them have four-poster beds. In the tastefully rustic restaurant a tiled stove provides welcoming warmth.

Sights nearby: Feldberg (9km west), Schluchsee (10km southeast), Hüsli local museum (16km southeast)

Access: At intersection of B 500 and B 317 between Titisee and Todtnau

31 LUDINMÜHLE

Frau Zimmermann

Brettental 31
79348 Freiamt-Brettental
Tel. (07645) 9 11 90
Fax (07645) 911999 – www.ludinmuehle.de

Open all year • 53 rooms, including 43 with balcony, 2 with disabled access and 35 non-smoking • Restaurant with terrace: set lunch 18-28€, set dinner 18-40€ • Children's play room, parking; dogs allowed • Wellness facilities, sunbathing lawn, bicycle hire, guided walks, wine tasting

122/204 €, Breakfast included
AE (D) VISA MC

An enchanting boat trip along the forgotten meanders of the Rhine

Do you want to relax but also indulge in some healthy exercise as well? If so, the Ludin Mill is definitely the place: there's a little health and beauty area and a range of guided walks to be enjoyed. Or you can head off under your own steam on foot or bike. If this is not enough, the live music provided will certainly get you tripping the light fantastic. The reception is friendly and the attractively furnished and comfortable rooms will enhance your stay here.

Sights nearby: Ettenheim Minster (15km northwest), Hochburg ruined castle (16km south)

Access: From Exit 59 on A 5 via Malterdingen, Freihof, Ottoschwanden

32 ZUR TANNE

Gernot Elmlinger

Altgasse 2
79112 Freiburg-Opfingen
Tel. (07664) 18 10
Fax (07664) 5303 – www.tanne-opfingen.de

Closed Jan, fortnight in Jun/Jul • 10 rooms, including 4 non-smoking • Restaurant with terrace: (closed Tue) set meals 29-34.50€ • Parking; dogs allowed by arrangement

43/84 €, Breakfast included

VISA MC

Losing oneself in the "Opfingen Maize Labyrinth"

Tranquil little Opfingen is located among the Tuniberg vineyards on the outskirts of Freiburg, and this characterful old inn of 1786 stands on the village's main street. The bedrooms on the top floor just beneath the roof are rather more spacious and the exposed beams lend them a particular charm. The dining rooms with their fine old tiled stoves are full of rustic character; one of the stoves was painted by hand in 1912. On fine days you can sit out in the prettily planted courtyard.

Sights nearby: Vita Classica thermal spa in Bad Krozingen (10km south), Freiburg Minster (11km east)

Access: From Exit 63 on A 5 via Tiengen

33 MÜHLENHOF

Familie Rottler

Oberweierer Hauptstr. 33
77948 Friesenheim-Oberweier
Tel. (07821) 63 20
Fax (07821) 632153 – www.landhotel-muehlenhof.de

Open all year • 32 rooms, including 30 with balcony • Restaurant with terrace (closed Tue, 10-27 Jan, 8-25 Aug): set lunch 7.50-32€, set dinner 22-32€ • Garden, parking; dogs allowed

52/72 €, Breakfast included

AE VISA MC

The half-timbered charm of Friesenheim

Beautifully adorned with flowers and other plants, this lovely country house will surely tempt you to extend your stay. The rooms feature light wood furnishings and most of them have their own balcony, so you can enjoy whatever fine weather comes your way from here as well as on the hotel terrace. In the wood-panelled restaurant with its tastefully decorated tables, friendly ladies - wearing traditional 'Dirndl' dresses - offer you a fine range of seasonal dishes from the establishment's extensive menu.

Sights nearby: Schuttern monastery (4km west), Ritterhaus Museum in Offenburg (14km north)

Access: In Oberweier, 1.5km east of B 3

34 HIRSCHEN-GÄSTEHAUS VERENA

Karl Amann

Kirchgasse 1
78343 Gaienhofen-Horn
Tel. (07735) 9 33 80
Fax (07735) 933859 – www.hoeri.de/hirschen

Closed 9 Jan to 4 Feb • 30 rooms, including 12 with balcony, 1 suite with disabled access • Restaurant with terrace (closed Wed, Thu, Nov-Mar): set meal 18-40€ • Garden, parking; dogs allowed • Sunbathing lawn, guided walks, organised boat trips, live music, Nordic walking

84/100 €, Breakfast included (WE: 90 €)
Credit cards not accepted

The extraordinary range of things to do, on water as well as on land

This historic inn stands on a peninsula at the western end of Lake Constance, opposite the famously beautiful island of Reichenau. The main building is linked to the guesthouse by a cobbled terrace, whose lovely planting gives it an authentically Mediterranean air. The rooms are in country style, and some of them have furnishings in dark oak. The holiday home with its tiled stove and lake views is particularly attractive. With decor evoking the different seasons, the restaurant has a cosy and welcoming atmosphere

Sights nearby: Reichenau island, Mainau island, Sea Life Konstanz (best reached by lake steamer)

Access: By the church in the centre of Horn

35 ZUM HECHT

Christine Uffhausen

Hauptstr. 41
78187 Geisingen
Tel. (07704) 2 81
Fax (07704) 6464 – www.zumhecht.de

Closed two weeks during Fasnacht festival • 7 rooms, 6 with shower on landing • Restaurant with terrace (closed Mon, Tue, Sat lunchtime): menu 25-44€; half board 25€ • Parking; dogs allowed in hotel but not in restaurant • Cookery and wine courses

62/72 €, Breakfast included
Credit cards not accepted

The fine location within easy reach of both the Black Forest and Lake Constance

Dating from the 19th century, this fine old inn in the middle of Geisingen boasts a bright red façade and a bold oriel window. The restaurant is a successful blend of old and new and its decor is changed according to the season. After sampling the establishment's classic cuisine, your impeccably kept bedroom in country-house style awaits you. Note however that most of the rooms have showers on the landing.

Sights nearby: Fürstenberg collections in Donaueschingen (15km west), Blumberg-Weizen preserved railway (18km southwest)

Access: Exit 38 on A 81; opposite Rathaus on main street in town centre

36 REICHSSTADT

Familie Hummel

Engelgasse 33
77723 Gengenbach
Tel. (07803) 9 66 30
Fax (07803) 966310 – www.reichsstadt-gengenbach.de

Closed from week before Carnival and early to mid-Jan • 6 rooms, including 2 with balcony • Restaurant with terrace (closed midday, Mon): set lunch 27.50-45.50€, set dinner 27.50-65€; half board 15€ • Garden, parking; dogs allowed • Bicycle hire, changing exhibitions in house and garden

96/120 €, Breakfast included

The picturesque old town centre of Gengenbach with its historic gateways and idyllic timber-framed buildings

The individually styled rooms of this establishment are a good indication of the lady owner's profession of interior designer. Right in the middle of Gegenbach's historic core, the building dating from 1795 has tasteful apartments where great attention has obviously been paid to detail. Designer furnishings and parquet floorings are standard, and a cheerful note of colour is added by the changing selection of contemporary works of art which are in the restaurant as well. Best of all, there is a real little paradise in the shape of the garden terrace, bounded by ancient walls.

Sights nearby: Schloss Ortenberg (6km northwest), Villa Haiss Museum of Contemporary Art in Zell am Harmersbach (12km south)

Access: By B 33 from Offenburg

37 TANNENMÜHLE

Guido Baschnagel

Tannenmühlenweg 5
79865 Grafenhausen
Tel. (07748) 2 15
Fax (07748) 1226 – www.tannenmuehle.de

Closed mid-Nov to mid-Dec • 20 rooms, including 17 with balcony • Cafe, restaurant with terrace (closed Tue Jan-May and Oct-Dec): set lunch 17-30€, set dinner 19-35€; half board 15€ • Parking; dogs allowed • Table tennis

73/90 €, Breakfast included
Credit cards not accepted

The fine old mill, rebuilt according to old plans in 1987, and where home-grown 'spelt' grain is once more being milled

If you fancy something out of the ordinary, the various extras provided in the typical Black Forest inn on the edge of the forest might well suit you. A mill was recorded here as long ago as the 11th century, and the present structure of 1832 was grinding corn right up to 1960. The rooms have a delightfully rustic character, enhanced in some of them by hand-painted country furniture. Meals make much use of the mill's own trout, meat from the establishment's own butchery, and there are home-made cakes as well. Children will love the animals in the enclosure outside.

Sights nearby: Hüsli local museum (2km north), Wutach Gorge (15km northeast)

Access: 3km east of Grafenhausen (turning off road to Birkendorf)

38 **ROMANTIK HOTEL STOLLEN**
Familie Jehli-Kiefer

Elzacher Str. 2
79261 Gutach-Stollen
Tel. (07685) 9 10 50
Fax (07685) 1550 – www.romantikhotels.com/gutach

Closed 1 week late Jan • 9 rooms, all with balcony, 3 non-smoking • Restaurant (closed Tue, midday Wed) with terrace: set lunch 14-28€, set dinner 28-51€; half board 22€ • Garden, parking; dogs allowed by arrangement • Bicycle hire, cookery and wine seminars

94/130 €, Breakfast included
VISA MC

A refreshing walk in the Elz valley

On the main road in the Stollen district of Gutach, this flower-bedecked, half-timbered property has been in the same family since 1847. It makes its guests welcome with comfortably appointed, well-carpeted rooms with laquer or period furniture and lavish use of harmoniously coloured fabrics. The charming restaurant consists of several separate little dining areas, with old beams, furnishings in dark wood, and elegantly decorated tables.

Sights nearby: Elztal Museum in Waldkirch (5km southwest), Augustinian Museum in Freiburg (20km southeast)

Access: On B 294 north of Waldkirch

39 DER LÖWEN

Ursula und Hans Bröcker

Hansjakobstr. 2
88709 Hagnau
Tel. (07532) 43 39 80
Fax (07532) 43398300 – www.loewen-hagnau.de

Closed Jan, Feb to mid-Mar, Nov, Dec • 16 rooms, including 5 non-smoking, 2 with balcony • Restaurant with terrace (closed Wed, midday Mon, Tue, Thu, and Fri): half board 18€ • Garden, parking; dogs allowed in restaurant, not in hotel • Private beach with sunbathing lawn, tour of Japanese garden, Sunday sausage meals and live music

90/105 €, Breakfast included
VISA MC

The oven-fresh breakfast rolls from the establishment's own bakery

You're bound to enjoy the very special ambience of this hotel, built around a timber-framed house dating from 1656. The setting itself is just naturally relaxing and the large garden, with a pond populated by fish, frogs and tortoises, looks enchanting when lit up at night. Just 300 metres away, the hotel's private beach, with bathing huts and showers, gives you no excuse not to go for a refreshing dip in Lake Constance. Beneath the venerable vaults of the restaurant, dishes are prepared largely with local, organic ingredients for a real flavour of the region.

Sights nearby: Mainau island (crossing via Meersburg 5km northwest), Salem monkey mountain (17km north)

Access: In centre not far from lakeside

40 **VILLA AM SEE**

Christine Erbguth

Meersburger Str. 4
88709 Hagnau
Tel. (07532) 4 31 30
Fax (07532) 6997 – www.villa-am-see.de

Open Apr-Oct • 7 rooms all non-smoking, 1 with air-conditioning and 5 with balcony • Garden, parking; dogs allowed • Sauna, solarium

130/220 €, Breakfast included

AE D VISA MC

The lake views from the balcony of the breakfast room

The expectations aroused by the name of this establishment will not be disappointed. The "Villa by the Lake" is a delightful, bright white building right by the water, and its rooms (non-smoking only) are light and welcoming, some with distinctive colour schemes, marble floors and tasteful furnishings. Well-stocked with flourishing plants and glorious flowers, the idyllic garden invites you to stretch out on your sunbed or in the shade of the pavilion and give yourself over to your dreams.

Sights nearby: Birnau pilgimage church (13km northwest), Friedrichshafen Zeppelin Museum (15km southeast), Schloss Salem and minster (17km north)

Access: On the lakeshore close to the Westhafen (West Harbour)

41 SCHWANEN

Chris Groen, Pablo Gonzales

Marktplatz 5
72401 Haigerloch
Tel. (07474) 9 54 60
Fax (07474) 954610 – www.schwanen-haigerloch.de

Open all year • 25 rooms, including 13 non-smoking • Restaurant with terrace : (closed Mon, Tue) set lunch 41-76€, set dinner 61-76€; half board 25€ • Parking; dogs allowed • Wine and cheese seminars; etiquette courses

120/195 €, Breakfast included

AE VISA MC

The homemade jams, pasta and chocolate truffles on sale in the "Schwanenboutique"

This establishment consists of two buildings in contrasting styles on either side of the road. The one dating from the 17th century boasts exposed beams and furnishings in natural wood, giving it an elegantly rustic ambience, while the "Leda" opposite has rooms in contemporary style. There are alternatives too in the choice of cuisine; the elegant restaurant with its ancient vaults has a lovely riverside terrace, while the inviting café-cum-bistro offers a tempting selection of home-made cakes.

Sights nearby: Jewish cemetery, St-Anna-Kirche

Access: In the Lower Town at the foot of the castle

42 LANDHAUS HECHTSBERG

Rüdiger Schmid

Hechtsberg 1
77756 Hausach-Hechtsberg
Tel. (07831) 9 66 60
Fax (07831) 9666200 – www.landhaus-hechtsberg.de

Closed 1 week in Jan, 24 Dec • 8 rooms, all non-smoking and 1 with balcony • Restaurant with terrace (closed Mon): set meal 16-39€; half board 10€ • Garden, parking; dogs allowed • Bicycle hire, cookery courses, wine and health seminars

89 €, Breakfast included

VISA

A stimulating session in the nearby spa park

Right in the heart of the Black Forest, this establishment welcomes its guests with attractive rooms in contemporary country-house style. But there's no trace of dusty nostalgia here, instead everything is fresh and stylish as well as cosy. The comfortable rooms are furnished in elegant cherrywood, and the careful choice of colours for walls and materials further enhance the attractive setting. Despite all this, you will not be able to resist the call of the outside, where you can sit beneath old trees and allow yourself to be pampered with gastronomic delights.

Sights nearby: Vogtsbauernhof open air museum (on B 33 southeast of Hausach), Black Forest costume museum in Haslach (7km west)

Access: By access to B 33/294 in western part of Haslach, south of main road

43 HOFGUT HOHENKARPFEN

Susanne Ritzi-Mathé

78595 Hausen ob Verena
Tel. (07424) 94 50
Fax (07424) 945245 – www.hohenkarpfen.de

Open all year • 21 rooms, including 5 with balcony • Restaurant with terrace: set meal 29-49€; half board 20€ • Garden, parking; dogs allowed • Art museum, art street, organised walks

98 €, Breakfast included (WE: 88 €)

AE Ⓓ VISA MC

The "art road" by the exit gets longer every year, as participants in the annual art symposium add a piece or two

This is really somewhere out of the ordinary, a fascinating combination of historic surroundings, magnificent setting, and a place where art is not only exhibited, but lived. More than 300 years old, the group of timber-framed buildings on their hilltop offer comfortable bedrooms with ancient beams and dark furnishings as well as a rustic restaurant with fine views and a blue-tiled stove in an adjoining room. Here too is a museum run by the Hohenkarpfen art foundation which puts on changing exhibitions of southwest German art of the 19th and 20th centuries. 850 metres up, the peace and quiet and the wide views down into the valley of the Elta contribute to the perfection of the place.

Sights nearby: Dreifaltigkeitsberg (9km northeast), Rottweil Dominican museum (20km north)

Access: 6km southwest of Spaichingen on B 14 by Angerstrasse, Karlstrasse and Hausener Strasse

44 BACKMULDE

Alex Schneider

Schiffgasse 11
69117 Heidelberg
Tel. (06221) 5 36 60
Fax (06221) 536660 – www.gasthaus-backmulde.de

Open all year • 19 rooms, including 2 with disabled access and 6 with shower on landing • Restaurant with terrace: (closed Sun, Mon midday) set meal 19-21€ • Parking; dogs allowed

70/110 €, Breakfast included

AE VISA MC

Some gentle shopping in Heidelberg's Old Town

This building in Heidelberg's Old Town looks back on a long and eventful past. Originally used as boatmen's lodgings, it was twice destroyed in the course of the 17th century, then rebuilt in its present form in 1698. Since then it has housed a brewery and a factory, and even today it is used by Heidelberg's bakers as their guildhall. Furnished in darkwood and with dark blue carpets, the bedrooms have a warm and comfortable ambience, though some have showers on the landings. The atmosphere in the restaurant, with its bright and cheerful tables, is of times gone by.

Sights nearby: Kurpfälzisches Museum/Electoral Palatinate Museum, Jesuit Church, German Packaging Museum

Access: Follow Heidelberg Hotel Route A

45 WEISSER BOCK

Herr Merz

Große Mantelgasse 24
69117 Heidelberg
Tel. (06221) 9 00 00
Fax (06221) 900099 – www.weisserbock.de

Closed 24 Dec • 23 rooms, including 1 with balcony and 23 non-smoking • Restaurant with terrace; set meal 49€ • Dogs allowed

110 €, Breakfast 10 €
VISA MC

Heidelberg Schloss - the embodiment of what a castle should be

The university city of Heidlelberg is famous for its student culture, and everywhere in the Old Town are the traditional pubs and drinking places where they congregate. This historic building was one such place, though nowadays its patrons enjoy relatively sophisticated offerings. The immaculate and tastefully furnished bedrooms feature exposed beams and are full of local atmosphere. The black and white photographs on the walls of the elegantly rustic restaurant serve as reminders of the "good old days".

Sights nearby: German Apothecary Museum (in the castle), Heiliggeistkirche, Student Jail

Access: Follow Route A of Heidelberg hotel direction system

46 GASTHOF LAMM

Sibylle Serafin

Pfarrgasse 3
69121 Heidelberg-Handschuhsheim
Tel. (06221) 4 79 30
Fax (06221) 479333
www.gasthof-lamm-heidelberg.de

Open all year • 11 rooms, all non-smoking • Restaurant and Weinstube (daily from 6pm; closed 24 Dec, New Year's Eve to Twelfth Night): set dinner 28-45€, main course 8-19€ • Garden; dogs allowed in hotel and Weinstube, not in restaurant

105/115 €, Breakfast 7 €
VISA MC

The original pictures which strike a stylish note in the rustic restaurant

Maybe Heidelberg's overcrowded Old Town with its ever-present tour groups is a bit too much for you ? But you would still like to stay in an historic setting close to the centre ? In that case we would recommend this old inn in the Handschuhsheim part of town, whose tradition of hospitality goes back to the 17th century. Some of the rooms are really spacious, and they are all very comfortable and well-kept. An especially attractive feature on fine days is the lavishly planted cobbled courtyard, where you can relax and just let your thoughts wander.

Sights nearby: Heidelberg Schloss, Weinheim exotic wood (17km north)

Access: By B 3 from centre towards Weinheim; on far bank of River Neckar take Brückenstrasse and Handschuhsheimer Landstrasse, then left into Pfarrgasse

47 LANDHOTEL KRONE

Familie Thoma

Hauptstr. 12
79423 Heitersheim
Tel. (07634) 5 10 70
Fax (07634) 510766 – www.landhotel-krone.de

Open all year • 31 rooms, all non-smoking, 20 with balcony • Restaurant with terrace (closed Tue, midday Wed): set lunch 12.80-46€, set dinner 30-46€; half board 23€ • Garden, parking; dogs allowed • Bicycle hire, exhibitions, cookery courses, wine seminars, organised walks

80/114 €, Breakfast included
Credit cards not accepted

Letting ourselves be pampered by the sun on the hotel terrace

This establishment takes its cue from the many museums and galleries in this corner of Germany, close to both France and Switzerland. Dating in its present form from the 18th century, the hotel features rooms bearing the stamp of great painters such as Renoir, Picasso and Matisse. And because the daughter of the Thoma family is an artist too, the charm of the establishment is further enhanced by several of her works. There's no doubt that the combination of taste and comfort, to say nothing of the friendly service, will make you feel perfectly at home here.

Sights nearby: Vita Classica thermal spa in Bad Krozingen (6km north), Staufenburg castle ruins at Staufen im Breisgau (6km east)

Access: Exit 64b on A 5, then follow signposted hotel route in Heitersheim

48 DER WATZENHOF

Manuel Konstantin Rücker

69502 Hemsbach-Balzenbach
Tel. (06201) 7 00 50
Fax (06201) 700520 – www.watzenhof.de

Closed Jan, 24 Dec • 12 rooms, including 3 with balcony and 2 non-smoking • Restaurant (closed Sun eve, midday Mon) with terrace: set meal 7.50-20€; half board 20€ • Garden, parking; dogs allowed in restaurant, not in hotel • Cookery courses

85/110 €, Breakfast included

AE D JCB VISA MC

Lingering over breakfast by the tiled stove

Deep in the country, this is about as far away as you can get from the stresses and strains of everyday life. Your well-being is paramount as far as Manuel Rücker is concerned: he's the third generation of the family to run the place, and has a long-standing reputation to keep up. He might even invite you to accompany him on his early-morning jog, but it takes will-power to leave those immaculately kept rooms, all with solid oakwood furnishings. Despite the remoteness of this spot, there's no chance of boredom setting in, thanks to the host's barbecue evenings and get-togethers in the garden.

Sights nearby: Heppenheim Old Town (9km north), Lorsch monastery (15km northwest)

Access: From Exit 32 on A5, then 3km east of Hemsbach

49 GASTHAUS ENGEL

Klaus Steiert

Alpersbach 14
79856 Hinterzarten-Alpersbach
Tel. (07652) 15 39
Fax (07652) 5481 – www.engel-hinterzarten.de

Closed 10-30 April, 15 Nov-18 Dec • 11 rooms, 10 with balcony • Restaurant with terrace (closed Thu): main courses 8-20€; half board 11€ • Play area, garden, car park; dogs allowed

60/76 €, Breakfast included
Credit cards not accepted

Specialities from the establishment's own smokehouse

The Steiert family have lived here since 1446, and this stately Black Forest farmstead, 1 010 metres up in a wonderfully peaceful location, is still run by them. Children will hardly be able to wait before making the acquaintance of cows and horses in the stables, and they can work off their energies in the play area or pool. Adults will be happy here too. Almost all the rooms - fitted with pale natural wood furnishings - have balconies with panoramic views. Then there is the rustic dining room in authentically local style where good solid food is served. A cross-country ski trail runs directly behind the building and the hiking possiblities are endless.

Sights nearby: Hinterzarten Ski Museum (5km east), Titisee (9km east)

Access: 5km west of Hinterzarten

50 WASSERSTELZ

Richard Wagner

Guggenmühle 15
79801 Hohentengen am Hochrhein
Tel. (07742) 9 23 00
Fax (07742) 923050 – www.wasserstelz.de

Open all year • 11 rooms, including 3 with disabled access and 2 non-smoking • Restaurant with terrace (open 3pm Mon-Fri): set lunch 18.50-39.50€, set dinner 18.50-46.50€; half board 18.50€ • Garden, parking; dogs allowed • Kayak trips, wine tasting

80/125 €, Breakfast included
VISA MC

A very special experience almost on the doorstep: a swim in the Rhine, which here is quite safe

This old tithe barn built in stone at the foot of the ruins of Weisswasserstelz Castle is a real delight, and not just for history lovers. The rooms are decorated in country style and furnished in natural wood. The rustic and welcoming restaurant also fits in well in these rural surroundings. Because the Upper Rhine is nearby, there is a good choice of fish dishes, best enjoyed on the terrace in summer.

Sights nearby: August Deusser museum in Zurzach (14km west), Wettingen Cistercian monastery (20km southwest)

Access: 3km northwest of Hohentengen via Engelhof vineyard and hamlet of Guggenmühle

51 ZUR WESEREI

Ullrich Kramer-Eichin

Hauptstr. 81
79400 Kandern
Tel. (07626) 70 00
Fax (07626) 6581 – www.weserei.de

Open all year • 24 rooms, including 18 with balcony and 1 with disabled access • Restaurant with terrace (closed Mon, midday Tue): set lunch 15-50€, set dinner 30-50€; half board 21€ (min. stay 3 days) • Garden, parking; dogs allowed • Sauna, jacuzzi

52/136 €, Breakfast included

VISA MC

Enjoying one of the summer events held in the courtyard

This historic inn with its guesthouse looks back on centuries of tradition: the local mining administration was once based here and the house brewed its own beer for the thirsty miners. The guesthouse was taken over by the Kramer family in 1877, and they have been running it ever since with proverbial Baden hospitality. The rooms - those in the guesthouse are rather more spacious - have knotwood furnishings and most have their own balcony. The authentically rustic restaurant is divided into a number of intimate spaces and is decorated in a really enchanting way.

Sights nearby: Local museum and ceramics museum, Schloss Bürgeln (7km north), Steinen bird park (10km southeast), Vitra design museum in Weil am Rhein (16km south)

Access: On main road through Kandern on edge of centre

52 ZUM REBSTOCK

Karl-Josef Hodapp

€€ Kutzendorf 1
77876 Kappelrodeck-Waldulm
Tel. (07842) 94 80
Fax (07842) 94820 – www.rebstock-waldulm.de

Closed Nov • 11 rooms, including 8 with balcony • Restaurant with terrace (closed Mon, midday Tue): set lunch 19-22€, set dinner 34-38€ • Garden, parking; dogs not allowed

64/84 €, Breakfast included
Credit cards not accepted

A trip to the foaming Allerheiligen waterfalls

On the edge of the built-up area, this old inn presents a fairy-tale façade to the world, almost in gingerbread cottage style. But you needn't worry, there's no witch lying in wait here for Hansel and Gretel: far from it. The place has been in the same ownership since 1750, so the warm family welcome comes from years of experience. Most of the well-kept rooms have a balcony, and the rustic "Bauernzimmer" also feature country-style furniture, tiled stoves, and lovely views over the vineyards. The cheerful atmosphere in the cosy dining rooms is enhanced by a collection of clocks and old wedding photographs.

Sights nearby: Schauenburg ruined castle in Oberkirch (6km south), Mariä Himmelfahrt pilgrimage church in Lautenbach (9km southeast)

Access: 2.5km southwest of Kappelrodeck towards Oberkirch

53 SCHEIDELS RESTAURANT ZUM KRANZ

Franz Scheidel

Offenburger Str. 18
79341 Kenzingen
Tel. (07644) 68 55
Fax (07644) 931077 – www.scheidels-kranz.de

Closed 2 weeks over Fastnacht, 2 weeks in Nov • 4 rooms • Restaurant with terrace (closed Mon eve, Tue): set meal 23-49€ • Parking; dogs allowed in restaurant, not in hotel

72/78 €, Breakfast included

AE VISA MC

A stroll through the picturesque centre of old Kenzingen

This inn of 1800 has been run by seven generations of the Scheidel family. The accommodation is limited but of a high standard. Awaiting visitors are impeccably kept double rooms and apartments with tasteful decor and furnishings. You dine in style in the restaurant which features darkwood panelling and beautifully decorated tables with immaculate white tablecloths. When the sun shines, there is the beer garden, where you can improve your tan or relax in the shade of venerable old trees.

Sights nearby: Oberrheinische Narrenschau Fastnacht museum, Rust Europa Park (12km northwest)

Access: On B 3 towards Offenburg northeast of Old Town

54 ZUM RÖSSLE

Mathieu Seltz

Dietenbach 1
79199 Kirchzarten
Tel. (07661) 22 40
Fax (07661) 980022
www.zumroessle.de

Open all year • 6 rooms • Restaurant with terrace (closed Mon lunchtime, Tue lunchtime, Wed): set meals 28-44€ • Garden, parking; dogs allowed

69/74 €, Breakfast included
Credit cards not accepted

Taking breakfast on a rug spread out on the meadow in front of the building

On the Brugga brook, this building with its jolly roofline dates from the 18th century, and it becomes clear that you are somewhere historic as soon as you climb the steep stairs and peer around the nooks and crannies of your bedroom. These are all furnished in country style, and the panelled parlour with its low beams and well-polished tables is full of rustic charm. The “Brugga” dining room with its white tablecloths is a touch more sophisticated. Summertime can be savoured to the full on the well-shaded garden terrace.

Sights nearby: Freiburg Muesum of Contemporary Art (9km west), St.Peter Benedictine monastery (10km northeast)

Access: 1km south of Kirchzarten

55 **RAUB'S RESTAURANT**

Wolfgang Raub

Hauptstr. 41
76456 Kuppenheim-Oberndorf
Tel. (07225) 7 56 23
Fax (07225) 79378 – www.raubs-restaurant.de

Closed one week I Jan, 2 weeks end Aug to early Sept • 5 rooms, one with balcony • Restaurant with terrace (closed Sun, Mon): menus 84-96€ • Garten, car park; dogs allowed in restaurant but not in hotel

97/120 €, Breakfast included

VISA

Lingering outside in the sun or in the shade of the old barn

This establishment bears its name with pride, the Raub family having provided their guests with good food here for over 150 years. Nowadays you can stay here too, in rooms fitted with timeless pale cherrywood furnishings. At breakfast you are pampered with home-made jams, and you are equally well catered for at other mealtimes, either in Raub's Restaurant with its touch of Art Nouveau, or in the cosily rustic "Kreuz-Stübl", still with its big table where locals traditionally gathered for a drink.

Sights nearby: Schloss Favorite (3.5km west); Schloss Rastatt (7km northwest)

Access: 2km east of Kuppenheim; follow signs to Gaggenau/Freudenstadt

56 ADLER

Otto Fehrenbacher

Reichenbacher Hauptstr. 18
77933 Lahr-Reichenbach
Tel. (07821) 90 63 90
Fax (07821) 906393 – www.adler-lahr.de

Closed 31 Jan to 17 Feb • 22 rooms, including 15 with balcony • Restaurant with terrace (residents only Mon, Tue): set meal 32.50-78€ • Garden, parking; dogs allowed

110/145 €, Breakfast included

AE VISA MC

The cheerful splashing of the little stream on the terrace

Easily identifiable because of its highly varied roofscape, this sturdy inn stands on the main road through Reichenbach. You'll like the functional but tasteful rooms with their attractive furnishings, but there is more to the "Eagle" than this; you can expect to be well and truly pampered when you descend to the elegantly rustic restaurant, for the establishment is proud of its excellent cuisine. You can also dine in the Mediterranean ambience of the part-canopied terrace.

Sights nearby: Hohengeroldseck castle (4km east), St. Landelin pilgrimage church in Ettenheimmünster (15km southwest)

Access: 3.5km east of Lahr on B 415 towards Biberach

ADLER

Susanne Hackl

€€ Weinstr. 24
97922 Lauda-Königshofen-Beckstein
Tel. (09343) 20 71
Fax (09343) 8907 – www.hotel-adler-beckstein.de

Open all year • 26 rooms, 10 with balcony, 4 non-smoking • Restaurant with terrace: main courses 6.50-13€; half board 10€ • Car park; dogs allowed • Health and fitness facilities: sauna, gym and steam bath, bicycle hire, guided hikes, wine tasting, tours of wine cellars

52/62 €, Breakfast included

VISA MC

The idyllic atmosphere of the wine village of Beckstein

This establishment strikes the visitor immediately with its picturesquely convoluted roof and its balconies and oriel windows in a variety of shapes and sizes. The comfortable bedrooms have dark, rustic furnishings in "Old German" style, and some of them have attractive little sitting areas tucked away in the oriel windows. The cosy vaulted dining room with its tiled stove offers local dishes which are best accompanied by a bottle of Beckstein wine. There's no need to have a guilty conscience about over-indulging; any excess of eating and drinking can be dissipated in the basement sauna and steam bath.

Sights nearby: Deutschordenschloss Bad Mergentheim (11km southeast); Stuppacher Madonna in Stuppach Parish Church (17km southeast)

Access: 2km southwest of Königshofen by B 292

58 ALTE POST

Siegfried Draganski

Andelsbachstr. 6
79725 Laufenburg (Baden)
Tel. (07763) 9 24 00
Fax (07763) 924040 – www.alte-post-laufenburg.de

Open all year • 12 rooms, including 5 non-smoking and 1 with balcony • Restaurant (closed Mon, midday Tue) with terrace: set lunch 7.10-9.80€, set dinner 25.50-32.50€; half board 15.50€ • Parking; dogs allowed • Guided town walks

75/95 €, Breakfast included

VISA MC

The riverside beer-garden with its enchanting view over the Swiss half of town

When Napoleon redrew the map of Europe, Laufenburg, which had previously belonged to Austria, suddenly found itself divided between Switzerland and Germany. But no wall separated the two halves of the town, rather they remained linked by the lovely waters of the Upper Rhine. Not far from the riverside, this fine 19th century town-house offers individual and stylishly decorated rooms; cheerful colours, attractive materials, wood floors and exposed beams are just some of the design features which are used in a variety of combinations to create a feeling of comfort and well-being. Guests can dine either in the authentically rustic parlour or the elegant conservatory.

Sights nearby: Trumpeter's Palace at Bad Säckingen (10km west), Waldshut Old Town (17km east)

Access: Between B 34 and the river east of the bridge over the Rhine

59 OCHSEN

Jochen Stehle

Dorfplatz 1
79853 Lenzkirch-Saig
Tel. (07653) 9 00 10
Fax (07653) 900170 – www.ochsen-saig.de

Closed mid-Nov to mid-Dec • 36 rooms, including 21 with balcony • Restaurant with terrace: main course 8-22€; half board 15€ • Children's play room, garden, parking; dogs allowed • Indoor pool, sauna, steam bath, tennis, billiards, mountain-bike hire, guided walks

80/120 €, Breakfast included

AE VISA MC

Room rates which include the use of tennis courts and mountain bikes

This sturdy 17th century Black Forest inn is a place for both young and old to unwind. The bedrooms with rustic furnishings and the charmingly traditional dining room with its low ceiling and tiled stove together form an attractive starting point for the enjoyment of country pleasures in the lovely setting of the Hochschwarzwald Nature Park. The inn's modern extension houses a leisure area with an indoor pool, and sauna, steam bath and massage facilities. Children will be pleased to find a playroom as well as an open air playground.

Sights nearby: Titisee (2km west), Löffingen Black Forest Park (18km east)

Access: 4km northwest of Lenzkirch by B 315

60 WALDFRIEDEN

Werner Roth

Insel Rott 2
76351 Linkenheim-Hochstetten
Tel. (07247) 17 79
Fax

Open all year • 10 rooms, including 5 with balcony • Restaurant with terrace (closed Mon, Tue): main course 4.90-9.40€ • Parking; dogs allowed • Bicycle hire

69 €, Breakfast included
Credit cards not accepted

The tasty eels and other fish from the establishment's own smokehouse

The location - an island among the watermeadows of the Rhine - is quite enchanting. The place is popular too, with many coming here to enjoy the array of fish dishes on offer. But you can also relax and enjoy peace and quiet in the lovely green setting. Accommodation is in solidly furnished bedrooms reached by a little staircase tower. Those in the know ask for the "Seerose" (water-lily) room with its spacious balcony overlooking the water. But there is also a little sun terrace high up on the roof for the use of everyone.

Sights nearby: Baden Regional Museum in Karlsruhe (20km south), Schloss Bruchsal (20km east)

Access: From B 36 to Linkenheim-Hochstetten, then 4.5km northwest via Hochstetten

61 LANDGASTHOF ZUM ADLER

Peter Vögele

Hauptstr. 44
88662 Lippertsreute
Tel. (07553) 8 25 50
Fax (07553) 825570 – www.landgasthofzumadler.de

Open all year • 16 rooms • Restaurant with terrace (closed Wed eve, Thu): main course 9.50-19.50€, set lunch 14.50-18.50€; half board 14.50€ • Garden, parking; dogs allowed • Sunbathing lawn, bicycle hire, cookery courses, wine tasting

62/86 €, Breakfast included

VISA MC

Home-made bread, sausages, jams and spirits

Authentic local character and unpretentious charm characterise this building in the heart of Lippertsreute in the back country around Lake Constance. Seven generations of the Vögele family have welcomed guests into their fascinating timber-framed house dating from 1635. The impeccably kept rooms are furnished in solid country style and the rustic dining room has gleaming maplewood tables, wooden panelling and a tiled stove. An adjacent building contains holiday apartments with cooking facilities.

Sights nearby: Schloss Salem (6km southeast), Uberlingen Lake Constance thermal spa (9km southwest)

Access: 9km northeast of Uberlingen by L 200

62 LANDHAUS KELLER

Jürgen Keller

Gartenstr. 21
79364 Malterdingen
Tel. (07644) 13 88
Fax (07644) 4146

Closed 3-6 Jan • 16 rooms, including 10 with balcony and 5 non-smoking • Restaurant with terrace: (closed midday Sat, Sun eve) set meal 23.50-35€; half board 24€ • Garden, parking; dogs allowed in restaurant, not in hotel • Bicycle hire, cookery courses

90/110 €, Breakfast included

AE JCB VISA MC

The delightful location at the foot of the vineyards

In a tranquil village-like residential area between the Black Forest and the Kaiserstuhl, this family establishment has good access to the autobahn but is well away from traffic noise and disturbance. The rooms are individually and stylishly furnished in country style and the use of fresh colours enhances the attractive ambience. You are accommodated in an annexe linked by a terrace to the main building, where you dine off prettily decorated tables in the panelled restaurant.

Sights nearby: Kenzingen Old Town (6km north), Rust Europa-Park (18km northwest)

Access: 2km east of Exit 59 on A 5

63 STRIFFLER'S HERRENKÜFEREI

Helmut Striffler

Marktplatz 2
71706 Markgröningen
Tel. (07145) 9 30 50
Fax (07145) 930525 – www.herrenkueferei.de

Open all year • 8 rooms, including 2 non-smoking • Restaurant with terrace: (closed Sat midday) set lunch 10-24€, set dinner 35-48€ • Parking; dogs allowed

110 €, Breakfast included (WE: 100 €)

The half-timbered heart of old Markgröningen

Its foundation stone laid as long ago as 1414, this lavishly restored building stands on the old town's historic marketplace. Ancient beams and stylish decor with lightwood furniture and carefully chosen accessories help the comfortable bedrooms fit harmoniously into this setting, as does the attractive restaurant. The adjoining "vinothek" offers a fine range of wines from many countries, and connoisseurs of cigars are well catered for too. To add to the variety, there are themed evenings and changing exhibitions of works of art.

Sights nearby: Hochdorf Celtic Museum (7km west), Schloss Monrepos (10km east)

Access: North of A 81/B 10 interchange

64 VILLA SEESCHAU

Sabine Ertl-Schneider

Von-Laßberg-Str. 12
88709 Meersburg
Tel. (07532) 43 44 90
Fax (07532) 434499 – www.hotel-seeschau.de

Cloesd Jan to 14th Feb • 18 rooms, all non-smoking, all with balcony • Garden, parking; dogs not allowed • Sauna, steam bath, solarium, massage, bicycle hire

99/137 €, Breakfast included

JCB VISA MC

The stylish atmosphere of the breakfast room

From the terrace and from many of the rooms of this establishment there is a wonderful view over the rooftops of old Meersburg to Lake Constance. The colours of the lake and the surrounding landscape are repeated in the decor of the bedrooms, each of which has been individually designed with great care and good taste. Each has a balcony, with a view either of the lake or the local vineyards. To take care of your bodily needs, there is a well-equipped leisure area, where you can also enjoy a relaxing massage.

Sights nearby: Castle (Altes Schloss), Unteruhldingen Prehistoric Stilt Dwellings Museum (5km northwest)

Access: Above the Old Town, from B 33 (Stettiner Strasse) turn into Daisendorfer Strasse, then right into Von-Lassberg-Strasse

65 **JAGSTMÜHLE**

Linda Hruby

Jagstmühlenweg 10
74673 Mulfingen-Heimhausen
Tel. (07938) 90 03 00
Fax (07938) 7569
www.jagstmuehle.de

Closed 1-31 Jan • 21 rooms • Restaurant with terrace (closed Mon to midday Fri): main course 10-15€; half board 15€ • Garden, parking; dogs allowed • Swimming in the River Jagst

78 €, Breakfast included

AE JCB VISA

The enchanting view from the breakfast room

Few will fail to respond to the idyllic landscape of the valley of the River Jagst, and here at Heimhausen is one of its most romantic spots. In its secluded setting, the old corn mill offers its guests rooms in a variety of rustic styles, with antique, natural wood and farmhouse furnishings. The dining rooms too breathe the atmosphere of the countryside, though when the sun shines you will want to spend time on the terrace by the water or on the island in the middle of the river.

Sights nearby: Langenburg German Auto Museum in Schloss Langenburg (10km southeast), Würth Museum in Künzelsau (12km southwest)

Access: 4km south of Mulfingen towards Buchenbach

66 OCHSEN

Gudrun Adam-Eglin

Bürgelnstr. 32
79379 Müllheim-Feldberg
Tel. (07631) 35 03
Fax (07631) 10935

Closed 2 weeks early Jan • 7 rooms, 6 with balcony • Restaurant with terrace (closed Thu): main courses 12.50-46€; half board 17.50€ • Car park; dogs allowed • Organised walks

62/86 €, Breakfast included

VISA MC

We most liked

The luxuriant country garden

This country inn on the road through the village was founded in 1763 and has been in the same family ownership ever since. It makes a pretty picture with its flower-bedecked façade and the wide, low-slung gateway leading to the court-yard. The elegant bedrooms feature furnishings in pale wood and most of them have a balcony. By contrast, the restaurant is authentically rustic in style, with rough-hewn wooden chairs and a splendid green-tiled stove. In summer you can sit out in the idyllic courtyard.

Sights nearby: Cassiopeia Baths in Badenweiler (10km north); Blauen (18km east)

Access: 6km southeast of Müllheim via Vögisheim or take the B 3 via Auggen

67 ROMANTIK HOTEL SPIELWEG

Karl-Josef Fuchs

Spielweg 61 (in Obermünstertal)
79244 Münstertal
Tel. (07636) 70 90
Fax (07636) 70966 – www.spielweg.com

Open all year • 48 rooms, including 26 with balcony, 20 non-smoking, 5 with disabled access • Restaurant with terrace: set meal 36-52€; half board 37€ • Children's play area, garden, parking; dogs allowed • Indoor pool, open-air pool, wellness facilities, tennis

123/246 €, Breakfast included

AE Diners VISA MC

The range of home-made cheeses

In a setting of woods and meadows high above the idyllic valley stands this venerable old establishment together with its two modern annexes, the "House by the Stream" and "Sunny Slope". Guests are accommodated in elegant modern rooms in country style. Families will appreciate what is on offer here; children have a playroom and playground at their disposal and in the summer they can play around in the nearby mountain brook. Then there are bikes to be borrowed, for adults as well as children. The cosy, rustic restaurant is graced by original works by Tomi Ungerer, the famous artist from Alsace.

Sights nearby: St. Trudpert Abbey (5km southwest), Belchen (19km south)

Access: About 5km northeast of the main settlement in the Münstertal district

68 BURG HORNBERG

Marcus Frhr. v. Gemmingen

74865 Neckarzimmern
Tel. (06261) 5001
Fax (06261) 2348 – www.burg-hornberg.de

Open all year • 20 rooms • Restaurant with terrace: set lunch 25-33€, set dinner 39-45€ • Garden, parking; dogs allowed • Wine tastings, cellar visits, mountain walks and cookery courses for groups, bicycle hire, boat hire

125/135 €, Breakfast included

AE ⓓ VISA MC

The restaurant in the old stables with its wall-paintings of knights a-jousting

The tale of the Knight with the Iron Hand draws many visitors to this spot in the valley of the Neckar. It was here in 1517 that the Imperial Knight Götz von Berlichingen - later immortalised in a play by Goethe - first settled in Hornberg Castle and it was here in 1562 that he ended his days. The spirit of chivalry lives on in the rustically-furnished bedrooms, some of which boast four-poster beds. The finest feature of the establishment on its vine-planted height is the wonderful view down into the valley of the Neckar, much appreciated by the many visitors savouring it either from the panoramic restaurant or from the café terrace.

Sights nearby: Guttenberg castle (5km south), Bad Wimpfen im Tal collegiate church

Access: On B 27, 1km south of Neckarzimmern

69 RÖSSLE

Maria Preußler

Hauptstr. 12
74676 Niedernhall
Tel. (07940) 98 36 60
Fax (07940) 9836640 – www.landhotel-roessle.com

Open all year • 21 rooms, all non-smoking, 1 with balcony • Restaurant with terrace (closed Sun eve): set meal 24-40€; half board 24€ • Parking; dogs allowed in restaurant, not in hotel • Cookery courses, cycle tours, walks

72/75 €, Breakfast included
VISA MC

A stroll through the tranquil streets of the old salt town of Niedernhall

This fine old 17th century half-timbered building on the Kocher offers its guests rooms (some in the house next door) with cherrywood furnishings, among them a number of lovely old wardrobes. The exposed beams and uprights in a number of rooms add an extra bit of historic character. The restaurant too has an attractively rustic ambience. But the most romantic part of the building is the cosy vaulted cellar with its ancient stone walls.

Sights nearby: Würth museum in Künzelsau (7km east), Schöntal monastery (14km northwest)

Access: 7km west of Künzelsau via Ingelfingen

70 KRONE

Dirk Marquardt

Marktplatz 3
97996 Niederstetten
Tel. (07932) 89 90
Fax (07932) 89960 – www.hotelgasthofkrone.de

Open all year • 32 rooms, including 6 non-smoking, 5 with balcony • Restaurant with terrace: main course from 7€; half board 14.40€ • Parking; dogs allowed • Sauna, steam bath, solarium, bicycle hire

81/92 €, Breakfast included (WE: 77/88 €)
AE D VISA MC

The value-for-money set meals on Sunday

In the heart of Niederstetten, this traditional inn invites its guests into a harmoniously designed, bright and cheerful interior in which subtle, warm colours create a welcoming and friendly effect. The breakfast buffet is laid out in the so-called glasshouse with its transparent roof and eaten in the adjacent elegantly decorated "Friedrich Witt Room". The other meals are taken either in the "Gute Stube" with lovely decor in red and orange tones or in the more rustic "Kronenstube".

Sights nearby: Schloss Weikersheim (11km north), Herrgottskirche near Creglingen (18km northeast)

Access: 5km east of B 290

71 DIE HALDE

Lucia Hegar

Halde 2
79254 Oberried-Hofsgrund
Tel. (07602) 9 44 70
Fax (07602) 944741
info@halde.com – www.halde.com

Open all year • 38 rooms, all non-smoking, 8 with balcony and 1 with disabled access • Café-restaurant with terrace: menu 23-45€; half board 18€ • Garden, car park; dogs allowed in hotel but not in restaurant • Health and fitness area: indoor pool, sauna and gym, boules

128/188 €, Breakfast included
Credit cards not accepted

The breakfast room with a panoramic view of the Feldberg

1147 metres up on the Schauinsland, Freiburg's local mountain, this venerable Black Forest farmhouse has a sensitively designed modern extension. The rooms are tastefully furnished and decorated, with good use made of native wood. The hosts concentrate on essentials to ensure your comfort and well-being, which are further enhanced by the characterful (and listed) dining rooms and by the wellness area with its lovely pool and panoramic views. You can catch your meal in the fishpond and have it prepared exactly as you want for supper.

Sights nearby: Schauinsland Mining Experience (2km north), Schniederlihof Farm Museum (2km)

Access: From Freiburg follow the signs for Schauinsland/Todtnau (via the Güntertal) or from Todtnau follow signs for Schauinsland

72 BLUME

Alfred Krammer

Weinstr. 160
77654 Offenburg-Rammersweier
Tel. (0781) 3 36 66
Fax (0781) 440603 – www.gasthof-blume.de

Closed 1 week in Jan and Feb • 6 rooms, all non-smoking • Restaurant with terrace (closed Sun eve, Mon): set meals 25-38€ • Garden, parking; dogs by arrangement

80/84 €, Breakfast included

VISA MC

The friendly reception by the owners

This attractive 18th century timber-framed building stands just down from the church in Rammersweier. The rooms are furnished in country style in rustic oak; each room is named after a flower and has a character all of its own. Warm colours and use of fine materials make a lovely setting for your stay. The cosy dining room features a tiled oven. In front of the building, the terrace in its green and leafy framework is a relaxing spot in which to dine on fine days.

Sights nearby: Hl.-Kreuz Kirche in Offenburg (3km southwest), Museum of Modern and Contemporary Art in Strasbourg (24km northwest)

Access: 3km northeast of Offenburg towards Durbach

73 LANDHOTEL ZUM HIRSCH

Familie Ermler

Hauptstr. 27
88356 Ostrach
Tel. (07585) 9 24 90
Fax (07585) 924949 – www.landhotel-hirsch.de

Closed during Baden-Württemberg autumn holiday • 16 rooms, including 5 non-smoking, 1 with disabled access • Restaurant with terrace (closed Fri, but open by arrangement): main course 7.50-16€, set lunch 19-24€; half board 18€ • Garden, parking; dogs not allowed • Bicycle hire

60/75 €, Breakfast included (WE: 60 €)
VISA

Exploring the countryside of the Pfrunger Ried on a bike provided by the inn

This is what a country inn should be: attractive, unfussy with impeccably kept rooms, and in addition a genuinely warm reception; now in their fourth generation, the Ermeler family have been providing a welcome for those trying to get away from the stress and anonymity of city life since 1904. So enjoy the friendliness and tranquillity of the countryside, and don't forget to sample the fresh and tasty wares from the next door butcher's, which belongs to the family.

Sights nearby: Pfullendorf Old Town (9km west), Siessen monastery (10km northeast)

Access: In the centre by the church

74 ART VILLA AM SEE

Astrid und Johannes Kögel

Rebsteig 2/2
78315 Radolfzell
Tel. (07732) 9 44 44
Fax (07732) 944410 – www.artvilla.de

Closed New Year to mid-Jan • 10 rooms, including 8 with balcony, 7 with disabled access and 9 non-smoking • Garden, parking; dogs allowed • Wellness and beauty facilities, bicycle and canoe hire, changing art exhibitions

130/195 €, Breakfast included

VISA MC

The outstanding wine cellar with more than 500 different vintages

The name of this establishment can be explained either by its permanent picture collection or because of the sculpture scattered around its park-like garden. But it could also refer to the way in which the art of living is practised here, on this tongue of land protruding into Lake Constance, where everything seems to invite you to dream your time away. The extremely stylish rooms are named after the world's great cities, and are decorated accordingly. One of them is based on the captain's cabin of a luxury yacht. So come aboard, and set off for new horizons!

Sights nearby: Konstanz Minster (20km southeast), garden island of Mainau (21km southeast)

Access: From Rudolfzell follow the signposted hotel route to the hotels on the Mettnau peninsula

75 ALTE MÜHLE

Familie Koch

Singener Str. 3
78239 Rielasingen-Worblingen
Tel. (07731) 91 13 71
Fax (07731) 911472 – www.muehle-rielasingen.de

Open all year • 6 rooms, including 1 non-smoking • Restaurant with terrace (closed midday Tue and midday Wed): set meal 27-40€; half board 20€ • Garden, parking; dogs allowed in restaurant, not in hotel • Organised walks, cookery courses

78/88 €, Breakfast included

VISA MC

The little "stream" flowing through the restaurant as a reminder of the old days

The first watermill here on the main road through Rielasingen was built 600 years ago, but the present listed structure dates from the 18th century. No fewer than four waterwheels once filled the air with their racket, but the mill finally closed down in 1984 and was converted into a hotel-restaurant. It still has plenty of character, with massive beams making a splendid feature in the restaurant which goes up through two floors. It's a pleasure to eat in one of the cosy little niches here. The hotel rooms are in straightforward country style with lightwood furnishings.

Sights nearby: Stein am Rhein Old Town (10km south), Schaffhausen Museum of Contemporary Art (18km west)

Access: In Rielasingen; 4km south of Singen, follow signs for Stein am Rhein

76 LANDGASTHOF ADLER

Josef Bauer

Ellwanger Str. 15
73494 Rosenberg
Tel. (07967) 5 13
Fax (07967) 710300 – www.landgasthofadler.de

Closed 3-28 Jan, 15 Aug to 3 Sep • 15 rooms, all non-smoking • Restaurant (closed Mon, Tue, midday Wed and Thu): set meal 24-75€ • Garden, parking; dogs not allowed

80/100 €, Breakfast included
Credit cards not accepted

The establishment's own spirits made from local ingredients

A sense of well-being is guaranteed by a stay in this historic inn of 1380, with its unfussy, almost Spartan character. The bedrooms, which are on the second floor, have timeless designer furnishings, contrasting attractively with massive old wardrobes and exposed timbers in various shades of grey. One floor lower down, modern pictures lend the restaurant a colourful air, while timber beams and wood floors help create a welcoming, bright and light atmosphere in this historic setting. The whole ambience is relaxed and service is friendly and attentive.

Sights nearby: Jakobuskirche in Hohenberg (3km south), Ellwangen collegiate church (11km southwest)

Access: 6km west of B 290 by Jagstzell

77 ENGEL

Herbert Decker

Talstr. 14
77887 Sasbachwalden
Tel. (07841) 30 00
Fax (07841) 26394 – www.engel-sasbachwalden.de

Open all year • 13 rooms, including 2 with balcony and 6 non-smoking • Restaurant with terrace: (closed Mon) set lunch 19-39€, set dinner 22-44€; half board 18.50€ • Garden; dogs allowed • Bicycle hire

78/90 €, Breakfast included
VISA MC

Getting out your sketchbook and drawing some of Sasbachwalden's pretty timber-framed buildings

With its flower-bedecked façade, the "Angel" on Sasbachwalden's main street is one of the most picturesque of the town's heritage of timber-framed buildings. The immaculate rooms are mostly furnished in pale natural wood in country style, and the attractive restaurant has elegantly rustic decor. It specialises in regional cuisine, best accompanied by one of the wines produced in the neighbourhood. Make sure you include an afternoon break in your programme of activities so that you can enjoy some of the establishment's home-made cakes and pastries.

Sights nearby: Hohenrode ruined castle, Achern-Ottenhöfen preserved railway (6km west)

Access: From Exit 53 on A 5 via Achern, or by B 500 via Freudenstadt (Black Forest High Road)

78 TALMÜHLE

Gutbert Fallert

Talstr. 36
77887 Sasbachwalden
Tel. (07841) 62 82 90
Fax (07841) 6282999 – www.talmuehle.de

Open all year • 27 rooms, including 15 with balcony and 11 non-smoking • Restaurants with terrace: set lunch 24-40€, set dinner 40-72€; half board 20€ • Garden, parking; dogs allowed in restaurant, not in hotel • Morning walks, cookery courses

90/142 €, Breakfast included

AE Ⓓ VISA MC

The romantic garden pavilion

The Fallert family welcomes guests to their venerable inn on the main road through Sasbachwalden. To the rear of the property is a lovely, park-like garden. Accommodation is in uncluttered but comfortable rooms - those in the extension have cherrywood furnishings and spacious balconies with a view over the leafy surroundings. The "Fallert" restaurant is classically elegant, while the "Talmühle-Stube", where you can have a light meal, is a cosy spot with a cheerful open fire.

Sights nearby: Mummelsee (12km east), Allerheiligen monastery ruins (16km southeast)

Access: From Exit 53 on A 5 via Achern, or from Freudenstadt by B 500 (Black Forest High Road)

79 HEGERS PARKHOTEL FLORA

Hugo Heger

Sonnhalde 22
79859 Schluchsee
Tel. (07656) 9 74 20
Fax (07656) 1433 – www.parkhotel-flora.de

Closed 20 Nov to 8 Dec • 34 rooms, all with balcony • Restaurant with terrace: main course from 11€, set meal 19-78€; half board 20€ • Garden, parking; dogs allowed in hotel, not in restaurant • Swimming pool, sauna, steam bath, gym, bicycle hire

110/160 €, Breakfast included

AE VISA

An evening in rustically elegant surroundings by the open fire

Overlooking the centre of Schluchsee from above, this little holiday hotel is run by the Heger family, who are particularly proud of the personal care they take of their guests. Bedrooms are in a wing extending into the lovely gardens; mostly furnished in tasteful country style, they all have a south-facing terrace or balcony and some benefit from a view of the lake. Among the other amenities is the establishment's own patisserie and a wellness and beauty area with a lovely swimming pool. The stylish restaurant with its delicate wrought-iron decor also has an inviting terrace giving on to the gardens.

Sights nearby: Domed church of St Blasien (15km south), Wutach Gorge (19km east)

Access: On B 500 between Titisee-Neustadt and Waldshut-Tiengen

80 DORER

Rolf Scherer

Franz-Schubert-Str. 20
78141 Schönwald
Tel. (07722) 9 50 50
Fax (07722) 950530 – www.hotel-dorer.de

Open all year • 15 rooms, all with balcony, 2 non-smoking • Restaurant with terrace: evening menus from 20€, main courses 17-22€; half board 20€ • Garden, car park; dogs allowed in hotel but not in restaurant • Indoor pool, tennis court, bicycle hire, wine tasting

92/115 €, Breakfast included (WE: 130/150 €)

AE D VISA MC

Relaxing on the grass surrounded by fine old trees

The comfortable accommodation here consists of rooms with dark wood panelling, some of them with exposed timbers. Equally rustic is the restaurant, divided into a number of separate little spaces and provided with a fine tiled stove. However, should you not want to spend your whole holiday snuggled up next to the stove, there are plenty of outdoor activities to tempt you. For example, there is a chairlift and a cross-country ski trail just outside the door. And even when it gets really cold, you can enjoy yourself wholeheartedly in the snow, secure in the knowledge that the stove is glowing away just inside.

Sights nearby: Triberg waterfall (7km north), Furtwangen Clock Museum (9km south)

Access: On the B 500 between Triberg and Furtwangen

81 MÜHLE ZU GERSBACH

Martin Buchleither

€€ Zum Bühl 4
79650 Schopfheim-Gersbach
Tel. (07620) 9 04 00
Fax (07620) 904050
hotel@muehle.de – www.muehle.de

Closed 10 Jan to 4 Feb • 15 rooms, including 8 with balcony • Restaurant with terrace (closed Tue, midday Wed): set lunch 17.60-48€, set dinner 19-48€; half board • Garden, parking; dogs allowed in hotel • Sauna, cookery courses, Nordic walking

38/58 €, Breakfast included (WE: 42/64 €)
VISA MC

The Wurlitzer in the parlour

In an old mill building - there's a little water-wheel in the garden - this family establishment is located downhill from the church, well away from through traffic. The decor of the rooms is contemporary, with solid furnishings in pale wood. The panelled roof studio is particularly attractive, offering plenty of space and boasting its own tiled stove. The restaurant is divided into a number of intimate spaces and has tasteful decor with much attention paid to detail. When the sun shines, there is an inviting terrace and well-kept garden to enjoy.

Sights nearby: Gersbach Weidepark, Todtnau MTB Fun Park (25km north)

Access: From B 317 north of Schopfheim via Raitbach-Schweigmatt 12km east

82 HIRSCH

Thomas Zimmermann

Hauptstr. 11
78713 Schramberg
Tel. (07422) 28 01 20
Fax (07422) 2801218
info@hotel-gasthof-hirsch.com – www.hotel-gasthof-hirsch.com

Closed 1 week over Fastnacht, 2 weeks early Jul • 6 rooms • Restaurant (closed Tue, midday Wed): set lunch 22-28€, set dinner 43-50€; half board 20€ • Dogs allowed in hotel, not in restaurant • 50% fee reduction at Königsfeld golf club

95/100 €, Breakfast included

AE JCB VISA MC

The vast selection of wines from here and abroad

This historic inn located in a traffic-calmed part of the town centre offers an out-of-the-ordinary experience to its guests. The elegant and comfortable bedrooms are exceptionally well-kept and are lavishly furnished, mostly with period pieces. Some have marble bathrooms and their own jacuzzi. The choice may be small, but it is perfectly formed! The restaurant on the first floor is stylishly elegant, with wall-panelling and fascinating features like pewter tableware.

Sights nearby: Schiltach Old Town (10km west), Alpirsbach monastery church (18km north)

Access: From Exit 34 on A 81 by B 462

83 FLOHR'S

Kirsten und Georg Flohr

Brunnenstr. 11
78224 Singen-Überlingen am Ried
Tel. (07731) 9 32 30
Fax (07731) 932323 – www.flohrs-restaurant.de

Open all year • 8 rooms, all with balcony, 2 non-smoking • Restaurant with terrace (closed Sun lunchtime, Mon lunchtime): set lunch 26-59€, set dinner 39-59€; half board available • Garden, parking; dogs allowed • Open-air pool, bicycle hire, cookery courses, exhibitions, wine events

113 €, Breakfast included

AE VISA MC

The pretty garden with its little pool

This centrally-located establishment is cared for by a friendly couple with great devotion and personal attention to the needs of their guests. He is responsible for everything that happens in the kitchen, she for the bedrooms, which are in the extension and look out over the tranquil garden. They have been decorated and furnished with sure taste and are suffused with a feeling of timeless elegance. The restaurant with its attractive panelling and traditional decor makes a stylish setting for the culinary delights on offer.

Sights nearby: Radolfzell Old Town (7km east), St George Monastery in Stein am Rhein (15km south)

Access: 5km southeast of Singen towards Radolfzell

84 HIRSCH

Gerd Windhösel

Im Dorf 12
72820 Sonnenbühl-Erpfingen
Tel. (07128) 9 29 10
Fax (07128) 3121 – www.restaurant-hotel-hirsch.de

Closed 1 week mid-Jan, 2 weeks early Nov • 11 rooms, including 2 with balcony, 1 with disabled access and 2 non-smoking • Dorfstube pub, restaurant with terrace (closed midday Mon; Tue): set meal 28-73€; half board 26€ • Garden, parking; dogs allowed in hotel, not in restaurant

73/102 €, Breakfast included

VISA MC

The idyllic garden restaurant in fine weather

There's no doubt that most people come here because of the restaurant forming part of this modernised inn, which is centrally located but well away from the main road. Gerd Windhösel pampers his guests with fine cuisine, which is served either in a stylish country ambience or in the homely village bar, its rustic atmosphere enhanced by wood panelling and floors. The guest accommodation is in sparklingly clean and impeccably kept bedrooms with comfortable furnishings in natural wood. Some have pleasant little sitting areas.

Sights nearby: Bärenhöhle cave (4km north), Schloss Lichtenstein (16km northeast)

Access: North of B 32/B 313 junction

85 KREUZ-POST

Michael Zahn

Hauptstr. 65
79219 Staufen
Tel. (07633) 9 53 20
Fax (07633) 953232 – www.kreuz-post-staufen.de

Closed 13-26 Jan • 5 rooms, all non-smoking • Restaurant with terrace: (closed Wed) set lunch 25-36.50€, set dinner 25-64€; half board 25€ • Parking; dogs allowed in restaurant, not in hotel

95/100 €, Breakfast included

JCB VISA MC

The crooked lanes and alleyways of the medieval core

Rich in tradition, this inn stands at the entrance to the traffic-free centre of "Faust's Town" - it was here in 1539 that the Devil is supposed to have snatched Dr Faustus away. The comfortable rooms have individual decor and furnishings. Because the place has belonged to the Schladerer family since 1844, and because this is where the famous fruit brandies that bear their name originated, the rooms are not numbered but given the names of types of fruit. With colourful panelling and tiled stoves, the attractive dining rooms in regional style radiate the welcoming atmosphere typical of Baden.

Sights nearby: Staufenburg castle, St Trudpert Abbey (8km east)

Access: From Exit 64a on A 5 via Bad Krozingen

86 ROMANTIK HOTEL TRAUBE

Romy Recknagel

Brabandtgasse 2
70599 Stuttgart-Plieningen
Tel. (0711) 45 89 20
Fax (0711) 4589220 – www.romantik-hotel-traube.de

Closed Good Friday to Easter Monday, fortnight in Aug, 23-31 Dec • 19 rooms, including 4 with balcony, 6 non-smoking and 1 with disabled access • Restaurant with terrace (closed Sun, Sat midday and Mon midday): main course from 12€, set meals 48-52.50€ • Parking; dogs allowed

105/195 €, Breakfast included (WE: 95/195 €)

VISA

"Recki's Bar and Bistro" in the old village smithy next door

Right by the church in Plieningen on the outskirts of Stuttgart, this old timber-framed building dating from around 1680 makes an attractive, historic setting for your stay. Some of the rooms are in a cheerfully rustic style, others are elegantly furnished with period pieces. A number of them have comfortable little sitting areas. The dining areas are also stylishly rustic, and the playful decor adds a certain something. The champagne breakfast is an especially good way to start the day.

Sights nearby: Palladium Theatre (musicals), State Gallery

Access: From Exit 53 on A 8

87 OCHSEN

Jeanette Bender

Ulmer Str. 323
70327 Stuttgart-Wangen
Tel. (0711) 4 07 05 00
Fax (0711) 40705099
info@ochsen-online.de – www.ochsen-online.de

Open all year • 22 rooms, all with air-conditioning, 6 with balcony and 16 non-smoking • Restaurant with beer garden: main course 8-28€; half board 18€ • Garden, parking; dogs allowed in restaurant, not in hotel

107/128 €, Breakfast included

AE JCB VISA

A cool drink in the beer garden

Wood is used to most attractive effect in this half-timbered establishment not far from the banks of the River Neckar, and the warm colours help create a comfortable and welcoming atmosphere. The rooms are stylish and unfussy and benefit from exceptionally good facilities. Some even boast whirlpool baths. You will appreciate the ambience of the bar, wine cellar and Alpine parlour, which features wall and ceiling panelling and offer a fine range of gastronomic delights. Note too the splendid tiled stove.

Sights nearby: Mercedes-Benz Museum, Wilhelma Zoo

Access: Close to Gottlieb Daimler Stadium, on far side of the River Neckar parallel to B 10

88 HIRSCHEN

Hans-Paul Steiner

Hauptstr. 69
79295 Sulzburg
Tel. (07634) 82 08
Fax (07634) 6717 – www.hirschen-sulzburg.de

Closed 10-27 Jan, 25 Jul to 11 Aug; reception not staffed Mon, Tue - check-in by special arrangement only • 9 rooms • Restaurant with terrace: (closed Sun, Mon) set lunch 36-98€, set dinner 74-98€ • Dogs allowed

92/128 €, Breakfast included
Credit cards not accepted

The attractive wood floors in the bedrooms

"Laughter and cheerful conversation obligatory" is how this establishment spells out its philosophy. So there is no TV or radio in the bedrooms and if you want a telephone you will have to ask for it. Much better just to relax and soak up the elegant country-house atmosphere, to which the lovely antiques make a special contribution. The restaurant also combines stylishness with authenticity. And the cuisine has one aim only - to maximize your enjoyment by providing you with very special culinary delights.

Sights nearby: Staufenburg castle (7km north), Cassiopeia thermal spa at Badenweiler (14km south)

Access: From Exit 64b on A 5 via Heitersheim

89 HISTORISCHER GASTHOF OCHSEN

Nadine und Markus Daxenbichler

Hauptstr. 40
71732 Tamm
Tel. (07141) 2 99 95 55
Fax (07141) 2999556 – www.ochsen-tamm.de

Closed 24 Dec • 17 rooms, including 4 non-smoking • Restaurant with terrace: set lunch 15.90€, set dinner 33-44€; half board 23€ • Parking; dogs allowed • Bicycle hire, organised walks, carriage rides, cookery courses, culinary wine tastings

89/112 €, Breakfast included (WE: 62 €)

AE VISA MC

An evening in the ancient vaulted cellars

With its trio of prominent gables, this pretty, timber-framed edifice dating in part from the 14th century stands opposite the historic town hall. There's an attractive country-style ambience in the bedrooms with their furnishings in natural wood and, in places, exposed beams. The stylish restaurant features fine wood-panelling, though head for the courtyard if there's a hint of sun. From the nearby station, the S-Bahn will whisk you into the centre of Stuttgart in around 20 minutes.

Sights nearby: Ludwigsburg Baroque palace (7km east), Porsche Museum in Stuttgart-Zuffenhausen (16km south)

Access: From Exit 15 on A 81 towards centre of Tamm

90 BIBERMÜHLE

Rolf Riemensperger

Untere Mühle 1
78250 Tengen-Blumenfeld
Tel. (07736) 9 29 30
Fax (07736) 9293140 – www.bibermuehle.de

Closed 3 weeks in Feb, 24 Dec • 31 rooms, including 1 with balcony • Cafe-restaurant with terrace: set meals 23-38€; half board 21€ • Garden, parking; dogs allowed • Sauna, steam bath

90/107 €, Breakfast included

VISA MC

The restored giant-sized millwheel, 12 metres in diameter

Idyllically sited where the River Biber pours over a waterfall, the old mill offers a measure of peace and quiet just beneath the town centre of Blumenfeld. The annexe has spacious rooms with cherrywood furnishings, while the rooms in the historic mill itself, where oak is used, have a more rustic character. The restaurant extends over two storeys of the mill building; it boasts an authentically traditional atmosphere, with rugged stone walls, a huge open fire and splendid timber columns which are protected by a conservation order.

Sights nearby: Blumberg-Weizen preserved railway (16km west), Rhine Falls at Schaffhausen (20km south)

Access: On B 34 between Tengen and Engen

91 HÄCKERMÜHLE

Claire Stier und Georg Häcker

Im Würmtal 5
75233 Tiefenbronn
Tel. (07234) 42 46
Fax (07234) 5769 – www.haecker-muehle.de

Closed 2 weeks early Feb • 15 rooms, including 8 with balcony and 1 with disabled access • Restaurant with terrace (closed Mon, midday Tue): set meal 25-60€; half board 20-25€ • Garden, parking; dogs allowed • Sauna, bicycle hire, organised walks and longer hikes, wine tasting

75/95 €, Breakfast included (WE: 70/95 €)
AE VISA MC

The staging of events under the heading "art and cooking"

The old mill tucked away in the leafy valley of the River Würm ground grain right up to 1972. Now it makes an idyllic setting for an elegantly rustic restaurant and a functional hotel. The bedrooms feature subtly coloured decor and furnishings in cherrywood or pale oak. Many guests appreciate the "Häckerbrot", a loaf made here in a wood-fired oven to a traditional family recipe. Then there are fresh and salt water tanks, from which fish and crustaceans are plucked and served as fresh as they could possibly be.

Sights nearby: St Maria Magdalena in Tiefenbronn (4km east), Pforzheim deer park (10km north)

Access: 4km west of Tiefenbronn towards Würm

92 OCHSEN-POST

D. und Th. Jost

Franz-Josef-Gall-Str. 13
75233 Tiefenbronn
Tel. (07234) 9 54 50
Fax (07234) 9545145
info@ochsen-post.de – www.ochsen-post.de

Closed 4 weeks Jan • 19 rooms • Restaurant with terrace (closed Tue): set lunch 16.80-160€, set dinner 42-96€ • Garden, parking; dogs allowed

68/85 €, Breakfast included

JCB VISA MC

The fine old ceiling timbers in the bedrooms

This impeccably maintained timber-framed building in a central location promises its guests a nostalgic excursion into the "good old days". In an attractive country style, the bedrooms are furnished in dark wood, supplemented by many a well-chosen antique piece. With their wood panelling, the dining rooms have a similar character. Snug, cosy, intimate, the words are hardly adequate! Such is the allure of the interior that it's difficult to tear yourself away on a sunny day and venture outside to sit in the delightful surroundings of the garden café.

Sights nearby: St. Maria Magdalena, Pforzheim Jewellery Museum (15km northwest)

Access: In the Würmtal 15km southeast of Pforzheim towards Weil der Stadt

93 SONNE-POST

Gerhard Wehrle

Landstr. 13
79822 Titisee-Neustadt
Tel. (07669) 9 10 20
Fax (07669) 910299 – www.sonne-post.de

Closed 4-22 Apr, 15 Nov-20 Dec • 19 rooms, including 15 with balcony • Cafe-restaurant with terrace: (closed Mon) set lunch 14-25€, set dinner 14-30€; half board 10€ • Children's play room and playground, garden, parking; dogs allowed in restaurant, not in hotel • Outdoor chess, table tennis, organised walks

72/89 €, Breakfast included (WE: 69/84 €)

VISA MC

The enchanting view from the bedroom balconies

After being burnt down, this establishment was completely rebuilt in 1992 but has lost none of its original authentic character. The wonderfully harmonious interior is deeply rooted in the traditions of Black Forest hospitality, not surprising, since the Wehrle family has been making guests welcome here since 1870. The rooms are comfortable and feature much attractive use of wood. There's plenty of wood too in the dining rooms, where painted panelling helps create a cheerful atmosphere.

Sights nearby: Hinterzarten Ski Museum (14km south), St Peter's Benedictine Monastery (17km northwest)

Access: In Waldau, 10km north from Neustadt by Titisee road or by B 500 towards Furtwangen

94 TRESCHERS SCHWARZWALD-ROMANTIK-HOTEL

H. J. Trescher

Seestr. 10
79822 Titisee-Neustadt
Tel. (07651) 80 50
Fax (07651) 8116
trescher@mail.pcom.de – www.schwarzwaldhotel-trescher.de

Open all year • 84 rooms, including 40 with balcony • Restaurants with terrace: set dinner 25-30€, main course 19-25€; half board 30€ • Garden, parking; dogs allowed in hotel, not in restaurant • Health and beauty area, massage, gym, indoor pool, open-air pool, sauna, skittles

130/200 €, Breakfast included

AE ⓓ VISA MC

Coffee and cakes on the lakeside terrace

This lakeside location is simply enchanting! Guests are accommodated in spacious bedrooms featuring warm colours or furnishings in lime-washed natural wood. Your well-being is catered for by a generous leisure area, with plenty of facilities and beauty treatments. Even when the weather isn't at its best, you can still enjoy the lake; there are panoramic views of it from the indoor pool. Enjoy the friendly service, allow yourself to be pampered and have your every wish fulfilled.

Sights nearby: Feldberg (13km southwest), Löffingen Black Forest Park (17km east)

Access: On the lakeside in Titisee

95 **RÖSSLE**

Thomas Maier

Kapellenweg 2
79682 Todtmoos-Strick
Tel. (07674) 9 06 60
Fax (07674) 8838 – www.hotel-roessle.de

Closed 2 Nov-20 Dec • 22 rooms, 10 with balcony, one with disabled access and 10 non-smoking • Café-restaurant with terrace (closed Tue) : menu 13-20€; half board 16€ • Garden, car park; dogs allowed • Health and fitness area: sauna and gym, tennis court, table tennis, billiards, boule, giant chess, Nordic walking, snow-shoe excursions

88/100 €, Breakfast included

VISA MC

The fine leisure facilities of the so-called "Black Forest Village of Well-Being"

A serpentine approach road leads up to this typical Black Forest inn, which was once a staging-post on the old pass road to the Hochkopf. The accommodation is in a pair of guesthouses idyllically located on the road through the village of Strick, a setting which is responsible for much of their charm. Much use is made of different woods in the decor of the comfortable country-style bedrooms. One of the guesthouses is designed in accordance with ecological principles and is entirely built of wood; some of its apartments have their own tiled stoves, guaranteeing a warm and friendly atmosphere.

Sights nearby: Hans Thoma Gallery in Bernau (3km northeast), St Blaise Cathedral (16km east)

Access: 2km northwest of Todtmoos; follow signs for Todtnau

96 SONNENALM

Familie Brender

Hornweg 21
79674 Todtnauberg
Tel. (07671) 18 00
Fax (07671) 9212 – www.hotel-sonnenalm.de

Closed 7 Nov to 15 Dec • 15 rooms, including 14 with balcony and 4 non-smoking • Restaurant for residents only: half-board 14-16€ • Sunbathing lawn, parking; dogs not allowed • Swimming pool, sauna, solarium, steam bath, fitness facilities, organised walks

72/104 €, Breakfast included

MC

The charmingly old-fashioned restaurant with its tiled stove

This establishment certainly deserves its name of "Sunny Meadow", located as it is among woods and pastures and basking in the sun on a south-facing slope. Here, high above the town, there is peace and quiet and, on clear days, a view extending as far as the Bernese Oberland. You can improve your tan by taking it easy on the balcony or stretching out on the grass of the idyllic lawn. The bedrooms feature hand-painted furniture and are impeccably kept.

Sights nearby: Steinwasenpark (9km north), Schauinsland visitor mine (17km north)

Access: 6km north of Todtnau via Aftersteg towards Schauinsland

97 WELLNESS- UND VITALHOTEL MANGLER

Helmut Mangler

Ennerbachstr. 28
79674 Todtnauberg
Tel. (07671) 9 69 30
Fax (07671) 8693 – www.mangler.de

Open all year • 30 rooms, including 24 with balcony and 6 non-smoking • Cafe-restaurant with terrace: set lunch 18-24€, set dinner 25-38€; half board 19€ • Garden, parking; dogs not allowed • Health and beauty area, aqua-fitness, morning gymnastics, relaxation and vitality training, organised walks, wine seminars

134/176 €, Breakfast included
VISA MC

The cheerful twitterings of the dawn chorus

This is the place to book into if you want to get close to the sun. More than 1 000 metres up on a south-facing slope in the superb high country around Todtnauberg, this family-run establishment offers attractive country-style rooms as well as right royal wellness and beauty facilities. The lavish use of glass means that the indoor spaces are flooded with glorious light and that you benefit from changing views of the landscape all around. The elegantly rustic restaurant with its well thought-out decor makes a fine setting for dining.

Sights nearby: Todtnau waterfalls, Feldberg (17km east)

Access: 6km north of Todtnau via Aftersteg towards Schauinsland

98 ROMANTIK PARKHOTEL WEHRLE

Georg Wiengarn

Gartenstr. 24
78098 Triberg
Tel. (07722) 8 60 20
Fax (07722) 860290 – www.parkhotel-wehrle.de

Open all year • 50 rooms, 19 with balcony, 35 non-smoking • Café, tea room, restaurant with terrace: lunch menu 18-22€, evening menu 29-43€; half board 29€ • Garden, car park; dogs allowed • Indoor and outdoor pools, sauna, solarium, fitness equipment

129/149 €, Breakfast included

AE VISA

The tea-room where more than 20 varieties of tea are dispensed from a samovar

This stately corner building with its mansard roof in the centre of Triberg straightaway makes a striking impression. Hidden behind it is a further guesthouse and, not to be overlooked, a pretty park with a little villa. The rooms in the main building are elegantly furnished with period pieces, while those in the guesthouse are in contemporary country style. The villa in the park, by contrast, features antique furnishings in Biedermeier style. There's a choice of places to eat: the rustic "Old Smithy" and the classically elegant "Ox Parlour" or "Red Salon". In addition, there is the Garden Café in the park where you can sample cakes and pastries made on the premises.

Sights nearby: Triberg waterfall; Furtwangen Clock Museum (16km south)

Access: On B 500 between Hausach and Furtwangen

99 STAUDE

Rolf Fleig

Obertal 20
78098 Triberg-Gremmelsbach
Tel. (07722) 48 02
Fax (07722) 21018 – www.gasthaus-staude.de

Closed early to late Nov, 1 week Mar • 12 rooms, 1 with balcony, 1 with shower on landing • Restaurant with terrace (closed Tue): main course 9.80-22€; half board 18€ • Garden, parking; dogs allowed • Sauna, fitness rooom, bicycle hire

68/76 €, Breakfast included
Credit cards not accepted

The inviting terrace in front of the building

On the forest edge, half-hidden among the upland meadows, this is a typical Black Forest house. Here, 900 metres above sea level, you will have no difficulty in giving yourself over to the peace and quiet of the idyllic countryside. When you go indoors, you will find interiors in tune with the natural world outside. The bedrooms feature lightwood country-style furnishings, and some have painted peasant-style pieces and even four-poster beds. The dining rooms are equally attractive, with wood floors and ceilings and tiled stoves. In the courtyard you can't miss the massive log cabin which houses the sauna.

Sights nearby: Black Forest Museum and Maria in der Tanne pilgrimage church in Triberg (9km southwest)

Access: 9km northeast of Triberg; first by B 33 towards St Georgen then turn left at the Sommerau watershed

100 LANDHOTEL HIRSCH

Brigitte Fischer

Schönbuchstr. 28
72074 Tübingen-Bebenhausen
Tel. (07071) 6 09 30
Fax (07071) 609360 – www.landhotel-hirsch-bebenhausen.de

Open all year • 12 rooms, all non-smoking • Cafe-restaurant (closed Tue) with terrace: main course 13-22.50€ • Parking; dogs allowed

128/145 €, Breakfast included

AE · VISA · MC

A punt trip around the islands in the River Neckar

A most convenient place to stay, this country hotel is located just outside Tübingen, which had the good fortune to escape from wartime destruction and has consquently preserved intact its wonderfully romantic townscape. The hotel offers country-style rooms with timeless and tasteful furnishings in light natural wood. The bathrooms feature much marble and reinforce the overall stylishness of the establishment. The restaurant too is special, partly in elegant country-style, partly of a more rustic character.

Sights nearby: Bebenhausen monastery, Hohentübingen Castle (6km south)

Access: 6km north of Tübingen, follow the brown Kloster Bebenhausen signs

101 ZUR TANNE

Claus Ruch

Alter Weg 4
79677 Tunau
Tel. (07673) 3 10
Fax (07673) 1000 – www.tanne-tunau.de

Closed 1-10 May, 20 Nov to 10 Dec • 13 rooms, including 4 non-smoking, 3 with balcony • Restaurant with terrace (closed Mon eve, Tue): set meal max. 35€; half board 15€ • Garden, parking; dogs allowed in hotel, not in restaurant • Indoor pool, sauna, tennis

80/90 €, Breakfast included (WE: 140/160 €)
VISA MC

The mild but stimulating climate here in the heart of the Black Forest

750 metres above sea level, overlooking the climatic resort of Schönau, this 400-year-old Black Forest house dispenses traditional hospitality in generous measure to its guests. The bedrooms are unpretentious but comfortable and immaculately looked after, the dining room's cosy and as homely as could be. Here, where the tarmac road gives out, you might think you were on the very edge of civilisation, and you certainly won't be disturbed by through traffic. But the cooking is far from unsophisticated, service is hearty, and the surroundings offer plenty of things to do all year round.

Sights nearby: Todtnau waterfalls (10km north), Belchen (15km northwest)

Access: 3km east of Schönau im Schwarzwald (on B 317) by valley road and Bischmatt

102 BÜRGERBRÄU

Manfred Metzler

Aufkircher Str. 20
88662 Überlingen
Tel. (07551) 9 27 40
Fax (07551) 66017
dorfwirt@aol.com – www.buergerbraeu-ueberlingen.de

Closed 15 Feb to 10 March • 12 rooms • Restaurant (closed Wed, Thu): main course 15-20€ • Parking; dogs allowed

78/82 €, Breakfast included

AE, D, VISA, MC

Mrs Metzler's collection of more than 1 000 thimbles

This pretty half-timbered building stands above the old core of Überlingen, in the so-called "village" between the two fortifications. It's a good location, with good access by road and only a short distance on foot to the lakeside promenade and the town park. With pine furnishings and colourful carpets and curtains, the rooms are comfortable, and some of them are further enlivened by playfully flowery wallpaper. The restaurant consists of a rustic bar where locals congregate at the "Stammtisch", plus the dining room itself in attractive country style.

Sights nearby: Minster, Unterhuldingen Stilt Dwellings Museum (7km south)

Access: Überlingen (Aufkirch) Exit on Singen-Lindau Autobahn which leads directly into Aufkircher Strasse.

103 ROMANTIK HOTEL JOHANNITER-KREUZ

Andreas Liebich

Johanniterweg 11
88662 Überlingen-Andelshofen
Tel. (07551) 6 10 91
Fax (07551) 67336 – www.romantikhotels.com/ueberlingen

Open all year • 25 rooms, including 12 with balcony and 2 non-smoking • Restaurant (closed Mon, midday Tue) with terrace: set meal 25-48€; half board 28€ • Garden, parking; dogs allowed by prior arrangement • Sauna, steam bath, jacuzzi, solarium, sunbathing lawn, bicycle hire

100/150 €, Breakfast included

VISA

Andelshofen when the orchards are in glorious blossom

Just below the church in the middle of the delightful fruit-growing village of Andelshofen, this farmstead was once the abode of the Knights of St John Jerusalem. The name of the 300-year-old establishment recalls those days, but the farmstead is now a hotel, with a modern annexe called the “Luisenhöhe”. With low ceilings, exposed timbers and period furnishings the old farmstead is full of historic character, while the new building has spacious rooms with cherrywood furnishings. There’s plenty of romantic atmosphere in the restaurant, which also features exposed timbers as well as a homely open fire.

Sights nearby: Birnau pilgrimage church (6km southeast), Affenberg Salem: a free-range Barbary ape park (12km east)

Access: Pfullendorf/Uberlingen exit on B 31, then towards Andelshofen

104 REBMANNSHOF

K. D. Besser

Maurach 2
88690 Uhldingen-Mühlhofen
Tel. (07556) 93 90
Fax (07556) 6555 – www.hotel-pilgerhof.de/rebmannshof

Open all year • 48 rooms, all with air conditioning, 33 with balcony and 8 non-smoking • Cafe-restaurant with terrace: set meal 16-35€; half board 16€ • Parking; dogs allowed • Sauna, solarium, jacuzzi, gym, bicycle hire

96/140 €, Breakfast included

VISA MC

The jacuzzi in its timber-framed setting

This historic 17th century fisherman's house profits from a peaceful location right on Lake Constance opposite the flower-bedecked island of Mainau. The half-timbered exterior is as it ever was, but the interior has been transformed. The bedrooms are furnished in contemporary style, and are enlivened with bold blue splashes of colour in bedding and curtains. Here and there, for example in the restaurant with its rustic roof-beams, the designers have played with the contrast between modern decor and venerable structure. To the rear of the building, a lovely terrace runs down to the water, which guests can make the most of, thanks to the hotel's own bathing place and landing stage.

Sights nearby: Birnau pilgrimage church, Unteruhldingen stilt dwelling museum (4km south)

Access: Klosterkirche Birnau Exit on B 31 between Uberlingen and Oberuhdingen

105 SCHIEFES HAUS

Frau T. Scholl

Schwörhausgasse 6
89073 Ulm
Tel. (0731) 96 79 30
Fax (0731) 9679333 – www.hotelschiefeshausulm.de

Closed 1-6 Jan, 25-31 Dec • 11 rooms, including 2 non-smoking • Parking; dogs allowed • Town tours

140 €, Breakfast included

AE VISA MC

The rustic look-out above the River Blau

Pisa has its Leaning Tower and Ulm its Crooked House. The name is no exaggeration; the building boasts an entry in the Guinness Book of Records as the "world's most crooked hotel". In the middle of Ulm's idyllic Fishermen's Quarter on the banks of the River Blau, the 15th century building has gained its present appearance through severe subsidence. It's equally out of the ordinary inside, with scarcely a right angle to be seen. Low ceilings, massive beams and exposed stonework have been successfully combined with tasteful contemporary design. This is a place that really has to be seen and experienced!

Sights nearby: German bread museum, Wiblingen monastery (7km south)

Access: In centre of Ulm between minster and Danube

106 LAMM

Sabine Bramm

Klosterbergstr. 45
71665 Vaihingen-Horrheim
Tel. (07042) 8 32 20
Fax (07042) 832250 – www.hotel-lamm-horrheim.de

Closed 1st week Jan • 23 rooms, including 1 with disabled access and 15 non-smoking • Restaurant with terrace: (closed Sun eve, Mon) set lunch 20-28€, set dinner 38-60€; half board 25€ • Parking; dogs allowed in hotel, not in restaurant • Bicycle hire, wine tasting, guided walks

76/98 €, Breakfast included

AE JCB VISA MC

Exploring the hilly landscape of the Kreichgau on one of the hotel's bikes

Next to the timber-framed town hall in the pretty wine village of Horrheim, the "Lamb" was rebuilt in 1994 on the foundations of its historic predecessor. It is now a modern hotel-restaurant with contemporary fittings. The bedrooms have functional wood furnishings and some of them are equipped with a kitchenette. Diners in the restaurant or on the sun terrace to the rear of the building can choose from an array of mostly regional dishes, best accompanied by a good Württemberg wine.

Sights nearby: Sweet Museum in Kleinglattbach (3km south), Maulbronn Monastery (14km west), Tripsdrill Leisure Park (16km northeast)

Access: 7km northeast of Vaihingen towards Heilbronn

107 STEINBUCK

Thomas Wernet

Steinbuckstr. 20 (in den Weinbergen)
79235 Vogtsburg-Bischoffingen
Tel. (07662) 91 12 10
Fax (07662) 6079 – www.hotel-steinbuck.de

Closed 3 Jan to 1 Feb, 31 Jul to 10 Aug • 18 rooms, including 5 with terrace • Restaurant with terrace (closed Tue, midday Wed): set meal 22-49€; half board 22€ • Garden, parking; dogs allowed • Sauna, tennis, bicycle hire, cookery courses, wine seminars

91/93 €, Breakfast included
Credit cards not accepted

Strolling through the vineyards and enjoying the fabulous ever-changing views

The "Steinbuck" welcomes its guests in an utterly tranquil, leafy setting high above the vines. Spreading out in front of it like a glorious garden are the vineyards of the Kaiserstuhl. The panorma is vast, and you can savour it from the rooms with their solid natural wood furnishings, from the glazed restaurant, and of course from the sun terrace. It's wonderful to sit here and allow your gaze to soar over the suroundings while being treated to fine local and international dishes. Life couldn't get much better!

Sights nearby: St. Michael Niederrotweil (4km south), Breisach Minster (13km south)

Access: From Exit 59 on A 5 by Riegel, Endingen, Königschaffhausen, Leiselheim

108 ROMANTIK HOTEL WALK'SCHES HAUS

Bernd Werner

Marktplatz 7
76356 Weingarten
Tel. (07244) 7 03 70
Fax (07244) 703740 – www.walksches-haus.de

Closed 1 week in Jan, fortnight in summer holidays • 26 rooms, including 3 with balcony • Restaurant with terrace (closed midday Sat; Tue): set lunch 26-62€, set dinner 32-62€; half board by arrangement • Parking; dogs allowed • Cookery courses

100/120 €, Breakfast included

AE D VISA MC

A hike across the Weingarten moorland

This picturesque timber-framed building dating from 1701 is the principal ornament of the market square in the community of Weingarten on the Walzbach stream. Guests are accommodated either in individually decorated rooms featuring darkwood furnishings in the main building, or in the guesthouse, where the rooms have standard furnishings in light maplewood. The establishment offers traditional cuisine either in the rustically elegant restaurant with its stylish panelling or, in good weather, in the pretty courtyard garden with its pergola.

Sights nearby: Schloss Bruchsal mechanical instruments museum (11km northeast), Karlsruhe state art gallery (14km southwest)

Access: By B 3 between Bruchsal and Karlsruhe-Durlach

109 GOLDENER PFLUG

Udo Stark

Obertorstr. 5
69469 Weinheim an der Bergstraße
Tel. (06201) 9 02 80
Fax (06201) 902829 – www.hotel-goldener-pflug.de

Closed 2 weeks in Jan • 14 rooms, including 2 with balcony • Restaurant (closed Thur, Fri midday); main course 9.90-16€; half board 13€ • Parking; dogs allowed

67/80 €, Breakfast included

JCB VISA MC

An evening stroll through the lovely old town centre of Weinheim

This most attractive old timber-framed building is right in the middle of the delightful town of Weinheim; St Lawrence's Church is nearby, and the famous town hall on the market square is not far away. You may well be tempted to prolong your stay in what the Stark family have made into a welcoming and impeccably run establishment. The comfortable rooms with cherrywood furnishings and the country-style restaurant with its green tiled stove may tempt you to make your stay a long one.

Sights nearby: Exotic arboretum, Windeck castle ruins, Heidelberg castle (17km south)

Access: Via Weinheim interchange on A 5

110 BERGGASTHOF SCHLÜSSEL

Monika Lafferentz

€€ Pfaffenberg 2
79669 Zell-Pfaffenberg
Tel. (07625) 92 48 61
Fax (07625) 924862 – www.berggasthof-schluessel.de

Closed 11 Jan-17 Feb, 24-25 Dec • 11 rooms, 9 with balcony • Café-restaurant with terrace (closed Mon, Tue except for residents): Lunch menu 22-30€, evening menu 22-36€; half board 14.50€ • Garden, car park; dogs allowed in restaurant but not in hotel • Exhibitions

53 €, Breakfast included
VISA MC

The home-made bread and cakes

You are sure to appreciate the many delights of this mountain inn, high up in the peace and quiet of the pretty village of Pfaffenberg with enchanting views of the Wiesental valley. Everything that you could expect of such an establishment is here; the cheerful, upland atmosphere, and an aura of real authenticity. There's no television or telephone in the bedrooms, which feature natural wood or painted furniture, and you dine on good solid food made from local ingredients, either in the rustic dining rooms or outside on the inviting sun terrace.

Sights nearby: Erdmansshöhle Hasel (17km south); Vogelpark Steinen (17km southwest)

Access: B 317 between Schönau and Zell via Mambach or Atzenbach

Bayern

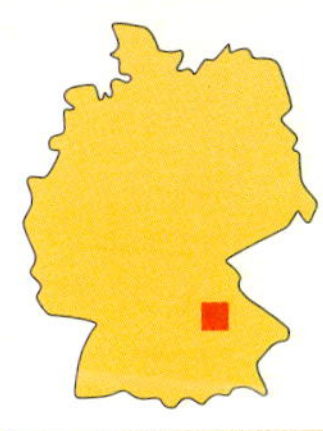

Bavaria is picture-book Germany at her most delightful and recognisable. Here you'll find the fairy-tale castles of King Ludwig in an incomparable alpine setting; glorious jewels of Baroque architecture like the great abbey of Ottobeuren, Weltenburg monastery on the Danube, and Passau cathedral rising on its peninsula between three rivers. Magic Munich herself was rebuilt in the early 19th century as a royal capital and boasts an array of world-class museums, while Rothenburg-ob-der-Tauber and the other exquisite little cities are strung like pearls along the country's most famous tourist route, the Romantic Road. Foremost among the proud cities of Franconia are the prince-bishops' capitals of Würzburg and Bamberg and Imperial Nuremberg, where Germany's past comes alive as nowhere else. Deep-rooted customs, the traditional costumes, the Oktoberfest...even to the Germans, there's a hint of cliché about this perfect picture. But if there's a deep local pride in these Bavarian archetypes, and plenty of truth to them, the region's charm can be felt in every part of life; enjoyable enough in the tourist hot-spots, it comes into its own in a host of out-of-the-way places too.

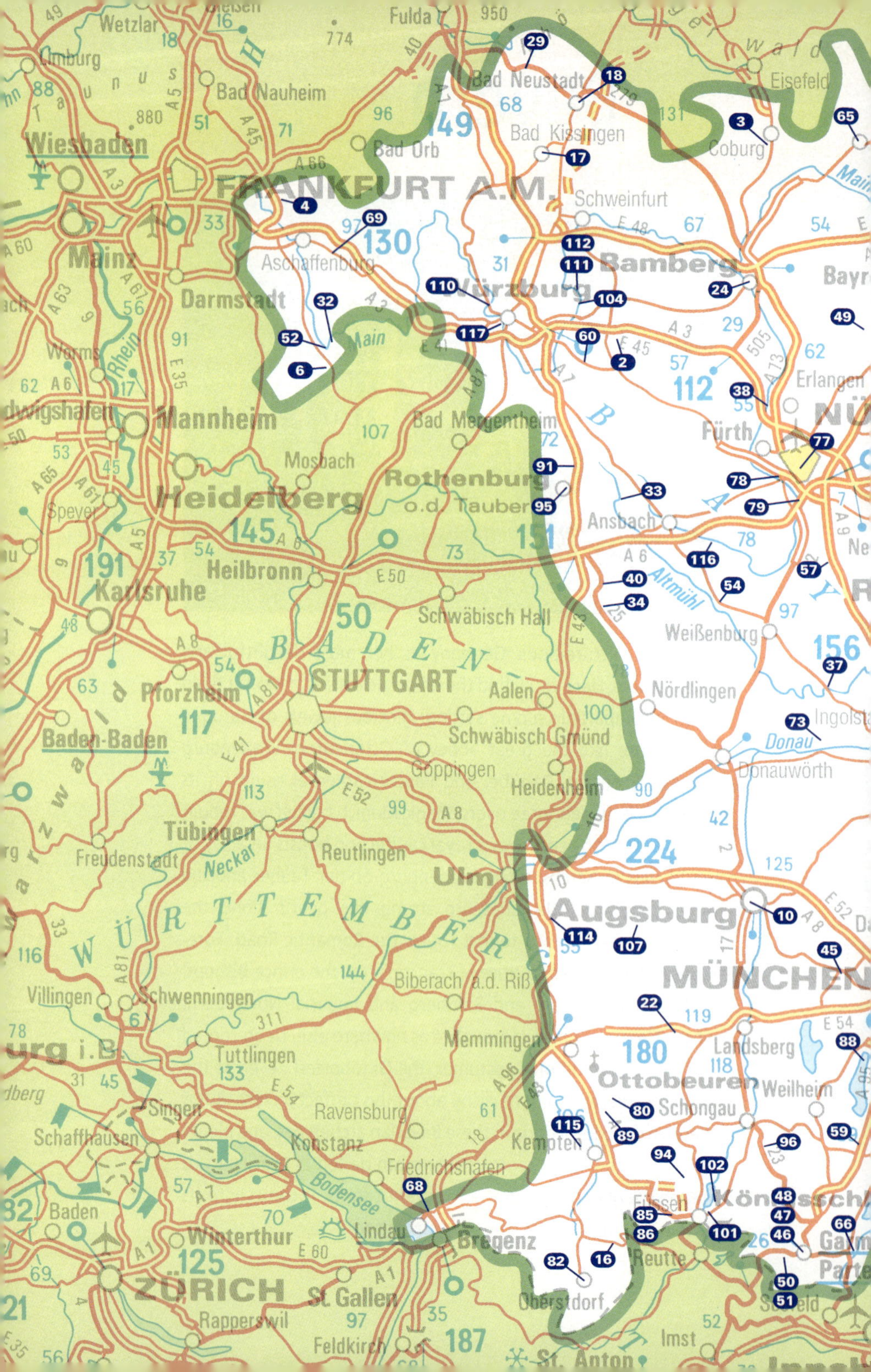

Wetzlar
Limburg
Bad Nauheim
Wiesbaden
FRANKFURT A.M.
Mainz
Darmstadt
Worms
Rhein
Ludwigshafen
Mannheim
Heidelberg
Speyer
Karlsruhe
Pforzheim
Baden-Baden
Freudenstadt
Tübingen
Neckar
Reutlingen
Villingen
Schwenningen
Tuttlingen
Singen
Schaffhausen
Konstanz
Bodensee
Winterthur
ZÜRICH
Rapperswil
St Gallen
Feldkirch
Lindau
Bregenz
Friedrichshafen
Ravensburg
Memmingen
Biberach a.d. Riß
Ulm
Göppingen
Heidenheim
Schwäbisch Gmünd
Aalen
STUTTGART
Schwäbisch Hall
Heilbronn
Mosbach
Bad Mergentheim
Rothenburg o.d. Tauber
BADEN-WÜRTTEMBERG
Fulda
Bad Neustadt
Bad Kissingen
Bad Orb
Schweinfurt
Coburg
Eisefeld
Aschaffenburg
Main
Würzburg
Bamberg
Erlangen
Fürth
Ansbach
Altmühl
Weißenburg
Nördlingen
Donau
Donauwörth
Ingolst
Augsburg
MÜNCHEN
Landsberg
Weilheim
Schongau
Ottobeuren
Kempten
Füssen
Königsschl
Reutte
Oberstdorf
Seefeld
Imst
St. Anton
Garm
Parte

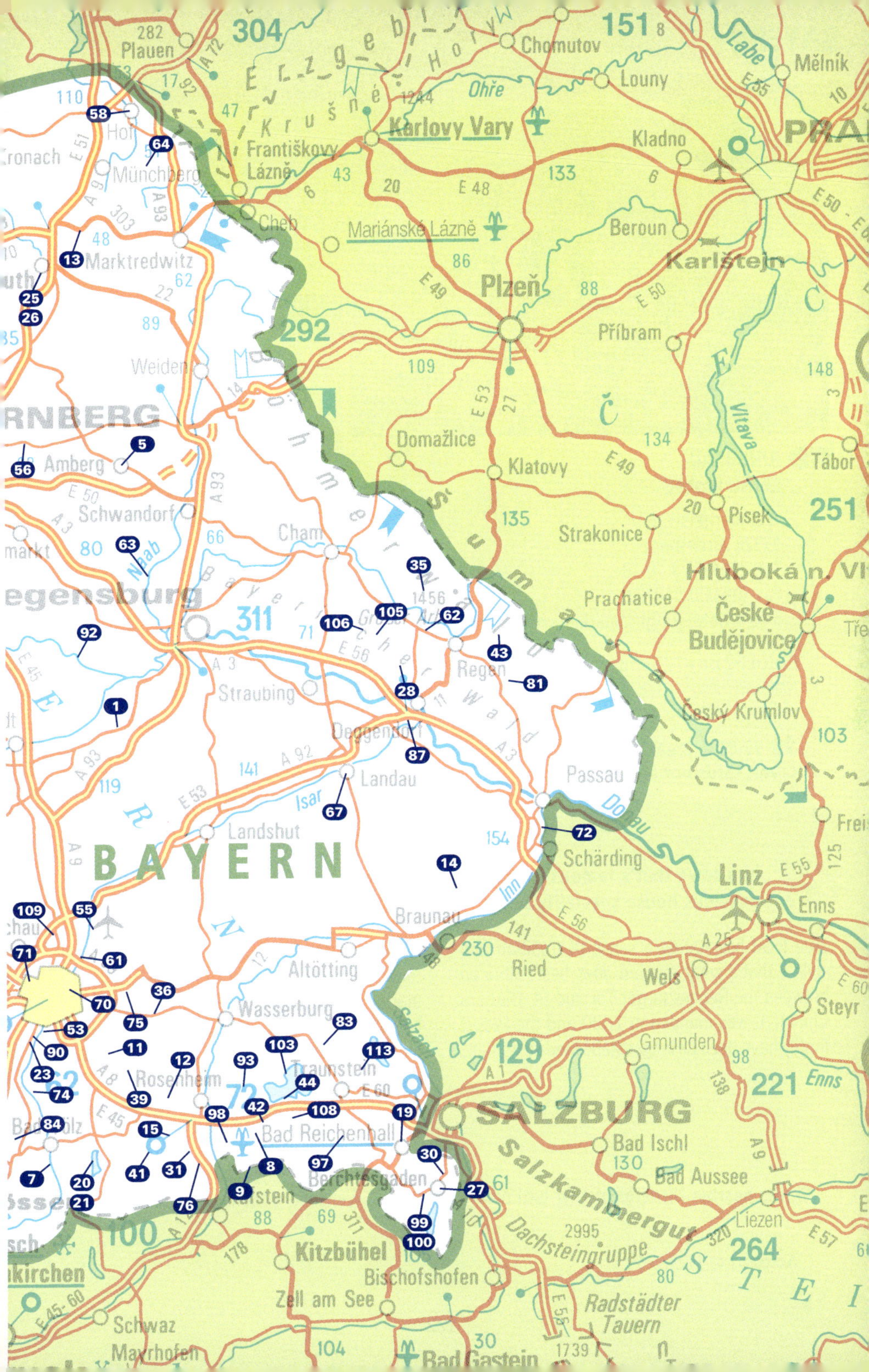

Plauen
Chomutov
Mělník
Louny
Labe
Ohře
Karlovy Vary
Kladno
Hof
Kronach
Münchberg
Františkovy Lázně
Cheb
Mariánské Lázně
Beroun
Karlštejn
Marktredwitz
Plzeň
Příbram
Weiden
Vltava
Domažlice
Klatovy
Tábor
Amberg
Schwandorf
Písek
Strakonice
Cham
Hluboká n. Vl.
Naab
Prachatice
České Budějovice
Regen
Straubing
Český Krumlov
Deggendorf
Passau
Landau
Isar
Donau
Landshut
Schärding
BAYERN
Linz
Inn
Braunau
Enns
Ried
Altötting
Wels
Steyr
Wasserburg
Gmunden
Traunstein
Rosenheim
Salzach
SALZBURG
Bad Reichenhall
Bad Ischl
Bad Tölz
Berchtesgaden
Bad Aussee
Salzkammergut
Liezen
Dachsteingruppe
Kitzbühel
Bischofshofen
Zell am See
Radstädter Tauern
Schwaz
Mayrhofen
Bad Gastein

1 JUNGBRÄU

Christl Probst

Weinbergerstr. 6
93326 Abensberg
Tel. (09443) 9 10 70
Fax (09443) 910733
info@hotel-jungbraeu.de – www.hotel-jungbraeu.de

Closed 1-2 Jan • 17 rooms, including 1 with balcony and 3 non-smoking • Restaurant with beer garden (closed Mon): set lunch 10-18€, main course 4.80-19€; half board 12.50€ • Garden, parking; dogs allowed • Free use of fitness centre for residents

75/85 €, Breakfast included
Credit cards not accepted

In a town that's famous for its asparagus, you should be able to guess the delicious house speciality here

True local hospitality, a sense of tradition and style - that's what this inn does best. Situated between the Regensburger Tor and St. Barbara Church, it was founded in 1620 and the Probst family have been its long-established custodians for over a century. In addition to the agreeable rooms in country house or rural rustic style, the marvellous beer garden and a really cosy pine breakfast room with solid, homely furniture are all very appealing and very typically Bavarian.

Sights nearby: Niederbayrischer bird park (2km south), Weltenburg monastery (15km north)

Access: Exit 49 on A 93

2 ZUR SCHWANE

Herbert Schäfer

Hauptstr. 10
97355 Abtswind
Tel. (09383) 60 51
Fax (09383) 6052 – www.gasthof-schwane.de

Open all year • 9 rooms, including 1 non-smoking • Restaurant with terrace (closed Mon): main course 5-15€; half board 13€ • Garden, parking; dogs allowed

67/78 €, Breakfast included

VISA MC

All of the bathrooms have natural light from the outside windows

'The Swan' is typically Franconian: unspectacular, no frills, but with an easy, immediately likeable charm to it. Dating back to 1739, the inn has been run by the Schäfer family since 1885. Things have remained simple and down-to-earth: a decent glass of beer is still here for the asking and traditional, regional specialities are the menu's forte. The cosy rooms, furnished with rustic bare-wood finish which seems to fit the original character of the place, are all in the new annex.

Sights nearby: Iphofen Knauf Museum: (12 km southeast), Maria im Weingarten pilgrimage church in Volkach (16 km northwest)

Access: From Exit 75 on A 3 via Rüdenhausen

3 SCHLOSS HOHENSTEIN

Michael Kötterl, Stefan Wandt

Hohenstein 1
96482 Ahorn-Hohenstein
Tel. (09565) 9 49 40
Fax (09565) 949460 – www.schloss-hohenstein.de

Open all year • 13 rooms, including 1 with balcony • Restaurant with terrace: set meal 29-62€; half board 25€ • Garden, parking; dogs allowed • Guided tours of castle, exhibitions, wine seminars, cookery courses

95/230 €, Breakfast included

AE VISA MC

The castle grounds and the romantic little temple folly

Although the grounds of the castle were laid out in the 16th and 18th centuries, their appearance today owes much to the Historicism in vogue in the 1800s. All this makes for a fascinating setting which is worth a visit in itself, but is further enhanced by tasteful interior design of the castle. As well as stuccoed ceilings, the period-styled furniture gives the rooms an elegantly formal atmosphere, but some parts of the house have been reworked in contemporary, clean-lined style - take your pick! See the fine period architecture from a different angle in the conservatory restaurant in the inner courtyard.

Sights nearby: Ehrenburg castle (9 km northeast), Banz monastery (22 km south)

Access: From B 4 south of Coburg via Triebsdorf and Haarth

4 SCHLOSSBERG

Familie Reising

Schlossberg 2
63755 Alzenau-Wasserlos
Tel. (06023) 9 48 80
Fax (06023) 948813 – www.reising-hotels.de

Open all year • 18 rooms, including 14 with balcony, 3 non-smoking, 1 with disabled access • Restaurant with terrace (closed Mon): set lunch 30-61€, set dinner 19.50-61€; half board from 19.50€ • Parking; dogs allowed • Wine tasting, guided walks

96/108 €, Breakfast included

AE VISA MC

Wandering through the vineyards

This sizeable hotel lies surrounded by hillside vineyards. Built in 1965 and comprehensively remodelled in 1997 it boasts practically equipped rooms with modern white baths. In addition to these features, some also have an individual terrace or balcony from where the view stretches away towards the Frankfurt skyline and beyond. The restaurant, designed in the style of a classic dining room, shares the same wonderful vistas and the outdoor tables are particularly delightful.

Sights nearby: Schönbusch castle and park (19 km south), Schloss Johannisburg at Aschaffenburg (21 km southeast)

Access: From Exit 45 on A 45 towards Alzenau

5 **DRAHTHAMMER SCHLÖSSL**

Margit Michel-Trettenbach

Drahthammer Str. 30
92224 Amberg
Tel. (09621) 70 30
Fax (09621) 88424 – www.hotel-drahthammer-schloessl.com

Closed 2-6 Jan, 23-24 Dec, 26-30 Dec • 43 rooms, including 3 with balcony • Restaurant with terrace: set meal 15-55€ • Parking; dogs allowed • Health and beauty facilities, bicycle hire, tours of the town

82/131 €, Breakfast included

AE (D) VISA MC

The delightfully light and airy conservatory

Some of this family-run establishment's accommodation is in an historic gentleman's residence of 1820 on the edge of the little town. The rooms here are well-kept and individually furnished and decorated, while those in the newer extension, in a pleasantly elegant style, are more spacious. The extension also houses apartments and a number of smaller attic rooms. Among the hotel's amenities are a cosmetics section where guests are pampered with a variety of treatments. Pampering of another kind is on offer in the "Michel" restaurant, which specialises in French cuisine.

Sights nearby: Schulkirche, Maria Hilf pilgrimage church

Access: From Exit 66 on A 6 towards Amberg-Haselmühl; establishment is on left c 5km after passing through Lengenfeld and Haselmühl

6 DER SCHAFHOF

Herbert Ullrich

63916 Amorbach
Tel. (09373) 9 73 30
Fax (09373) 4120 – www.schafhof.de

Open all year • 16 rooms and 8 suites, including 3 with terrace and 3 with disabled access • Restaurants with terrace: Abtstube (closed Mon, Tue), Benedikter-Stube (closed Wed, Thu); set meal 43.50-76.50€; half board 40€ • Garden, parking; dogs allowed • Health and beauty facilities, natural bathing pool, tennis, table tennis, boccia, bicycle hire, guided walks, wine tasting

130/275 €, Breakfast included

AE VISA

The home-made aromatic Bavarian honey makes a great gift to take home

This former monastery which once belonged to the Benedictine order is located in a tranquil setting: it has a rich history and has kept much of the exceptional atmosphere and charm that you would expect from a venerable old estate. The former storeroom offers cosy little guest-rooms, but with their light and tasteful furniture and medieval timbering the lavish suites in the carefully restored wine-pressing house boast rather grander comforts. The restaurant offers fine classic cuisine: with its imposing red sand-stone walls, the elegant rural character of the 'Abbot's room' is very appealing; so too is the beautiful wooden ceiling adorning the Benedictine room in the neighbouring building.

Sights nearby: Amorbach abbey church (3 km east), Eulbach Englischer Garten animal park (13 km west)

Access: In the Otterbach valley 3 km west of Amorbach via Amorsbrunner Strasse

7 **BENEDIKTENHOF**

Veronika Bichler

Alpenbadstr. 16
83646 Arzbach
Tel. (08042) 9 14 70
Fax (08042) 914729 – www.benediktenhof.de

Open all year • 11 rooms, all with balcony • Children's play area, garden, parking; dogs not allowed • Sauna, solarium, aromatic steam bath, gym, bio swimming pool

75/100 €, Breakfast included
Credit cards not accepted

A spa bath in front of an open fire

In a peaceful setting, well away from Arzbach's main road, this is the very model of a well-run family place. It's taken great efforts to turn the former farmstead into a handsome little country hotel, but it's been a labour of love for Herr Bichler, who put his training as a carpenter to good use in redesigning the rooms: they're now light and welcoming, with comfortable furnishings in natural wood. His finest work was in the lovely conservatory; you can have breakfast here, or in the cosy lounge. And if you're still not entirely relaxed, a pretty garden and a bathing pond - all 100% natural and eco-friendly - will soon take care of that!

Sights nearby: Brauneck (5 km south), Benediktbeuern monastery (20 km west)

Access: 6 km south of Bad Tölz

8 ALPENGASTHOF BRUCKER

Hermann Max

Schlossbergstr. 12
83229 Aschau im Chiemgau
Tel. (08052) 49 87
Fax (08052) 1564 – www.gasthofbrucker.de

Closed 15 Jan to 10 Feb • 10 rooms, including 3 with balcony, 2 with showers on landing • Cafe-restaurant with terrace (closed Wed, Thu): main course 6.50-12.50€ • Garden, parking; dogs allowed in restaurant, not in hotel

50/64 €, Breakfast included

VISA

The bedrooms themselves and the painted rustic furniture - a lovely, typically southern German touch.

Long established and impeccably run, this family owned Gasthof - on a family scale - strikes just the right note with its welcoming and relaxing atmosphere: it helps that it's in a quiet spot on the edge of the town. It really is every inch the typical Bavarian inn, and the team take real pride in its trim yet comfortable bedrooms: the furniture in pale, natural wood and the bright checked fabrics add a pretty touch, and the laminated wood floors are always swept spotless. The little parlour is intimate and cosy - just as you would expect around here - and serves up good, honest cooking in the best local tradition from a concise menu.

Sights nearby: Kampenwand, Schloss Herrenchiemsee (ferry from Prien, 11 km north), Marquartstein Fairytale theme park (16 km east)

Access: From Exit 105 on A 8 via Frasdorf or Exit 106 via Bernau

9 **POSTHOTEL SACHRANG**

Jörg Wilhelm

Dorfstr. 7
83229 Aschau-Sachrang
Tel. (08057) 9 05 80
Fax (08057) 905820 – www.posthotel-sachrang.de

Closed 8-28 Nov • 14 rooms, including 13 non-smoking • Restaurant with terrace (closed Mon-Wed): set meal 18-45€; half board 18€ • Garden, parking; dogs allowed • Sauna, massage, ayurveda, cosmetic treatments, bicycles, cookery courses

70/105 €, Breakfast included

VISA MC

The beer garden: traditional 'Brotzeit' snacks, good beer and a children's play area, all under the chestnut trees.

For over 500 years the old coaching inn has stood at the centre of this sleepy little village. It's now a small and undeniably contemporary hotel, but its developers have managed to keep much of its easy country character. Its fresh, modern look keeps in surprisingly close harmony with the original building, while the elegant design of the bedrooms makes each one a real gem in itself: a warm palette of colours and plenty of real wood set the tone here, while rustic furnishings, wood panelling and a delicately pretty decorative style give the lounges a character all of their own.

Sights nearby: Ebbs foal farm (10 km south), Kufstein fortress (18 km south)

Access: 13 km southwest of Aschau towards Kufstein

10 ROMANTIK HOTEL AUGSBURGER HOF

Ruth Meder

Auf dem Kreuz 2
86152 Augsburg
Tel. (0821) 34 30 50
Fax (0821) 3430555 – www.augsburger-hof.de

Open all year • 36 rooms • Restaurant with terrace: set meal 18-45€; half board 18€ • Parking; dogs allowed • Sauna, solarium

80/130 €, Breakfast included (WE: 80/110 €)

AE D JCB VISA MC

The summer terrace

One of Augsburg's longest-established hotels is only a short walk from the famous landmarks of the old city centre - in fact, it can almost lay claim to being one itself. The sound, elegant good taste of the interior recalls the country houses of the good old days, and there's an pleasant hint of nostalgia about the place. Warm wood tones add to the relaxing and intimate feeling of the rooms - some of which are fitted out in local pine - and you'll find the same reassuring cosiness in the lounges and restaurant, which specialises in dishes from south-west Germany. The handsome 'Zirbelstube' has a particularly fine atmosphere.

Sights nearby: Fuggerei, Art Gallery, Augsburg Puppet Museum

Access: Nearly opposite Mozarthaus, north of cathedral

11 BRAUEREIGASTHOF AYING

Angela Inselkammer

Zornedinger Str. 2
85653 Aying
Tel. (08095) 9 06 50
Fax (08095) 906566
brauereigasthof@ayinger-bier.de – www.ayinger-bier.de

Open all year • 34 rooms, including 6 with balcony, 7 non-smoking and 2 with disabled access • Restaurant with terrace: set lunch 18.20-56€; half board available • Garden, parking; dogs allowed • Gym, sauna, skittles, bicycle hire, brewery tours

135/180 €, Breakfast included
AE Diners VISA MC

A fresh draft beer tastes better in the open air - especially when the sky is Bavarian blue and white!

A brewery and inn with a wealth of tradition behind it, where the owners greet you with a smile, just as their family has always done for over 200 years. The rooms are styled with natural wood or painted country furniture, and some even have their old fireplaces: each in its own way is tasteful and comfortable. The rustic restaurant is just what you'd hope for in deepest Bavaria, with hearty local cooking to match, and sampling one of the many house beers in the garden is an absolute must. A tour of the 'Brewery Experience' reveals a blend of tried-and-tested brewing lore and state-of-the-art technology.

Sights nearby: Sixthof local museum, Blindham mountain fauna park (3 km south)

Access: Exit 96 on A 8

12 ROMANTIK HOTEL LINDNER

Gabi Jung

Marienplatz 5
83043 Bad Aibling
Tel. (08061) 9 06 30
Fax (08061) 30535 – www.romantikhotels.com/bad-aibling

Open all year • 26 rooms, including 18 non-smoking • Restaurant with terrace: set lunch 9.50-49€, set dinner 20-49€; half board 25€ • Garden, parking; dogs by arrangement • Bicycle hire

100/160 €, Breakfast included

AE D VISA MC

The elegant baths in green marble

A real gem in the heart of Bad Aibling. What was once Prantshausen Castle is now the Romantik Hotel Lindner, family owned for over 150 years. Even from the outside, the handsome curved gables and striped shutters announce that this is no ordinary place, but the harmonious blend of elegant design on historic foundations is at its finest inside. Period-styled furniture, plus some antique pieces, beautiful fabrics and materials, crystal chandeliers and many a fine architectural detail within the 1000 year-old walls are all remarkable in themselves, but quite enchanting as a whole. The classically tasteful ambience of the restaurant sets the same stylish standards.

Sights nearby: St Nikolaus parish church and Locomotive shed exhibition centre in Rosenheim (11km east)

Access: Exit 100 on A 8

13 LINDENMÜHLE

Tatiana Hartl

Kolonnadenweg 1
95460 Bad Berneck
Tel. (09273) 50 06 50
Fax (09273) 5006515 – www.lindenmuehle.de

Open all year • 30 rooms, including 3 with balcony and 4 non-smoking • Restaurant with terrace: set lunch 6-12€, set dinner 8-20€; half board 11€ • Garden, parking; dogs allowed • Pool, sauna, mini-golf, mountain bikes, archery, medieval banquets, open-air theatre

50/98 €, Breakfast included

AE VISA

The café and beer garden on the Mühlbach

Let there be light! This could be the motto of the Lindenmühle, a converted 17C water-mill with a bright and radiantly friendly atmosphere. Well-proportioned rooms are comfortable, with a sunny, almost Mediterranean style to them, and breakfast is served under the skylight of the 'Atrium'; as light and airy as the name suggests. The converted stables - still with a touch of their original, down-to-earth atmosphere - and the soft-toned restaurant both offer tempting meals, while 'James Choice', a German take on the Irish pub, gives you another option!

Sights nearby: Colonnades, Bayreuth opera house (15 km south), Plassenburg castle in Kulmbach (19 km northwest)

Access: At entrance to Kurpark

14 SAMMAREIER GUTSHOF

Albrecht Vogel

Pfarrkirchner Str. 22
84364 Bad Birnbach
Tel. (08563) 29 70
Fax (08563) 29713

Open all year • 44 rooms, all with balcony or terrace • Restaurant with terrace: set lunch 15-85€, set dinner 15-45€; half board 17€ • Garden, parking; dogs allowed • Health and fitness area: gym, indoor pool and sauna

68/126 €, Breakfast included

AE MC

The unusual entrance to the cellar bar

These two houses in the centre of Bad Birnbach both have something special in store for their guests. The hotel itself provides comfortable rooms in country style, furnished in natural blond wood: they also share a small kitchen, but you may not spend much time in here once you've eaten next door! 'Café Gugelhupf' specialises in, well, 'Gugelhupf', a delicious cake originally from Alsace, and the restaurant itself is made up of snug little booths and parlours: it's very easy to settle in for a cosy, convivial evening. There's also a lovely garden, perfect for soaking up summer sun

Sights nearby: Rottal spa, Asbach monastery (11 km east)

Access: By B 388 between Pfarrkirchen and Ruhstorf

15 GUNDELSBERG

Carsten Schumann

Gundelsberger Str. 9
83075 Bad Feilnbach
Tel. (08066) 9 04 50
Fax (08066) 904519 – www.hotel-gundelsberg.de

Open all year • 11 rooms, including 7 with balcony • Restaurant with terrace (closed Mon, midday Tue): set lunch 16-21€, set dinner 16-30€; half board 16€ • Garden, parking; dogs allowed • Sauna, steam bath, rasul treatments, solarium, massage, bicycle hire

80/102 €, Breakfast included

VISA MC

The steam bath with a touch of the Orient

Above the town of Bad Feilnach, surrounded by woodland, you'll find a typical Bavarian mountain inn with a terrace and a number of balconies, all with impressive views across the mountains, rising away in the distance towards the Alps. The good-sized rooms are fitted out with modern wood furniture and decorated in cheerful colours - some also have a little kitchenette. More wood furnishings in the restaurant lend it the same bright, fresh country style.

Sights nearby: Wendelstein (18km south), Schliersee (21km southwest)

Access: Exit 100 on A 8

16 ROMANTIK HOTEL SONNE

Peter Schneider

Marktstr. 15
87541 Bad Hindelang
Tel. (08324) 89 70
Fax (08324) 897499 – www.sonne-hindelang.de

Open all year • 57 rooms, including 45 with balcony and 17 non-smoking • Restaurant with terrace: set lunch 12.50-15€, set dinner 14.50-18€; half board 23€ • Garden, parking; dogs allowed • Swimming pool, health and fitness area, bicycle hire

114/156 €, Breakfast included (WE: 177/192 €)

AE ⓓ VISA MC

An affectionate welcome from the hotel cat

The beautiful murals and the gleaming golden sun on the pale pink façade are proof enough that this is a place where little details count for a lot. Individually chosen combinations of fine antiques and oil paintings lend the rooms a distinguished touch and blend perfectly with the tasteful furnishings and fittings. The restaurant, though smart, has a proper feel of the countryside to it: the menu combines specialities from the Allgäu with culinary excursions further south to Switzerland.

Sights nearby: Obermaiselstein caves (18 km southwest), Nebelhorn (21 km south)

Access: In town centre

17 ROMANTIK PARKHOTEL LAUDENSACK

Hermann Laudensack

Kurhausstr. 28
97688 Bad Kissingen
Tel. (0971) 7 22 40
Fax (0971) 722444
laudensacks-parkhotel@t-online.de – www.laudensacks-parkhotel.de

Closed 1-23 Jan • 21 rooms, including 14 with balcony • Restaurant with terrace (eve only Wed-Sun; midday Mon, Tue also a la carte for residents): set meal 38-76€; half board 21€ • Garden, parking; dogs allowed • Health and fitness area with sauna and gym; cookery courses, bicycle hire, organised walks, exhibitions

124/160 €, Breakfast included
AE, Diners, JCB, VISA, MC

The romantic lily pond in the garden

An establishment with style and comfort! Fully and cosily furnished rooms are ready for your stay, the restaurant, noted for its modern elegance, welcomes you to its culinary delights and the 'beauty farm' on the third floor will take care of your physical and emotional well-being - its for men as well as women! Regularly changing art exhibitions accentuate its charm: the hotel also has a conservatory with a bar area, not forgetting the terrace, which leads into the idyllic park behind the hotel.

Sights nearby: Bismarck museum, KissSalis spa, Luitpold Casino

Access: By station on edge of town

18 KUR- UND SCHLOSSHOTEL

Michael Erichsen

Kurhausstr. 37
97616 Bad Neustadt an der Saale
Tel. (09771) 6 16 10
Fax (09771) 2533 – www.hotel-schloss-neuhaus.de.vu

Open all year • Cafe; restaurant with terrace: set lunch 15-22.50€, set dinner 22.50-47.50€; half board 17.50-25€ • Garden, parking; dogs allowed

95/145 €, Breakfast included

AE, Diners, JCB, VISA, MC

The coffee break with dainty cakes from the castle cake shop and the view of the splendid park

The castle, designed by the German-Italian, Todesco, in the 18C Late Baroque style, nestles in idyllic parkland - such a magnificent setting is a real invitation to relax, unwind and forget about everyday life for a while. The rooms are tastefully furnished, partly with period furniture, and the bathrooms are in marble. The restaurant will also win you over with its classical elegance. Don't miss the wonderful Mirror Room on the first floor, which is available for functions, take a look at the castle chapel.

Sights nearby: Maria Himmelfahrt church, Salzburg

Access: In spa district on the edge of the town

19 NEU-MERAN

Franz Weber

83435 Bad Reichenhall-Nonn
Tel. (08651) 40 78
Fax (08651) 78520 – www.hotel-neu-meran.de

Closed 15 Jan to 5 Feb, 1-30 Nov • 19 rooms, all with balcony, 3 non-smoking • Cafe; restaurant with terrace (closed Tue, Wed): set meal 25-45€; half board 18€ • Garden, parking; dogs allowed • Gym, bicycle hire, wine tasting, organised walks, swimming pool, sauna, solarium, sunbathing lawn, massage, cosmetic treatments

114/164 €, Breakfast included

VISA MC

A fine wine in the very cosy wine cellar

From the outside the building with the balcony façade looks like many others in the region. But the pleasant atmosphere and, above all, the lovely location at the edge of the woods above Bad Reichenhall distinguishes it from the crowd. All the rooms, attractive in their elegant rural furnishings, are south-facing for extra sun. The view of the town with the Predigtstuhl in the background is wonderful and can also be enjoyed from the balcony terrace of the restaurant, which has a sophisticated rustic design and many a cosy little spot to spend an evening.

Sights nearby: Minster, Old Saltworks, Bad Reichenall Bavarian Casino, Salzburg Old Town (15 km northeast)

Access: On left bank of Saalach by Alte Luitpoldbrücke (bridge) and Nonner Strasse

20 AM SONNENBICHL

Kathrin Frömling

Sonnenbichlweg 1
83707 Bad Wiessee
Tel. (08022) 9 87 30
Fax (08022) 8940 – www.amsonnenbichl.de

Open all year • 22 rooms, including 18 with balcony, 4 with terrace • "Patrizierhof" restaurant with terrace (eve only; closed Sun, Mon): set meal 48-60€; Bauernstube pub (closed Mon) • Parking; dogs allowed • Direct access to ski-lift and footpaths

110/123 €, Breakfast included

AE VISA MC

The restaurant table with its hovering guardian angel

830 metres up on the ski-slopes of the Sonnenbichl, this most attractive hotel-restaurant commands superb views over the valley of the Tegernsee. The elegant rooms have been lavishly furnished and decorated in the best possible taste, with much use of warm and welcoming colours: you are certain to enjoy your stay here. In a fresh and tasteful rustic style, the two-part restaurant offers outstanding traditional cuisine as well as local specialities. The sun terrace is for the exclusive use of hotel guests, enabling you to enjoy your coffee or cocktail in peace and quiet.

Sights nearby: Bad Wiessee iodine/sulphur spa, Schliersee (17km east)

Access: Exit 97 on A 8

21 **LANDHAUS MIDAS**

Horst Scheurer

Setzbergstr. 12
83707 Bad Wiessee
Tel. (08022) 8 11 50
Fax (08022) 99577 – www.landhaus-midas.de

Closed 8-30 Jan, 4-22 Dec • 12 rooms, all with balcony • Restaurant (closed Sun): limited choice dinner menu for residents • Garden, parking; dogs allowed in hotel, not in restaurant • Bicycle hire, bio-magnetic treatment

65/96 €, Breakfast included
VISA MC

The superb wood-panelled breakfast room

The Midas country house looks so pretty with its flower bedecked balcony façade, and the inside lives up to the expectations set by the typical Alpine exterior. Nicely designed rooms in country style seem to give out a comfortable warmth: they are furnished in a homely manner with natural wood, mainly cherry, and are very well-kept. As the establishment is situated in a quiet residential area, close to the village centre, you can relax in total peace.

Sights nearby: Tegernsee, Bad Wiessee Bavarian Casino

Access: Exit 97 on A 8

22 SONNENBÜCHL

Christa Brutscher

Sonnenbüchl 1 (am Freibad)
86825 Bad Wörishofen
Tel. (08247) 95 99 00
Fax (08247) 959909 – www.cafe-restaurant-sonnenbuechl.de

Closed 8 Jan to 1 Feb • 4 rooms, including 1 with balcony • Cafe-restaurant with terrace (closed Sun eve, Mon): main course 11-16.50€, set lunch 22.50-27.50€; half board 20€ • Garden, parking; dogs allowed

88/95 €, Breakfast included

AE VISA MC

The delightful location on the Sonnenbüchlsee, opposite an open-air pool

This welcoming inn, whose façade is partially panelled with dark wood, is at the edge of the woods, above Bad Wörishofen's spa. You can tell there's natural local character here just by looking at the outside. The internal rooms are also designed in calm but cheerful style: light wood and intricate decoration create a homely atmosphere in the rooms. The lounges are in a smart country style, which matches the regionally orientated cuisine, and the terrace seats in front of the establishment will rate highly with any true Bavarian!

Sights nearby: Bad Worishofen spa, Sebastian Kneipp Museum

Access: From Exit 20 on A 96

23 WALDGASTHOF BUCHENHAIN

Christa Kastner

Am Klettergarten 7
82065 Baierbrunn-Buchenhain
Tel. (089) 7 93 01 24
Fax (089) 7938701 – www.hotelbuchenhain.de

Closed 21-31 Dec • 40 rooms, including 4 with balcony and 5 non-smoking • Restaurant with beer garden (closed Fri): set meal 7.50-9.80€; half board on application • Children's play area, garden, parking; dogs allowed in hotel, not in restaurant

85/117 €, Breakfast included (WE: 75/85 €)
AE VISA MC

The waitresses wearing traditional Dirndl dresses

Just the location of the establishment makes it interesting - it's situated in the south of Munich not far from the Starnberger See at the forest edge in the middle of the countryside. You can, however, reach the Bavarian capital comfortably and quickly by public transport from the S-Bahn stop nearby. But the rustically cosy rooms are also recommended, lovingly designed in country style and partly furnished with old country furniture. The dishes served in the four handsomely furnished lounges are mainly local ones and of course, this being Bavaria, there's also a traditional beer garden shaded by old chestnut trees.

Sights nearby: Geiselgasteig Bavaria Film Town (4 km north), Schäftlarn monastic church (5 km south), Hellabrunn zoo (9 km north)

Access: On B 11 between München-Pullach and Baierbrunn

24 ST. NEPOMUK

Waltraud Grüner

Obere Mühlbrücke 9
96049 Bamberg
Tel. (0951) 9 84 20
Fax (0951) 9842100
gruener@hotel-nepomuk.de – www.hotel-nepomuk.de

Open all year • 47 rooms, including 23 non-smoking, 1 with disabled access • Cafe; restaurant: set meal 20-47€; half board 20€ • Parking; dogs allowed • Bicycle hire

112/270 €, Breakfast included

VISA

The traditional breweries of Bamberg Old Town

This is the ideal starting point for walks through Bamberg's old town, now a UNESCO World Heritage Site. The individually designed rooms are divided between the main building, a former mill, built on the Regnitz river, and the two guest houses. Exposed beams give them a rustic, romantic charm, and many are also fitted with period furniture or antiques. The restaurant is a sophisticated setting for your meals, offering a wonderful view of the river and old town.

Sights nearby: Diocesan museum, Michaelsberg

Access: On an island in the Regnitz south of the Bischofsmühl bridge

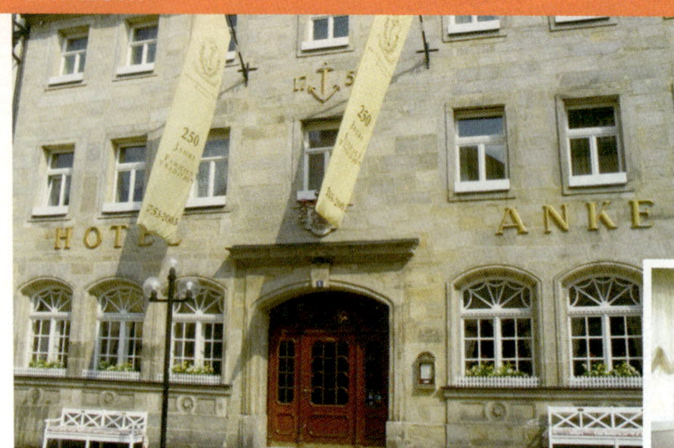

25 GOLDENER ANKER

Eva Graf-Handel

Opernstr. 6
95444 Bayreuth
Tel. (0921) 6 50 51
Fax (0921) 65500 – www.anker-bayreuth.de

Closed New Year's Day to mid-Jan, 23 Dec to New Year's Eve • 35 rooms • Restaurant (eve only; closed Mon, Tue): main course 20.50-32€ • Garden, parking; dogs allowed in hotel, not in restaurant

95/175 €, Breakfast included

AE Diners VISA MC

The bathrooms with freestanding baths

Do you love opera? Then you're sure to like this traditional establishment in Bayreuth town centre. The setting is enchanting and the stylish rooms, their ambience occasionally verging on the baroque, could serve as the scenery for a comic opera - canopies over the beds, fabric wallpaper, and antiques are the accessories for a successful staging of your stay. Incidentally, the restaurant furnishings are still the originals from 1927. Enjoy the convivial nostalgia of the location!

Sights nearby: Opera house, Richard Wagner museum

Access: Next to opera house

26 GOLDENER LÖWE

Jörg Schöner

Kulmbacher Str. 30
95445 Bayreuth
Tel. (0921) 74 60 60
Fax (0921) 47777 – www.goldener-loewe-bayreuth.de

Open all year • 12 rooms • Restaurant with beer garden (closed Sun eve, midday Mon): set lunch 9.50-11.50€, set dinner 14-20€; half board 14.50 • Beer garden, parking; dogs allowed

95/105 €, Breakfast included

AE JCB VISA MC

Home-made jams for breakfast

An unpretentious Franconian inn - simple in style yet enchanting in atmosphere. The lounges, which are typical of a brewery inn, are rustically designed in wood and intricately decorated with all sorts of ornamentation, and it goes without saying that Franconian specialities take pride of place on the menu. The Bayreuth Festival Orchestra has met at its regular tables in the Golden Lion since 1959. The bedrooms also reflect traditional cosiness, furnished rustically in light natural wood, except for some, which are slighly more sophisticated, with dark furniture.

Sights nearby: Neues Schloss and Hofgarten, Schlosskirche

Access: In a side street off the Hohenzollernring in the northwestern part of the city centre not far from the Rotmaincenter

27 KRONE

Jörg Grafe

Am Rad 5
83471 Berchtesgaden
Tel. (08652) 9 46 00
Fax (08652) 946010 – www.hotel-krone-berchtesgaden.de

Closed 1 Nov-20 Dec • 20 rooms, including 19 with balcony and 15 non-smoking • Cafe; restaurant for residents only (closed midday, Mon): half board 11€ • Garden, parking; dogs not allowed • Sauna, steam bath, freshwater jacuzzi

72/88 €, Breakfast included
VISA MC

The especially comfortable rooms lined with Swiss pine wood

Here on the edge of the village in a peaceful, slightly elevated position you can enjoy the fabulous views over the village and the Berchtesgaden countryside with the majestic Watzmann, the Obersalzberg and the Kehlsteinhaus. The Alpine style hotel has very cosy rooms ready for you, some of which are rustically designed and completely panelled with wood, and some fitted out in a very contemporary style. The lounges also are aglow with local colour and the traditional cosiness you would expect in the heart of the Bavarian Alps.

Sights nearby: Castle, Salt Mine, Königsee (5 km south)

Access: Bad Reichenall Exit on A 8

28 REBLINGER HOF

Peter Krauß

Rebling 3
94505 Bernried-Rebling
Tel. (09905) 5 55
Fax (09905) 1839 – www.reblingerhof.de

Open all year • 25 rooms, all with balcony, 4 non-smoking • Cafe; restaurant with terrace: main course 9.90-20€; half board 15€ • Garden, parking; dogs allowed in hotel, not in restaurant • Indoor pool, sauna, mini golf, paddling, tennis, mountain bikes, cookery courses, canoe trips, paragliding

84/132 €, Breakfast included
VISA MC

The ecological swimming pond fed by spring water

There are so many charming things about this place that it's hard to know where to start. Its location is special enough: it sits on a slope above the fallow deer reserve, and its indoor pool has a fine view over the Danube valley. The rooms - in many of which you can even start dreaming in four-poster beds - are furnished in an elegant country style or with original country furniture from the Bavarian Forest. The cosy lounges are equally as rustic. And, last of all, an 'in-house' cake shop is bound to win over anyone with a bit of a sweet tooth.

Sights nearby: Egg castle (9 km southwest), Metten Benedictine abbey (12 km southwest)

Access: Deggendorf-Rusel Exit on A 92, then towards Bernried/Egg; after Egg do not continue towards Bernried but via Edenstetten and Leithen

29 RHÖNHÄUSCHEN

Marlene Schmidt

Rhönhaus 1
97653 Bischofsheim a. d. Rhön
Tel. (09772) 3 22
Fax (09772) 912033 – www.rhoenhaeuschen.de

Open all year • 20 rooms, including 5 with balcony and 2 with shared bath • Restaurant with terrace: set meal 13,50-21,60 € ; half board from 15 € • Parking, dogs allowed in hotel, not in restaurant

70/87 €, Breakfast included (WE: 77/87 €)

Rhön trout from the establishment's own pond

The border between Hessen and Bavaria runs through the middle of a natural moorland landscape, touching heights of over 1 500 feet. The former tollhouse and customs house hasn't collected taxes for many a year, and feels so right as a small, lovely country hotel that it's almost hard to imagine it as anything else. Because of its isolated position in the Rhön Biosphere Reserve, it needs its own water and electricity supply, but still manages to supply every modern comfort. The building itself has retained its local, original charm and is now makes a lovely place to get away from it all; close to nature and with a inviting, nostalgic ambience.

Sights nearby: Ev.Church Gersfeld (8 km west); German glider museum (16 km north)

Access: 5 km north of Bischofsheim via the B 278 towards Ehrenberg

30 HUNDSREITLEHEN

Markus Selbertinger

Quellenweg 11
83483 Bischofswiesen
Tel. (08652) 98 60
Fax (08652) 986160
hundsreitlehen@t-online.de – www.hundsreitlehen.de

Closed provisionally 1 Nov to 20 Dec • 19 rooms, all with balcony, 5 non-smoking • Restaurant with terrace (eve only; closed Mon): set meal 12.50-18€; half board 13€ • Garden, parking; dogs allowed in hotel, not in restaurant • Kneipp spa, sunbathing lawn, guided walks, 'Nordic' walking

84/104 €, Breakfast included
Credit cards not accepted

The outdoor Kneipp spa with fresh mountain spring water

A genuinely traditional establishment in a particularly beautiful part of the world. The hotel is situated in a solitary spot above Bischofwiesen, surrounded by fragrant meadows, with fantastic views of the Kehlstein. The farm, which is part of the hotel, is still managed and as it has its own stables children can still ride here under instruction. Accommodation is in rooms fitted with light, solid country house style furniture and good plain cooking is served in the country restaurant. Just as you would imagine your holiday in the country to be!

Sights nearby: Berchtesgaden salt mine (5km southeast), Obersalzberg and Kehlstein (9km east)

Access: On B 20 between Bad Reichenhall and Berchtesgaden just outside Bishofswiesen towards Loipl

31 SCHLOSSWIRT

Irmgard Schmidt-Widmann

Kirchplatz 1
83098 Brannenburg
Tel. (08034) 7 07 10
Fax (08034) 7071128 – www.schlosswirt.de

Closed 10-17 Mar, mid-Nov to 1st week Dec • 17 rooms, including 5 with balcony • Restaurant with terrace (closed Tue May-Sep, Tue and Wed Oct-Apr): main course 6.80-13.20€; half board 11€ • Parking; dogs allowed

66/70 €, Breakfast included

AE VISA MC

The "Artists' Studio" once welcomed Wilhelm Busch, the illustrator and poet famous for the tales of Max and Moritz.

This old-established inn can be found in the village square with the venerable lime-trees and church, in the heart of Brannenburg. The long-standing building is not, however, an outmoded country hotel, but has refreshingly modern and very well-kept rooms. In no way, however, do the furnishings deny its rustic roots. As the hotel has its own hunting preserve, hunting trophies are spread all over the house. And the tables for the regulars in the lounges are still, as ever, the focus of village life. A tradition-conscious family business, which changes with the times!

Sights nearby: Wendelstein (3 km south), Rosenheim locomotive shed exhibition centre (15 km north)

Access: Exit 58 on A 93

32 WEINHAUS STERN

Heidi Martin und Klaus Markert

Hauptstr. 23
63927 Bürgstadt
Tel. (09371) 4 03 50
Fax (09371) 403540 – www.hotel-weinhaus-stern.de

Open all year • 11 rooms, including 2 non-smoking • Restaurant with terrace (closed Wed, Thu): set dinner 24-70€; half board 20€ (min 3 days stay) • Garden, parking; dogs allowed • Bicycle hire, wine tours

70/105 €, Breakfast included

AE VISA MC

The fine wines and spirits made from local berries and fruits

The spruce property in the village centre, built in 1638 and typical of the local sandstone and timber-frame buildings still seen around the area, offers elegantly, individually furnished rooms and bathrooms. Some of the antiques distributed throughout the buildings - from furniture to craftwork and prints - are even for sale, so if you like something, just ask! Mainly regional specialities are served in the wood-panelled restaurant - when the sun shines, though, you can also eat in the romantic arbour in the shade of vines.

Sights nearby: Miltenberg Old Town (2 km south), Amorbach Benedictine abbey (13 km south)

Access: By B 469 via Miltenberg

33 BURG COLMBERG

Otto Unbehauen

91598 Colmberg
Tel. (09803) 9 19 20
Fax (09803) 262 – www.burg-colmberg.de

Closed Feb • 26 rooms • Cafe-restaurant with terrace (closed Tue): main course 8.50-22.50€ • Playground, garden, parking; dogs by arrangement • 9-hole golf course

74/130 €, Breakfast included

AE VISA MC

The game specialities from its own estate

This former Hohenzollern fortress on a 500-metre mountain peak is pure castle romance. It has a fantastic view over the valley, a timber-frame façade intertwined with ivy in the inner courtyard, natural stone walls in some of the rooms and restaurant. The furnishing of the guests' 'apartments' ranges from elegantly baroque to historically rustic to simple and contemporary. A playground at the foot of the keep, and the castle's game preserve, will interest the little guests, and a private golf-course will keep some older ones busy!

Sights nearby: Ansbach Residenz (17km southeast), Rothenburg ob der Tauber Old Town (18km west), Franconian open air museum in Bad Windsheim (25km north)

Access: On direct road between Ansbach and Rothenburg ob der Tauber

34 KUNST-STUBEN

Arthur Appelberg

Segringer Str. 52
91550 Dinkelsbühl
Tel. (09851) 67 50
Fax (09851) 553527 – www.kunst-stuben.de

Closed 24-25 Dec • 5 rooms, all non-smoking • Cafe with terrace • Garden, parking; dogs not allowed

55/70 €, Breakfast included

AE JCB VISA

The coffee break in the tranquil inner courtyard

The name doesn't raise too many expectations. This establishment at the Segringer Tor, close to the town wall, houses two studios. Look over the shoulders of the artistic married couple, who run this establishment, when they are working - he produces fine art prints on historic printing presses and she makes individually designed ceramics, not just on the potter's wheel. You will especially appreciate the secluded character of the establishment. Only a few rooms are available, all furnished with hand-painted furniture in country house style. If you want to curl up with a good book you can withdraw to the intimate atmosphere of the library.

Sights nearby: Georgskirche, Kinderzeche children's festival (Jul), Feuchtwangen Bavarian Casino (11 km north)

Access: On B 25 between Nördlingen and Feuchtwangen

35 SPORT- UND FERIENHOTEL RIEDLBERG

Familie Grassl

Riedlberg
94256 Drachselsried
Tel. (09924) 9 42 60
Fax (09924) 7273 – www.riedlberg.de

Closed mid-Nov to mid-Dec • 38 rooms, including 35 with balcony and 5 non-smoking • Restaurant with terrace: set dinner 20-25€, main course 6-13€; half board 5€ • Garden, parking; dogs allowed in hotel, not in restaurant • Health and beauty facilites with beauty treatments and physiotherapy, ski lifts, bicycle hire, guided walks, 'Nordic' cross-country walking

108/155 €, Breakfast included (WE: 108/155 €)
Credit cards not accepted

Ski-ing under floodlights

There are so many tempting leisure activities on offer here that it is really difficult to choose - a solar heated open-air pool, a beautiful garden with a small pond, an elegant spa-area, which meets every requirement, and even private ski-lifts make time fly. As the establishment is in an isolated position in a large private wood, you can simply enjoy the beauty and peace of the Bavarian Forest. The hotel rooms have rustic, unfussy furnishings, some even with their own tiled stove. Apartments with rooms for children are also provided.

Sights nearby: Silberberg visitor mine in Bodenmais (8km south), fortress church at Kötzing (20 km northwest)

Access: 6 km east of Drachselsried via Oberried

36 HÖLZERBRÄU

Katharina Huber

Sieghartstr. 1
85560 Ebersberg
Tel. (08092) 2 40 20
Fax (08092) 85258944
hotel.gasthof@hoelzerbraeu.de – www.hoelzerbraeu.de

Closed 8-28 Aug • 50 rooms, including 20 with balcony and 8 non-smoking • Restaurant with beer garden: main course 8.90-19.50€; half board 14.90€ • Garden, parking; dogs allowed • Health and fitness facilities with sauna, gym

82/120 €, Breakfast included (WE: 64/82,50 €)

VISA

The Bavarians' most beloved spot - the beer garden

A seasoned inn and a fine advertisement for Bavarian lifestyle - the Hölzerbräu, in the centre of Ebersberg, is obviously doing something right! Outstandingly well-kept rooms with rustic natural wood furniture, contrasting prettily with the strong colours of the carpets, are ready for your overnight accommodation. Your culinary requirements are well catered for in the restaurant's three cosy lounges. The gnarled beams of the ceiling in the "Georgi room" came originally from the old loft and have been successfully "recycled".

Sights nearby: Forest and environment museum, Poing deer park (19km northwest)

Access: On B 304 between Munich and Wasserburg

37 GÄSTEHAUS ABTEI ST. WALBURG

Äbtissin Franziska Kloos OSB

Walburgiberg 6
85072 Eichstätt
Tel. (08421) 9 88 70
Fax (08421) 988740
st-walburg.ei@kirche-bayern.de – www.bistum-eichstaett.de/abtei-st-walburg

Closed 1-6 Jan • 19 rooms, all non-smoking, 1 with disabled access • Garden, parking; dogs not allowed

54 €, Breakfast included
Credit cards not accepted

Breakfast under a historic vault in the convent

The guest house of the Benedictine convent is, in keeping with its environment, more of a pilgrims' hostel than a hotel. And, naturally, it's something quite special to live inside convent walls, whose origins date back to the 11C. The rooms are light and friendly with parquet floors, some have old furniture and exposed beams, creating a pleasant atmosphere. There's no point in looking for a telephone and TV, but precisely because of that your stay will be especially relaxing, giving you the opportunity to take stock and communicate with the inner rather than the outside world: spiritual guidance is always on hand, but never an obligation.

Sights nearby: Cathedral, Willibaldsburg castle and Jurassic Museum

Access: On northern edge of town centre towards Weissenburg

38 SCHWARZER ADLER

Christiane Müller-Kinzel

Herdegenplatz 1
91056 Erlangen-Frauenaurach
Tel. (09131) 99 20 51
Fax (09131) 993195 – www.hotel-schwarzer-adler.de

Closed 24 Dec to 7 Jan • 8 rooms, including 4 non-smoking • Restaurant with terrace (closed Sat, Sun, midday Mon-Fri): main course 20-22€, set dinner 37-60€ • Garden, parking; dogs allowed

95/105 €, Breakfast included

AE D VISA MC

The oak spindle staircase giving access to the rooms in the original house

The smart 17C timber-framed building right next to the church in the centre of the village of Frauenaurach welcomes you. Here, and in the adjacent building, the rooms are indivdually furnished with country or natural wood furniture. Exposed beams create a rustic atmosphere. The attic rooms are especially lovely, their ceilings reaching to the gables. To restore bodily strength you can have a set meal in the cosy wine bar or on the inner courtyard terrace, or if you would like something more hearty and uncomplicated, you can enjoy Franconian snacks - the traditional 'Brotzeit' - in the bar.

Sights nearby: Stately home garden in Erlangen (5 km east), German National Museum in Nuremberg (22 km south)

Access: Frauenaurach Exit on A 3, then by Niedendorfer Strasse, Erlanger Strasse, Brückenstrasse and Wallenroderstrasse

39 BERGHOTEL ASCHBACH

Dorothee Lechner

83620 Feldkirchen-Westerham
Tel. (08063) 8 06 60
Fax (08063) 806620 – www.berghotel-aschbach.de

Closed 10-25 Feb, 23-24 Dec • 20 rooms, including 14 with balcony • Cafe-restaurant with terrace: set lunch 11.50-20€, set dinner 20-39€ • Parking; dogs allowed

83/108 €, Breakfast included

AE VISA MC

The large selection of home-made cakes and gateaux

This inn was built after the Second World War in a superb position, and later extended with a new building in the same typical regional style. The spacious rooms, many with a south-facing balcony, have homely natural wood furniture and the fresh fabrics give them an especially comfortable atmosphere. The lounges also have a welcoming country feel. Breakfast is served in the 'Joseph Room' furnished in natural Swiss pine, from where you can enjoy the panoramic view of the Bavarian Alps.

Sights nearby: Aying Brewery Experience (9 km northwest)

Access: Exit 98 on A 8, then 3 km northwest of Feldkirchen towards Aying

40 ROMANTIK HOTEL GREIFEN-POST

Birgit Becker-Plaha

Marktplatz 8
91555 Feuchtwangen
Tel. (09852) 68 00
Fax (09852) 68068 – www.greifen.de

Closed 3-9 Jan • 35 rooms, including 6 non-smoking • Restaurant with terrace (closed Mon, Sat from 3pm): set meals 23.20-45€; half board 25€ • Parking; dogs allowed • Indoor pool, sauna, steam bath, solarium, bicycle hire

99/140 €, Breakfast included
AE VISA MC

A small snack in the snug Fireside Room

Over the course of time many crowned heads have stayed at this establishment in the market square of the pretty, small Franconian town. And you can feel like a king here today, not least because of the warm and attentive service. Four categories of room are available, their design's central theme ranging from Renaissance to Rococco and Biedermeier to English country house style. The original 'Bath House' was for the mail-coaches passing through - and even just 100 years ago stables were accommodated under the arches. You can enjoy regionally orientated cuisine in the rustically smart gourmet restaurant.

Sights nearby: Collegiate church, Casino, Cloisters Festival (May-Aug)

Access: Exit 49 on A 6 or Exit 111 on A 7

41 **CAFÉ WINKLSTÜBERL**
Thekla Mairhofer

Leitzachtalstr. 68
83730 Fischbachau-Winkl
Tel. (08028) 7 42
Fax (08028) 1586
www.winklstueberl.de

Open all year • 8 rooms, including 6 with balcony and showers on landing • Restaurant with terrace: main course 6-15€ • Garden, parking; dogs allowed

44/50 €, Breakfast included
Credit cards not accepted

The lovely view out over the Chiemgau region

Come and try the superb home-made delicacies which have made Café Winklstuberl famous throughout Bavaria and beyond: they need over 1000 eggs a day for their cakes and patisseries, but on a fine summer afternoon it seems barely enough to keep up with demand - an empty seat on the terrace or in the garden won't stay free for very long! You may decide that the only way to do justice to the amazing list of cakes is to book yourself in for the night: you'll have your choice of spotless little rooms, but note that most are not ensuite. The traditonal character of the old inn itself is wonderfully well preserved, and a collection of over 500 coffee mills is worthy of a museum.

Sights nearby: Wendelstein (8km southeast), Schliersee (10 km west)

Access: From Exit 100 on A 8 via Bad Feilnach and Hundham; 1 km north of Fischbachau

42 LANDGASTHOF KARNER

Christl Karner

Nussbaumstr. 6
83112 Frasdorf
Tel. (08052) 40 71
Fax (08052) 4711 – www.landgasthof-karner.de

Closed 24-25 Dec • 26 rooms, including 1 with balcony • Restaurant with terrace: set lunch 26€; set dinner 40-60€; half board 28€ • Garden, parking; dogs allowed • Indoor pool, sauna, bicycle hire, cookery course

95/125 €, Breakfast included

AE VISA MC

An excursion to the Kampenwand to take in the enchanting panorama of the Bavarian Alps

Proper country hospitality, straightforward and generous, with no airs and graces, is a matter of real pride in the south-east. Nowhere is that more true than in this archetypal alpine inn; from the moment you open the heavy wooden door, everything, from the flagged floor to the imaginative décor, tells you that this could only be Bavaria. Bright, cheerful rooms look the part with their wooden, country-style furniture, and the intimate, richly decorated parlour offers refined cooking with a pronounced local flavour: you can also eat on the charming terrace.

Sights nearby: Chiemsee (12 km east), Marquartstein Fairytale theme park (20 km southeast)

Access: Exit 105 on A 8

43 ST. FLORIAN

Michaela und Bernd Koller

Althüttenstr. 22
94258 Frauenau
Tel. (09926) 95 20
Fax (09926) 8266 – www.st-florian.de

Open all year • 32 rooms, including 26 with balcony, 1 with disabled access and 11 non-smoking • Restaurant with terrace: main course 7.80-13.80€; half board 13€ • Garden, parking; dogs allowed • Indoor pool, Finnish sauna, Roman steam bath, massage, cosmetic treatments

68/80 €, Breakfast included
Credit cards not accepted

Bathing in sunlight in the bright indoor swimming pool, then basking in the long grass all afternoon

A holiday location that's perfect at any time of year. Frauenau, known as Bavaria's 'heart of glass' on account of its glass industry, is surrounded by the Bavarian Woods: it offers an almost infinite variety of hiking trails, and in winter there are many different ways of making the most of the slopes and snowfields. This dependable, immaculately kept house is a perfect base from which to start exploring: comfy rooms in fine fabrics and local wood are lovely to come back to after a day in the open air, a wood-floored lounge with a traditional stove provides feel-good atmosphere, Bavarian style and a candlelit restaurant sets a more refined tone.

Sights nearby: Glass museum, Zwiesel forest museum (7km northwest)

Access: 7km southeast of Zwiesel

44 ZUR LINDE

Maria Erlacher

83256 Fraueninsel im Chiemsee
Tel. (08054) 9 03 66
Fax (08054) 7299 – www.inselhotel-zurlinde.de

Open all year • 14 rooms • Café-restaurant with terrace (closed 6 Jan to end of Mar): set meals 6.80-17.50 € • Dogs allowed

110 €, Breakfast included

VISA MC

Making time for traditional coffee and cakes on the waterside terrace

A truly special place, over 600 years in the making! The origins of this inn go right back to 1396, and there's enough living tradition here to enchant any visitor. Historic lounges and parlours and a private bathing platform are reasons enough to stay, but the unique atmosphere of the Fraueninsel, with its beautiful and unspoilt fishing village and the ancient, peaceful dignity of its convent buildings, is really best enjoyed when the last of the day-trippers have gone back to the mainland and the island is yours to explore. Cosy, wood-furnished rooms allow you to do just that, then relax in style!

Sights nearby: Frauenchiemsee monastery, Schloss Herrenchiemsee (on Herreninsel)

Access: No cars allowed on Fraueninsel. Ferry from Gstadt (5 min) or Prien (20 min)

45 ROMANTIK HOTEL ZUR POST

Ludwig Weiß Jun.

Hauptstr. 7
82256 Fürstenfeldbruck
Tel. (08141) 3 14 20
Fax (08141) 16755 – www.hotelpost-ffb.de

Closed 22-31 Dec • 41 rooms, including 2 with disabled access • Restaurants with terrace (closed Sat, Sun eve): main course 8-25€ • Parking; dogs allowed

90/130 €, Breakfast included

AE D JCB VISA MC

The hotel's 'Hausgebrannten': powerful, 'home-distilled' digestifs to try here or take home.

Incredibly, the Weiß family have been attending to their guests' every need since 1590, although the inn as we see it today 'only' dates back to 1872. Stucco ceilings and handsome furnishings that wouldn't look out of place in an elegant 19C townhouse lend period tone to some of the rooms: even the finely finished old doors are the work of a real craftsman. Other accommodation is in more timeless style with solid wood furniture. There's a mood of discreet, comfortable good taste in the restaurant, with its traditional tiled stove as a focal point, though don't pass up a seat in the leafy courtyard on a fine evening.

Sights nearby: Fürstenfeld monastery church, Ammersee (16 km southwest)

Access: Exit 30 on A 96 or Exit 78 on A 8

46 BERGGASTHOF PANORAMA

Stefan Kitzmüller

St. Anton 3
82467 Garmisch-Partenkirchen
Tel. (08821) 25 15
Fax (08821) 4884 – www.gapinfo.de/berggasthof-panorama

Closed mid-Nov to mid-Dec • 16 rooms, including 12 with balcony • Cafe-restaurant with terrace: main course 6.40-16.60€; half board 14€ • Parking; dogs allowed

66/85 €, Breakfast included

VISA MC

The Saturday dance evening with Bavarian music and folk dancers

Its location at the foot of the Wank, about 80 metres above the roofs of Partenkirchen, allows you a fantastic view over the Loisach valley and the Wetterstein with the Zugspitze. And, of course, there's a large terrace with a beer garden. Here, and in the typically Bavarian lounges, you can sample good solid Bavarian fare, and home-made pastries and cakes. Accommodation is in cosily rustic rooms, each of which have small corner seats.

Sights nearby: St Anton pilgrimage church, Wank, casino

Access: In Patenkirchen; halfway up slope towards lower station of Wank cable railway

47 GASTHOF FRAUNDORFER

Barbara und Andrea Fraundorfer

Ludwigstr. 24
82467 Garmisch-Partenkirchen
Tel. (08821) 92 70
Fax (08821) 92799 – www.gasthof-fraundorfer.de

Closed between 9th Nov to 2nd Dec. • 30 rooms, including 10 with balcony • Restaurant with terrace (closed Tues, Wed lunchtime): set meal 12-23 €; half board 14 € • Parking, dogs allowed • Sauna, steam bath, solarium, bicycle hire

76/86 €, Breakfast included

JCB VISA MC

The profusion of flowers on the windowsills and balconies

A long-established inn, where traditions are cultivated, as well as flowers! This much is clear from the paintings on the exterior walls and the beer benches outside. Folk evenings with yodellers, folk dancers and musical interludes in rustic wood-panelled rooms are popular with tourists. The down-to-earth character of the establishment is also highlighted in the menu, with its substantial Bavarian dishes, and in the rooms, furnished in a pleasant country style, in both the original house and guest house.

Sights nearby: Olympic ski resort, Schachenhaus; Eibsee (8 km west)

Access: In the centre of Partenkirchen not far from the church

48 STAUDACHERHOF

Peter Staudacher

Höllentalstr. 48
82467 Garmisch-Partenkirchen
Tel. (08821) 92 90
Fax (08821) 929333 – www.staudacherhof.de

Closed 3-20 Apr, 20 Nov to 5 Dec • 41 rooms, including 40 with balcony and 4 non-smoking • Restaurant with terrace: set dinner 18-25€, main course 11.50-22€; half board 22.50€ • Children's play area, garden, parking; dogs allowed in hotel, not in restaurant • Health and beauty facilities and lectures, bicycle hire, organised hikes and bicycle tours

120/212 €, Breakfast included

JCB VISA MC

The weekly 'Bavarian Evening' with its plentiful 'Snack Buffet'.

This long-standing favourite with its two prominent small towers is a stylish and attractive place to stay. Quietly located in a side-street it offers the comforts of a luxurious spa-area and tastefully designed rooms with elegant country style furnishings, some with a slight Mediterranean touch. The ever-innovative Staudacher family look after their guests well, and the rustically smart restaurant serves good nourishing fare.

Sights nearby: Old Church, Partnach gorge, Ettal monastery (13 km north)

Access: On edge of Garmisch town centre

49 ZUR POST

Otmar Wölfel

Balthasar-Neumann-Str. 10
91327 Gößweinstein
Tel. (09242) 2 78
Fax (09242) 578 – www.zur-post-goessweinstein.de

Closed 2 Nov to 10 Dec • 15 rooms, including 4 with balcony and 4 non-smoking • Cafe; restaurant with terrace (closed Mon): main course from 4.50€, set meals 16-30€; half board 13€ • Garden, parking; dogs allowed • Bicycle hire

52/54 €, Breakfast included
Credit cards not accepted

The breakfast buffet selection with its many home-made products

Run by the Wölfel family, this charmingly simple, town-centre inn in the heart of 'Swiss Franconia' welcomes you in with its comfortable, down-to-earth atmosphere. The well-kept rooms have natural wood furnishings and the restaurant has a traditionally rustic atmosphere.

Relaxing on the terrace you can enjoy not only the establishment's good regional cuisine, but in the afternoons you can also yield to the sweet temptations of home-made cake. Children especially will adore the small farm with rabbits, pigs and kid goats, which is part of the establishment.

Sights nearby: Holy Trinity pilgrimage church, castle, Marienfelsen rocks, Teufelshöhle caves, Pottenstein (7 km east)

Access: From Exit 8 on A 73 via Forcheim and Ebermannstadt or from Exit 44 on A 9 via Pottenstein

50 GASTHAUS AM ZIERWALD

Familie Hagenmeyer

Zierwaldweg 2
82491 Grainau
Tel. (08821) 9 82 80
Fax (08821) 982888 – www.zierwald.de

Closed 13-27 Jan, 14-21 Apr • 5 rooms, all with balcony • Cafe-restaurant with terrace (closed Wed): main course 8.50-14.50€ • Garden, parking; dogs not allowed • Bicycle hire

74/78 €, Breakfast included

AE D JCB VISA MC

A walk to the idyllic Badersee

This sun-drenched inn on the road to the Eibsee welcomes you with its simple, yet tasteful setting. The rooms are cosily furnished in light wood, with a rustic touch - as is the comfortable lounge, with its ordered décor, the home of the café and restaurant. As the Hagenmeyer family comes originally from the Black Forest it's not only Bavarian fare that's served up here; you can also try Swabian favourites like 'Maultaschen' - filled pasta squares, a bit like ravioli. Meals on the terrace overlooking the wonderful mountain scenery are especially uplifting.

Sights nearby: Schachenhaus (walk from Garmisch-Partenkirchen, 8 km northeast), Wank mountain (8 km northeast)

Access: 8 km southwest of Garmisch-Partenkirchen towards Eibsee

51 **ROMANTIK HOTEL WAXENSTEIN**

Helmut Toedt

Höhenrainweg 3
82491 Grainau
Tel. (08821) 98 40
Fax (08821) 8401 – www.waxenstein.de

Open all year • 48 rooms, including 40 with balcony and 20 non-smoking • Restaurant with terrace: set meals 12-24 € • Garden, parking, dogs allowed in hotel, not in restaurant • Health and beauty facilities: indoor pool, sauna, fitness room; bicycle hire, organised walks

92/175 €, Breakfast included

AE VISA

Climbing the mountains by mountain bike

The majestic panorama of the Bavarian Alps unfolds impressively before you, a little outside the village, in an elevated position on the road to the Eibsee and the Zugspitze railway: the breathtaking prospect of the Waxenstein and the Zugspitze massif is almost too much to take in! You could sit on the terrace for hours and be spoilt from breakfast to supper, but there's more to the hotel than just the view: the rooms, furnished in a nostalgically elegant country style or with timeless cherry wood, and the attractive leisure area with its light-filled indoor pool, are also points in its favour.

Sights nearby: Eibsee (4 km southwest); Partnach gorge in Garmisch-Partenkirchen (8 km northeast)

Access: 8 km southwest of Garmisch-Partenkirchen towards Eibsee

52 **ZUR KRONE**
Ralph Restel

Miltenberger Str. 1
63920 Großheubach
Tel. (09371) 26 63
Fax (09371) 65362 – www.gasthauskrone.de

Closed 5-13 Feb • 8 rooms • Restaurant with terrace (closed Mon, midday Fri): set meals 32-45€ • Garden, parking; dogs allowed

70 €, Breakfast included
VISA MC

The charming and attractive decoration throughout the establishment

This pretty country inn on the main road through the village, idyllically situated on the Main, has a genuine, natural feel, which encourages you to stay. The well-maintained rooms have natural wood furniture and modern white bathrooms. You can enjoy the good cuisine in the sophisticated ambience of the rustic restaurant, or if the sun is shining, in the pretty landscaped inner courtyard. The attractive setting of the very cosy 'Urbanusstube' with its wood panelling and tiled stove makes breakfast a double pleasure.

Sights nearby: Engelberg Franciscan monastery, Miltenberg Old Town (4 km south), Amorbach abbey church (11 km south)

Access: From Exit 64 on A 3 via Rohrbrunn, Eschau, Mönchberg and Röllbach

53 ALTER WIRT

Familie Portenlänger

Marktplatz 1
82031 Grünwald
Tel. (089) 6 41 93 40
Fax (089) 64193499 – www.alterwirt.de

Open all year • 52 rooms, including 10 with disabled access and 25 non-smoking • Restaurant with terrace: set lunch 9-45€, set dinner 16-45€; half board 25€ • Garden, parking; dogs allowed • Bicycle hire, natural food shop

95/140 €, Breakfast included
AE VISA MC

The natural food shop 'Naturell' in the inn.

This long-standing inn in the market place has remained down-to-earth in two senses - on the one hand, the lounge areas, some of which are very traditional, are in the typical regional style; on the other hand, several rooms have been refurbished on the principles of 'organic architecture'. They are designed only with natural materials - wooden floors in the bedrooms and Solnhofen stone tiles in the bathrooms creating an attractive sense of comfort. In contrast, other rooms are furnished in an almost ornate style. The choice is yours!

Sights nearby: Bavaria Filmstadt at Geiselgasteig, Schäftlarn monastery church (10km south), State Antiquities Collection in Munich (13km north)

Access: Oberhaching/Grünwald Exit on A 99

54 ZUR POST

Natascha Loos

Bahnhofstr. 7
91710 Gunzenhausen
Tel. (09831) 6 74 70
Fax (09831) 6747222 – www.hotelzurpost-gunzenhausen.de

Closed 1 week in Jan • 26 rooms, including 10 non-smoking • Restaurant with terrace (closed Sun eve, Mon): main course 7-23€; half board 16€ • Parking; dogs allowed

85/95 €, Breakfast included

AE VISA MC

When the sun shines you have the choice of the terrace at the side of the building or the green garden.

With such lovely streets and houses, anyone would be proud to call this beautiful little place their home town. It offers numerous health and leisure activities - on foot, by bike, as well as on and in the water - due to its location in the Franconian Lake region. This traditional inn, centrally situated between the station and the marketplace - even Goethe and King Ludwig I of Bavaria have spent the night here - has tasteful rooms, in a timeless-homely design.

Sights nearby: Evangelical town church, Altmühlsee, Brombachsee (10km east)

Access: At junction of B 13 and B 466

55 DANIEL'S

Helga Held

Hauptstr. 11
85399 Hallbergmoos-Goldach
Tel. (0811) 5 51 20
Fax (0811) 551213 – www.hotel-daniels.de

Closed 1-6 Jan, Christmas • 28 rooms, including 2 with balcony and 10 non-smoking • Garden, parking; dogs allowed • Bicycle hire

69/79 €, Breakfast 9 € (WE: 65/79 €)

AE VISA

The easy access, only 10 minutes by car to Munich Airport

You will be enchanted by this intensively run family business at the first glimpse of the gleaming white façade with the smart little oriel towers. The rooms, furnished in an elegant Italian style, are spacious, homely, and above all, tasteful. The completely white bathrooms are second to none. Both the friendly atmosphere in the Breakfast Room, decorated in pastel colours, and the buffet, stocked, of course, with very good products, guarantee a good start to the day.

Sights nearby: Cathedral and Weihenstephan Bavarian State Brewery in Freising (13 km north)

Access: Grüneck Exit on A 92

56 KAINSBACHER MÜHLE

R. Herzog

Mühlgasse 1
91230 Happurg-Kainsbach
Tel. (09151) 72 80
Fax (09151) 728162
hotel-muehle@t-online.de – www.kainsbacher-muehle.de

Open all year • 38 rooms, including 36 with balcony and 8 non-smoking • Restaurant with terrace: set lunch 26-32€, set dinner 29-36€; half board 23€ • Garden, parking; dogs by arrangement • Wellness facilities including indoor pool, sauna and gym, bicycle hire, organised walks

118/144 €, Breakfast included

VISA

The swimming pool overlooking the working millwheel

Enjoy the relaxing atmosphere of this former mill on the edge of the village! The rooms are furnished in a very homely manner with dark oak, and most have their own corner seat. Being family run the rooms are immaculately maintained. In the restaurant you will be sitting under a historic vaulted ceiling in a congenial country style setting. The idyllic park grounds with pond, pavilion and the small bread baking house are particularly pretty. The charm and unspoilt nature of the surrounding Swiss Hersbruck area also has a tempting range of sport and leisure activities.

Sights nearby: German shepherd museum and Frankenalb spa in Hersbruck (7km northwest)

Access: 7km south of Hersbruck; Happurg Exit on B 14, turn right at reservoir beyond Happurg

57 BRAUEREIGASTHOF ZUM SCHWARZEN ROSS

Constanca Schaffrath

Marktstr.10
91161 Hilpoltstein
Tel. (09174) 4 79 50
Fax (09174) 479528 – www.hotelschwarzesross.de

Open all year • 12 rooms, including 5 non-smoking • Restaurant with terrace (closed Wed): set meal 6.90-8€ • Garden, parking; dogs allowed

62/68 €, Breakfast included

VISA MC

The labyrinth of cellars under the property with eight rooms

The origins of the establishment go back to the 12C, but its current design dates from the beginning of the 19C, creating a pleasant historically rustic ambience. Rooms are furnished individually, mostly in a country style, but some also have period furniture. The Wedding Suite, in a small separate timber-framed house, has an especially intimate character. The restaurant, with its wooden floor and traditional cosiness, radiates the typical charm of a brewery inn. You can, by the way, still look round the historic brewery (in operation until 1870) in the 'Museum Schwarzes Ross' (Black Horse Museum).

Sights nearby: Castle, Rothsee (3 km north)

Access: Exits 55, 56 on A 9

58 BURGHOF

Anita Hartmann

Bahnhofstr. 53
95028 Hof
Tel. (09281) 81 93 50
Fax (09281) 81935555 – www.hotel-burghof.com

Open all year • 22 rooms, including 4 non-smoking • Parking; dogs allowed in hotel, not in restaurant • Sauna

80/90 €, Breakfast included (WE: 72 €)

AE D VISA MC

Underfloor heating in the bathrooms

The Burghof is extremely well situated, not far from the station and only a short walk to the town centre. This building with its elegant façade has been used as a hotel since 1909. Following a general overhaul in 1998 it now offers modern comfort combined with a tradition-conscious, dignified atmosphere. The rooms are uniformly fitted with period furniture and laminated floors, but vary slightly in size and colour. Look forward to a stylish stay!

Sights nearby: Zoo, Fernweh park, Hof film festival (late Oct)

Access: From Exit 34 on A 9, Exit 2 or 3 on A 72, or Exit 4 on A 93

59 LANDGASTHOF OSTERSEEN

Barbara Link

Hofmark 9
82393 Iffeldorf
Tel. (08856) 9 28 60
Fax (08856) 928645
www.landgasthof-osterseen.de

Closed 17 May to 3 Jun • 24 rooms, including 9 with balcony and 12 non-smoking • Cafe; restaurant with terrace (closed Tue): set lunch 16.50-25€, set dinner 25-35€; half board 18€ • Parking; dogs allowed • Sauna, bicycle hire

88/118 €, Breakfast included

AE, D, JCB, VISA, MC

The temptations of the home made cakes and pastries

The comparatively more intimate character of the so-called Osterseen, south of the Starnberger See, gives them a charm of their own. This country inn right at their water's edge invites you to a relaxing stay. On one side the inn has a typical Alpine outlook, along the road through Iffeldorf, and on the other, the welcoming terrace offers extensive views over the idyllic countryside. The rooms are pretty to look at with their whitewashed natural wood furniture. Together with the restaurant and its various lounges, they impart an elegant rural atmosphere.

Sights nearby: Buchheim Museum in Bernried (14 km north), Franz Marc Museum in Kochel am See (21 km southeast)

Access: Exit 8 on A 95

60 **ROMANTIK HOTEL ZEHNTKELLER**

Heinrich Seufert

Bahnhofstr. 12
97346 Iphofen
Tel. (09323) 84 40
Fax (09323) 844123 – www.zehntkeller.de

Closed 24-25 Dec • 47 rooms, including 25 non-smoking • Restaurant with terrace: set meals 20-60€; half board 20€ • Garden, parking; dogs allowed • Wine tasting

103/200 €, Breakfast included

AE · VISA · MC

Strolling through the idyllic lanes of Iphofen with its well preserved medieval ramparts

This former official seat of the prince-bishop will welcome you with Franconian hospitality. The Seufert family has looked after the well-being of its guests for three generations. The 18C baroque building, a typical court, has elegant rooms, some with period furniture, and all with modern, light bathrooms. In the dining areas you will be served sophisticated regional cuisine and good wine from their own estate. The grapes are processed and the wine bottled in the extensive cellars, three floors below ground level.

Sights nearby: Knauf museum, Craft and Farm museum in Mönchsondheim fortress church (6 km south)

Access: By B 8 southeast of Kitzingen

61 **FREY**

Frau Frey

Hauptstr. 15
85737 Ismaning
Tel. (089) 9 62 42 30
Fax (089) 96242340 – www.hotel-frey.de

Open all year • 23 rooms, including 3 with balcony • Parking; dogs allowed • Sauna, solarium, fitness equipment, billiard room

100/130 €, Breakfast included (WE: 80/100 €)
AE ⓓ VISA MC

The short walk to the S-Bahn stop for Munich

The Frey family welcomes you to the secluded atmosphere of their establishment in the traffic calming zone in the very centre of Ismaning. A tradition-conscious, Bavarian style characterises the rooms of this small hotel, once part of a farmhouse, at the gateway to Munich. Solid natural wood creates an agreeable and homely atmosphere in the outstandingly well-kept rooms. A good start to the day is guaranteed in the pleasant setting of the light and rustic Breakfast Room with its stylish, stained-glass skylight.

Sights nearby: Schloss Schleissheim (13 km west), Pinakothek der Moderne in Munich (13 km southwest)

Access: Exit 71 on A 9

62 OSWALD

Alfons Oswald

Am Platzl 2
94244 Kaikenried
Tel. (09923) 8 41 00
Fax (09923) 841010
info@hotel-oswald.de – www.hotel-oswald.de

Closed 4-10 Apr, 17-24 May, 6-27 Nov • 17 rooms, all non-smoking and with balcony • Cafe; restaurant with terrace (open from 3pm): set dinner 18-35€; half board 18€ • Garden, parking; dogs allowed in hotel, but not in restaurant • Sauna, solarium, skittles, shooting range, bicycle hire, organised walks

79/90 €, Breakfast included

AE D JCB VISA MC

The Bavarian cuisine of the establishment with products from its own butcher's shop, which has won several awards.

Although built in the town centre in 1982, this spruce inn in the town centre has a down-to-earth atmosphere, as if its roots have been in the heart of the Bavarian Forest for centuries. The furnishings are predominantly in wood, creating a warm, homely atmosphere throughout the rooms and restaurant. A shooting range and a skittles alley offer indoor sporting activity and outdoors the national park presents numerous leisure activities in all seasons- on foot, by bike or on the cross country ski-run.

Sights nearby: Weissenstein ruined castle near Regen (10 km southeast), Silberberg visitor mine at Bodenmais (13 km northeast)

Access: By B 85 between Viechtach and Regen

63 ZUM GOLDENEN LÖWEN

Richard Luber

Alte Regensburger Str. 18
93183 Kallmünz
Tel. (09473) 3 80
Fax (09473) 90090

Open all year • 7 rooms, one with disabled access • Restaurant with terrace (Tue-Sat evenings only, Sun from 11am. Closed Mon): Menu 23-30 € • Garden, private parking, dogs not allowed • Bicycle hire, exhibitions

65 €, Breakfast included

AE VISA MC

The home-brewed, unfiltered dark beer.

A charming, local inn with regional cuisine, where hospitality is what matters! The rustic furnishings of this country inn with its pretty courtyard terrace have retained the intimate, welcoming charm of its 17C origins. The rooms, housed in the annexe, some of which are maisonettes, have been lovingly and individually adorned with old country furniture. You can see from the works of art spread over the walls that the innkeepers have an eye for art. Each year they give a month's "Food, drink and accommodation" to an artist of their choice.

Sights nearby: Castle ruins; Burglengenfeld Old Town (9km northeast)

Access: Exit 95 or 96 from A 3 or Exit 35 from A 93

64 JAGDSCHLOSS FAHRENBÜHL

Angelika Raeithel

95158 Kirchenlamitz-Fahrenbühl
Tel. (09284) 3 64
Fax (09284) 358 – www.jagdschloss-fahrenbuehl.de

Open all year • 15 rooms, including 3 with balcony, 2 non-smoking • Restaurant with terrace, residents only: set meal from 14.90€; half board 8.50€ • Garden, parking; dogs allowed • Indoor pool, sauna

56/62 €, Breakfast included

Walking tours in the Fichtel Mountains.

The 19C 'Prince of the Schönburg Hunting Lodges', is still a gem, with its peaceful, idyllic position in a splendid park, The style of its wood panelled façade indicates its origins as a feudal hunting lodge. The rooms are individually furnished in different schemes, ranging from baroque to rustic. In turn, the restaurant evokes a sophisticated ambience, complete with period furniture. There is a riding yard in the former forestry building next door, where the business of horse dealing and breeding is still alive and well.

Sights nearby: Selb (porcelain town) (17 km east), Upper Franconia Farm Museum in Kleinlosnitz bei Zell (20 km southwest)

Access: 5 km northeast of Kirchenlamitz between Niederlamitz and Martinlamitz

65 STADTHOTEL PFARRHOF

Karin Holzmann

Amtsgerichtsstr. 12
96317 Kronach
Tel. (09261) 50 45 90
Fax (09261) 5045999 – www.stadthotel-pfarrhof.de

Open all year • 15 rooms, including 12 with air-conditioning and 6 non-smoking • Restaurant serving snack meals • Parking; dogs allowed • Cosmetic studio

87/132 €, Breakfast included (WE: 74/132 €)

AE VISA

The cosy breakfast room with a tiled stove and wood panelling

This former vicarage was built in 1520 in the picturesque Old Town of Kronach, the so-called Upper Town, at the foot of the fortress of Rosenberg. Its historical framework was filled with elegant furnishings when it was converted into a hotel. The rooms are now individually designed,with period furniture or antiques, complemented by paintings on the walls. Beautiful materials enhance the homely aspect. And you don't have to miss out on modern comfort - all bathrooms have underfloor heating.

Sights nearby: Rosenberg fortress, Marktrodach rafting museum (6 km east), Plassenburg castle at Kulmbach (22 km southeast)

Access: At junction of B 173 and B 85

66 **ALPENHOF**

Georg Schober

Edelweißstr. 11
82494 Krün
Tel. (08825) 92 02 40
Fax (08825) 1016
hotel@alpenhof-kruen.de – www.alpenhof-kruen.de

Closed 4-28 Apr, 7 Nov to 15 Dec • 40 rooms, including 33 with balcony, 6 with air conditioning, 3 with disabled access and 10 non-smoking • Restaurant with terrace (closed Sun): set lunch 11-15€, set dinner 11-18€; half board 7€ • Playroom, garden, parking; dogs allowed in hotel, not in restaurant • Indoor pool, sauna, gym, table tennis, bicycle hire, cross-country and downhill skiing

70/112 €, Breakfast included

AE VISA

The wonderful sunbathing lawn

Krün's location in the upper Isar valley, between Wetterstein and Karwendel, could not be better. It affords wonderful views over both mountain ranges and there is no limit on relaxation here, close to nature. The Alpenhof is in a quiet side street in the village centre. The ambience is informal and cosy, the typical country style of the rooms and restaurant creating a congenial atmosphere of well-being. They even serve home-made cake in the afternoons - what more could you wish for?

Sights nearby: Mittenwald violin museum (8km south), Walchensee (10km north)

Access: At junction of B 2 and B 11

67 GÄSTEHAUS NUMBERGER

Liselotte Spranz

Dr.-Aicher-Str. 2
94405 Landau an der Isar
Tel. (09951) 9 80 20
Fax (09951) 980220
www.gaestehaus-numberger.de

Closed 1 Jan, 24-31 Dec • 19 rooms, including 10 non-smoking, 3 with balcony • Garden, parking; dogs not allowed

60/70 €, Breakfast included

AE VISA MC

The smart breakfast room with access to the garden

The former villa built in 1936 on the edge of the town above the Old Town makes a truly idyllic picture with its interworked façade, and still retains its noble air. The rooms are tastefully and cosily furnished, mainly in cherry wood. The whole establishment has been lovingly developed with many small details, which the dedicated lady of the house is personally responsible for. In short, it's an extremely attractive setting in which to switch off from everyday stress!

Sights nearby: Lower Bavarian archeological museum, Bayern Park in Reisbach (17 km southwest)

Access: Exit 19 on A 92

68 **VILLINO**

Reiner Fischer

Hoyerberg 34
88131 Lindau-Hoyren
Tel. (08382) 9 34 50
Fax (08382) 934512 – www.villino.de

Closed Christmas • 17 rooms, including 15 with balcony and 5 non-smoking • Restaurant with terrace (eve only, closed Mon): set meals 68-78€ • Garden, parking; dogs by prior arrangement • Sauna, massage, wine seminars, cookery courses

140/200 €, Breakfast included

VISA MC

The pictures of the contemporary artist Manfred Scharpf in the restaurant

The name itself conveys the reason for the establishment - the Italian term can be translated as a small villa, a summer house. And that's exactly what you'll find here. A small country house, with an all-embracing Italian atmosphere, nestles in a dreamlike garden, whose enticing blossom display spreads its own special charm. The rooms have been very tastefully fitted with period furniture, the warm colours creating a Mediterranean atmosphere. And just the sound of their names is enough to inspire dreams - Paradiso, Mare, Stella, Fiore... An outstanding restaurant with a light-filled conservatory rounds off the proposal.

Sights nearby: Municipal Museum, Lindau Bavarian Casino, Pfänder (8 km south)

Access: In Lindau take the Friedrichshafener Strasse and Schönauer Strasse, turning off later into the "Hoyerberg" road

69 SCHLOSSHOTEL

Michaela Weber

Schlossallee 25
63875 Mespelbrunn
Tel. (06092) 60 80
Fax (06092) 608100 – www.schlosshotel-mespelbrunn.de

Open all year • 40 rooms, including 20 with balcony and 20 non-smoking • Restaurant with terrace: main course 7.50-15€; half board 15€ • Garden, parking; dogs allowed in hotel, in restaurant by arrangement • Jacuzzi, steam bath, solarium

85/145 €, Breakfast included

AE JCB VISA MC

Finish the day with a nightcap in the snug hotel bar

In 1910 a timber-framed house was built as a castle inn, close to the idyllic moated castle of Mespelbrunn. Several extensions later it has grown into an impressive hotel complex, which, with its small towers and gables, still fits in romantically with the Spessart forest scenery. The rooms are furnished in a homely manner, varying colours and shapes giving each a personal touch. The restaurant with its hunting trophies has a cosily rustic feel. The "Fireside Room" and the "Knight's Hall" are also available for use.

Sights nearby: Schloss Mespelbrunn, Schloss Johannisburg in Aschaffenburg (19km northeast)

Access: Exit 63 on A 3 via Hessenthal and Mespelbrunn

70 **FREISINGER HOF**

Michaela Wallisch

Oberföhringer Str. 189
81925 München-Oberföhring
Tel. (089) 95 23 02
Fax (089) 9578516 – www.freisinger-hof.de

Closed 24 and 31 Dec • 13 rooms, including 4 non-smoking • Restaurant with terrace: main course 10.10-22€ • Garden, parking; dogs allowed • Finnish sauna, steam sauna, gym, bicycle hire, wine tasting

130/220 €, Breakfast included (WE: 100/180 €)

AE VISA

The cuisine featuring Bavarian and Austrian specialities

This welcoming, traditional inn, whose origins go back to 1875, is in the beautiful Isar valley, northeast of Munich town centre.The conventionally rustic lounge and the wonderful beer garden display a fresh, original cosiness. The rooms are unparalleled, furnished with bright light natural wood in an appealing, uncomplicated style, their charm further emphasized by warm colours and beautiful materials. An enchanting place to stay, from where "the international city with a small-town charm" can be explored at your leisure!

Sights nearby: Englischer Garten, Deutsches Museum (6km southwest)

Access: From Frankfurter Ring Exit on A 9, via Föhringer Ring, take the Unterföhring/Oberföhring Exit after 2km, then right after lights

71 JAGDSCHLOSS

Inge Schmidtlein

Alte Allee 21
81245 München-Obermenzing
Tel. (089) 82 08 20
Fax (089) 82082100
jagdschloss@t-online.de – www.weber-gastronomie.de

Open all year • 26 rooms, including 5 with balcony • Restaurant with beer garden: set lunch 6.50€, main course 5-20€ • Garden, parking; dogs allowed

90/150 €, Breakfast 8 € (WE: 85/150 €)
VISA MC

The beer garden with its fresh, hospitable atmosphere

The intimate and rural character of the hunting lodge, which can look back on more than 100 years of eventful history, is alluring. Although it didn't awake from its slumber until 1990, when it was lovingly revived, it still boasts the captivating charm of an establishment rich in tradition. Homely yet functional rooms, light and well-kept, await your arrival. The lounges are rustic, almost basic, with bare tables and an air of the romance of the hunt - simply real Bavarian!

Sights nearby: Schloss Nymphenburg, Alte and Neue Pinakothek (9km east)

Access: At end of A 8 autobahn turn right into Pippinger Strasse, then right again into Alte Allee just before the bridge under the railway

72 SCHLOSS NEUBURG

Sebastian Ott

Am Burgberg 5
94127 Neuburg am Inn
Tel. (08507) 91 10 00
Fax (08507) 911911
info@schlossneuburg.de – www.schlossneuburg.de

Closed 1-6 Jan, open from 24 Dec by arrangement • 34 rooms, 1 with disabled access • Restaurant with terrace: main course from 12€, set meal 26-48€; half board 25€ • Garden, parking; dogs allowed • Sauna, solarium, guided tour of castle, climbing wall, bicycle tours, rubber dinghy trips

125/145 €, Breakfast included

AE D VISA MC

A tour along the Inn valley bicycle path

The 11C castle buildings, which underwent changes in Renaissance and Baroque times, soar majestically above the green thread of the river Inn. The rooms, housed in the former malt house and castle stables, offer stylish living. Clear lines and high-quality materials characterise the ambience, marble bathrooms giving a perfect finishing touch to the tasteful furnishing. The cross vault of the "Court Tavern" emphasizes the historical atmosphere, dating back to the 15C.

Sights nearby: Schärding Old Town (8 km south), Passau Cathedral (11 km north), Fürstenzell monastery (13 km west)

Access: Exit 117 on A 3

73 ROMANTIK HOTEL ZUM KLOSTERBRÄU

Otto Böhm

Kirchplatz 1
86633 Neuburg-Bergen
Tel. (08431) 6 77 50
Fax (08431) 41120 – www.zum-klosterbraeu.de

Closed 1-5 Jan and 1 week from late Aug to early Sept • 24 rooms, all non-smoking • Restaurant with terrace (Closed Sun eve and Mon): Menu 20-36€, half board by arrangement • Children's play area, garden, private parking; dogs allowed • Sauna, table tennis, pony rides, bicycle hire, organised walks

72,50/89 €, Breakfast included
VISA MC

The special atmosphere of the terrace in the monastery garden.

You will be warmly welcomed into an inviting short-term home near the monastery church in the centre of Bergen. The Böhm family has looked after its guests since 1746. The accommodation is attractive with tasteful, uncomplicated furnishing. Light natural wood furniture and mainly marble bathrooms create a homely atmosphere. By the way, the entrance to the rooms, with its elongated glass façade, is part of the former cloister. You'll be pampered with a regional seasonal cuisine in the old Bavarian style lounges with their tiled stoves and wood panelled ceilings.

Sights nearby: Burg Nassenfels (7km east); Pfalz-Neuburg Castle in Neuburg and der Donau (8km southeast)

Access: 8km northwest of Neuburg an der Donau via Ried; turn off to the left in the Iglstetter Wald

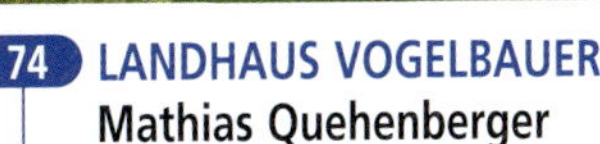

74 LANDHAUS VOGELBAUER

Mathias Quehenberger

Schanzenstr. 4
82544 Neufahrn bei Egling
Tel. (08171) 2 90 63
Fax (08171) 22671 – www.vogelbauer.de

Closed 24 Dec • 12 rooms, including 2 with balcony • Restaurant with terrace (open Sat and Sun only): main course 17-28€, set dinner 35-65€ • Garden, parking; dogs allowed • Bicycle hire, cookery courses

95/145 €, Breakfast included

AE JCB VISA MC

Nine golf courses within easy reach

The Vogel family farm, which dates back to the 17C, was effortlessly redesigned in 1992 into the "Vogelbauer" - now a country house instead of a farm! The restaurant now has its home in the former stables where you can enjoy the imaginative and varied cuisine in a sophisticated rustic atmosphere. The rooms, some of which are maisonettes, are furnished in a beautiful country house style with natural wood, each one having its own personal touch. Breakfast can be served in bed at request, on the balcony and in the garden.

Sights nearby: Starnberger See (14 km west), Bad Tölz Old Town (24 km south)

Access: From Exit 6 on A 95 via Wolfratshausen and Egling, or from Exit 96 on A 8 via Sauerlach, Endlhausen and Egling

75 STANGL

Herr Katzensteiner

Münchener Str. 1
85646 Neufarn bei Anzing
Tel. (089) 90 50 10
Fax (089) 90501363 – www.hotel-stangl.de

Open all year • 56 rooms, including 1 with balcony and 3 with disabled access • Restaurant with beer garden: set meal 21-25€ • Garden, parking; dogs allowed • Deer enclosure

99/209 €, Breakfast included (WE: 85/129 €)

AE DC VISA MC

In keeping with an old tradition, free soup is served to guests on festival days.

This former estate in eastern Munich combines Bavarian practicality with the festive mood of Art Nouveau. It still gives a strong impression of the lifestyle of the Bavarian upper classes at the beginning of the 20C. Some of the furnishings, such as the wood carvings, are still the originals, and the Art Nouveau furniture in many of the rooms in the original house creates a special atmosphere. In contrast, the accommodation in the guest house is simpler. The dining areas, where you can enjoy the regional cuisine, are cosily rustic.

Sights nearby: Poing deer park (3km north), Deutsches Museum in Munich (20km west)

Access: From Exit 9 on A 94 via Parsdorf, or from Exit 10 via Anzing

76 ALPENHOF

Josef Schmid

Rosenheimer Str. 97
83080 Niederaudorf
Tel. (08033) 30 81 80
Fax (08033) 4424
alpenhof-oberaudorf@t-online.de – www.alpenhof-oberaudorf.de

Open all year • 16 rooms, all with balcony • Restaurant with terrace (closed Thu): set meal 13.50-23.50€; half board 11€ • Garden, parking; dogs allowed • Bicycle hire

75/78 €, Breakfast included

JCB VISA MC

Sunbathing on the lawn or enjoying a piece of cake on the terrace

Here, you can have a holiday on a farm, with every wish being granted! In the wonderful countryside of the Inn valley in Bavaria, surrounded by the Alpine panorama, nature lies at your feet - walks, bicycle tours or a refreshing swim in a mountain lake, a wide range of winter sports and a farm with a large fruit garden await you. The pampering starts at breakfast with fresh milk, quark and home-made jam. The rooms, like the house itself, are designed in the style typical of the region - enchanting and with rustic cosiness!

Sights nearby: Tatzelwurm waterfall (8 km west), Kufstein fortress (14 km south)

Access: Exit 59 on A 93, 2 km north of Oberaudorf towards Flintsbach

77 **DREI RABEN**

Dr. Daniela Hüttinger und Werner Deibel

Königstr. 63
90402 Nürnberg
Tel. (0911) 27 43 80
Fax (0911) 232611 – www.hotel-drei-raben.de

Open all year • 25 rooms, including 15 non-smoking, 3 with air-conditioning • Dogs allowed • City tours

120/185 €, Breakfast included

AE, Diners, JCB, VISA, MC

The lounge with its imaginative design and multi-media facilities - a breakfast room, cafe and cocktail bar all in one.

Are you looking forward to discovering the enchanting old imperial town of Nürnberg? Then you can start straightaway with the rooms of this original hotel. You can trace the myths of the great past, but also current phenomena from the life of the town. Subjects such as Albrecht Dürer, the first German railway or indeed the famous Nürnberg football club - sometimes in the top division, sometimes not - are presented imaginatively and with much attention to detail: even typical Nürnberg sandstone is part of the display. And wonderfully, it's accomplished with taste and elegance. The Junior suites with the free-standing vintage baths also have a unique quality.

Sights nearby: New Museum/State Museum of Art and Design, Germanisches Nationalmuseum, St Lorenz Church

Access: In the city centre not far from the station, follow orange signs indicating "9 Hotels"

78 ROMANTIK HOTEL ROTTNER

Stefan Rottner

Winterstr. 17
90431 Nürnberg-Großreuth bei Schweinau
Tel. (0911) 65 84 80
Fax (0911) 65848203 – www.rottner-hotel.de

Closed 1-10 Jan • 37 rooms, including 2 with disabled access and 18 non-smoking • Restaurant with terrace (closed Sat midday, Sun and public holidays): set lunch 44€, set dinner 54-58€ • Garden, parking; dogs allowed • Bicycle hire, cookery courses

140/155 €, Breakfast included

AE (D) VISA MC

The unusual round showers

The historic inn with its timber frame façade, extremely cosy lounges and shady garden seats has been enlarged by two modern buildings, which are available for your overnight accommodation - the “Breakfast Pavilion” with conference rooms, and the “Bed House” on the other side of the street. These modern rooms have been tastefully designed with great style. Modern art, three-piece suites and stylish colour combinations create an attractive at-home feeling. Minibar drinks are inclusive, by the way.

Sights nearby: Kaiserburg, Toy Museum in Nuremberg (6 km west)

Access: Gebersdorf/Grossreuth Exit on A 73

79 ZIRBELSTUBE

Maria und Erhard Kunkel

Friedrich-Overbeck-Str. 1
90455 Nürnberg-Worzeldorf
Tel. (0911) 99 88 20
Fax (0911) 9988220 – www.zirbelstube.com

Closed 2 weeks in Jan, last week in Jul, 1 week in Aug • 8 rooms • Restaurant with terrace (closed Sun, midday Mon): set meals 22-49€; half board 21€ • Garden, parking; dogs not allowed • Bicycle hire, organised walks

95/130 €, Breakfast included (WE: 90 €)
VISA MC

Home-made jams and jellies for breakfast.

The sandstone building, listed as an historical monument, is an attractive place to stay in the south of Nürnberg. As the name suggests, the restaurant does, of course, have a Swiss pine room. It also has the "vault" and a pretty terrace, and both regional and international dishes are served. Rooms are furnished in a country house style with unobtrusive colours. The matching bedspreads and wallpapers give the rooms a unified look. As there are only a few rooms the atmosphere is informal.

Sights nearby: Sebalduskirche, Zoo, Nuremberg Rally documentation centre (10 km north)

Access: Exit Nürnberg-Zollhaus on A73, turn right in Worzeldorf towards Kornburg

80 **GOLDENER HIRSCH**
Harald Holfelder

Marktplatz 4
87634 Obergünzburg
Tel. (08372) 74 80
Fax (08372) 8480 – www.holfelder.info

Closed 1 week after Fasching (Carnival week before Lent), last 2 weeks Aug • 5 rooms • Restaurant with terrace (closed Mon): set lunch 9.50-16€, set dinner 18-35€; half board 18€ • Parking; dogs not allowed • Cookery courses

66 €, Breakfast included
VISA MC

The readiness to listen to guests' requests

An historic inn in a tranquil market community in the Allgäu. Here in the valley of Günz the peaceful and hospitable rural life awaits you in countryside which is still largely unspoilt and off the beaten track. Rooms furnished in light wood, simply and with no frills, are ready for your stay.The lounges are of rustic design with wood panelling and green-tiled stoves.You should pay special attention to the "Museum room", which is adorned with items collected by Captain Nauer, who was born in Obergünzburg and spent his life on the high seas.

Sights nearby: Ottobeuren Benedictine Abbey (15 km northwest), Kaufbeuren Puppet Theatre Museum (18 km east)

Access: Exit 132 on A 7

81 BERGGASTHOF GROBAUER

Marianne und Alois Grobauer

Kreuzbergstr. 8
94518 Oberkreuzberg bei Spiegelau
Tel. (08553) 9 11 09
Fax (08553) 91110 – www.hotel-grobauer.de

Closed mid to 24 Apr, Nov to 19 Dec • 35 rooms, including 25 with balcony • Restaurant with terrace (closed midday Tue, midday Wed): main course 6.80-14.50€; half board 8€ • Parking; dogs allowed in restaurant, not in hotel • Indoor pool, sauna, steam bath, gym, guided walks, weekly bingo and dance evenings

50/70 €, Breakfast included
Credit cards not accepted

The wonderful Bavarian dance and music evenings

This inn with its extensive views, not only over the beautiful Bavarian forest, but also as far as the Alps in good visibility, has been run since 1910 by the Grobauers - now in the third generation. The rooms in the original house and in the guest house are just as down-to-earth as the owners. The cosily rustic furnishings in light wood match the rural village setting. The inn's own butcher's shop ensures that delicious sausage and ham specialities are fresh on the table for breakfast.

Sights nearby: Spiegelau glass works (7km north), Bavarian Forest National Park information centre and native animal enclosure in Neuschönau

Access: 7km south of Spiegelau by Hauptstrasse and Grafenauer Strasse, turn left in Steinbüchl

82 SCHEIBENHAUS

Sabine Horlacher

Scheibenstr. 1
87561 Oberstdorf
Tel. (08322) 95 93 02
Fax (08322) 959360 – www.scheibenhaus-oberstdorf.de

Closed Nov to mid-Dec, early/mid-Apr to early/mid-May • 8 rooms, including 6 with balcony • Restaurant with terrace for residents only (closed lunchtime and all day Tue): half board 18€ • Garden, parking; dogs not allowed • Sauna, steam bath, massages, ayurvedic yoga, bicycle hire, organised walks

98/112 €, Breakfast included
Credit cards not accepted

The Spa suite with whirlpool and waterbed.

100% holiday! You will be lovingly looked after here and will enjoy the many comforts that this idyllically situated establishment offers you. The rooms are individually and very tastefully designed. You can even choose the mattress which appeals to you most - the selection ranges from horse hair to Latex. You'll also appreciate the free drinks and home-made cake. And above all, of course, the nature garden which allows you wonderful views of the Trettach valley and the Allgäu Alps. Time to ask for more holiday when you get back to work: if the Schiebenhaus has rooms free, how about 52 weeks a year?

Sights nearby: Breitach Gorge, Heini Klopfer ski jump, ceremonial descent of cattle from alpine meadows (13 Sept)

Access: Southern edge of built-up area by the Loretto Chapel

83 MICHLWIRT

Rudolf Trinkberger

Steiner Str. 1-3
83349 Palling
Tel. (08629) 9 88 10
Fax (08629) 988181 – www.michlwirt.de

Closed 2 weeks in Jan, 3 weeks in Sep • 42 rooms, including 7 with balcony, 9 non-smoking, 17 with air conditioning and 19 with disabled access • Cafe; restaurant with terrace (closed Sun): main course from 6€ • Garden, parking; dogs allowed • Pool, health and beauty facilities, skittles, bicycle hire

59/71 €, Breakfast included

VISA MC

Breakfast by the cosy fireside

This long-standing inn with its own butcher's shop offers tremendous value for money. The original house and the new houses, conforming to the same design, have pretty country style rooms. The light wood furniture is rustic, as is usual in Upper Bavaria. As a complement to that the carpets and materials have been lovingly matched with one another. You will really feel at home here! The different sized lounges and dining rooms offer an appropriate setting for every occasion - whether it's an intimate supper or a large function.

Sights nearby: Stein an der Traun cliff fortress (8 km west), Tittmoning castle (16 km northwest)

Access: By B 304 between Wasserburg and Traunstein to Stein an der Traun and from there to Palling

84 HOISL BRÄU

Maria Gattinger

€€ Promberg 1
82377 Penzberg
Tel. (08856) 9 01 73 30
Fax (08856) 3179 – www.hoisl-braeu.de

Open all year • 19 rooms, all non-smoking, 10 with balcony • Restaurant with terrace (closed Mon, Tue, 3 weeks early Jan): main course 6-16€ • Garden, parking; dogs allowed • Massage

65/105 €, Breakfast included

VISA MC

The beer garden in the countryside

A traditional establishment in a small idyllic hamlet in the countryside, where you'll be given a warm welcome - this couldn't be a more accurate description of the Hoisl-Bräu. Beer was still brewed here until 1960 - hence the name. In 2002 a country hotel was created by extending the upper floors above the country lounges, some genuinely rustic, some elegant. So you can now really relax in a natural environment, in rooms which have been designed in a modern and tasteful country house style using natural wood.

Sights nearby: Benediktbeuern monastery (12 km southeast), Kochelsee (20 km south)

Access: From Exit 7 on A 95 via Beuerberg then towards Penzberg, turning right c 5 km beyond Beuerberg

85 BERGHOTEL SCHLOSSANGER-ALP

Bernhard Ebert

Am Schlossanger 1
87459 Pfronten-Meilingen
Tel. (08363) 91 45 50
Fax (08363) 91455555 – www.schlossanger.de

Open all year • 30 rooms, including 28 with balcony, 1 with disabled access and 3 non-smoking • Restaurant with terrace: set lunch 14.80-20.50€, set dinner 20.50-58€; half board 20€ • Garden, parking; dogs allowed • Wellness facilities, cookery courses, painting courses, whisky, cigar and running courses

140/204 €, Breakfast included

VISA MC

The clear and aromatic air of the alpine pastures.

This mountain hotel, situated in seclusion at 1130 metres, amid meadows and woods, has a warm welcome for everyone. Miles away from everyday life you'll have enough time here to enjoy the fine things in life. The rooms furnished in a homely, elegant country house style, the good cuisine with its emphasis on regional dishes, served on the terrace or in the rustic lounges, and the comfortable spa area with its complete range of facilities provide plenty of opportunity to do so. Anyone who can't relax here must be doing something wrong!

Sights nearby: Schloss Neuschwanstein and Schloss Hohenschwangau (19km east)

Access: Look for the ruined castle by the Falkenstein mountain east of Pfronten-Meilingen

86 BURGHOTEL AUF DEM FALKENSTEIN

Anton Schlachter

Falkenstein 1
87459 Pfronten-Meilingen
Tel. (08363) 91 45 40
Fax (08363) 9145444 – www.burghotel-falkenstein.de

Open all year • 10 rooms, including 8 with balcony and 2 non-smoking • Cafe-restaurant with terrace: set lunch 19-45€, set dinner 25€; half board 20€ • Garden, parking; dogs allowed • Guided walks, snowshoe tours, rafting, canyoning

138/190 €, Breakfast included

AE (D) JCB VISA MC

The Wedding Suite is like a dream from 1001 nights

The fairytale king, Ludwig II, sought out the most beautiful places in his kingdom to carve out his dreams in stone. He also constructed a "Robber Baron Castle" from the Falkenstein ruins. The king's decision reveals everything there is to say about the position of the Castle Hotel, at 1250 metres, at the foot of the ruins - it's simply like a fairytale! The mountain inn offers cosily furnished rooms, mainly in natural wood (some with cooking facilities). It's wonderful to sit in the pavilion annexe of the restaurant with the panoramic windows, and of course, even lovelier on the terrace. When the weather's good you can even see as far as Neuschwanstein castle.

Sights nearby: Falkenstein castle ruins, Hohes Schloss in Füssen (15km east)

Access: Look for the ruined castle by the Falkenstein mountain east of Pfronten-Meilingen

87 LANDHOTEL HUTTER

Siegfried Hutter

Altholz 6
94447 Plattling-Altholz
Tel. (0991) 73 20
Fax (0991) 382887 – www.landhotel-hutter.de

Closed 1 week Aug • 11 rooms • Restaurant with terrace (Closed Sat lunchtime, Sun eve): lunch menus 18.80-19.80€, evening menus 18.80-38€ • Garden, parking; dogs allowed • Indoor pool, sauna, bicycle hire, organised walks

120 €, Breakfast included (WE: 100 €)

AE VISA

The private hotel park with its mature trees

The estate in the countryside still exudes the chic atmosphere of a manor house. The rooms are designed in an elegant country house style, the bathrooms are pleasantly light. And the spacious and tasteful leisure area allows for plenty of relaxation. The restaurant is opposite, its various lounges displaying either rural sophistication or rustic cosiness with wooden floors and tiled stoves. The natural Lower Bavarian hospitality lends them an additional charm.

Sights nearby: Benedictine abbeys of Metten (10km north) and Niederalteich (13km southeast)

Access: Exit 23 from A 92 towards Plattling, then follw the signs to Altholz

88 FORSTHAUS AM SEE

Bernhard Graf

Am See 1
82343 Pöcking-Possenhofen
Tel. (08157) 9 30 10
Fax (08157) 4292 – www.forsthaus-am-see.de

Open all year • 22 rooms, including 15 with balcony, 1 with disabled access • Restaurant with terrace: main course 13.50-26.50€ • Garden, parking; dogs allowed • Bicycle hire, cookery courses

120/175 €, Breakfast included

AE VISA MC

Enjoying the lake view from the balconies of the rooms

If you wanted to you could even arrive by boat! There is a small landing stage in front of this establishment situated on the bank of the Starnberger Lake. The country house style of the Alpine region characterises the rooms - the elegant Suite having a whirlpool bath - and the restaurant. The light wood and panelling creates a rustically refined ambience. The tables have pretty tablecloths, true to the motto "It's a feast for the eyes too". It is especially lovely to eat on the terrace overlooking the water: you'll find yourself wishing that time could stand still!

Sights nearby: Bernried Buchheim Museum (13 km south), Andechs monastery (13 km west)

Access: 1.5 km southeast of Pöcking by Hindenburgstrasse

89 **LANDHAUS HENZE**

Pia und Christian Henze

Wohlmutser Weg 2
87463 Probstried
Tel. (08374) 5 83 20
Fax (08374) 583222 – www.landhaus-henze.de

Open all year • 9 rooms, including 8 with balcony • Restaurant with terrace (eve only weekdays, closed Thu): set lunch 42-72€, set dinner 46-72€; half board 30€ • Parking; dogs allowed in hotel, not in restaurant • Cookery courses, wine seminars

80/129 €, Breakfast included
VISA MC

The extravagant number of staff to look after you

A pretty country house in the foothills of the Alps! The rooms continue the rustic theme with their elegant country house style wood furnishings. And in the three restaurant lounges, lavishly decorated in Alpine style, the chef, also well-known on television, indulges the guests with his creations. The seats around the walled white stove are especially romantic. There is a tranquil garden with a small pond area behind the house for relaxation.

Sights nearby: Cambodunum archeological park in Kempten (15 km south), Ottobeuren Benedictine abbey (17 km north)

Access: Exit 132 on A 7; on a sloping site in a side street off the main road in Probstried

90 **SEITNER HOF**

Stephanie Köhler

Habenschadenstr. 4
82049 Pullach
Tel. (089) 74 43 20
Fax (089) 74432100 – www.seitnerhof.de

Closed 1-7 Jan, Christmas to New Year's Eve • 40 rooms, including 12 with terrace, 1 with disabled access and 7 non-smoking • Restaurant with terrace (closed Mon): main course 13-29€ • Garden, parking; dogs allowed in hotel, not in restaurant • Sauna, bicycle hire

125/150 €, Breakfast included

AE VISA MC

The impressive glass lift in the lobby

In the south of Munich a former farmhouse has become a smart country hotel. Although the farmhouse has been modernised and a new building added to it, the style of the furnishings is reminiscent of the time when Pullach was still a village in the countryside. A refined country house style characterises the tastefully furnished rooms - natural wood furniture and wood panelling conjure up a rustic atmosphere with an elegant touch. The prettily decorated breakfast room is in the same guise, the terrace being an alternative on sunny days.

Sights nearby: Hellabrunn Zoo (5 km north), Pinakothek der Moderne in Munich (12 km north)

Access: In centre of Pullach; from B 11 (Wolfratshausener Strasse) by Münchener Strasse

91 **LANDWEHRBRÄU**

Roland Hausmann

Reichelshofen 31
91628 Reichelshofen
Tel. (09865) 98 90
Fax (09865) 989686 – www.landwehr-braeu.de

Closed 3-28 Jan • 37 rooms • Restaurant with terrace: set meal 19-25€; half board 19.90€ • Garden, parking; dogs allowed • Brewery tour and beer tasting

79/95 €, Breakfast included

VISA MC

A stylish tour through the Tauber valley in the establishment's 1948 Bentley

Hospitality has been cultivated here since 1387 and the proud timber-framed façade proclaims the long tradition of the establishment. The homely rooms are individually furnished, enhanced by beautiful antiques - collector's items of the owner. The bathrooms are also lavishly appointed, partly in marble. A selection of four cosy lounges, ranging from rustically rural to Biedermeier, cater for your gastronomic requirements. You can book a tour - including beer tasting - of the private "in-house" brewery next door. But you can, of course, "sample" the beer independently at any time in the lounges.

Sights nearby: Rothenburg Old Town (7 km south), Franconian Open Air Museum in Bad Windsheim (17 km northeast)

Access: From Exit 107 on A7 via Endsee

92 SCHLOSS EGGERSBERG

Familie Schwarz

93339 Riedenburg-Obereggersberg
Tel. (09442) 9 18 70
Fax (09442) 918787 – www.schloss-eggersberg.com

Closed Christmas, Jan, Feb • 15 rooms, including 6 non-smoking • Restaurant with terrace (closed Sun eve, Mon): set lunch 13-23€, set dinner 18-33€; half board by arrangement • Garden, parking; dogs allowed • Stables

70/125 €, Breakfast included
Credit cards not accepted

The park terrace with its extensive views.

Stucco decorations, wooden and parquet floors as well as antiques - all this in a castle built around 1600 during the Late Renaissance. Rooms so big they almost remind you of ball-rooms, and an individual furnishing style with a nostalgic touch. If all of that doesn't win you over, then maybe the historic restaurant rooms will, with their soft lighting in the "Chapel" and the "Knight's Cell" or under the beautiful vaulted ceiling of the "Marstall". Talking of riding - the establishment's own riding arena and show-jumping course will at least please those who are horse-mad.

Sights nearby: Hofmark Museum (in castle), Prunn castle (4 km east), Schulerloch dripstone cave (11 km east), Kelheim Hall of Liberation (18km east)

Access: From Exit 59 on A 9 via Dörndorf, Pondorf, Neuses, Thann and Georgenbuch

93 DER WEINGARTEN

Otto Ackermann

Weingarten 1
83253 Rimsting-Ratzingerhöhe
Tel. (08051) 17 75
Fax (08051) 63517 – www.gasthof-weingarten.de

Open all year • 23 rooms, including 18 with balcony, 1 with disabled access and 10 non-smoking • Restaurant with terrace (closed Fri): main course 6-18€; half board 12€ • Playground, garden, parking; dogs allowed • Gym, sauna, sunbathing lawn

58,80/90 €, Breakfast included

JCB VISA MC

The warmth-filled atmosphere

This delightful inn sits regally on a hill above the Chiemgau. It has a lovely view across the Alpine foothills, which lie in front of the onlooker like an open book: you could read endlessly, watching the effects of the light on the majestic Chiemsee or the mountain panorama. The rooms in the original house and in the new guest house are furnished in rustic country house style, making an attractive retreat for you. Rural cosiness is also the dominant theme in the Bavarian lounges.

Sights nearby: Schloss Herrenchiemsee (ferry from Prien, 3km southeast), Bedaium Roman museum in Seebruck (17km northeast)

Access: From Exit 52 on A 8 via Prien, turn left in Sankt Salvator and continue straight on

94 HAFLINGER HOF

Iris Linder

Vordersulzberg 1
87672 Rosshaupten-Vordersulzberg
Tel. (08364) 9 84 80
Fax (08364) 984828 – www.haflingerhof.com

Open all year • 9 rooms, including 7 with balcony • Restaurant with terrace (closed Tue Jan to Mar and Nov to 15 Dec): set meal 9.90-15.90€ • Children's playground, garden, parking; dogs not allowed • Swimming pool, riding lessons, carriage drives

68/78 €, Breakfast included
Credit cards not accepted

The riding lessons and carriage rides with the powerful Haflinger horses

The inn sparkles with as much original joie-de-vivre as the sturdy, blond-maned Haflinger horses, which are bred here. The inn chiefly serves its own home-grown products - at breakfast you can enjoy farmers' butter and milk, home-made sausages and home-baked bread. There is still more to delight in: homely rooms with rustic oak wood furnishings, apartments with cooking facilities and a cosy restaurant with a tiled stove make an attractive setting for your stay.

Sights nearby: Schloss Neuschwanstein (14km south), Wieskirche (19km northeast)

Access: On B 16

95 **ROMANTIK HOTEL MARKUSTURM**

Stephan Berger

Rödergasse 1
91541 Rothenburg ob der Tauber
Tel. (09861) 9 42 80
Fax (09861) 9428113 – www.markusturm.de

Open all year • 25 rooms, including 1 with balcony and 22 non-smoking • Restaurant with terrace (eve only, closed Tue): set meal 24-60€; half board 25€ • Parking; dogs allowed • Bicycle hire, brewing courses

125/165 €, Breakfast included

AE JCB VISA

The glass cabinets containing old pewter lids and other collector's items.

This former customs house, built in 1264 in the inner ring wall of the old town, now offers, in the unique atmosphere of medieval Rothenburg, attractive accommodation in a wide range of different designs. Whether you prefer Biedermeier or country furniture, whether you appreciate small floral patterns or an elegant country house style, you'll certainly find something to your taste. And the restaurant with its smart wood-panelling is also distinguished by its comfortable ambience.

Sights nearby: St Jacobskirche, Käthe Wohlfahrt Christmas Village, Reichstadt museum

Access: By the tower of the same name in the centre of the Old Town

96 MOOSBECK-ALM

Hans Gruber

Moos 38
82401 Rottenbuch-Moos
Tel. (08867) 9 12 00
Fax (08867) 912020 – www.moosbeck-alm.de

Open all year • 18 rooms, all with balcony, 3 non-smoking, 1 with disabled access • Cafe; restaurant with terrace (closed midday Tue): set meal 15-18€; half board 15€ • Garden, parking; dogs allowed • Gym, swimming pool, sauna, massage, tennis, solarium, table tennis, bicycles

60/76 €, Breakfast included

The model of Neuschwanstein castle in the garden

The former, now extended, farmhouse hasn't lost any of its delightful charm. Its isolated location in the countryside means that you can really relax here. The rooms have typical Bavarian Christian names and their furnishings are just as individual. The combination of country furniture and antiques creates a special atmosphere. The restaurant with the "King Ludwig Lounge" is cosily rustic, and also has a modern light-filled winter garden extension. The heated open-air pool is in a sheltered position in the large garden area, therefore also suitable for nudist bathing.

Sights nearby: Mariä Geburt church in Rottenbuch (2 km southeast), Wies pilgrimage church (14 km southwest), Steingaden Minster (14 km southwest)

Access: By B 23 between Schongau and Oberammergau, 2 km northwest of Rottenbuch

97 BERGGASTHOF WEINGARTEN

Franz Haßlberger

Weingarten 1
83324 Ruhpolding
Tel. (08663) 92 19
Fax (08663) 5783

Closed 4-5 Apr, 17 Oct to 25 Dec • 13 rooms, all with balcony • Restaurant with terrace: set meal 9.50-16€; half board 10€ • Garden, parking; dogs allowed in restaurant, not in hotel • Bicycle hire

38/50 €, Breakfast included
Credit cards not accepted

The sunny terrace seats, which have a view as magnificent as from a balcony.

A picture-perfect Bavarian mountain inn! An extensive panorama of the village and the Chiemgau is revealed from its solitary position on a hill above Ruhpolding. Rustic and original is an apt description for this still down-to-earth inn and its similarly styled adjacent building.The rural style furnishings of the rooms and holiday apartments encourage you to really enjoy the peace of the location. Good, hearty cooking is served in the wood-panelled lounges with the cosy fireside. Enjoy the genuine Bavarian lifestyle!

Sights nearby: Ruhpolding leisure park, Vita Alpina swimming centre

Access: 3 km southwest of Ruhpolding

98 BERGGASTHOF DUFTBRÄU

Markus Wallner

Duft 1
83122 Samerberg-Duft
Tel. (08032) 82 26
Fax (08032) 8366 – www.duftbraeu.de

Open all year • 15 rooms, all non-smoking • Restaurant with terrace: set lunch 9-15€, set dinner 12-25€; half board 13€ • Children's play area, garden, private parking; dogs allowed • Petting zoo, bicycle hire, guided walks, torchlight walks, mountain hut evenings

50/55 €, Breakfast included
Credit cards not accepted

The "Pigsty" guest room with its enchanting, original design

An ideal residence for hikers! A guide is provided for tours around the Duftbräu and they'll send you off with a packed lunch to give you strength on the way! But even if you don't feel the urge to be on the move this is a pleasant place to relax in - you can enjoy the beauty of the Alpine foothills in the peaceful setting at the edge of the woods. The rooms are furnished in an attractive country manner, and you quickly feel at home in the secluded atmosphere. The substantial fare and home-made cakes, served in the cosy guest rooms or on the welcoming terrace, take care of your culinary needs.

Sights nearby: Kampenwand (14 km east), Tatzelwurm waterfall (17 km southwest)

Access: Exit 104 on A 8, then towards Achenmühle and follow signs

99 **GEORGENHOF**

Hans Weindl

Modereggweg 21
83471 Schönau-Oberschönau
Tel. (08652) 95 00
Fax (08652) 950200 – www.hotel-georgenhof.de

Closed 10 Nov to 15 Dec • 25 rooms, all with balcony, 6 non-smoking, 2 with disabled access • Cafe; restaurant with terrace (evenings only, residents only); half board 11-14€ • Garden, parking; dogs allowed in hotel, not in restaurant • Sauna, solarium, massage, bicycle hire

90/110 €, Breakfast included (WE: 66/104 €)

AE VISA

A restorative massage for your aching muscles after a strenuous mountain walk

Situated on the edge of the woods, the whole property seems to stretch towards the sun. The extension built onto the original mountain inn has a very long façade creating enough rooms with balconies or terraces - all designed in a smart country style - from which you can enjoy the wonderful mountain view. The restaurant, furnished in a cosy lounge style has been expanded with an attractive winter garden, where, just as from the garden terrace, even at mealtimes the wonderful mountain views are not to be missed.

Sights nearby: Berchtesgaden salt mines (6 km northeast), Obersalzberg and Kehlstein (10 km northwest), Hallein Celtic museum (20 km northeast)

Access: From Exit 115 on A 8 via Bad Reichenhall and Berchtesgaden, then by B 305 towards Ramsau and finally follow signs to Schönau

100 ZECHMEISTERLEHEN

Hans-Michael Angerer

Wahlstr. 35
83471 Schönau-Oberschönau
Tel. (08652) 94 50
Fax (08652) 945299
info@zechmeisterlehen.de – www.zechmeisterlehen.de

Closed 10 Nov to 24 Dec • 42 rooms, including 41 with balcony and 11 non-smoking • Cafe, restaurant with terrace (eve only): set meal 12-40€; half board 12€ • Garden, parking; dogs allowed in hotel, not in restaurant • Health and beauty area with indoor and outdoor pools, sauna, jacuzzis, solariums, fitness studio, table tennis, billiards, bicycle hire, organised walks

140/190 €, Breakfast included

AE VISA MC

The open-air pool with its view of the majestic mountain scenery

It's lovely here, at the edge of the village of Oberschönau in the middle of Berchtesgaden National Park. The mountain inn which seems to emerge from the surrounding meadows has much more to offer than "just" the beautiful view. You can also look forward to the spa area, which has everything you could possibly want. Practical Bavarian furnishings prevail in the rooms and restaurant, light natural woods creating a cosy ambience. It's especially pleasant to sit in the "Bauernstube" with its tiled stove and panoramic view, or to have a night-cap in the genninely rustic "Watzmann Bar".

Sights nearby: Königsee (5km southeast), Berchtesgaden Schloss (6km northeast), salt mines in Salzburg/Bad Dürrnberg (18km northeast)

Access: From Exit 115 on A 8 via Bad Reichenhall, Berchtesgaden; from Berchtesgaden by B 305 towards Ramsau then follow signs to Schönau

101 RÜBEZAHL

Familie Thurm

Am Ehberg 31
87645 Schwangau-Horn
Tel. (08362) 88 88
Fax (08362) 81701 – www.neuschwanstein-hotel.com

Open all year • 40 rooms, including 38 with balcony and 10 non-smoking • Cafe-restaurant with terrace (closed Wed): set dinner 20-45€, main course 10-40€; half board 21€ • Children's playroom, garden, parking; dogs allowed • Health and beauty facilities, Kneipp spa, bicycle hire, guided walks, nordic walking courses, wine seminars

110/130 €, Breakfast included
VISA MC

The "Roman thermal baths" with their refreshing saunas and whirlpools

Where else can you find this? An unimpeded view from the "Rübezahl" to the fairytale castle of Neuschwanstein, surrounded by majestic mountain scenery. The two houses of the establishment have immaculately maintained rooms, some in a more rustic style and some along more elegant lines. Most have a balcony with a panoramic view. In the dining area you also have the choice between a country setting - in the best Bavarian tradition - or something more timelessly smart. You can enjoy the scenic view from the conservatory bar.

Sights nearby: Schloss Neuschwanstein and Schloss Hohenschwangau (2km south), Steingaden minster (19km northeast)

Access: In a side road off B 17

102 GASTHOF AM SEE

Rainer Schneidberger

Forggenseestr. 81
87645 Schwangau-Waltenhofen
Tel. (08362) 9 30 30
Fax (08362) 930339 – www.hotelgasthofamsee.de

Closed 28 Feb to 17 Mar, 14 Nov to 15 Dec • 22 rooms, including 20 with balcony • Cafe; restaurant with terrace (closed Tue): set meal 7.60-13.70€; half board 13€ • Garden, parking; dogs allowed • Rowing boats for hire

58/77 €, Breakfast included

JCB VISA MC

It has to be the rooms overlooking the lake

The name says it all - hospitality characterised by an informal atmosphere and, of course, its position right on the bank of the Forggensee gives it a special charm. The rooms are light and friendly, some with large wooden balconies. The restaurant also has a cosy rustic design in light wood. When the sun is shining head for the terrace with the wonderful view of the lake. And there are sun-loungers and rowing boats ready for you on the shore.

Sights nearby: Royal Kristall spa, Neuschwanstein and Hohenschwangau castles (3 km south)

Access: On the lakeside in the middle of Waltenhofen

103 LANDGASTHOF LAMBACH

Gisela Betz

Lambach 8
83358 Seebruck-Lambach
Tel. (08667) 8 79 90
Fax (08667) 8799199 – www.hotel-lambach.de

Open all year • 34 rooms, including 5 with balcony and 15 non-smoking • Restaurant with beer garden (closed Tue): main course from 7€; half board 15€ • Garden, parking; dogs allowed in restaurant, not in hotel • Pool, aromatic sauna, solarium, bathing beach

90/130 €, Breakfast included
Credit cards not accepted

Lazing in the meadow by the Chiemsee under a blue and white Bavarian sky

What could be more beautifully, quintessentially Bavarian than this? A pretty country inn decorated with listed murals and right on the shore of the Chiemsee: it even has an absolutely wonderful beer garden, where you'll find the locals enjoying a glass or two as the wind rustles the leaves of the linden trees. Inside, the rooms are furnished in sturdy wood, just as you'd expect out in the country, and the parlours and lounges, whether you're sitting under a wood-clad ceiling or vaulted arches, have a proper rural feel too. In these simple surroundings, there's a pleasant, smart surprise waiting: a stylishly designed swimming area which still manages to feel like a proper part of the place.

Sights nearby: Bedaium Roman Museum in Seebruck (4 km northeast), Schloss Herrenchiemsee (ferry from Gstadt, 6 km south)

Access: 3 km southwest of Seebruck towards Rosenheim

104 VILLA SOMMERACH

Marianne und Holger Denecke

Nordheimer Str. 13
97334 Sommerach
Tel. (09381) 80 24 85
Fax (09381) 802484 – www.villasommerach.de

Closed 1st 2 weeks in Aug, Christmas • 6 rooms • Cafe (open 2pm-7pm Sun and public holidays) • Garden, parking; dogs not allowed

87/108 €, Breakfast included
Credit cards not accepted

Breakfast is also served in the garden, weather permitting of course!

A beautifully restored property, polished up like a new penny! The Deneckers have turned the old house at the heart of the former wine-growing estate into a real gem. The preservation of the original structure and features - including some fine stuccoed ceilings - and a sensitive, tasteful updating of the rest has brought truly extraordinary results. What sets this place apart from the competition is not only the year-round schedule of cultural events but also the "Villa Café", which is open on Sundays and Bank Holidays. It's time to rediscover your taste for the finer things in life...

Sights nearby: Maria im Weingarten pilgrimage church (6km north), Maria im Sand pilgrimage church (10km southwest)

Access: From Exit 74 on A 3 towards Volkach

105 ANGERHOF

Franz Wagnermayr

Am Anger 38
94379 St. Englmar
Tel. (09965) 18 60
Fax (09965) 18619 – www.angerhof.de

Closed end Nov to end of 1st 2 weeks in Dec • 80 rooms, all with balcony or terrace, 3 non-smoking • Cafe; restaurant with terrace: set lunch 20-35€, set dinner 21-38€; half board 20€, 25€ at weekends • Children's playroom, garden, parking; dogs not allowed • Health and beauty facilities, mountain bikes, climbing wall, archery, curling, table tennis, squash, billiards, tobogganing.

146/200 €, Breakfast included
Credit cards not accepted

Health resort facilities and walking the paths in the 3 hectare nature park

You would be hard pushed to exhaust all the luxuries on offer here, but if there's one thing the Angerhof is designed to avoid, it's over-exertion! Relax instead into a variety of reviving spa treatments: try a Rasul mud pack, discover the beneficial properties of salts or a "bath" in a hay wrap, or just bathe in the solar-heated, open-air bio-pool. No need to come prepared: just make sure you have plenty of free time to be properly pampered. The accommodation and cuisine won't disappoint either: homely rooms, in classically elegant or smartly maintained rural style, and a panorama restaurant with wine cellar and fireplace comprise the other stylish ingredients for a revitalising stay.

Sights nearby: Viechtach crystal museum (13km north), Bogenberg pilgrimage church (21km southwest)

Access: From Exit 107 on A 3 via Hunderdorf, Neukirchen and Grün, or from Exit 108 via Schwarzach

106 MAIBRUNN

Beate Attenberger

Maibrunn 1
94379 St. Englmar-Maibrunn
Tel. (09965) 85 00
Fax (09965) 850100 – www.berghotel-maibrunn.de

Open all year • 52 rooms, all with balcony, 6 with disabled access and 6 non-smoking • Restaurant with terrace: set meal 17€; half board 22€ • Garden, parking; dogs not allowed • Health facilities, tennis, ski-lift with snow-making equipment, halfpipe, deer feeding

88/144 €, Breakfast included
Credit cards not accepted

The unspoilt surroundings of "Peters Alm" - Peter's Alpine Pasture - in the hut belonging to the house

The tasteful ambience of the setting will take your breath away: pretty, impeccably decorated rooms commanding spectacular views await you - at a height of over 2 700ft. Further attractive features include reviving options to improve your health and well-being, an elegant, Mediterranean restaurant, the choice of tasteful country décor or rustic simplicity in the rooms and the fruit thoughtfully provided to sweeten your stay. The icing on the cake, however, are the winter sports facilities; the hotel's own double-tow lift, natural half-pipe for snowboarders and floodlit pistes!

Sights nearby: Whit Monday "Englmarisuchen", Windberg abbey (9 km south)

Access: From Exit 107 on A3 via Hunderdorf, Neukirchen and Grün

107 SCHREIEGG'S POST

Dr. Nils Goltermann

Postgasse 1
86470 Thannhausen
Tel. (08281) 9 95 10
Fax (08281) 995151 – www.schreieggs-post.de

Closed Jan • 10 rooms, including 2 with disabled access and 5 non-smoking • Restaurant with terrace (closed Mon, midday Tue): set lunch 9.80-85€, set dinner 32-85€ • Parking; dogs allowed • Solarium, Finnish sauna, gym, bicycle hire, wine seminars, cookery courses

120 €, Breakfast included

AE VISA MC

The chance to try your luck in the hotel's own fishing waters on the Mindel

This former brewery, perched high above the centre of Thannhausen, is like your very own private escape from everyday life. The bedrooms benefit from the individual touch of the landlady, who personally selected the tasteful classic furnishings, including the antiques. Tradition and hospitality are of the essence here, as you would expect from a former coaching house that dates back to the days of the Kingdom of Bavaria. The beautifully decorated "post room" boasts an open fireplace, the "brewery" has a real touch of rural elegance and the "Hunters room" and "Schreiegg's room" are decorated in 19C Biedermeier style. The finishing touch is the wonderful garden with its chestnut trees.

Sights nearby: Edelstetten convent (7km west), Roggenburg monastery (23km west)

Access: From Exit 69 on A 8 via Burtenbach and Münsterhausen

108 ALPENHOF
Martin Bachmann

Westerbuchberg 99
83236 Übersee-Westerbuchberg
Tel. (08642) 89 40 00
Fax (08642) 894033 – www.alpenhof-chiemgau.de

Closed Nov to early Dec • 10 rooms, all with balcony • Cafe; restaurant with terrace (closed Tue, Wed): main course from 9.50€, set meal 18-35€ • Garden, parking; dogs allowed • Cookery courses, wine seminars

60/100 €, Breakfast included
VISA MC

Breakfast on the terrace in front of a picturesque mountain view

In a part of the beautiful Chiemgau that's particularly well-known for its clean, bracing air, this is the kind of place that makes you feel that all's right with the world. Right next to the church of St Peter and Saint Paul, which is over 1000 years old, the venerable alpine inn has a unique atmosphere and familiar feel to it. This is one of the few places where they still distill their own schnapps and the sound home cooking respects the famous Bavarian love of tradition! A cosy and snug charm pervades the rooms thanks to the homely warming, tiled stoves. The bedrooms and holiday flatlets in the extension sport solid lightwood furnishings.

Sights nearby: Marquartstein Fairytale theme park (10 km south), Schloss Herrenchiemsee (ferry from Prien, 18 km northwest)

Access: From Exit 108 on A 8 to Ubersee, continue 500 metres towards Grassau and turn right

109 ALTER WIRT

Steffi Leimböck

Hauptstr. 36
85716 Unterschleissheim
Tel. (089) 3 70 73 40
Fax (089) 37073424 – www.alterwirt-ush.de

Open all year • 10 rooms, all with air-conditioning and 5 with balcony • Restaurant with terrace: main course 9-30€ • Parking; dogs allowed

90/105 €, Breakfast included

AE VISA

The 2nd floor rooms with exposed ceiling beams

Look for the pretty little yellow church, and you've found its near-neighbour, the Alter Wirt. The name - "The Old Innkeeper" - is well-earned indeed; the first in a long line of landlords welcomed travellers here back in the 16th century. After being ravaged by fire in 1920, however, only the main walls of the building remained, but despite this, a trimly kept place in the style of a prosperous townhouse was to arise from the flames. There's a touch of the rustic inn to it - in the lounges and in the lovely beer garden - but the rooms are modelled on tasteful country house style: each is individually furnished with antiques.

Sights nearby: Schloss Schleissheim and Aircraft Museum (4 km south), Englischer Garten in Munich (17 km south)

Access: Exit 3 on A 92

110 **SPUNDLOCH**
Sascha Obert

Kirchstr. 19
97209 Veitshöchheim
Tel. (0931) 90 08 40
Fax (0931) 9008420 – www.spundloch.com

Open all year • 9 rooms, 2 with balcony • Cafe; restaurant with terrace: main course from 6.50€, set meals 10-42€; half board 15€ • Parking; dogs allowed • Massage, baths, natural cosmetic treatments, ayurveda

80 €, Breakfast included
AE VISA

The wide range of wines on offer

Located in the centre of Veitshöchheim, the Spundloch is a beautiful example of Main-Franconian hospitality. The 300 year-old half-timbered house offers cosy rustic bedrooms, and the jewel in the crown is the "wedding room", which would, of course, hardly be complete without a four-poster bed. The first floor offers a variety of health treatments to guests who feel their well-being needs a little top-up, and the traditional lounges on the ground floor have been designed with the same aim in mind - there's more than one path to well-being, after all! The decorative wine utensils adorning the walls should whet your appetite for the local Franconian wines available.

Sights nearby: Schloss and Schlosspark, Marienberg fortress in Würzburg (10 km southeast)

Access: 10 km north of Würzburg by B 27

111 ROMANTIK HOTEL ZUR SCHWANE

Andreas Poth

Hauptstr. 12
97332 Volkach
Tel. (09381) 8 06 60
Fax (09381) 806666 – www.schwane.de

Closed 22-28 Dec • 28 rooms, including 5 non-smoking • Restaurant with terrace (closed midday Mon): set lunch 24-67€, set dinner 24-67€; half board 25€ • Garden, parking; dogs allowed • Sauna, bicycle hire, boat trips, wine tasting, wine seminars, cookery courses

85/185 €, Breakfast included

AE VISA MC

The paved terrace of the inner courtyards

You don't have to be a wine lover to appreciate this hotel in the heart of Volkach, but those who are couldn't have chosen better: the hotel has its own vineyard and the fine wines it produces naturally find their way into your glass in the bar. A feature of the town since the 15th century, the inn boasts a splendid restaurant, and its beautiful tiled stove and painted coffered ceilings bring a sense of the historic past a little closer. The bedrooms, most of them facing into the inner courtyard, are elegantly decorated with a rustic air and some boast the odd antique.

Sights nearby: Maria im Weingarten pilgrimage church, Würzburg Diocesan Museum in Astheim (1 km west)

Access: From Exit 74 on A 3

112 VIER JAHRESZEITEN

Christina Fuchsberger

Hauptstr. 31
97332 Volkach
Tel. (09381) 8 48 40
Fax (09381) 848444 – www.vierjahreszeiten-volkach.de

Open all year • 20 rooms, including 12 non-smoking • Parking; dogs by arrangement • Bicycle hire, organised walks, cookery courses

89/119 €, Breakfast included
AE VISA MC

Spiralling art - A collection in the inner courtyard tower

Find your romantic refuge in the magnificent Renaissance grounds of 1605. The historic building has a special ambience, of course, but so too do the individual, tastefully furnished rooms, adorned with exquisite antiques. Alternatively, the "Vogteihaus", as it's known, gives you the option of a complete holiday flat. The stylish breakfast room is certainly not put in the shade by the high standards of the bedrooms but, speaking of shade, you can also find yourself an outside table and enjoy the first meal of the day on the quaint courtyard terrace.

Sights nearby: Boat trips on River Main, Maria im Sand pilgrimage church in Dettelbach (14km southwest)

Access: Exit 74 on A 3

113 LANDHAUS TANNER

Franz Tanner Jun.

Aglassing 1
83329 Waging am See
Tel. (08681) 6 97 50
Fax (08681) 697549 – www.landhaustanner.de

Closed 10 days Feb/Mar and Nov • 7 rooms, all with balcony, 2 with disabled access • Restaurant (closed Tue) with terrace: set lunch 13.50-22€, set dinner 22-38€; half board 19€ • Children's play area, garden, parking; dogs allowed • Luxury sauna

68/78 €, Breakfast 8 €
VISA MC

The luxurious and tastefully styled sauna area

A neat country house style sets apart this secluded estate in a lovely green setting. You can hardly miss the radiant blue façade, but a combination of warm-toned wood and a blend of fine fabrics and materials make for a soothingly comfortable atmosphere indoors. The rooms are arranged as apartments with individual kitchens and separate baths and WCs. The menu is based on regional cuisine and the rustic restaurant with its simply set tables has a delightful and actually quite refined décor. It's relaxing both inside and out here, particularly on the peaceful rear terrace.

Sights nearby: Lake Waging, Tittmoning castle (20 km north)

Access: Just outside Waging on Teisendorf road

114 ZUM LÖWEN

Andreas und Wolfgang Ländle

Martin-Kuen-Str. 5
89264 Weißenhorn
Tel. (07309) 9 65 00
Fax (07309) 5016 – www.der-loewen.de

Open all year • 24 rooms • Restaurant with terrace (closed Sun): set meals 21-28€ • Parking; dogs allowed • Bicycle hire

70/80 €, Breakfast included (WE: 60/72 €)

JCB VISA MC

Taking a wander through the historic old-town of Weißenhorn

The lion, glittering like gold, gleams a welcome on the sign of this inn, nestled in the beautiful old centre of Weißenhorn. Guests have been welcomed in since the 16th century, today there is a choice of a room in the older section or in the guesthouse, with its spacious and contemporary rooms furnished in cherry wood. A cosy atmosphere predominates in the smart dining room - its ornate decorations really are a feast for the eyes - and friendly, obliging service instantly makes you feel you're in good hands.

Sights nearby: Roggenburg monastery (7 km east), Wiblingen monastery (16 km west), Ulm Minster (22 km northwest)

Access: From Exit 123 on A 7

115 GOLDENES KREUZ

Richard Zeller

Marktplatz 1
87487 Wiggensbach
Tel. (08370) 80 90
Fax (08370) 80949
hotel-goldenes-kreuz@t-online.de – www.hotel-goldenes-kreuz.de

Open all year • 23 rooms, including 12 with balcony, 1 with disabled access and 2 non-smoking • Restaurant with terrace (residents only Mon): set lunch 14-25€, set dinner 15-35€; half board 18€ • Garden, parking; dogs allowed in hotel, not in restaurant • Sauna, gym equipment, golf course, tennis, nordic walking

90/130 €, Breakfast included

AE VISA MC

The intimate mood of the hotel bar by candlelight

This guesthouse, dating back to 1593, strikes a balance of elegance, no-nonsense simplicity and local pride. The Bavarian flag greets you from the half-timbered façade and the atmosphere of lovingly upheld tradition continues inside. Sporting solid wood furniture the rooms are rustic but undeniably smart and you're bound to fall in love with the pretty decoration. The lounges are in an attractively rural style and staff members are apparelled in country house dress to complete the picture.

Sights nearby: Cambodunum archeological park in Kempten (10km southeast)

Access: 10km northwest of Kempten

116 ALTE VOGTEI

Georg Dörr

Hauptstr. 21
91639 Wolframs-Eschenbach
Tel. (09875) 9 70 00
Fax (09875) 970070 – www.alte-vogtei.com

Closed Christmas • 18 rooms • Restaurant with beer garden (closed Mon; Mon and Tue Nov to Mar): set lunch 13.40€, set dinner 28€ • Garden, parking; dogs allowed

57/62 €, Breakfast included

VISA

The home-made biscuits on the breakfast buffet

This long-established and centrally located inn is a real institution in Wolframs-Eschenbach, a town long associated with the medieval poet of the 'Parzival' legend that inspired Wagner. Dating back to the 1300s, the house - the old governor's residence, according to the name at least - boasts picturesque façades and the "knights' hall"on the first floor, with its Gothic wood ceiling, has survived since the early days. The rooms are homely and simple and filled with country house furniture, all are impeccably maintained. The rustic restaurant, with its painted stucco ceiling, sets a wonderfully characterful scene for dinner.

Sights nearby: Altmühlsee (11 km south), Ansbach castle (16 km northwest)

Access: From Exit 52 on A6

117 ZUR STADT MAINZ

Margarethe Schwarzmann

Semmelstr. 39
97070 Würzburg
Tel. (0931) 5 31 55
Fax (0931) 58510 – www.hotel-stadtmainz.de

Closed 1-10 Jan • 15 rooms • Restaurant (closed Sun eve): set meals 15-50€ • Parking; dogs allowed

110 €, Breakfast included

AE JCB VISA MC

The wide range gifts to take home for friends or as souvenirs

So how did this Franconian inn, in the heart of the old bishop's capital of Würzburg, come to be called "The City of Mainz"? It seems that it acquired the name around the beginning of the 19th century when boats sailing upriver from Mainz would weigh anchor in the town, so that all hands could make straight for their favourite inn. The lounges have stayed true to the charming style that you only find in the upper reaches of the Main, all prettily decorated in country style; bedrooms are fitted in more contemporary natural wood, but have their own little touches of nostalgia too.

Sights nearby: Residenz, Marienberg fortress, Käppele pilgrimage church

Access: In a city centre side street off Theaterstrasse halfway between the station and the Residenz

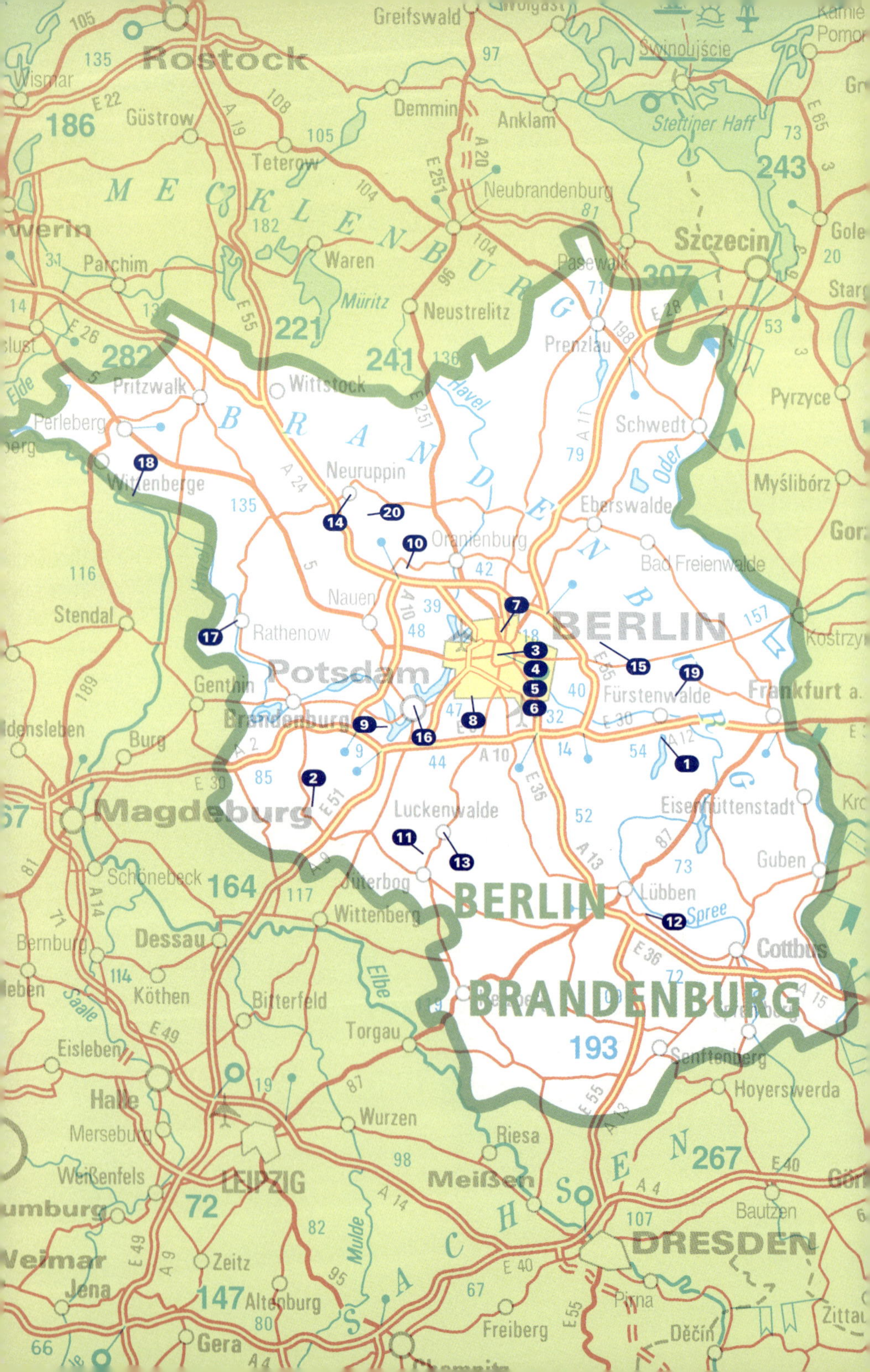
Rostock
Greifswald
Wismar
Güstrow
Demmin
Anklam
Świnoujście
Stettiner Haff
Teterow
Neubrandenburg
MECKLENBURG
Parchim
Waren
Müritz
Neustrelitz
Pasewalk
Szczecin
Prenzlau
Pritzwalk
Wittstock
Havel
Perleberg
Wittenberge
Schwedt
Oder
Pyrzyce
Myślibórz
Neuruppin
Eberswalde
Oranienburg
Bad Freienwalde
Stendal
Nauen
Rathenow
BERLIN
Kostrzyn
Potsdam
Genthin
Brandenburg
Fürstenwalde
Frankfurt a.
Burg
Magdeburg
Luckenwalde
Eisenhüttenstadt
Schönebeck
Jüterbog
Guben
Lübben
Spree
Wittenberg
Dessau
Bernburg
Cottbus
Köthen
Elbe
Saale
Bitterfeld
BERLIN BRANDENBURG
Torgau
Senftenberg
Eisleben
Hoyerswerda
Halle
Merseburg
Wurzen
Riesa
Weißenfels
LEIPZIG
Meißen
SACHSEN
Bautzen
DRESDEN
Zeitz
Mulde
Jena
Altenburg
Pirna
Freiberg
Děčín
Gera
Zittau
1 2 3 4 5 6 7 8 9 10 11 12 13 14 15 16 17 18 19 20

Berlin/ Brandenburg

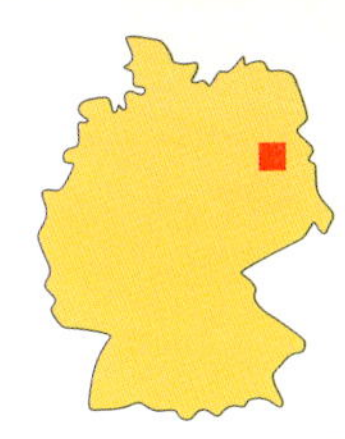

No other great city is evolving with such verve and style as Germany's new capital, now a showcase of contemporary architecture. The cranes will be part of the skyline for some time yet, and though Berlin is well into its second decade as a reunified city, the reminders of forty very different years in the East and West add another layer of diversity to its fascinating, evolving neighbourhoods. Its pulse beats fast, not least because of the hours it keeps; there's no such thing as closing time, and the sheer quality, variety and dynamism of its cultural and social scene can make it hard to keep up. Berlin is also a green capital, with parks, woods, even farmland within its city limits: the urban area merges seamlessly with the Brandenburg countryside. Watered by meandering rivers and the braided, willow-shaded streams of the Spreewald, this part of Germany is little known to visitors from abroad, but its churches, castles and quiet towns will delight anyone prepared to slow their pace and get to know them. Far more famous are the splendours of Potsdam, where, at the gates of Berlin, the Hohenzollern rulers fashioned a Prussian arcadia of palaces in a glorious natural setting.

1 LANDHAUS ALTE EICHEN

Jörn und Ragnhild Peters

Alte Eichen 21
15526 Bad Saarow
Tel. (033631) 41 15
Fax (033631) 2058
info@landhaus-alte-eichen.de – www.landhaus-alte-eichen.de

Open all year • 38 rooms, including 4 with balcony, 2 with air-conditioning • Restaurant with terrace: main course 9.20-14.90€ • Garden, parking; dogs by arrangement • Gym, open-air pool, sauna, solarium, massage, bicycle hire, rowing boats

92/149 €, Breakfast included

AE VISA MC

Coffee and cakes on the terrace overlooking the lake

There could hardly be a more idyllic spot than this spit of land projecting into the lake known as the Scharmützelsee. The rooms are located in a number of separate buildings and have been furnished and decorated with great attention to detail, with the use of pale natural wood completing the tasteful country-house atmosphere. This theme is successfully continued in the rustic restaurant with its lake views. Friendly, competent service helps guests feel at home straightaway. And with the hotel boats and its own bathing place at your disposal, you can enjoy all the pleasures of the water.

Sights nearby: Saarow spa, boat trips on the Scharmützelsee

Access: Exit 4 on A 12; in Bad Saarow follow the green hotel direction signs

2 SPRINGBACH-MÜHLE

Gabriel Muschert

€€ Mühlenweg 2
14806 Belzig
Tel. (033841) 62 10
Fax (033841) 62111 – www.springbachmuehle.de

Open all year • 22 rooms, including 3 with balcony and 7 with disabled access • Restaurant with terrace: main course from 7€, half board 11€ • Garden, parking; dogs allowed • Bicycle hire, children's zoo, fallow deer park

66/77 €, Breakfast included

JCB VISA MC

The coypu which have colonised the surrounding area and have become almost tame.

There has been a mill here since the 18th century, and its waterwheel still turns, though nowadays its role is to contribute to the idyllic atmosphere which visitors find so appealing. Further contributions to the rustic ambience are made by the nearby woodland, pools and ponds, an animal enclosure and a children's zoo. The comfortable guest rooms in the two buildings have attractive pine furnishings, while the restaurant's massive beams and country-style decor make an attracitve setting for dining. Motor caravans have their own parking spaces.

Sights nearby: Hoher Fläming Nature Park, Eisenhardt castle

Access: 2km north of Belzig close to B 102

3 ART NOUVEAU

Christine Schlenzka

Leibnizstr. 59
10629 Berlin
Tel. (030) 3 27 74 40
Fax (030) 3277440 – www.hotelartnouveau.de

Open all year • 22 rooms, all non-smoking • Dogs not allowed • Bicycle hire, organised tours

110/150 €, Breakfast included

AE VISA MC

Rising through the floors in the well-preserved lift of 1906

This well-run hotel is on the fourth floor of a restored town house dating from the early years of the 20th century. The rooms are tastefully furnished, some of them with antique pieces. High ceilings, rich plasterwork and wood floors add to the stylish atmosphere. Some of the rooms have a “colour” or “country” theme and are decorated accordingly. In addition, there's the location: the Ku'damm, Berlin's most prestigious boulevard, is almost on the doorstep.

Sights nearby: Zoo, Berggruen “Picasso and his time” collection, Kaiser Wilhelm memorial church

Access: In a side street off the Kurfürstendamm

4 AUGUSTINENHOF

Herr Ochs

Auguststr. 82
10117 Berlin
Tel. (030) 30 88 60
Fax (030) 30886100 – www.hotel-augustinenhof.de

Open all year • 63 rooms, including 8 with disabled access and 34 non-smoking • Restaurant with terrace: set lunch 10-15€, set dinner 10-20€; half board 17€ • Parking; dogs allowed • Sauna, solarium, massage, cookery courses, town walks and tours

140/190 €, Breakfast included (WE: 117 €)

AE JCB VISA MC

Breakfast in the courtyard when the sun shines

Run by the Berlin city mission, this old Christian hospice now makes your comfort its first priority. The comfortable rooms are decorated in warm colours and benefit from natural wood floors. Breakfast is taken in the bistro-like "Bias" restaurant. A special feature of the Augustinenhof are the 165 paintings by the contemporary abstract artist Karl-Heinz Kautzinski, who painted them specially for the hotel. And there's something else too - hotel guests are entitled to reductions on Deutsche Bahn/national railway tickets.

Sights nearby: Hackesche Höfe, Pergamon museum, Reichstag

Access: From Unter den Linden by Friedrichstrasse and Oranienburger Strasse

5 KRONPRINZ

Kurt Hermandung

Kronprinzendamm 1
10711 Berlin
Tel. (030) 89 60 30
Fax (030) 8931215 – www.kronprinz-hotel.de

Open all year • 76 rooms, including 17 with balcony, 35 non-smoking and 1 with disabled access • Beer garden, garden, underground parking; dogs allowed • Bicycle hire, city tours arranged

145/205 €, Breakfast included (WE: 109/125 €)

AE D JCB VISA MC

The complementary cup of tea or glass of sherry served in the afternoon

Dating from 1894, this establishment is close to the trade-fair grounds. It makes its guests feel welcome straightaway, with an elegant foyer featuring inviting places to sit and linger. Most of the rooms have solid cherry- or maplewood furniture. The tasteful "Romantik" rooms are especially comfortable, with Provençal-style decor and rustic natural wood furniture. Breakfast is taken in the conservatory or, in fine weather, beneath the trees in front of the building.

Sights nearby: Schloss Charlottenburg, Radio Tower, Brücke Museum

Access: Kurfürstendamm Exit on A 100 or A 115, then left at Rathenauplatz, left at first traffic lights after roundabout (Bornimer Str.), then first right

6 LUISENHOF

H. Förstermann

Köpenicker Str. 92
10179 Berlin
Tel. (030) 2 41 59 06
Fax (030) 2792983
info@luisenhof.de – www.luisenhof.de

Open all year • 27 rooms, including 15 non-smoking • Restaurant with terrace: set lunch 5.50-25€, set dinner 12.50-25€; half board 20 € • Parking; dogs allowed

120/195 €, Breakfast included

AE (D) VISA MC

A visit to the bears in the nearby park

The attractive façade of this neo-Classical town house dating from 1822 boasts clean lines and delicate colouring. This theme is continued inside, where the comfortable, elegant rooms have white laquered furniture, high ceilings and striped wallpaper. The bathrooms with their white marble tiles are of an equally high standard. Breakfast - including homemade cakes - is taken in the pleasant conservatory, an excellent start to your day's exploration of the sights of central Berlin.

Sights nearby: Märkisches Museum, Old National Gallery, Nikolai district, East Side Gallery

Access: Close to Märkisches Museum in a street running parallel to the River Spree

7 MYER'S HOTEL

Sascha Hilliger

Metzer Str. 26
10405 Berlin
Tel. (030) 44 01 40
Fax (030) 44014104 – www.myershotel.de

Open all year • 41 rooms, including 27 non-smoking and 2 with disabled access • Garden; dogs allowed

110/165 €, Breakfast included

AE VISA MC

The elegant "Red Salon" or a pleasant break in the "Tea-Room"

This many-storeyed establishment with its neo-Classical façade is located in the old working-class quarter of Prenzlauer Berg, now one of the trendiest parts of the capital. Only a short distance from the centre, it's ideal for visitors who relish the challenge of exploring a city. When pounding the pavements begins to pall, it's a simple matter to retire to your room, relax in the garden or on the roof terrace, or enjoy a drink in the stylish lobby bar with its parquet floor. The next day, after breakfast in the Yellow Salon or on the courtyard terrace, you can start all over again!

Sights nearby: TV Tower, Kulturforum Gallery, Prenzlauer Berg Jewish Cemetery

Access: In a side street west of Prenzlauer Allee (B 109) towards city centre

8 VILLA TOSCANA

Ingeborg Schulze-Gundelach

Bahnhofstr. 19
12207 Berlin-Lichterfelde
Tel. (030) 7 68 92 70
Fax (030) 7734488 – www.villa-toscana.de

Open all year • 16 rooms, including 3 with balcony • Garden, parking; dogs not allowed

100/120 €, Breakfast included

AE, Diners, JCB, VISA, MC

The colourful koi carp in the garden pool

No need to cross the Alps in order to experience some of the allure of the Mediterranean, since here in Lichterfeld in Berlin's southern suburbs is this splendid Tuscan-style villa, built in 1885. A glance from the windows of the breakfast room will confirm the impression of Italy, as the garden has a delightful array of statuary and sculpture. The bedrooms are elegant and dignified, with fine plasterwork, chandeliers, and imported Baroque-style furniture.

Sights nearby: Dahlem museums - World Art and Cultures, Jewish Museum, German Technical Museum

Access: Close to Lichterfelde-Ost S-Bahn station

9 HAUS AM SEE

Brigitte Stein

Neue Scheune 19
14548 Ferch
Tel. (033209) 7 09 55
Fax (033209) 70496 – www.hotel-hausamsee.de

Closed 10 Jan to 7 Feb • 21 rooms, including 7 with balcony and 1 non-smoking • Restaurant with terrace: main course 6-18€; half-board 15€ • Garden, parking; dogs not allowed • Bicycle, surfboard and boat hire, sunbathing lawn, own motor yacht

72/93 €, Breakfast included

VISA MC

The home-made rolls at breakfast-time

Only 15km south of the busy city of Potsdam there awaits an altogether different world, where the idyllic lakeside of the Schmielowsee forms a lovely setting for this hotel. To relax beneath fine old trees on the lakeside terrace in front of the hotel is quite delightful. The lake itself can be experienced more directly, as the hotel has its own landing stage as well as rowing boats and surfboards. The traditionally styled rooms have dark wood or lacquered furniture; ask for one facing the lake.

Sights nearby: Neuer Garten in Potsdam (15km northeast), Babelsberg Filmpark (16km northeast)

Access: Exit 18 on A 10

10 **SCHLOSS ZIETHEN**

Edith von Thüngen

Alte Dorfstr. 33
16766 Gross-Ziehten bei Kremmen
Tel. (033055) 9 50
Fax (033055) 9559 – www.schlossziethen.de

Closed 23-24 Dec. • 39 rooms, including 35 non-smoking and 1 with balcony, • Restaurant with terrace: main course 9.90-17.50€; half board 23€ • Garden, parking; dogs allowed • Sauna, boccia, table-tennis, badminton, bicycle hire, organised walks, exhibitions, wine seminars

97/142 €, Breakfast included

AE JCB VISA MC

The "Suite d'Amour" with its four-poster for special occasions

The castle's Baroque façade conceals a medieval residence full of character. Once through the door you find yourself in another world, with a splendid double staircase and a whole range of different interiors, including a library and a little concert hall. You can stay in the castle itself or in the apartments in the adjoining guesthouse. The comfortable rooms - some are 4 metres from floor to ceiling! - have contemporary decor and facilities and are enhanced by well-chosen antiques. You dine in the light and airy Orangerie or on the terrace overlooking the park with its ancient trees.

Sights nearby: Wustrau Museum of Brandenburg-Prussia (22km northwest), Ruppin Lake (22km northwest)

Access: Via Staffelde from Exit 25 on A 24

11 ROMANTIK HOTEL ALTE FÖRSTEREI

Roland Frankfurth

Markt 7
14913 Jüterbog / Kloster Zinna
Tel. (03372) 46 50
Fax (03372) 465222 – www.romantikhotels.com/kloster-zinna

Open all year • 18 rooms, including 2 non-smoking • Restaurant with terrace: set meal 23-29€ • Garden, parking; dogs allowed • Bicycle hire

95/105 €, Breakfast included

AE VISA MC

The austere beauty of the nearby monastery of Zinna

Framed by formal groups of trees, this old forestry building of 1765 makes an attractive picture, its façade like a face peeping out from beneath the cap of its cheerful red-tiled roof. Inside, there are country-style rooms with exposed beams. Delightful details and choice antiques lend a further romantic touch. Breakfast is taken in the old stables, which also serves as the “12 Monks” bar. Full meals are served here too, as well as in the richly decorated “Friedrichsstuben” restaurant.

Sights nearby: Jüterbog Old Town (4km south), Luckenwalde high-wire adventure course (9km north)

Access: 4km north of Jüterbog by B 101 towards Luckenwalde

12 SCHLOSS LÜBBENAU

Guido Graf zu Lynar

Schlossbezirk 6
03222 Lübbenau
Tel. (03542) 87 30
Fax (03542) 873666 – www.schloss-luebbenau.de

Closed 3-14 Jan • 46 rooms, including 4 non-smoking • Restaurant with terrace: set meal 24.50-57€; half board 22€; cafe-restaurant Orangerie (closed Mon) • Garden, parking; dogs allowed • Sauna, bicycle hire, punt trips, canoe trips, cookery courses

84/134 €, Breakfast included (WE: 104/134 €)
AE VISA MC

A romantic stroll in the park

A castle set among the woods and waterways of the idyllic Spreewald - what more could the heart desire? In its lovely landscape park, the early-19th century neo-Classical building with its two wings offers a choice of elegant rooms and suites, mostly with traditional furnishings. Then there is the elegant, English-style restaurant, the rustic “Huntsman’s Parlour”, the café-restaurant in the Orangery, and last but not least the terrace facing the park, just right for relaxing on a sunny day.

Sights nearby: St Nikolai Stadtkirche, punt trips in the Spreewald

Access: From Exit 9 on A 13 follow signs to Lübbenau, Altstadt, Schlosspark and Schloss Lübbenau

VIERSEITHOF

Herma Gruenewald

Haag 20 (Eingang am Herrenhaus)
14943 Luckenwalde
Tel. (03371) 6 26 80
Fax (03371) 626868
info@vierseithof.com – www.vierseithof.com

Open all year • 43 rooms, including 12 non-smoking, one with balcony, one with disabled access • Restaurant with terrace: set lunch 18-30€, set dinner 29-50€; half-board 18-28€ • Garden, parking; dogs allowed • Indoor pool, sauna, bowling, bicycle and skate hire, cookery courses, brunch

95/105 €, Breakfast included (WE: 90/95 €)
AE VISA MC

The lovely courtyard

This old linen mill has been transformed into a place where hospitality goes hand in hand with art. Production ceased in 1990, and the mill together with the millowner's stately residence has become a hotel of striking individuality. The machine room is now a gallery with changing exhibitions of modern art. There are other contemporary works in the elegant, brick-vaulted restaurant - with the informal "Weavers' Parlour" - and in the rooms around the courtyard, the art complementing the stylish traditional decor and homely pine furnishings.

Sights nearby: St. Johanniskirche, Fläming thermal spa, high-wire climbing course, Zinna monastery (9km south)

Access: On B 101 in centre of Luckenwald

14 UP-HUS-IDYLL

Gabriele Lettow

Siechenstr. 4
16816 Neuruppin
Tel. (03391) 39 88 44
Fax (03391) 652050
lettow@up-hus.de – www.up-hus.de

Closed 3-7 Jan • 17 rooms • Restaurant with terrace (closed Mon lunchtime; open eve only Mon-Fri Jan to Mar): set dinner 18-30€, main course 7-15€; half board 15€ • Garden, parking; dogs allowed in hotel, not in restaurant • Private chapel with concerts, readings, lectures and exhibitions; bicycle hire, guided town walks

65/85 €, Breakfast included
Credit cards not accepted

A steamer trip on Ruppin Lake

With its chapel dedicated to St Lazarus, the old hospice once provided shelter for the town's poor, as did the little 17th century timber-framed building called "Up Hus", the only structure to survive the great fire of 1787. Nowadays, with its gnarled beams and authentically historic atmosphere, "Up Hus" is part of a hotel, with three apartments, each with a bedroom and living room. The pleasant restaurant, with something of the character of a wine-cellar, is here too, while the hotel's other accommodation, consisting of functional, well-cared for rooms, is in a new purpose-built structure.

Sights nearby: St Trinitatis monastery church, museum of Brandenburg Prussia in Wustrau (15km south)

Access: From Exit 22 on A 24 follow hotel route in Neuruppin

15 LANDGASTHOF ZUM MÜHLENTEICH

Nicole Schössow

Karl-Marx-Str. 32
15345 Petershagen-Eggersdorf
Tel. (03341) 4 26 60
Fax (03341) 426666 – www.landgasthof.de

Open all year • 20 rooms, 2 non-smoking, 2 with balcony • Restaurant with terrace: menu 19.90-27.50€ • Garden, parking; dogs allowed • Bicycle hire, guided hikes and cycle tours, carriage rides, shuttle to the golf course

73/100 €, Breakfast included (WE: 130/185 €)
AE JCB VISA MC

Relaxing by the millpond and on the meadow

The very model of a country hotel. The reception is friendly, the staff wear traditional dress, and the comfortable rooms have pine furnishings. The bridal suite even has rustic painted furniture. Comprising the "Farmer's Parlour" and "Hunter's Room", the restaurant has lots of appeal, in a style reminiscent of the Alps; you would hardly think you were just a stone's throw from Berlin! There's a tiled stove for cold days, and a beer garden for when the sun comes out. Relax and enjoy a slice of country life!

Sights nearby: St Marienkirche Strausberg (5km northeast), Altlandsberg Old Town (6km northwest); Rüdersdorf mining museum (11km south)

Access: In Eggersdorf; take Exit 10 from A 4 and follow signs to Strausberg via Tassdorf

16 AM LUISENPLATZ

Ralf Winstroth

Luisenplatz 5
14471 Potsdam
Tel. (0331) 97 19 00
Fax (0331) 9719019
info@hotel-luisenplatz.de – www.hotel-luisenplatz.de

Open all year • 30 rooms, including 19 with balcony • Half board in nearby restaurants 17.50€ • Garden; dogs allowed

119/169 €, Breakfast included

AE, Diners, VISA, MC

Breakfast on the terrace overlooking the square

If the idea of staying right by the Brandenburg Gate appeals, you don't necessarily have to go to Berlin. This establishment on the Luisenplatz in the centre of Potsdam has rooms looking out onto the square and Potsdam's version of the famous Gate, while some of the suites have a view of the park of Schloss Sanssouci. Inside, stylish darkwood furnishings and warm colours create a classically comfortable ambience. The cool design of the breakfast room adds its own elegant touch.

Sights nearby: Sanssouci palace and park, Potsdam Film Museum, Mosque (Sanssouci pumping station)

Access: In Potsdam town centre between Havel and Sanssouci Park via B 1 (Zeppelinstrasse)

17 **FÜRSTENHOF**

Hans Koch

Bahnhofstr. 13
14712 Rathenow
Tel. (03385) 55 80 00
Fax (03385) 558080
www.hotel-fuerstenhof-rathenow.de

Closed 23-31 Dec • 35 rooms, including 3 with balcony and 30 non-smoking • Restaurant (open 6pm-10pm Mon-Fri): set meal 13.80-24.50€; half board from 10€ (by arrangement) • Parking; dogs allowed • Massage

80/110 €, Breakfast included

AE VISA MC

The elegant breakfast room with its splendid tiled stove

This stately structure with its corner tower dates from 1902, and its interior decor has been carried out very much in the spirit of that golden age. The comfortable rooms have bedsteads in cherrywood and are given an individual note through other well-chosen items of furniture, some of them antiques. The bathrooms are convincingly contemporary in style, with careful use of marble and granite. This exemplary taste finds further expression in the immaculate restaurant with its lovely chandeliers and fine furnishings.

Sights nearby: St Marien und Andreas Stadtkirche, steamer trips on River Havel

Access: Near station in Rathenow at junction of B 102 and B 188

18 **SCHLOSS RÜHSTÄDT**

Diana Glass

19322 Rühstädt
Tel. (038791) 8 08 50
Fax (038791) 808529 – www.schlosshotel-ruehstaedt.de

Closed 5-27 Jan, 24-26 Dec • 14 rooms, including 12 non-smoking • Garden, parking; dogs allowed • Health and fitness facilities including sauna and solarium, fitness equipment, riding lessons and excursions, carriage drives, bicycle hire, stork-watching

89/109 €, Breakfast included

VISA MC

The very special atmosphere of the village which boasts the most storks' nests in Germany

It's a surprise to learn that this castle has only 14 rooms to offer its guests. But this is as it should be; it means they are airy and spacious, and there is room too for a library and a generous wellness area. Within the castle walls the decor is stylish, with lovely carpets in the public spaces and parquet floors in the bedrooms. Well-chosen antiques complete the tasteful atmosphere, while outside, pools and parkland make an inviting prospect.

Sights nearby: Kristall saline spa at Bad Wilsnack (12km northeast), Havelberg cathedral (23km southeast)

Access: 15km southeast of Wittenberge via Hinzdorf

19 SCHLOSS STEINHÖFEL

Evelyn und Frank John

Schlossweg 4
15158 Steinhöfel
Tel. (033636) 27 70
Fax (033636) 27777 – www.schloss-steinhoefel.de

Open all year • 30 rooms, including 2 with balcony • Cafe, restaurant with terrace: set meal 22-39€; half board 15€ • Garden, parking; dogs allowed • Sauna, organised walks, wine seminars

100/130 €, Breakfast included

AE VISA MC

A picnic in the park

This old aristocratic residence was given its present castle-like character in the course of a late-18th century rebuilding, and this has been reinforced and confirmed by its recent meticulous restoration. Great attention to detail has been paid in the remodelling of the rooms, some in Biedermeier, others in country-house style. Well-chosen antiques add to their allure. You could spend your whole stay here exploring the romantic, 42-hectare park which extends all around, and then recover in the "Castle Parlour" ("Schlosstube"), the Valentin restaurant or the Café Luise, all of them furnished with impeccable taste.

Sights nearby: "Schwapp" swimming and water paradise in Fürstenwalde (7km southwest), Müncheberg Old Town (14km north)

Access: 7km northeast of Fürstenwalde via Neuendorf

20 SEESCHLÖSSCHEN

Peter Lange

Am Schloss 8
16818 Wustrau-Altfriesack
Tel. (033925) 88 03
Fax (033925) 88055 – www.wustrau.de

Open all year • 11 rooms, all non-smoking and all with balcony • Restaurant with terrace (closed Jan): main course 8.50-19.50€ • Garden, parking; dogs allowed • Sauna, bicycle and rowing-boat hire, carriage rides

90/120 €, Breakfast included

AE Diners VISA MC

The wealth of paintings and sculpture by contemporary artist Matthias Zágon Hohl-Stein

The "Seeschlösschen" (Little Castle on the Lake) stands at the southern end of the lake known as the Ruppiner See. It's really a villa in Mediterranean style rather than a castle, but this doesn't in any way diminish its appeal as a place to stay. Inside, terracotta floors and indirect lighting create a warm and welcoming atmosphere throughout. The tastefully styled bedrooms with their iron bedsteads are all on the first floor; those with lake views are particularly inviting. This is a place to relax in style!

Sights nearby: Lifting bridge, Museum of Brandenburg-Prussia

Access: Exit 23 on A 24, then via Dammkrug and Langen

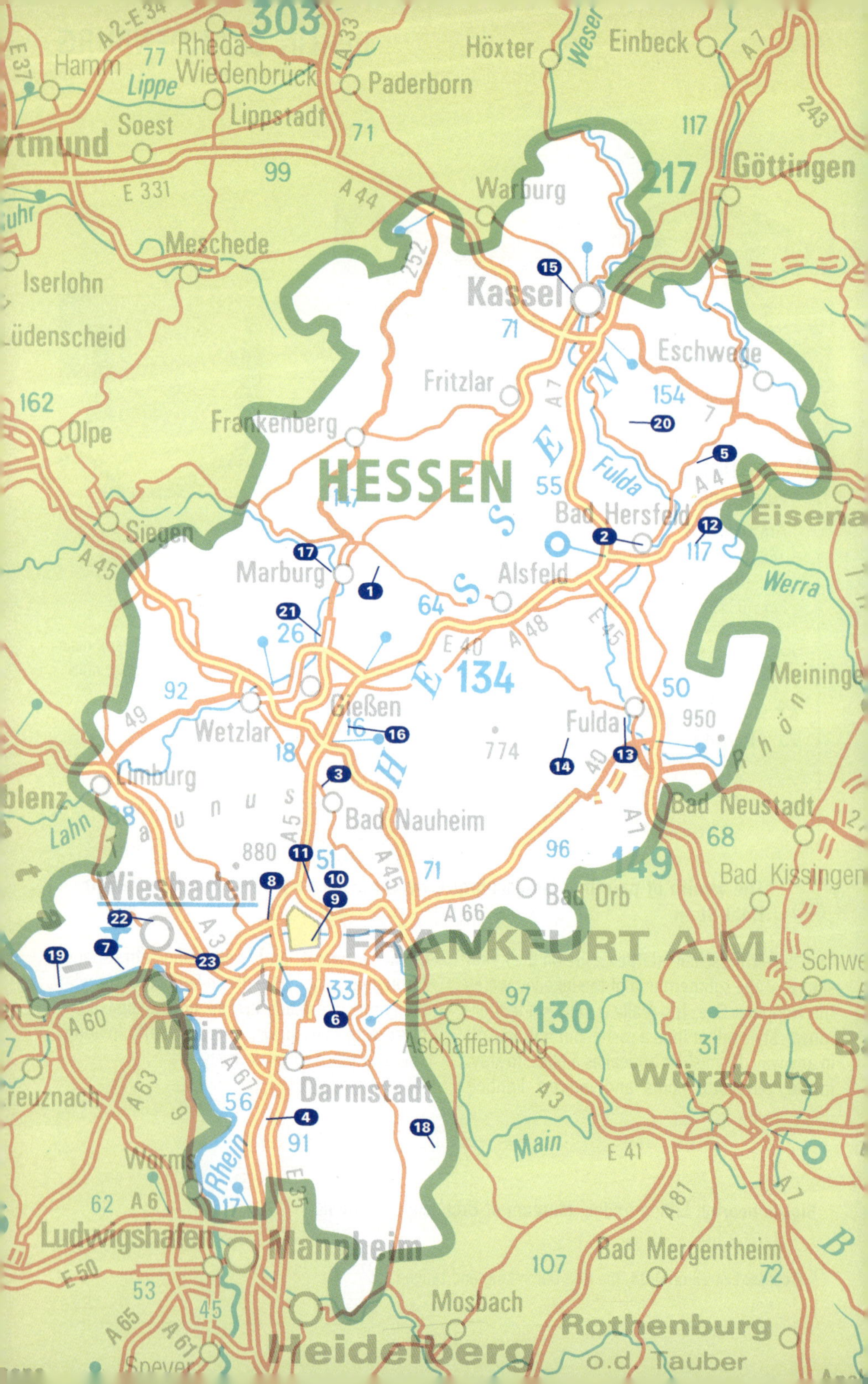

HESSEN
Kassel
Fritzlar
Frankenberg
Eschwege
Bad Hersfeld
Marburg
Alsfeld
Gießen
Wetzlar
Fulda
Limburg
Bad Nauheim
Wiesbaden
Frankfurt A.M.
Bad Orb
Mainz
Darmstadt
Aschaffenburg
Mannheim
Heidelberg
Ludwigshafen
Worms
Höxter
Einbeck
Paderborn
Lippstadt
Soest
Hamm
Rheda-Wiedenbrück
Warburg
Göttingen
Meschede
Iserlohn
Lüdenscheid
Olpe
Siegen
Meiningen
Bad Neustadt
Bad Kissingen
Würzburg
Bad Mergentheim
Mosbach
Rothenburg o.d. Tauber
Lippe
Weser
Fulda
Werra
Lahn
Main
Rhein
Taunus
Rhön
880
774
950

Hessen

In the not-so-distant past, the map of Hessen resembled a patchwork quilt of sovereign statelets, each of them jealously guarding its distinctive identity and particular privileges. This explains the region's array of castles and palaces, and why so many of its medium-sized towns have kept their own special allure. A tour could take in Wiesbaden, famous for its spa; Darmstadt, with a unique heritage of Art Nouveau buildings, and Kassel, where the Documenta exhibition can be counted on to rock the art world to its roots. The Rhine wines of Rüdesheim and the famous sparkling "Sekt" from Eltville are not to be missed, while historic Fulda is known as the gateway to the Rhön, one of several glorious upland massifs which invite walkers to savour their fresh air and peace and quiet. But all of this takes second place to the great metropolis of Frankfurt on the River Main. Jokingly referred to as "Mainhatten", its soaring skyscrapers proclaim the city's role as the country's financial centre, but Frankfurt has its down-to-earth side too, best sampled in one of its cider pubs. And stretching along the river banks is a "Museum Mile" which is the envy of many a capital city.

1 DOMBÄCKER

Petra Krohn

Am Markt 18
35287 Amöneburg
Tel. (06422) 9 40 90
Fax (06422) 94097
www.dombaecker.de

Closed 1 week in Jan • 5 rooms, including 2 with balcony • Restaurant with terrace (closed Mon, midday Tue): set meal 30-58€ • Garden, parking; dogs allowed • Wine seminars, cookery courses, town tours

105 €, Breakfast included

The really cosy wine cellar - it's been here since 1630

This attractive half-timbered house, built in 1725, boasts a particularly interesting setting; it stands on the marketplace of a small town which is perched high up in line of hills. The rooms are furnished in rustic country house style; some even boast four-poster beds. Exquisite decoration highlights its elegance and lends a gentle air of nostalgia. The restaurant is in keeping with the rustic theme, adding a touch of old German style with exposed timbers, and is no less cosy and snug. During summer time seating is available on the marketplace in front of the house.

Sights nearby: Elisabethkirche and Schloss in Marburg (14km west)

2 ROMANTIK HOTEL ZUM STERN

Familie Kniese

Linggplatz 11
36251 Bad Hersfeld
Tel. (06621) 18 90
Fax (06621) 189260 – www.zumsternhersfeld.de

Open all year • 45 rooms, including 1 with balcony, 1 with disabled access and 20 non-smoking • Restaurant with terrace: set lunch 15-20€, set dinner 21-44€; half board 20€ • Parking; dogs allowed • Indoor pool, sauna, bicycle hire, organised walks

97/134 €, Breakfast included

AE D VISA MC

Unwinding in the "little world of baths"

In the historic city centre, this venerable building from the 15th century is still long on character, even after a number of alterations and extensions over the centuries. Individually furnished rooms are always spacious and luxurious yet still homely, regardless of whether you prefer a rustic look, a dash of country house style or the noble ambience of period-style furniture. Low ceilings, exposed timbers and rough-sandstone walls give the place "das gewisse Etwas", or, as we say in English, a certain "je ne sais quoi"! Similarly, the style of the restaurant takes in a little of every look, from rustic to elegant.

Sights nearby: Ruined collegiate church, Bad Hersfeld Festival (Jun-Aug), Salzberg theme park (18km northwest)

Access: Head for town centre, follow signs indicating "Parkhaus Stadtmitte", drive round the car park and via Webergasse to hotel car park

3 **HERRENHAUS VON LÖW**

Jürgen Seim

Steinfurther Hauptstr. 36
61231 Bad Nauheim-Steinfurth
Tel. (06032) 9 69 50
Fax (06032) 969550 – www.herrenhaus-von-loew.de

Closed 1st week Jan • 20 rooms, including 2 with balcony, 3 with disabled access, and 5 non-smoking • Restaurant with terrace (eve only, closed Sun): set meal 49-54€ • Garden, parking; dogs allowed • Sauna, steam bath, solarium, gym, bicycle hire, Art Nouveau architecture tour of Bad Nauheim

105/139 €, Breakfast included (WE: 105 €)

AE VISA MC

The elegant, rustic restaurant under the vaulted ceiling of the old cellar bar

Situated in the centre of Steinfurth, the "village of roses", this manor house from the 19th century has lost none of its aristocratic allure in its transformation into a hotel. The rooms have been furnished with exquisite taste and in fresh and well-chosen colours. They are unique in their finely honed ambience and tasteful, homely atmosphere, with baths stylishly fashioned from marble. The breakfast room - the 'Vivaldi' - fits seamlessly into this handsome scene, and there's a little of its cheery, friendly character throughout.

Sights nearby: Castle and church in Friedberg (7 km south), Münzenberg castle (8 km north)

Access: Exit 14 on A 5

4 PARKHOTEL HERRENHAUS

Thilo Patzelt

Im Staatspark Fürstenlager
64625 Bensheim-Auerbach
Tel. (06251) 7 09 00
Fax (06251) 78473 – www.parkhotel-herrenhaus.de

Open all year • Rooms, including 1 with balcony • Restaurant with terrace (reservations required for dinner): set dinner 32-37€; main course 14-19€; half board 23€ • Garden, parking; dogs allowed • Wine tasting

120/160 €, Breakfast included
VISA MC

A jog in the park - a treat for the body and soul

Located in the Fürstenlager park, the former summer retreat of the Landgrave of Hessen, you'll find this stylish hotel set among exotic trees and charming monuments. The impeccably maintained rooms are furnished along elegant Biedermeier lines, partly with antiques and always with good taste. The restaurant is striking with its elegant, classic furnishings. Together with the wonderful parks on the estate, they evoke a true princely ambience: it's hard not to get a little caught up in the charming grandeur of it all...

Sights nearby: Lorsch monastery (11km southwest), exotic wood in Weinheim (22km south)

Access: Exit 30 on A 5; 2km northeast of Bensheim

5 KLOSTER CORNBERG

Rolf W. Behrend

Am Steinbruch 1 (an der B 27)
36219 Cornberg
Tel. (05650) 9 69 60
Fax (05650) 969622 – www.kloster-cornberg.de

Closed 1 week Feb, 1 week Nov • 9 rooms • Restaurant with terrace (closed Sun eve): set meal 20-25€; half board 16.50€ • Parking; dogs allowed • Skittles

71/88 €, Breakfast included

JCB VISA MC

The golden glow of the sandstone in the evening sunlight

This old Benedictine monastery had, at one point, been left in serious disrepair, but between 1990 and 1994 it was carefully restored at great expense. Today the estate still has all the charm, even the romantic aura of an ancient and historic building. It was built from local grey-gold sandstone and for those who have a thirst for knowledge about the material, it even houses a "Sandstone Museum" in the west wing, while accommodation and kitchens are to be found in the east wing. The rooms have natural stone walls and are equipped with functional yet homely wood-furnishings. The beamed restaurant and the terrace in the inner courtyard, with its rough cobblestones, add the finishing touch.

Sights nearby: Bebra water-tower (10 km southwest), Rotenburg an der Fulda Old Town (15 km southwest)

Access: On B 27, 10 km northeast of Bebra

6 ALTE BERGMÜHLE

Angelika Emmer

Geisberg 25
63303 Dreieich-Dreieichenhain
Tel. (06103) 8 18 58
Fax (06103) 88999 – www.altebergmuehle.de

Closed 24 Dec • 14 rooms • Restaurant with terrace: lunch menu 25.50-30.50€, evening menu 42.50-49.50€ • Car park; dogs allowed

100/125 €, Breakfast included

AE Diners VISA MC

The window set in the floorboards of the restaurant, revealing a view of the cellar

It doesn't take long to appreciate that interior decoration is treated as a serious art and a labour of love in this house. The bedrooms have been furnished with impeccable attention to detail and with no expense spared. The accommodation has a touch of elegance combined with a quaint country house feel, while clever colour combinations ensure a homely atmosphere. This former mill has been enjoying the patronage of customers from as early as the 15th century and with its appealing fireplace and tiled stove, it looks likely to attract them for some time to come.

Sights nearby: German Leather Museum (13km north); Kranichstein hunting lodge (16km south)

Access: Langen Exit from A 661, then B 486 towards Deburg/Offenthal for 5km, then follow sign left for Götzenhain/Dreieich

7 ZUM KRUG

Josef Laufer

Hauptstr. 34
65347 Eltville-Hattenheim
Tel. (06723) 9 96 80
Fax (06723) 996825 – www.hotel-zum-krug.de

Closed 1-20 Jan • 8 rooms, all non-smoking • Restaurant with terrace (closed Sun eve to midday Tue): set lunch 17-24€, set dinner 28-40€ • Parking; dogs allowed

110 €, Breakfast included
VISA MC

Home-produced wines and a selection of souveniers

"The Jug" is a perfect ambassador for the Rhine town of Hattenheim, which stands at the foot of the famous wine-growing hillsides. The sense of long-established tradition, dating back to the year 1720, is visible immediately from the ornate, painted timbered façades, and the dedicated family who run the place take a traditional approach to housekeeping: you can be sure that the rooms, furnished in natural rustic wood, will be impeccably maintained. Since the family also own a vineyard, this is the perfect chance to relax in the parlour bar, with its wooden wainscoting, beamed ceilings and tiled stove and choose a wine from their list of over 600 items - not all home-produced, of course!

Sights nearby: Eltville Old Town (4km east), Kiedrich church (7km north)

Access: From western end of A 66 near Wiesbaden continue on B 42 towards Rüdesheim

8 BOMMERSHEIM

Marianne Bommersheim

Hauptstr. 418
65760 Eschborn-Niederhöchstadt
Tel. (06173) 60 08 00
Fax (06173) 600840 – www.hotel-bommersheim.de

Closed 1-5 Jan, Christmas to New Year's Eve • 35 rooms, including 10 non-smoking • Restaurant with terrace (closed Sat, Sun, public holidays, mid-May to mid-June): main course 7-19.50€ • Parking; dogs allowed

120/195 €, Breakfast included (WE: 90 €)
AE JCB VISA MC

The terrace of the inner courtyard with its little pond

The two buildings look very different from the outside, but once inside you'll see how well they go together - on the one hand, the small restaurant with its alpine-style timbered façade and wood panelling, and on the other, the bigger, gabled extension added in 1998. You'll find the accommodation in this newer part: rooms here are simple yet homely; most with a rustic feel and a bit of Tyrolean character to them. Two rooms have their own whirlpool and one even has a sauna. Breakfast is served in a pleasant, light room with a glass front facing the surrounding greenery.

Sights nearby: Frankfurt Cathedral Museum and Museum of Applied Arts (13km southeast)

Access: Eschborner Dreieck Exit off A 66; 2km beyond Eschborn

9 LIEBIG-HOTEL

Rufino Rondoni

Liebigstr. 45
60323 Frankfurt am Main
Tel. (069) 72 75 51
Fax (069) 727555 – www.hotelliebig.de

Closed 1-2 Jan, 20-31 Dec • 20 rooms, including 5 non-smoking, 10 with air conditioning, 3 with balcony • Garden; dogs not allowed

128/179 €, Breakfast 12 € (WE: 86/110 €)
AE VISA MC

Taking a stroll to the nearby palm tree garden

In the exclusive residential area in the west end of Frankfurt this building, from the prosperous years of the late 1800s, fits in seamlessly with the other prestigious townhouses. Much style is also evident indoors. A few rooms on the first floor are more simply furnished, but on the next two floors there's a plushly comfortable feel; lavish and tastefully chosen designs incorporate classic features like parquet flooring and attractive materials set off the fine furnishings. Even the bathrooms have a nostalgic touch.

Sights nearby: Städelsches Art Institute and City Gallery, Senckenberg Natural History Museum, Deutsche Bundesbank Museum

Access: From Bockenheimer Landstrasse between Palmengarten and Alte Oper by Siesmayerstrasse and Feldbergstrasse

10 VILLA ORANGE

Christiane Hütte

Hebelstr. 1
60318 Frankfurt am Main
Tel. (069) 40 58 40
Fax (069) 40584100
contact@villa-orange.de – www.villa-orange.de

Open all year • 38 rooms, including 8 with balcony and 18 non-smoking • Parking; dogs allowed • Library

140/150 €, Breakfast included

AE D VISA MC

The romantic bathtubs in the "orange-deluxe" rooms

This hotel, like many others in Frankfurt, is well-suited to business guests, and welcomes plenty of them through its doors. The difference here, though, is that the staff understand that their clientèle - despite number-crunching day-in, day-out - also know how to appreciate the finer things in life, and might like to forget the office for once. Anyone who enjoys a touch of style will have no trouble finding something to suit them: rooms and bathrooms are well designed along fine modern lines. Four-poster beds in some rooms, a well-stocked library and a breakfast room with sun terrace are just a few of the plus points of this hotel, in which taste is paramount.

Sights nearby: Frankfurt Zoo, musuem of modern art, cathedral

Access: On a side street west of Friedberger Landstrasse on northern edge of Old Town

11 LANDHAUS ALTE SCHEUNE

Klaus-Peter Mast

Alt Erlenbach 44
60437 Frankfurt-Niedererlenbach
Tel. (06101) 54 40 00
Fax (06101) 544045 – www.alte-scheune.de

Closed 1-10 Jan, Christmas to New Year's Eve • 33 rooms, including 6 with balcony and 5 non-smoking • Bierstube, restaurant with terrace (open 5pm Tue-Fri, 6pm Sat): set meal 22-36€ • Garden, parking; dogs allowed

125/165 €, Breakfast included (WE: 89/98 €)
AE JCB VISA MC

An excellent glass of Pilsner in the cosy taproom

This long-established estate was once a thriving farm, with this house at its centre. Thanks to careful restoration from 1986 onwards it has been transformed into an inviting country hotel. Rooms and apartments with kitchen facilities await you: with sturdy, generous wooden furniture in country house style they offer a homely atmosphere. The restaurant, with its rustic brick vaulting and exquisitely pretty decoration, radiates a warm peaceful atmosphere, and acacia blossom mingles with the greenery of the inner courtyard.

Sights nearby: German film museum and Liebieghaus sculpture museum in Frankfurt (14km south)

Access: From Preungesheimer Dreieck interchange on A 661 take B 3 towards Bad Vilbel; leave B 3 at Bad Vilbel-Massenheim Exit and turn left

12 ZUM LÖWEN

R. Draeger

Hauptstr. 17
36289 Friedewald
Tel. (06674) 9 22 20
Fax (06674) 922259
zum-loewen-friedewald@t-online.de – www.zum-loewen.de

Open all year • 32 rooms, including 2 with balcony and 11 non-smoking • Restaurant with terrace: set lunch 16-35€, set dinner 25€; half board 19€ • Garden, parking; dogs allowed • Tennis, firing range, guided walks, art exhibitions, wine tasting, shuttle service to golf courses

65/92 €, Breakfast included

AE VISA

The "forgotten corner" - a cosy little spot for unwinding after a long day

Wherever you look, there's something to catch the eye: the glass roof of the foyer is striking enough, but the stunning features continue throughout the house, with various items of fine art by contemporary artists. The spirits, whiskies, jellies and jams in display windows look marvellous and can be sampled too, while awaiting you on the basement level is a wine cellar with over 1400 different vintages from all over the world. There's plenty to tantalise the senses in the restaurant: situated in the original building, it exudes a rustic ambience and serves international cuisine. The bedrooms are homely and practical.

Sights nearby: Werra potash mining museum in Heringen (15km east), collegiate church ruins in Bad Hersfeld (18km west)

Access: Exit 33 on A 4

13

BRAUHAUS WIESENMÜHLE

Wilfried Renner

Wiesenmühlenstr. 13
36037 Fulda
Tel. (0661) 92 86 80
Fax (0661) 9286839 – www.wiesenmuehle.de

Open all year • 24 rooms, including 2 non-smoking • Restaurant with beer garden: set meal 13€, main course 8.50-20.20€; half board 13€ • Garden, parking; dogs allowed

77/87 €, Breakfast included
AE VISA MC

Live music events in the beer garden

Though the origins of the mill in this idyllic area date back to the 14th century, the millwheel keeps on turning: today it generates electricity, which powers the brewery based here. The beer goes down well and can be enjoyed to the full in the rustic brewery bars and taprooms, the out-and-out traditional 'Mill Room' and outdoors in the huge beer garden. And if all that beer appreciation means you decide to stay the night, then rooms with solid, pale wood furniture are ready and waiting for you.

Sights nearby: Michaelskirche, Schloss Fasanerie (6km south)

Access: Southwest of cathedral on edge of Old Town

14 SIEBERZMÜHLE

Waldemar Neidert

€€ 36154 Hosenfeld
Tel. (06650) 9 60 60
Fax (06650) 8193 – www.sieberzmuehle.de

Closed 10-28 Jan • 31 rooms, including 20 with balcony and 3 non-smoking • Restaurant with terrace (closed Mon): set lunch 12-35€, set dinner 14-45€; half board 46€ • Garden, parking; dogs allowed • Bathing pool, skittles, animal enclosure

70 €, Breakfast included

AE VISA MC

The mill wheel, which can still be seen turning behind a glass window in the restaurant

A place where real relaxation means getting back to nature! Set in the midsts of unspoilt greenery, the extended mill from the 16th century is so idyllic that you can't help but unwind. Brooks, ponds and meadows as far as the eye can see are all located on this 30-hectare area and the activity of the organic farm - including a fallow deer reserve and a herd of Highland cattle - adds to the picture of a working but well-balanced landscape. The rooms, apartments and holiday flats are furnished with solid, light wood and offer a homely setting for your stay.

Sights nearby: Michaelskirche in Fulda (14km northwest), Schloss Fasanerie (17km east)

Access: 14km southwest of Fulda via Giesel, c 3km before Hosenfeld

15 ELFBUCHEN

Angelika Fischer

34131 Kassel
Tel. (0561) 96 97 60
Fax (0561) 9697633 – www.waldhotel-elfbuchen.de

Open all year • 11 rooms, all with disabled access, 3 non-smoking • Restaurant with terrace (closed Fri): set meal from 19.80€; half board 15€ • Garden; dogs allowed • Gym, indoor pool, bicycle hire, guided walks, carriage rides, wine appreciation and cookery courses

80 €, Breakfast included (WE: 115 €)
VISA MC

A coach ride to the monuments of Wilhelmshöhe and 'Herkules', the symbol of Kassel, on Mondays and Tuesdays

This "guesthouse in the woods" was welcoming guests way back in 1879 and is currently run by the fourth generation of the Fischer family. This spot is particularly popular with ramblers and walkers, the range of treats to sample from the house cake shop is reason enough to stop in and certainly boosts morale for the next mile or two! As the hotel is at the end of a private drive, in its own secluded woodland clearing, a sound night's sleep is virtually guaranteed. Rooms are furnished to modern standards in a country house style; some of the baths are equipped with a whirlpool option.

Sights nearby: Schloss Wilhelmshöhe and park, Hessen Regional Museum

Access: Exit 68 on A 44; turn left off Konrad-Adenauer-Strasse at "Herkules" sign, follow signs to Parkplatz, then signs to "Elfbuchen"

16 ALTE KLOSTERMÜHLE

Peter Schönberg

35423 Lich-Arnsburg
Tel. (06404) 9 19 00
Fax (06404) 919091 – www.alte-klostermuehle.de

Open all year • 14 rooms, including 5 non-smoking • Restaurant with terrace: main course from 12€, set meal 22.80-28€ • Garden, parking; dogs allowed

97/123 €, Breakfast included

AE ⓓ VISA MC

Barbecues on Monday evenings with live music

On the grounds of the Arnsburg monastery, founded in the 12th century, the "old monastery mill" awaits you with its romantic church ruins. There's good food and drink to be had and it's lovely sitting in the cosy parlour - its furnishings were originally from an Austrian church - or on the terrace under an old spinney of trees. The rooms are to be found in the former hostel building and sport individual flavour: here a touch of elegance with dark cherry wood, there some lighter pale wood for a more rural look. Whichever you choose, your stay here will be couched in style and made even more enjoyable by the enchanting setting.

Sights nearby: Münzenberg castle (7km south), Altes Schloss in Giessen (19km northwest)

Access: From Exit 10 on A 5 via Lich, or from Exit 36 on A 45 via Eberstadt

17 LANDHAUS LA VILLA

Karl-Ludwig Kuhl

Sylvester-Jordan-Str. 22
35039 Marburg
Tel. (06421) 17 50 70
Fax (06421) 1750720
www.la-villa-kuhl.de

Open all year • 15 rooms, all with ventilation, 3 with balcony • Garden, parking; dogs not allowed

92/102 €, Breakfast included

AE MC

The sensational breakfast buffet with numerous home-made treats

Run with exemplary dedication, this hotel offers a taste of stylish Italian life. The bedrooms are furnished with much thought and attention to detail: the furniture exudes good taste, but so too does the painstakingly detailed decoration and a harmoniously blended palette of colours. Get the day off to a good start by enjoying breakfast in the inviting breakfast room with its conservatory and fireplace. After that, it's easy to let go all your troubles and enjoy the simplicity of life.

Sights nearby: Elisabethkirche, Marburg University Museum of Fine Art

Access: From Marburg-Mitte Exit on B 3, then by Kurt Schumacher bridge and Weintrautstrasse

18 **GEIERSMÜHLE**

Familie Wewetzer

Im Ohrnbachtal
64720 Michelstadt-Vielbrunn
Tel. (06066) 7 21
Fax (06066) 920126

Closed 3 weeks in Jan, 2 weeks in Mar • 8 rooms • Restaurant with terrace (closed Mon, Tue, and Wed and Fri lunchtime): main course from 14€; half board 20€ • Garden, parking; dogs allowed • Sauna

80 €, Breakfast included
Credit cards not accepted

A revitalising walk through the green Ohrnbach valley

The former mill makes a reassuring refuge from the world! Offering bed and board - and real relaxation too - it's an uplifting sight, nestling by its old millstream. The rooms in the original building and the annex are cosily kitted out with stylish yet contemporary furniture; some even have bare-wood floors. The restaurant could hardly be bettered for cosy country charm: soft lighting and a warm, homely tiled stove play their part in a comfortable atmosphere, enhancing the enjoyment of good international cuisine with regional specialities.

Sights nearby: Englischer Garten game park in Eulbach (7km south), Michelstadt Old Town (15km southwest)

Access: 15km north of Michelstadt; towards Walldürn on B 47, left after c 8km towards Vielbrunn; then 2km east

19 RÜDESHEIMER SCHLOSS

Heinrich Breuer

Steingasse 10
65385 Rüdesheim am Rhein
Tel. (06722) 9 05 00
Fax (06722) 905050 – www.ruedesheimer-schloss.com

Closed 1-8 Jan, Christmas to New Year's Eve • 26 rooms, including 5 with balcony, 1 with disabled access and 11 non-smoking • Restaurant with terrace: set meal 16-33€; half board 20€ • Garden, parking; dogs allowed • Table tennis, bicycle hire, vineyard walks, wine tasting, wine seminars, Dine Around

145 €, Breakfast included

AE · D · JCB · VISA · MC

The glockenspiel in the castle garden

The Archbishops of Mainz certainly had good taste! Back in 1729, one of them ordered the construction of this castle in central Rüdesheim between the Rhine and its celebrated grape-growing slopes. It's near the world-famous Drosselgasse, but it's not only the location that makes it special. The house itself boasts tasteful furnishings in modern designs, works by contemporary artists adorn the walls, and old and new are melded into a fine balance of complement and contrast. The restaurant is different again, in the style of a classic wine bar from the old days; very traditional but certainly no less charming. Naturally, wines from the surrounding hills are here for the asking.

Sights nearby: Brömserburg, Niederwald memorial, Eberbach monastery (16 km northwest)

Access: From western end of A 66 near Wiesbaden continue along the Rhine on B 42

20 SCHLOSS SPANGENBERG

Angela und Wilfried Wichmann

Schloss 1
34286 Spangenberg
Tel. (05663) 9 39 80
Fax (05663) 7567 – www.schloss-spangenberg.de

Closed 2 weeks in Jan • 24 rooms, including 6 non-smoking • Cafe-restaurant with terrace (closed Sun eve): set meal 29-49€; half board 22€ • Garden, parking; dogs allowed in hotel, not in restaurant • Guided forest walks, cookery courses

99/145 €, Breakfast included

VISA

The sweet temptations of the cake shop

This romantic residential estate sits in splendour above Spangenberg, a smart town of quaint half-timbered houses. The castle's origins can be traced back to the 13th century, but serious damage was sustained during the Second World War and only the main walls were left standing. Despite this it has lost none of its former allure thanks to careful reconstruction, which remained faithful to the original. The mighty walls and picturesque timbering combine to give a harmonious first impression: indoors you'll discover individually furnished rooms in romantic style, while the restaurant feels classically luxurious with all its fine dark wood.

Sights nearby: Melsungen Old Town (10km west)

Access: From Exit 83 on A 7 via Melsungen

21 BURGHOTEL STAUFENBERG

Stephan Lohbeck

Burggasse 10
35460 Staufenberg
Tel. (06406) 30 12
Fax (06406) 3014004 – www.burg-hotel-staufenberg.com

Closed 1 week in Jan, 24 Dec • 30 rooms, including 1 with balcony and 8 non-smoking • Restaurant with terrace: set meal 25-49€ • Parking; dogs allowed • Castle tours

90/120 €, Breakfast included

AE Diners JCB VISA MC

Gleaming knightly armour makes unusual - but very appropriate - decoration!

The view from the hotel Staufenberg stretches far across the Lahn valley. This prospect may have once been a vital strategic advantage in the turbulent Middle Ages, but today you can simply take in the view as a guest in the romantic old buildings, without worrying about who might appear on the horizon! The rooms are furnished with style and elegance: four-poster beds and carpets woven with fleur-de-lys lend a noble and dainty touch. Similarly appealing is the rustic restaurant, where you can take a seat beneath barrel- or cross-vaulted ceilings. The inviting terrace is there for your enjoyment too, not only at main meal times but also for tea, coffee and home-made biscuits or ice cream.

Sights nearby: Altes Schloss in Giessen (12km south), Elisabethkirche in Marburg (18km north)

Access: By B 3 between Giessen and Marburg

22 LANDHAUS DIEDERT

Oreste Diedert

Am Kloster Klarenthal 9
65195 Wiesbaden-Alt Klarenthal
Tel. (0611) 1 84 66 00
Fax (0611) 18466030 – www.landhaus-diedert.de

Open all year • 14 rooms, including 10 with balcony • Restaurant with terrace (closed Mon, midday Sat): set lunch 20-25€, set dinner 25-45€ • Garden, parking; dogs allowed • Bicycle hire with deposit

80/150 €, Breakfast included

AE VISA MC

The terrace in the shade of the plane trees

Wander wherever your spirit takes you through this pleasant country house near the Klarenthal monastery and virtually on the doorstep of the local capital, Wiesbaden. A green and tranquil setting and an almost spine-tingling feeling of authenticity make this historic estate a captivating place. The rooms have been furnished with great taste: country house style is naturally on the cards and pretty materials and colours highlight the homely ambience. Even the restaurant joins style and comfort to good effect: rustic ceiling beams, terracotta floors and soft lighting all play their part.

Sights nearby: Russian Orthodox church, Kaiser Friedrich spa

Access: From Wiesbaden-Stadtmitte Exit on A 66 towards city centre, left by the Ringkirche into Klarenthaler Strasse, then follow signs

23 DOMÄNE MECHTILDSHAUSEN

Christoph Zentgraf

65205 Wiesbaden-Erbenheim
Tel. (0611) 7 37 46 60
Fax (0611) 737479

Closed early to mid-Jan • 15 rooms, including 3 with balcony • Cafe; restaurant with terrace (closed Sun eve, Mon): set meals 34-43€ • Garden, parking; dogs allowed

130 €, Breakfast included

AE VISA MC

Watching the foals trotting across the meadow

There's been an estate here for at least 800 years, and probably since the days of the Merovingian kings, in fact, but the place is still brimming with life. Eco-friendly farming and a number of other successful cottage industries, including the butchers, bakery and dairy, ensure that goods of the highest quality arrive fresh on your plate. Cows, pigs, poultry and horses are all part of the life of the farm. Waiting for you among all this is the guesthouse, which provides trim and pretty rooms. Thanks to the restaurant and a combined café and wine bar, you'll want for nothing.

Sights nearby: Wiesbaden Museum (4 km north), Gutenberg Museum in Mainz (15 km south)

Access: Exit Fort Biehler/Domäne Mechtildshausen on B 455 between expressways Wiesbaden-Erbenheim (A 66) and Mainz-Kastel (A 671), then follow signs

Mecklenburg-Vorpommern

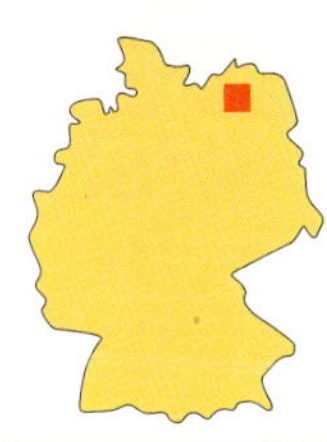

The spirit of the sea is never far away in the most northeasterly region of Germany. Along its sandy Baltic coast, and on holiday islands like Usedom, its chic resorts have kept much of the elegance of former times. Germany's largest island, Rügen, is also known for its beaches and boasts the gleaming white cliffs made famous by the Romantic painter Caspar David Friedrich. Looking to the sea for their living – and to Scandinavia for much of their history – the World Heritage cities of Wismar and Stralsund are fascinating to explore, while Rostock, the most important harbour on the Baltic, boasts its own delightful seaside resort at Warnemünde. All these places take pride in their unique heritage of "Brick Gothic" architecture, an intriguing style which still fascinates with its elegance and austerity. Further inland you'll find more than 1 000 lakes, many of them linked by streams and rivers: the largest is the Müritzsee, its broad waters and wooded banks offering endless delights to its visitors. These are still fairly few in number, making the whole region especially attractive for those in search of tranquility and undiscovered Nature.

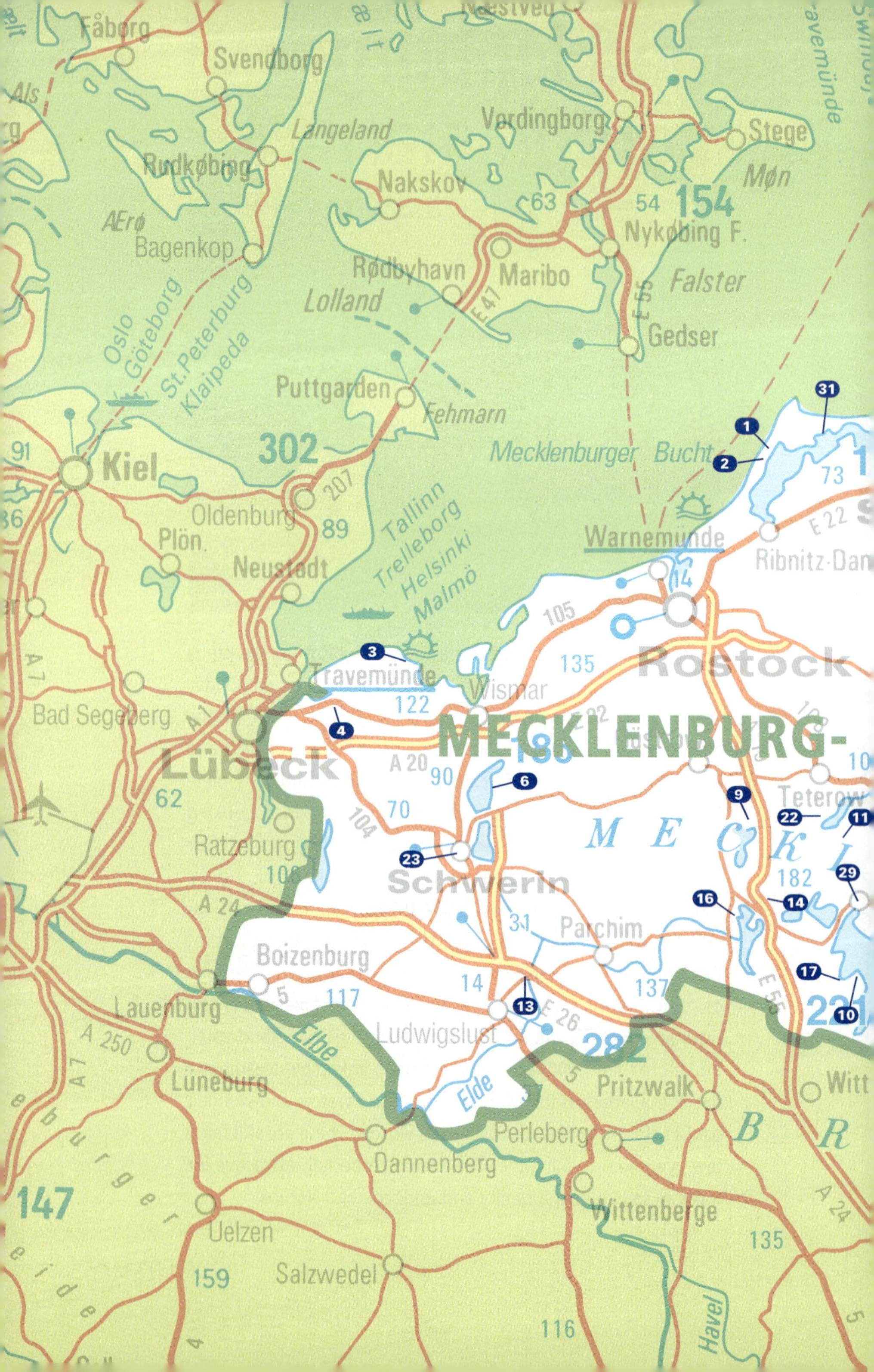

Fåborg
Svendborg
Als
Langeland
Rudkøbing
Ærø
Bagenkop
Vordingborg
Stege
Møn
Nakskov
63
54
154
Nykøbing F.
Rødbyhavn
Maribo
Lolland
E 47
Falster
E 55
Gedser
Oslo
Göteborg
St.Peterburg
Klaipeda
Puttgarden
Fehmarn
Kiel
91
302
207
Mecklenburger Bucht
73
Oldenburg
89
Plön
Tallinn
Trelleborg
Helsinki
Malmö
Warnemünde
E 22
Ribnitz-Dan
Neustadt
14
105
135
Rostock
Travemünde
Wismar
122
Bad Segeberg
A 1
A 7
Lübeck
MECKLENBURG-
A 20
90
70
62
104
Teterow
Ratzeburg
M E C K L
182
Schwerin
A 24
31
Parchim
Boizenburg
14
137
5
117
Lauenburg
E 26
Ludwigslust
282
A 250
Elbe
Elde
5
Lüneburg
Pritzwalk
Witt
A 7
Perleberg
B
R
Dannenberg
147
Wittenberge
A 24
Uelzen
135
159
Salzwedel
Havel
116
5

Rønne
København
Travemünde
M
E
Saßnitz
Rügen
Bergen
Göhren
Stralsund
Pommersche
Bucht
København
Malmö
Kołobrzeg
Wolgast
Greifswald
Kamień
Pomorski
Świnoujście
Gryfice
VORPOMMERN
Stettiner Haff
243
Nowogard
Neubrandenburg
Goleniów
Szczecin
Pasewalk
307
Stargard Szczeciński
Müritz
Neustrelitz
Prenzlau
241
Havel
Pyrzyce
Schwedt
Barlinek
Oder
Myślibórz
Strzelce
Eberswalde
Gorzów Wielkopolski
Oranienburg
Bad Freienwalde
Neuruppin

1 ROMANTIK HOTEL NAMENLOS & FISCHERWIEGE

Familie Fischer

Schifferberg 2
18347 Ahrenshoop
Tel. (038220) 60 60
Fax (038220) 60630
info@hotel-namenlos.de – www.hotel-namenlos.de

Open all year • 35 rooms, including 11 with balcony or terrace and 11 non-smoking • Cafe-restaurant with terrace: set dinner 29-49€, main course 12-22€; half board 22€ • Garden, parking; dogs allowed • Library, indoor pool, sauna, massage, billiards, bicycle hire, wicker beach-chair hire, organised walks, cookery courses

110/170 €, Breakfast included

AE VISA MC

Exhibitions of work from the Ahrenshoop painters' colony, on show in the 'Dune-house Gallery' during the summer

Four eye-catching houses - each a typical example of traditional architecture - make up this property: in the "Fischerwiege", a smart thatched house, the majority of the rooms, in cosy country style, are arranged into suites. Built around the end of the 19C, the top floor of the little "dune house" is home to a pair of cosy apartments. Further tasteful, albeit somewhat smaller guestrooms, are to be found on the particularly pretty grounds of the "Bergfalke", while the elegant Café Namenlos - the "Café With No Name" - is anything but anonymous-looking: these days it's a pleasantly formal restaurant.

Sights nearby: "Art Cottages" and Neues Kunsthaus in Ahrenshoop

Access: By B 105 northeast of Rostock via Dierhagen and Wustrow

2 LANDHAUS MORGENSÜNN

Susanne und Stefan Radszuweit

Bauernreihe 4d
18347 Ahrenshoop-Niehagen
Tel. (038220) 64 10
Fax (038220) 64126 – www.landhaus-morgensuenn.de

Open all year • 25 rooms, including 7 with terrace, 4 non-smoking, 3 with disabled access • Wine bar; cafe; restaurant with terrace: main course 10.50-22€, set dinner 20-40€; half board 18€ • Garden, parking; dogs allowed • Indoor pool, sauna, steam bath, solarium, beauty and wellness facilities, gym, bicycle hire, organised walks, nordic walking

100/130 €, Breakfast included
VISA MC

The wicker beach chairs in the garden

At the beginning of the 20th century, the unspoiled landscape between the Baltic Sea and the lagoon of the Saaler Bodden drew many creative spirits to Ahrenshoop, where they founded an artists' colony. Among the inviting dwellings with their traditional roofs of thatch which still form part of this idyll stands" "Morgensünn" together with its annexe " "Susewind", offering rooms in elegant country style. A good start to the day is guaranteed in the snug breakfast room with its open fire, and afternoon coffee and cakes are also available.

Sights nearby: "Art Cottages" and Neues Kunsthaus in Ahrenshoop

Access: By B 105 northeast of Rostock via Dierhagen and Wustrow

3 GUTSHAUS REDEWISCH

Ole Lueder

Dorfstr. 46
23946 Boltenhagen-Redewisch
Tel. (038825) 37 60
Fax (038825) 37637 – www.gutshaus-redewisch.de

Closed 3 Jan to 3 Mar • 21 rooms, including 4 with balcony, 2 non-smoking, 1 with disabled access • Restaurant with terrace (closed Mon, Tue in low season): set meal 15-19€; half board 15€ • Garden, parking; dogs allowed • Gym, steam bath and sauna, cold plunge, table tennis, darts, bicycle hire

100/140 €, Breakfast included
VISA MC

The staircase with its gallery of fascinating old family photographs

Standing on its own outside the seaside resort of Boltenhagen, this lovingly restored manor house has now recovered all its long-lost allure and once more casts a spell on all who come here. It is, of course, surrounded by its own idyllic park, which is also certain to enchant you, not least because of the lovely terrace where meals are provided in fine weather from early until late. It's perhaps the best place to really appreciate the peace and quiet of the place and enjoy the fresh sea air. The rooms are solidly furnished, some of them with the high ceilings one would expect in such an historic building.

Sights nearby: Schloss Bothmer near Klütz (4km south), Wismar Old Town (26km southeast)

Access: From Exit 6 on A 20 via Grevesmühlen, Damshagen and Klütz

4 SCHLOSS LÜTGENHOF

Katharina Stinnes-Mauch

Ulmenweg 10
23942 Dassow
Tel. (038826) 82 50
Fax (038826) 82522 – www.schloss-luetgenhof.de

Closed Nov • 30 rooms, all non-smoking, 23 with air conditioning, 2 with disabled access • Restaurants with terrace: Schloss Restaurant (closed Mon, Tue, midday), Terrazza (closed Mon, eve): main course from 21€, set dinner 43-59€; half board 35€ • Garden, parking; dogs allowed in hotel, not in restaurant • Swimming pool, bio- and steam sauna, ayurveda, bicycle hire, canoe trips

129/190 €, Breakfast 13 €

VISA

The ayurveda treatments and meals

The clever use of contemporary design has breathed new life into the architecture of this venerable neo-Classical castle. Rather than setting out to create a contrast with the existing building, the sensitively designed furnishings and tasteful pastel colour schemes blend in harmoniously and help create an exceptionally welcoming ambience. The elegant restaurant features a coffered ceiling and chandeliers, while the "Terrazza" bistro is more informal, with - as it name implies - a lovely terrace overlooking the neighbouring nature reserve.

Sights nearby: Schloss Bothmer in Klütz (18km north), Lübeck Old Town (21km west)

Access: By B 105 east of Lübeck towards Wismar

5 LANDHAUS STÖCKER

H. Sondermann

Strelitzer Str. 8-10
17258 Feldberg
Tel. (039831) 27 10
Fax (039831) 271113 – www.landhaus-stoecker.de

Open all year • 8 rooms, including 1 with balcony • Wine bar; cafe; restaurant with terrace: set meal 25-70€; half board 25€ • Garden, parking; dogs not allowed • Indoor pool, sauna, wellness facilities, cosmetic treatments, private bathing beach, rowing boat, cookery courses, wine seminars, organised walks and canoe trips

110/140 €, Breakfast included

AE

The coolly contemporary design of the bathrooms

With woods, meadows, moorland and water, the Feldberg lakeland is a natural paradise, home to the otter, the sea eagle and the lesser spotted eagle. Among all these glories, this establishment of 1912 on the lakeshore in the centre of Feldberg is a fine place to stay. A simple elegance characterises both the building and its furnishings; the individually designed and spacious rooms are well kept and have something of an aristocratic air about them. The restaurant is equally stylish, and in addition provides diners with a charming view of the lake.

Sights nearby: Stargard castle (24km north), Woldegk windmills (24km northeast)

Access: From B 198 via Möllenbeck

6 **SEEWISCH**
Sabine Börner

Am Schweriner See 1d
19067 Flessenow
Tel. (03866) 4 61 10
Fax (03866) 461116 – www.seewisch.de

Closed 2 Jan to 4 Feb • 23 rooms, including 17 with balcony, 1 with disabled access and 12 non-smoking • Restaurant with terrace: set dinner 16-68€, main course 9.50-19€; half board 16€ • Garden, parking; dogs allowed in hotel, not in restaurant • Wellness area with outdoor pool and sauna, table tennis, bathing beach, beach chairs, boat and canoe hire

88/142 €, Breakfast included
AE VISA MC

The separate barbecue building for outdoor feasts in summer

On the eastern shore of Schwerin's lake, surrounded by a 2-hectare park, this brick and timber-framed building with its stately hipped roof makes a colourful splash in a landscape otherwise characterised by the greens and blues of woods and water. Guests here will enjoy the wide open spaces and the chance to indulge in all kinds of leisure pursuits, not least because the establishment has its own private bathing beach. Accommodation is in elegantly appointed rooms with tasteful country-style furnishings. The attractively rustic restaurant extends out onto a sun-trap of a terrace.

Sights nearby: Schloss and state museum in Schwerin (19km south)

Access: From northern end of A 241 continue for short distance on B 104 towards Schwerin, then north from Rampe by lakeside road via Retgendorf

7 BORNMÜHLE

Britta Budeus-Wiegert und Richard Wiegert

Bornmühle 35
17094 Groß Nemerow
Tel. (039605) 6 00
Fax (039605) 60399 – www.bornmuehle.com

Closed 3-21 Jan • 66 rooms, including 26 non-smoking • Restaurant with terrace: set meal 20-46€; half board 18€ • Garden, parking; dogs allowed in hotel, not in restaurant • Indoor pool, sauna, solarium, gym, beauty treatments and thalassotherapy, physiotherapy, bicycle hire, cookery courses

90/105 €, Breakfast included

AE VISA MC

A bike ride around the Tollensee

From the higher land on the eastern shore of the Tollensee there is a fine view over the idyllic natural setting of lake and glorious parkland, animated by the presence of the horses bred here. But it's not only the privileged location which makes a stay here so pleasant; with their lime-washed furniture, the rooms are comfortable and certain to make you feel at home straightaway. The leisure area with its inviting swimming pool makes its contribution too. The stylishly traditional restaurant is particularly proud of its game and fish specialities, which can also be savoured on the panoramic terrace.

Sights nearby: Neubrandenburg Old Town (10km north), Schloss Hohenzieritz (15km southwest)

Access: By B 96 between Neubrandenburg and Neustrelitz

8 SCHLOSS GROSS PLASTEN

C. Walloschke

Parkallee 36
17192 Groß Plasten
Tel. (039934) 80 20
Fax (039934) 80299 – www.schlosshotel-grossplasten.de

Open all year • 54 rooms, including 14 with balcony • Restaurant with terrace: set meals 38-41€; half board 21€ • Garden, parking; dogs allowed in hotel, not in restaurant • Indoor pool, sauna, jacuzzi, cosmetic treatments, massage, sunbathing lawn by private lake, bicycle and rowing boat hire, wine tastings

90/150 €, Breakfast included

AE VISA MC

The restaurant terrace with its idyllic prospect of the lake

A castle with all the trimmings! The edifice and its outbuildings were laid out on the banks of the Klein Plastener See in 1751 and still convey the authentic atmosphere of that era. The Baroque splendour of the "theme" rooms is particularly striking, but the other accommodation in romantic country-house style is just as attractive in its own way. Some of rooms in the "Coachman's House" enjoy a view of the castle. Completing the princely offerings are the inviting leisure area, the wood-panelled "Royal" piano bar, and a number of sumptuous dining rooms.

Sights nearby: Heinrich Schliemann Museum in Ankershagen (14km southeast), Fritz Reuter Literature Museum in Stavenhagen (19km north)

Access: 10km east of Waren, firstly by B 192 towards Neubrandenburg then from Klein-Plasten by B 194 towards Stavenhagen

9 ICH WEISS EIN HAUS AM SEE

Petra König

Altes Forsthaus 2
18292 Krakow-Seegrube
Tel. (038457) 2 32 73
Fax (038457) 23274 – www.hausamsee.de

Open all year • 10 rooms, including 6 with balcony and 8 non-smoking • Restaurant (eve only; closed Mon; closed Sun as well Nov to Feb): set meal 57.50-78€ • Garden, parking; dogs allowed • Boat and bicycle hire, carriage rides, cookery courses, wine tasting

110/135 €, Breakfast included
Credit cards not accepted

The variety of the waterfowl that flock to the Krakower See

In the heart of Pomerania, standing alone on the shore of the Krakower See in the middle of a nature reserve, is the "Lake House"; its elegant country ambience fills the rooms which scan the lake or peer into the depths of the wood. Away to one side, right on the water's edge, you'll come across a little beach house, which you're welcome to use, or you can just sun yourself on the private lakeshore or in the meadow and enjoy the perfect peace of your unspoilt surroundings. There are also two mooring jetties for boats. Striking but also reassuringly comfortable and appealing, the restaurant's style makes it an appropriate setting for Chef Laumen's excellent classical cooking.

Sights nearby: Schloss and cathedral in Güstrow (16km northwest)

Access: From Exit 14 on A 19 towards Krakow; turn left in c 7km

10 GUTSHAUS LUDORF

Keril und Manfred Achtenhagen

Rondell 7
17207 Ludorf
Tel. (039931) 84 00
Fax (039931) 84620 – www.gutshaus-ludorf.de

Closed 24 Jan to 18 Feb, 19-28 Dec • 23 rooms, all non-smoking • Restaurant with terrace (closed midday, except 15 May to 15 Oct): set meals 20-40€; half board 23€ • Garden, parking; dogs allowed in hotel, not in restaurant • Sauna, gym, ayurveda, bicycle hire, guided tours of Müritz National Park, sailing and canoe trips

98/125 €, Breakfast included

VISA MC

The storks' nest in the park

This historic manor house has hardly changed since it was built at the end of the 17th century, and it still welcomes its guests in the manner of the Mecklenburg nobility of old. Painted ceilings, parquet floors, and exposed beams give the stylish bedrooms a flair all of their own, while the the restaurant is a successful combination of elegance and rusticity. All the amenities of the lake can easily be enjoyed, thanks to the landing stage and bathing beach within walking distance.

Sights nearby: Village church, estate museum, St. Nicholai-Kirche in Röbel (5km west)

Access: From Exit 18 on A 19 via Dambeck and Röbel

11 SCHLOSS ULRICHSHUSEN

Frhr. von Maltzahn

Seestr. 14
17194 Lupendorf-Ulrichshusen
Tel. (039953) 79 00
Fax (039953) 79099 – www.gut-ulrichshusen.de

Closed 1 Jan to 20 Mar • 30 rooms, all non-smoking • Restaurant with terrace: main course 5-14€; half board 12€ • Garden, parking; dogs allowed • Bicycle and rowing boat hire, castle tours, Mecklenburg-Vorpommern Festival venue

90/110 €, Breakfast included

JCB VISA MC

Breakfast in the tower with its fabulous view over the surrounding countryside

This 16th century Renaissance castle could hardly have a more picturesque location, romantically sited as it is between the waters of the fish ponds and the Ulrichshusenersee. It offers beautifully appointed, spacious rooms in elegant country style, distributed among three buildings. The rustic restaurant occupies the former stables. The nearby "Culture Barn" is the setting for the splendid offerings of the Mecklenburg-Vorpommern Festival. What more could you ask for?

Sights nearby: Müritz-See (19km south), Stadtkirche in Malchin (20km northeast)

Access: From B 108 between Waren and Teterow via Moltzow

12 **TERNER**

Gerlinde Terner

Greifswalder Str. 40
17498 Mesekenhagen
Tel. (038351) 55 40
Fax (038351) 554433

Closed 1 Jan-20 Mar, 1 Nov-31 Dec • 14 rooms, including 11 non-smoking • Garden, parking; dogs not allowed

98/108 €, Breakfast included

AE Diners VISA MC

The hot or cold evening snacks provided on demand

The Hotel Terner is well located to the northwest of Greifswald close to the B 96. It is not only a convenient place to stay while exploring the old Hansa city, but also provides a pleasantly relaxing environment, with exemplary attention paid to running and upkeep of the establishment. The Terner family will certainly do all they can to make your visit a pleasant one. The rooms have stylishly traditional furnishings and decor and contemporary fittings, and altogether the accommodation is solid, comfortable, and welcoming.

Sights nearby: Regional Museum of Pomerania in Greifswald (7km southeast), ruins of Eldena monastery (12km southeast)

Access: 7km northwest of Greifswald by B 96 towards Stralsund

13 GRAND HOTEL MERCURE

Jens Ludwig

Schlossfreiheit 1
19306 Neustadt-Glewe
Tel. (038757) 53 20
Fax (038757) 53299 – www.schloss-mv.de

Open all year • 27 rooms, including 3 non-smoking • Restaurant with terrace: set meal 18.50-28.20€; half board from 12€ • Parking; dogs allowed • Sauna, solarium, bicycle hire, canoe trips

90/191 €, Breakfast 10 € (WE: 65/124 €)

AE D VISA MC

The culinary specialities that are changed monthly

This restored 17th century Baroque castle in the centre of Neustadt-Glewe gives its guests a right royal experience of time-travel. The truly splendid deluxe rooms have high walls and parquet floors, but their most magnificent feature is the glorious ceiling and fireplace stuccowork created by Italian master-craftsmen. The other rooms are simpler, but no less tasteful in their furnishings and decor. The vaulted basement houses the elegantly laid tables of “Wallenstein’s”.

Sights nearby: Alte Burg, Schloss and town church in Ludwigslust (10km southwest)

Access: Exit 14 on A 24

14 GUTSHOF SPAROW

Ernst Matheis

17214 Nossentiner Hütte
Tel. (039927) 76 20
Fax (039927) 76299
gutshof.sparow@t-online.de – www.hotel-gutshof-sparow.m-vp.de

Open all year • 50 rooms, including 24 with balcony, 14 with disabled access and 13 non-smoking • Restaurant with terrace: set meal 18-33€; half board 18€ • Garden, parking; dogs allowed • Wellness and beauty facilities, tennis, badminton, skittles, squash, bicycle hire, guided walks, chapel concerts, hunting, carriage rides

85/150 €, Breakfast included
AE VISA MC

The delightful estate chapel

Active relaxation is the keynote of this establishment. Tennis, squash, badminton and skittles are all available, and in addition there is a splendid leisure area with swimming pool and sauna. Accommodation is in comfortable rooms and apartments in the restored gentleman's residence as well as in a trio of timber-framed houses in the old orchard. Beyond the estate there's an almost infinite choice of things to do; all around stretch the heathlands of the Nature Park and the lakes and waterways of the Mecklenburg Seenplatte are within easy reach. With so much on offer, you will find a single stay here is simply not enough!

Sights nearby: Swing bridge and Monkey Forest in Malchow (6km south)

Access: From Exit 16 on A 19 towards Schwerin, turn right in Alt-Schwerin

15 VILLA KNOBELSDORFF

Jörg Pommerening

Ringstr. 121
17309 Pasewalk
Tel. (03973) 2 09 10
Fax (03973) 209110 – www.villa-knobelsdorff.de

Open all year • 18 rooms, one with balcony and one with disabled access • Restaurant with terrace (Mon-Fri from 5.30pm, Sat-Sun from 11.30am): main courses 8.15-15.10€ • Garden, cark park; dogs allowed

73/78 €, Breakfast included

AE VISA MC

A glass or three of the local beer, Pasewalk's "Pasenelle"

On the edge of the town centre between the defensive wall and the Kürassier Park, this establishment was once the residence of the regimental commander of Pasewalk's garrison, and owes its name to one of them, General Hans-Friedrich von Knobelsdorff, who lived here until 1945. Beyond the historic façade of the 1896 villa there are rooms with tasteful contemporary furnishings and decor, while the vaulted wine cellar houses a restaurant in beer-hall style

Sights nearby: St Marien, Museum im Prenzlauer Tor

Access: Exit 35 from A 20

16 LANDHOTEL ROSENHOF

Familie Rose

August-Bebel-Str. 10
19395 Plau-Quetzin
Tel. (038735) 8 90
Fax (038735) 89189 – www.landhotel-rosenhof.de

Open all year • 31 rooms, including 8 with balcony • Cafe-restaurant with terrace; half board from 12€ • Garden, parking; dogs allowed • Sauna, rowing-boat and bicycle hire

75/88 €, Breakfast included
Credit cards not accepted

Fresh fish from the lake

You are sure to appreciate the peace and quiet and other amenities of this country hotel built on the site of an old farmstead on the banks of the Plauer See. The natural surroundings can be enjoyed to the full by going for a ride on one of the establishment's bikes or by taking a boat out from its landing stage. You are accommodated in attractive rooms lavishly decorated in rustic country style; some of them pamper you further with an enticing view of the lake from terrace or balcony. The welcoming dining rooms with their dark timbers are also attractively rustic in style.

Sights nearby: Lifting bridge in Plau (4km south)

Access: 4km north of Plau by B 103

17 LANDHAUS MÜRITZGARTEN

Marlene Neu

Seebadstr. 45
17207 Röbel
Tel. (039931) 88 10
Fax (039931) 881113 – www.landhaus-mueritzgarten.m-vp.de

Open all year • 40 rooms, including 16 with balcony • Afternoon and evening snack meals for residents • Garden, parking; dogs not allowed • Sauna, solarium, bicycle hire, organised walks

90/110 €, Breakfast included
Credit cards not accepted

Coffee or a snack in the "Landhausstuben"

Consisting of six separate buildings, this delightful establishment on the outskirts of town is located by woodland close to the banks of the Müritzsee. The two main houses have comfortable rooms with solid furnishings in natural wood, while the stylish garden buildings are completely furnished and panelled in wood. You can loll on the grass of the extensive grounds, play around by the lake, or set off on a borrowed bike to explore the many and varied delights of the unspoiled landscape all around.

Sights nearby: Müritz spa, St-Nicholai-Kirche

Access: Exit 18 on A 19

18 SOLTHUS AM SEE

Hans-Martin Steber

Bollwerkstr. 1
18586 Baabe
Tel. (038303) 8 71 60
Fax (038303) 87169 – www.solthus.de

Open all year • 39 rooms, including 30 with balcony, 2 with disabled access and 28 non-smoking • Restaurant with terrace: set meal 38€; half board 28€ • Parking; dogs allowed • Wellness facilities with indoor pool and sauna, bicycle hire, organised walks

140/155 €, Breakfast included

AE VISA

The wood-panelled library with its fireplace

There are plenty of reasons for spending your holiday in Baabe, not least because it's so easy to relax here between the sandy shore and the wooded countryside. The thatched-roofed building too is most inviting, idyllically located as it is just outside the village by a tiny harbour. The rooms have a terrace or balcony and are furnished in tasteful country style with warm colour schemes. The welcoming restaurant is partly built as a log cabin and features a panoramic window. Any urban stress still outstanding can soon be dispersed by a visit to the attractive wellness area.

Sights nearby: Sellin pier (3km north), Granitz hunting lodge (9km west)

Access: From Stralsund by B 96 and from Bergen by B 196

19 ROMANTIK HOTEL KAUFMANNSHOF

Uwe Hermerschmidt

Bahnhofstr. 6-8
18528 Bergen
Tel. (03838) 8 04 50
Fax (03838) 804545 – www.kaufmannshof.com

Open all year • 18 rooms, all non-smoking, 2 with balcony • Restaurant with terrace: set lunch 18-30€, set dinner 18-55€; half board 18€ • Garden, parking; dogs allowed • Sauna, bicycle hire, bicycle and boat tours

85/120 €, Breakfast included

AE VISA MC

The beer-garden beneath the mighty linden-tree

This establishment began life as a business enterprise at the start of the 20th century and they still keep up a steady trade selling things are still sold here, including gifts and ladies' and gentlemen's clothing, among other things. But since 1996 the establishment has also housed a hotel, which offers rooms in a timelessly straightforward style. The "Kontor" restaurant has a nostalgic, bistro-like atmosphere, and here, as in the bedrooms, there are many attractive details recalling the place's mercantile heritage. Breakfast is served in the bright and airy conservatory.

Sights nearby: Schloss Ralswiek (8km north), Jasmund National Park and Königsstuhl clifftop viewpoint (23km northeast)

Access: By B 96 from Stralsund; towards station in centre of Bergen

20 GUT TRIBBEVITZ

Dr. Renate Dettmering

18569 Neuenkirchen-Tribbevitz
Tel. (038309) 70 80
Fax (038309) 708138 – www.gut-tribbevitz.de

Closed 3 Jan to 28 Feb, Christmas • 19 rooms, including 2 non-smoking • Restaurant with terrace: set lunch 25-29€, set dinner 25-56€; half board 22€ • Garden, parking; dogs allowed • Library, sauna, solarium, gym, riding hall and paddocks, horse-boxes, bicycle hire, cookery courses, art seminars

100/135 €, Breakfast included

JCB VISA MC

Imagining you are the lord of the manor as you relax in the library with a good book

This fine old manor house with its delightful stepped gables was rescued from near-fatal decay when it was comprehensively restored and opened as a hotel in May 2002. At the same time a stud was accommodated (there are guest stalls for four-legged guests in the stables too). The place is surrounded by a fine old park with ancient trees, ideal for just sitting and dreaming. The spacious bedrooms are individually decorated and furnished with bright and colourful pieces. Antiques enhance the stylish restaurant, which in fine weather is extended onto an outdoor terrace.

Sights nearby: Rügenpark in Gingst (11km southwest), Hiddensee island (ferry from Schaprode, 18km west)

Access: From Stralsund, B 96 to Samtens, then Gingst; towards Bergen, Schaprode, Neuenkirchen; at entry to Neuenkirchen turn right towards Tribbevitz

21 WREECHER HOF

Ulla Jürgens

Kastanienallee
18581 Putbus-Wreechen
Tel. (038301) 8 50
Fax (038301) 85100 – www.wreecher-hof.de

Open all year • 43 rooms, including 16 with terrace and 3 with disabled access • Restaurant with terrace (6pm-8pm only, Sun and public holidays also 12pm-2pm): set dinner 25-50€, main course 14-26€; half board 23€ • Health and fitness facilities with pool, steam bath and sauna, bicycle hire

110/130 €, Breakfast included

AE D VISA MC

The fact that the whole establishment is a no-smoking area

This group of seven thatch-roofed houses was designed especially for holiday-makers. The architecture pays tribute to the vernacular traditions of the island, and the spacious accommodation consists mostly of units of several rooms, furnished in cherrywood with attractive trimmings. Dining is a pleasant experience, whether in the restaurant with its conservatory or in fine weather on the terrace by the garden pool. You are served with dishes mostly inspired by international cuisine. Attractive wellness facilities round off the establishment's range of amenities.

Sights nearby: Schlosspark in Putbus (2km northeast), "Rasender Roland" steam train

Access: By B 96 from Stralsund via Bergen to Putbus; at "Circus" in Putbus 1st road on right towards Wreechen

22 SCHLOSS SCHORSSOW

Thomas Rachel

Am Haussee
17166 Schorssow
Tel. (039933) 7 90
Fax (039933) 79100 – www.schloss-schorssow.de

Open all year • 44 rooms, including 2 with balcony and 1 with disabled facilities • Restaurant with terrace: set meal 48-60€; half board 28€ • Garden, parking; dogs allowed • Indoor pool, sauna, cosmetic treatments, massage, library, bicycle and pedalo hire, cookery courses

125/289 €, Breakfast included (WE: 175/275 €)

AE D VISA MC

The tastefully designed leisure facilities

A castle straight out of a dream, on the banks of its own lake and surrounded by the greenery of an English-style landscape park. The building itself is in neo-Classical style and dates from the beginning of the 19th century. The elegant interior features tastefully appointed rooms, where materials have been harmoniously coordinated with great success. An equally stylish ambience is to be found in the restaurant, next to which there is a welcoming conservatory where breakfast is taken. There is also a vaulted wine cellar full of authentic atmosphere.

Sights nearby: Church of St Peter and St Paul in Teterow (14km north), Town Church in Malchin (21km northeast)

Access: From Exit 15 on A 19 towards Malchin/Teterow via Vollratsruhe, Kirch Grubenhagen and Gross Luchow

23 NIEDERLÄNDISCHER HOF

Jürgen Wilkens

Karl-Marx-Str. 12-13
19055 Schwerin
Tel. (0385) 59 11 00
Fax (0385) 59110999
hotel@niederlaendischer-hof.de – www.niederlaendischer-hof.de

Open all year • 33 rooms, including 4 with balcony and 12 non-smoking • Restaurant with terrace: set lunch 10-28€, set dinner 26-30€; half board 22€ • Garden, parking; dogs allowed in hotel, not in restaurant • Bicycle and boat hire

128/140 €, Breakfast included

AE VISA MC

The crackling open fire in the library

This sophisticated town-mansion of 1901 will cast its spell on you at first sight. The mahogany reception desk is approached across a marble floor, and a tastefully appointed library opens off the classically stylish lobby. Guests are whisked upstairs aboard a glass-sided lift; each room is elegantly and individually designed, with four-poster beds and much use of marble in the bathrooms. Warm colour schemes enhance the comfortable, welcoming atmosphere. The traditional-style restaurant too is most attractive, not least because of the huge mirror which makes an immediate impression. The dishes offered are based on a contemporary interpretation of regional cuisine.

Sights nearby: Castle island, cathedral

Access: On west bank of Pfaffenteich pond north of Old Town

24 GUTSHAUS STOLPE

Karsten von der Heide

Dorfstr. 37
17391 Stolpe
Tel. (039721) 55 00
Fax (039721) 55099 – www.gutshaus-stolpe.de

Closed 10-30 Jan • 33 rooms, including 9 with balcony • Restaurant with terrace (closed Mon and lunchtime): main course 22-35€, set dinner 52-82€; half board 35€ • Garden, parking; dogs allowed in hotel, not in restaurant • Sauna, gym, tennis, bicycle hire

130/225 €, Breakfast included

AE VISA MC

The stylish ambience of the bar with its library

This fine old 19th century residence stands on the site of Lower Pomerania's very first Benedictine monastery, destroyed in the Thirty Years War. It's a stylish place to stay, surrounded as it is by a 150-hectare estate with meadows, ancient trees, and a variety of historic buildings. The well-appointed rooms feature antique pieces and include elements from all over Europe, in English style in the main building, with a touch of the Mediterranean in the "Remise". There's a festive atmosphere in the restaurant, where the establishment provides its guests with tempting traditional fare.

Sights nearby: Otto Lilienthal Museum in Anklam (10km east)

Access: By B 110 between Demmin and Anklam

25 VILLA AUGUSTE VIKTORIA

Petra Schultz

Bismarckstr. 1
17419 Ahlbeck
Tel. (038378) 24 10
Fax (038378) 24144 – www.auguste-viktoria.de

Closed Jan • 16 rooms, including 3 with balcony and 3 non-smoking • Cafe; restaurant with terrace: set dinner 15-29€; half board 18€ • Garden, parking; dogs allowed • Sauna, gym, bicycle hire, organised walks, barbecues

100/150 €, Breakfast included

Breakfast in the cheerful surroundings of the courtyard

The glory days of the late 19th century seaside seem still alive here. You will be enchanted by the two linked Art Nouveau villas (one of them in private use) with their lovely façades, sited a convenient 50 metres from the beach but in a quiet and peaceful location. The rooms are in an elegantly timeless style with tasteful apricot-coloured furnishings. Little sitting areas in the oriel windows enhance the welcoming atmosphere. The Mediterranean-style restaurant is in the glass-roofed conservatory-like structure linking the villas.

Sights nearby: Pier, Ostsee spa

Access: By B 110 from Anklam or B 111 from Wolgast; in a side road off promenade in Ahlbeck

26 ROMANTIK STRANDHOTEL ATLANTIC

R. Seelige-Steinhoff

Strandpromenade 18
17429 Bansin
Tel. (038378) 6 05
Fax (038378) 60600 – www.seetel.de

Open all year • 26 rooms, 5 with balcony, 5 with air-conditioning, 4 non-smoking • Pub, restaurant with terrace: main courses 10-35€, half board 35€ • Parking; dogs allowed in the hotel but not in the restaurant • Indoor pool, steam bath, sauna, solarium, skittle alley, billiards

130/165 €, Breakfast included

AE VISA MC

In complete contrast to the hotel, the informal atmosphere in the pub, with billiards, skittles and occasional live music

This is the place to recapture the festive seaside atmosphere of Kaiser Wilhelm's time. Right on the promenade in the westernmost of Usedom Island's three aristocratic resorts, the charming villa has been welcoming a new generation of guests since 1994 with elegantly appointed rooms featuring walnut furnishings and marble bathrooms. Some of the rooms enjoy views of the Baltic breakers, as does the stylish restaurant with its glittering chandeliers. The best prospect of all is from the terrace, where you can also benefit from the refreshing sea breeze. Attractive leisure facilities complete the alluring picture.

Sights nearby: Baltic baths (6km southeast), Schloss Mellenthin (14km southwest)

Access: Via B 111 from Wolgast or B 110 from Anklam to Ahlbeck, then B 111; the hotel is in Bansin, on the promenade

27 FORTUNA

Uwe-Heinz Hedel

Kulmstr. 8
17424 Heringsdorf
Tel. (038378) 4 70 70
Fax (038378) 470743 – www.hotel-fortuna.kaiserbaeder.m-vp.de

Closed 1-30 Nov • 21 rooms, including 6 with balcony and 4 non-smoking • Parking; dogs allowed • Sauna

75/90 €, Breakfast included
Credit cards not accepted

A barefoot stroll along the beach

Extending for more than 10km along the shore between the resorts of Bansin, Heringsdorf and Ahlbeck, the promenade is overlooked by countless aristocratic villas. There are further charming examples of sophisticated seaside architecture in the parallel street behind, among them the Hotel Fortuna with its neo-Classical façade. Generous windows allow plenty of light into the interior, whose bright and airy quality is further enhanced in the timelessly elegant bedrooms by attractive furnishings and the use of colourful fabrics. The attractive bistro-style breakfast room has an almost Mediterranean ambience.

Sights nearby: Villa Irmgard, Casino

Access: In a street parallel to the beach promenade in Heringsdorf; from Wolgast by B 111, or from Anklam to Ahlbeck by B 110, then B 111

28 STRANDHOTEL

Andreas Harder, Thomas Güde

Strandpromenade 1
17449 Karlshagen
Tel. (038371) 26 90
Fax (038371) 269199 – www.strandhotel-usedom.de

Closed 1 Nov to 27 Dec • 20 rooms, all non-smoking, including 7 with balcony and 1 with disabled access • Restaurant with terrace (lunch offered only Jul, Aug): set meal 14.50 - 70€; half board 14.50€ • Underground garage; dogs by arrangement • Jacuzzi, sauna, steam bath, bicycle hire, cycle tours, cookery courses, wine seminars

90/120 €, Breakfast included
VISA MC

The open fireplaces in lobby and restaurant

At the northern end of Usedom Island, this establishment opened its doors to guests in 2002. Eschewing the nostalgic charm of traditional seaside architecture, it is built in a confident contemporary style with tasteful interior decor. The accommodation, some of it in the form of maisonettes, is enhanced by the presence of modern works of art. It's a fine place to settle down for a while, particularly when you return from a long walk to be greeted by its welcoming atmosphere. The bathrooms are especially attractive, with generous mirrors, marble tiling and underfloor heating.

Sights nearby: Historical-Technical Information Centre Peenemünde (7 km northwest), St Petri Kirche in Wolgast (12 km southwest)

Access: By B 111 from Wolgast via Bannemin and Trassenheide

29 VILLA MARGARETE

Ulrich Pöhl

Fontanestr. 11
17192 Waren (Müritz)
Tel. (03991) 62 50
Fax (03991) 625100 – www.villa-margarete.de

Open all year • 30 rooms, including 11 with balcony, 10 non-smoking • Cafe; restaurant with terrace: set meals; half board 19€ • Garden, parking; dogs allowed • Wellness facilities, bicycle hire, walks, carriage rides

109/125 €, Breakfast included

AE JCB VISA MC

A walk in the wonderfully natural surroundings of the Müritz National Park

This villa stands among others on the edge of the National Park well away from the hustle and bustle of town yet only a short distance from the lake. The 19th century novelist Theodor Fontane lived for a while in the same road, and tribute is paid to him in the the establishment's pride and joy, the "Fontane Suite" with its lavishly appointed bathroom. The other rooms also have attractive decor and furnishings in timeless style, whether in the 19th century villa itself or in the modern extension.

Sights nearby: Müritz Museum, Wisent animal enclosure near Damerow (11km west)

Access: Exit 17 on A 19; in Waren from B 192 towards "Ecktannen"

30 ROMANTIK HOTEL BORCHARD'S ROOKHUS AM SEE

Alexander Borchard

Am Großen Labussee
17255 Wesenberg
Tel. (039832) 5 00
Fax (039832) 50100 – www.rookhus.de

Open all year • 45 rooms, including 10 with balcony, 1 with disabled access and 16 non-smoking • Restaurants with terrace: set dinner 28-52€, main course 12-24€; half board 25€ • Playroom, garden, parking; dogs allowed • Log cabin sauna, bathing beach, sunbathing lawn with beach chairs, billiards, guided walks, hire of bicycles, rowing boats, motorboats, canoes, quad bikes and Trabants

100/140 €, Breakfast included

AE JCB VISA MC

Enjoying the peace and quiet of the lakeside

This establishment once served as a youth hostel. The dormitory atmosphere is now a thing of the past, but many other attractions of the place remain, among them the leafy lakeside setting by the Grosser Labussee. The comfortable atmosphere of the tastefully decorated and furnished English-style rooms is enhanced by the colour-coordinated curtains and bedcovers. The country-style "Storks' Nest" restaurant contrasts with the stylishly traditional "Prince Nicholas".

Sights nearby: Neustrelitz Old Town (20 km northeast), Schloss Rheinsberg (30 km south)

Access: On B 198 4.5 km north of Wesenberg on west bank of the Grosser Labussee; follow signs from Wesenberg

31 HAFERLAND

Bernd Evers

Bauernreihe 5a
18375 Wieck auf dem Darß
Tel. (038233) 6 80
Fax (038233) 68220 – www.hotelhaferland.de

Open all year • 49 rooms, including 2 with disabled access and 32 non-smoking • Restaurants with terrace (closed lunchtime except Sun and public holidays from Nov to before Easter): set dinner 23-43€, main course 14-21€ • Garden, parking; dogs allowed • Indoor pool, saunas, solarium, bicycle hire, cookery courses

103/143 €, Breakfast included
Credit cards not accepted

The home-made stone-baked bread

On the outskirts of Wieck, these three linked thatch-roofed buildings make a welcoming sight on the idyllic peninsula between the Baltic and the lagoon of the Bodstedter Bodden. The attractive country-style bedrooms have pleasant furnishings in natural fir, and those on the ground and top floors have access to a terrace. The "Gute Stube" restaurant with its homely tiled stove is a bright and cheerful place, while the "Fass 36" is an unusual cellar establishment, featuring an enormous wine barrel and what must be the biggest corkscrew in the area. The food available ranges from refined to straightforwardly tasty.

Sights nearby: Ahrenshoop (13 km southwest)

Access: On the Darss peninsula northeast of Rostock

Niedersachsen/ Bremen/Hamburg

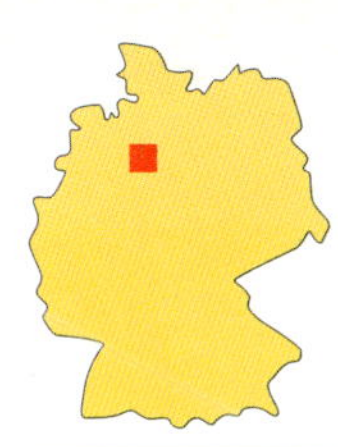

For centuries, the old Hansa trading centres of Hamburg and Bremen have been Germany's gateways, and the ships of the world still sail up the Elbe and Weser rivers to their quays. Both cities have evolved into modern metropolises but remain proud of their impressive heritage. Stretching from the North Sea coast to the hills of central Germany, Lower Saxony encompasses pretty Frisian fishing villages and the bracing dunes of Norderney, climbing trails and cycle tours through the Harz uplands, and Lüneburg Heath, one of Europe's oldest cultural landscapes. The distinctive architectural style known as Weser Renaissance is seen at its best in lovely castles like the Hämelschenburg or the sumptuous town mansions of Hamelin, whose children, as everyone knows, were charmed away by the legendary rat-catching Piper. Hannover once gave Britain a line of kings; its Baroque Great Garden is a reminder of such times, but today the regional capital is better known as a vibrant contemporary city and a commercial driving force. Equally emblematic of the modern age is Wolfsburg, the home of Volkswagen, while Bremen boasts the pioneering Universum Science Center.

Ostfriesische Inseln
Bucht
Harwich
Cuxhaven
Norden
Wilhelmshaven
Bremerhaven
Aurich
Emden
Nordenham
Delfzijl
Leer
Bad Zwischenahn
Oldenburg
Groningen
NIEDERSACHSEN
BREMEN
Delmenhorst
Weser
Assen
Emmen
Cloppenburg
Verden
Meppel
Nienburg
Lingen
Diepholz
Zwolle
Almelo
Nordhorn
Deventer
Hengelo
Enschede
Rheine
Osnabrück
Minden
Herford
Bielefeld
Winterswijk
Ems
Münster
Gütersloh
Detmold
Bocholt
Rhein
Rheda-Wiedenbrück
Paderborn
Wesel
Hamm
Lippe
Lippstadt
Soest
Ruhrgebiet
Dortmund
Duisburg
Essen
Ruhr
Meschede
Krefeld
Hagen
Iserlohn
Wuppertal

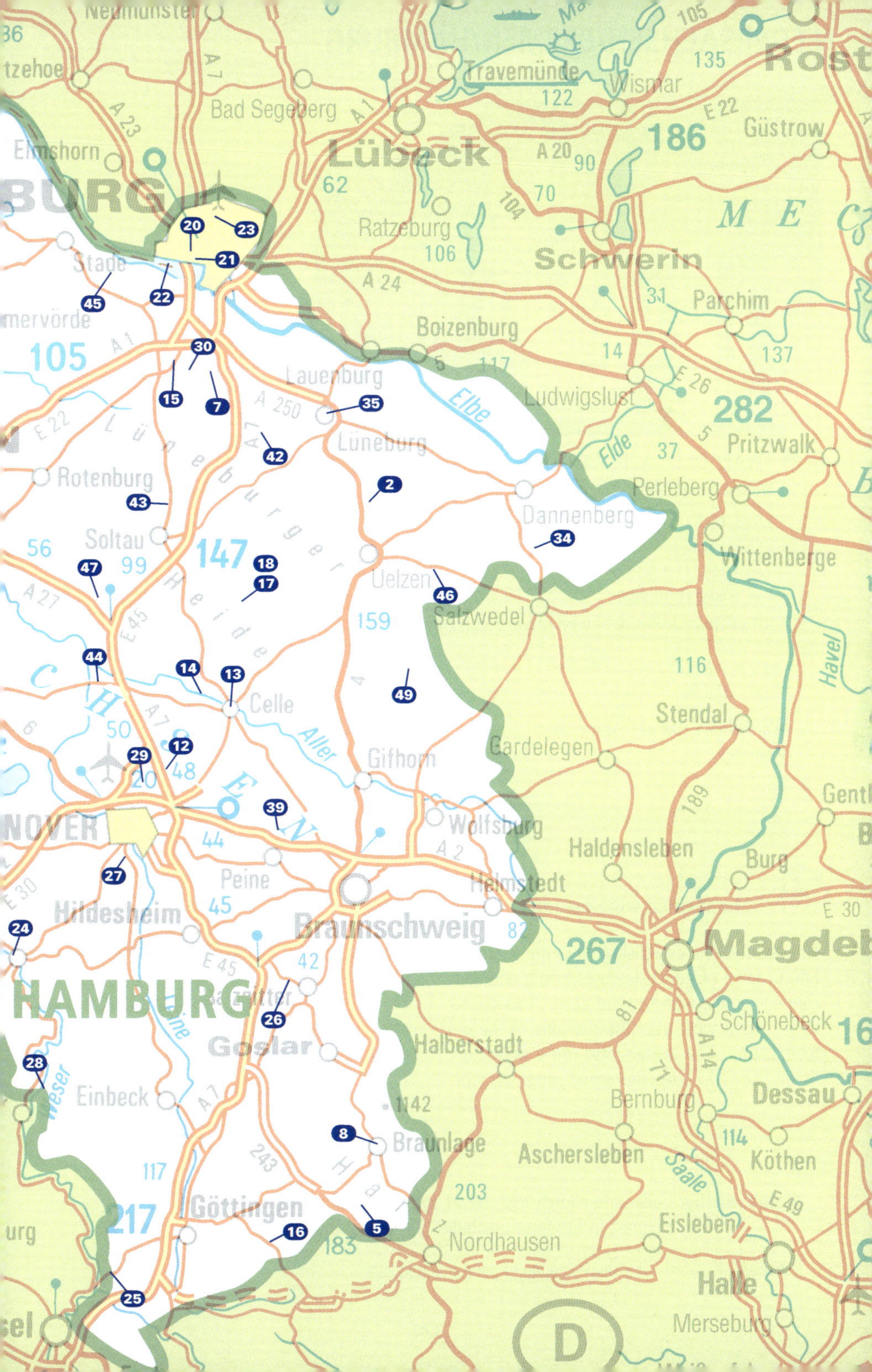

Travemünde
Wismar
Bad Segeberg
Lübeck
Güstrow
Elmshorn
Ratzeburg
Schwerin
Stade
Parchim
Boizenburg
Lauenburg
Ludwigslust
Elbe
Lüneburg
Elde
Pritzwalk
Rotenburg
Perleberg
Dannenberg
Soltau
Lüneburger Heide
Wittenberge
Uelzen
Salzwedel
Havel
Celle
Aller
Stendal
Gifhorn
Gardelegen
Wolfsburg
Haldensleben
Peine
Burg
Helmstedt
Hildesheim
Braunschweig
HAMBURG
Goslar
Halberstadt
Schönebeck
Einbeck
Bernburg
Dessau
Braunlage
Aschersleben
Köthen
Saale
Göttingen
Eisleben
Nordhausen
Halle
Merseburg
Weser
Harz
D

1 TWARDOKUS-ALTE KANTOREI

Nicole Sobczak

Kirchstr. 6
26603 Aurich
Tel. (04941) 9 90 90
Fax (04941) 990929
info@twardokus.de – www.twardokus.de

Open all year • 27 rooms, including 12 non-smoking and 1 with disabled access • Cafe-restaurant with terrace (closed 6pm Sun in winter): set lunch 7.50€, main course 11.80€ • Dogs by arrangement • Wine seminars

70/95 €, Breakfast included
VISA MC

The themed wine-tastings on Monday evenings

This comfortable establishment in the charming Frisian town of Aurich features bright and welcoming rooms, with tasteful decor, four-poster beds, and a view over the rooftops of the old town centre. The owners also run a bookshop, the source of the latest literary offerings thoughtfully provided in the bedrooms, so there's every reason to start brushing up on your German! There is an inviting cafe-restaurant and an attractive garden for relaxing in - or reading a good page-turner - when the sun comes out.

Sights nearby: Collegiate church mill, Henri and Eske Nannen Collection and Otto van de Loo Bequest in Emden Kunsthalle (23 km southwest)

Access: In Aurich Old Town on edge of pedestrianised zone

2 GRÜNINGS CHALET

Lothar Grüning

Haberkamp 2
29549 Bad Bevensen
Tel. (05821) 9 84 00
Fax (05821) 984041 – www.hotel-gruening.de

Closed 5-23 Jan, 1-18 Dec • 24 rooms, all with balcony • Café, restaurant with terrace (closed Mon, Tue): lunch 16.50€, evening menu 24-35€ ; half board 10€ • Garden, car parking; dogs allowed in restaurant but not in hotel • Health and beauty area with indoor pool, sauna, bicycle hire, organised hikes

108/164 €, Breakfast included
Credit cards not accepted

The cosy hall with its open fire

Soak up the peace and quiet of the spa area while enjoying the benefits of the abundant natural light which pours into the rooms of this establishment through the big windows. The bright and welcoming atmosphere is further enhanced by the furnishings, the work of a master-carpenter from the Alps. The restaurant too is most inviting, with tasteful decor in country-house style and much use made of floral displays. Or you can dine outside, where the garden terrace features beautifully decorated tables with gleaming white tablecloths.

Sights nearby: Ebsdorf monastery (13km southwest), Uelzen station, designed by Friedrich Hundertwasser

Access: Follow the olive-green 'Nr 5' signs in Bad Bevensen

3 **LANDHOTEL BUCHENHOF**

Jürgen Horstmann

Bergstr. 22-26
49152 Bad Essen
Tel. (05472) 93 90
Fax (05472) 939200 – www.landhotel-buchenhof.de

Open all year • 26 rooms • Garden, car park; dogs allowed • Sauna

90/95 €, Breakfast included

AE D VISA MC

A trip on the vintage railway from Bad Essen to Bohmte

Extending a hearty welcome to all its guests and making sure they are well looked after, this establishment consists of a listed group of timber-framed buildings in an idyllic parkland setting. The bedrooms are individually furnished and decorated, and not one of them resembles another. A country-house atmosphere comes in part from a subtle selection of materials while the carefully chosen antiques here and there lend a further touch of refinement. For something even more special, ask for a four-poster or a waterbed. Don't miss the chance to try some real local specialities at the breakfast table.

Sights nearby: St Peter's Cathedral and the Felix Nussbaum Museum, designed by Daniel Libeskind, both in Osnabrück (24km southwest)

Access: Via B 218/65 between Brahmsche and Lübbecke

4 LANDHAUS STUKENBROCK

Manfred Merk

Erdfällenstraße
31812 Bad Pyrmont
Tel. (05281) 9 34 40
Fax (05281) 934434 – www.landhaus-stukenbrock.de

Open all year • 11 rooms, including 5 with balcony, 1 with disabled access and 4 non-smoking • Restaurant with terrace (closed Thu and midday Mon,Tue): main course 10.20-16.80€; half board 29€ • Garden, parking; dogs allowed • Sauna, solarium, bicycle hire

102/165 €, Breakfast included
AE VISA MC

Getting closer to the flora and fauna all around

In a lovely setting high above the town on the forest edge, this long-established inn has evolved into an attractive hotel-restaurant. The pretty, half-timbered building with its delightful thatched roof has been given an extension in the form of a big conservatory; from here, as well as from the garden terrace, there is a wonderful panorama over Bad Pyrmont and the gently rolling countryside. Lime-washed pine furniture enhances the bedrooms with their solid, comfortable, country-style decor. They too look out over the valley, providing views which you are unlikely ever to tire of.

Sights nearby: Kurpark, Hämelschenburg (13 km northeast)

Access: 1 km north of centre by Bahnhofstrasse

5 SONNENHOF

M. und L. Rockendorf

Glasebergstr. 20a
37441 Bad Sachsa
Tel. (05523) 9 43 70
Fax (05523) 943750 – www.sonnenhof-bad-sachsa.de

Cloesd 5 Nov-1 Dec • 17 rooms, including 3 non-smoking, all with balcony • Garden, parking; dogs allowed • Gym, sauna, bicycle hire, carriage rides

70/122 €, Breakfast included

MC

The wine coolers and tea-making facilities in the rooms

In a side street just beyond the centre, this well-run family establishment enjoys pleasant views over the town thanks to its elevated position. The building itself is attractive, its balconies almost overflow with flowers in summer. Inside it's just as charming; you are made to feel welcome at once as you enter the hotel foyer with its cosy corner by the fireplace, while the bedrooms - most of them arranged as mini-suites with sitting areas - have cherrywood furnishings and colourful fabrics.

Sights nearby: Salztal-Paradies swimming centre, Walkenried monastery ruins (6km east)

Access: By B 242 between Herzberg and Nordhausen

6 HOF VON BOTHMER

Stephan Graf von Bothmer

Dreiberger Str. 27
26160 Bad Zwischenahn-Meyerhausen
Tel. (04403) 9 36 30
Fax (04403) 936310 – www.hof-von-bothmer.de

Open all year • 13 rooms, including 6 with terrace and 8 non-smoking • Café, bar • Garden, parking, dogs allowed • Sauna, solarium, bicycle hire, organised cycle tours and walks

113/128 €, Breakfast included

AE D VISA MC

The 30% discount on the green fees on the neighbouring golf course

In the protected landscape of the sunny northern bank of Zwischenahn Lake, this old farmstead offers its guests a number of maisonnette-apartments accommodating up to six people. Their names - Fox's Den or Hedgehog Nest - give some idea of their cosy character. Each of them is individually furnished in a contemporary country style, while in the main building, exposed beams help create an attractive ambience. Completing the picture is a welcoming breakfast room, a sitting room with open fire and a terrace.

Sights nearby: Ammerländer Farm; Oldenburg Augusteum (18km east)

Access: From exit 8 on A 28 towards Bad Zwischenahn and follow the signposts to Dreibergen

7 LANDHAUS MEINSBUR

Nicol Cordes

Gartenstr. 2
21227 Bendestorf
Tel. (04183) 7 79 90
Fax (04183) 6087 – www.meinsbur.de

Open all year • 12 rooms • Restaurant with terrace: set lunch 30-40€, set dinner 36-40€ • Garden, parking; dogs allowed • Bicycle hire, walks, jazz brunch

115/160 €, Breakfast included
AE JCB VISA MC

Exploring the unique landscape of the heathlands

More than 400 years old, this thatched timber-framed building offers its guests accommodation in which loving care has been taken with every detail. Oak, leather, and tasteful antiques help create an elegant and stylish atmosphere. In addition, there is a garden house with room for five, built in English country-house style. The park-like garden with its little pool is a fine place in which to relax and stretch your legs. The delightfully decorated restaurant has a special feature: in autumn and winter special dishes are prepared before your very eyes at the open fire.

Sights nearby: Film museum, Butterfly park in Buchholz-Seppensen (11km southwest)

Access: From Hittfeld Exit on A 1 towards Jesteburg, or from Ramelsloh Exit on A 7, then via Harmstorf

8 ROMANTIK HOTEL ZUR TANNE

Hans und Rüdiger Fleischhacker

Herzog-Wilhelm-Str. 8
38700 Braunlage
Tel. (05520) 9 31 20
Fax (05520) 3992 – www.tanne-braunlage.de

Open all year • 21 rooms, including 13 with balcony and 8 non-smoking • Restaurant (eve only): set meal 21-49€; half board (3 days or more) 20€; Brunos Marktwirtschaft bistro 10am-6pm • Parking; dogs allowed • Gym, sauna, steam bath, solarium, jacuzzi, bicycle hire

80/149 €, Breakfast included
VISA MC

A trip to the top of the Brocken, scene of the famous Witches' Sabbath

Hospitality has been dispensed here in the Kurpark - Braunlage is an upland spa - since 1725, though the original building with its charming timber façade has been supplemented by two annexes. The rooms are in refined country-house style and offer a tasteful and comfortable ambience for your stay. As far as dining is concerned, you have a choice of a traditional restaurant, a rustic taproom for a decent beer, and a bistro, "Brunos Marktwirtschaft", which features an attractive gallery section.

Sights nearby: Samson silver mine at St Andreasberg (13km west), Wernigerode Old Town (22km northeast)

Access: At junction of B 4 and B 27

9 LANDHAUS HÖPKENS RUH

Lutz Arnhold

Oberneulander Landstr. 69
28355 Bremen-Oberneuland
Tel. (0421) 20 58 53
Fax (0421) 2058545
www.hoepkensruh.de

Closed 1-10 Jan • 8 rooms, including 3 with balcony and 2 non-smoking • Restaurant with terrace (closed Mon): set lunch 30€, set dinner 40-55€ • Garden, parking; dogs allowed • Bicycle hire

100 €, Breakfast included

AE JCB VISA MC

The sitting room with its cheerfully crackling open fire

In its idyllic parkland setting, this country house is on the eastern edge of Bremen, at the point where the city ends and the countryside begins. In 1877, its wealthy owner, the patrician Johann Höpken, bequeathed it to his native city. Nowadays you don't have to be Bremen born and bred to reside here and enjoy the place's intimate atmosphere. Hotel guests are accommodated in individually decorated rooms which feature richly ornamental wall coverings and are partly furnished with antique pieces. The overall feeling is reminiscent of the way country-house life used to be lived; the dining room is no exception, while in summer a lovely terrace invites guests to admire the view of the park.

Sights nearby: Focke Museum and Schnoorviertel in Bremen (10km west)

Access: 10km east of Bremen city centre by Kurfürstenallee and Franz-Schütte-Allee

10 **FORSTHAUS HEILIGENBERG**

Adelheid Brüning

Heiligenberg 3
27305 Bruchhausen-Vilsen
Tel. (04252) 9 32 00
Fax (04252) 932020 – www.forsthaus-heiligenberg.de

Open all year • 12 rooms, including 8 non-smoking • Restaurant with terrace (closed Mon): set lunch 15-19.60€, set dinner 28-39€; half board • Garden, parking; dogs allowed • Sauna, wellness facilities, stables, woodland playground, organised walks, readings

84/120 €, Breakfast included

AE VISA MC

The use of fresh flowers from the hotel's own garden

Though the Premonstratensian monastery of Heiligenberg disappeared long ago, its name has been preserved and its medieval defensive walls are still intact. Within them, the old forester's house has been converted into an idyllically located hotel-restaurant, its timber-framed façade making a delightful picture in its green setting. The bedrooms, some with exposed timbers, are equally attractive, with furnishings in precious woods. The rustic restaurant with its lovely open fire is extended in summer onto a splendid terrace.

Sights nearby: Branch line railway museum of Lower Saxony, Bücken collegiate church (19km southeast)

Access: By B 6 in Heiligenberg

11 GROSSE KLUS

Harald Strüwe

Am Klusbrink 19
31675 Bückeburg-Röcke
Tel. (05722) 9 51 20
Fax (05722) 951250 – www.kluesker.de

Open all year • 29 rooms, including 9 with balcony and 13 non-smoking • Pub, restaurant with terrace; set lunch 15-25 €, set dinner 17-39,50 €, half board 16,50 € • Garden, parking, dogs allowed • Bicycle hire

82/107 €, Breakfast included (WE: 75 €)

AE VISA MC

A cool glass of "Klüsker Waldbräu", the unfiltered local beer

In 1794 Princess Juliane of Schaumburg-Lippe had a summer residence built here. Originally intended for "Travellers of High Rank", it now houses an attractive, timber-framed country restaurant with an open fire and a beer parlour. Since 1994, in a revival of tradition, visitors can once more stay overnight: they are accommodated in a modern hotel building, its comfortable, well-kept bedrooms furnished in solid wood. Breakfast is taken in a bright and welcoming conservatory.

Sights nearby: Castle and helicopter museum in Bückeburg (5 km east); Minden cathedral and canal crossing (7 km northwest)

Access: 5km west from Bückeburg in the direction of Minden

12 OLE DEELE

Elfrun Kühn

Heinrich-Wöhler-Str. 14
30938 Burgwedel-Grossburgwedel
Tel. (05139) 9 98 30
Fax (05139) 998340

Closed 22 Dec to 5 Jan • 15 rooms, including 4 non-smoking and 1 with disabled access • Garden, parking; dogs allowed • Indoor pool, sauna, gym

65/95 €, Breakfast included (WE: 65/75 €)

VISA MC

The breakfast room with its decor evoking a long-vanished era

This old farmstead dating from 1828 features a lovely half-timbered brick façade and an idyllic cobbled courtyard. It's a place to settle down on a bench and let the peace and quiet of the place work its calming magic. The rooms are all in the same attractive, straightforward style, in places with exposed timbers. The whole street in which the building is located is subject to a preservation order.

Sights nearby: Sprengel Museum and Zoo in Hanover (22km southwest)

Access: Exit 54 on A 7

13 UTSPANN

Ursula Meihs

Im Kreise 13
29221 Celle
Tel. (05141) 9 27 20
Fax (05141) 927252
info@utspann.de – www.utspann.de

Closed 1-2 Jan • 22 rooms, including 4 with balcony, 1 with air conditioning and 3 non-smoking • Restaurant with terrace (Mon-Sat eve only): set meal 20-25€; half board 15€ • Garden, parking; dogs allowed in hotel, not in restaurant • Sauna, solarium

100/130 €, Breakfast included (WE: 90/110 €)
AE D VISA MC

The picture-postcard beauty of Celle's Old Town

These three restored 17th century timber-framed buildings with their inviting courtyard really are something out of the ordinary. Inside, the individually designed rooms have contemporary furnishings complemented by antique pieces, while exposed beams lend a rustic air. What distinguishes the establishment from other places is its exuberant decor featuring an extraordinary array of objects - some nostalgic, some distinctly offbeat and likely to raise a smile. If you have a taste for the unusual, this is the place for you!

Sights nearby: Schloss, Wienhausen monastery (10km south)

Access: At eastern end of inner ring road on the continuation of the Nordwall

14 KÖLLNER'S LANDHAUS

Andreas Köllner

Im Dorfe 1
29223 Celle-Boye
Tel. (05141) 95 19 50
Fax (05141) 9519555
info@koellners-landhaus.de – www.koellners-landhaus.de

Open all year • 6 rooms, including 5 non-smoking • Restaurant with terrace: set lunch 15-40€, set dinner 40-43€; half board 22€ • Garden, parking; dogs by arrangement • Bicycle hire, boat hire, wine seminars, cookery courses

106/156 €, Breakfast included

AE ⓓ VISA MC

A canoe trip on the River Aller

A rural idyll such as you might conjure up in your dreams; a thatched timber-framed building, built as a farmstead in 1589, with a park-like garden stretching down to the river. Fine old trees and a pond make the ambience all the more romantic, and if you stay here you may find yourself wishing that time would stand still: if you settle down on the lovely terrace and relax you may well feel it has! But it's not just the outdoors here that appeals; inside, the restaurant features a vinotheque, while the bedrooms are tastefully decorated in subtle colours.

Sights nearby: Bomann Museum and Stadtkirche in Celle (4km southeast)

Access: 4km northeast of Celle town centre via Harburger Strasse (B 3) and John-Busch-Strasse

15 GÄSTEHAUS ULMENHOF

Hannelore Stöver

Am Sööl'n 1
21244 Dibbersen
Tel. (04181) 9 99 70
Fax (04181) 97103 – www.gaestehaus-ulmenhof.de

Open all year • 16 rooms, including 4 non-smoking • Garden, parking; dogs not allowed

50/57 €, Breakfast included

We most liked

Time spent dreaming away in the lovely garden

This brick-built farmhouse rose from its foundations in 1914, at a time when Germany was still ruled by the Kaiser, and it has kept its authentic country charm ever since. Lavishly furnished in wood' the bedrooms are in the old hayloft and are all named after birds. Walls and ceilings are mostly panelled and, together with the country-style furniture, create a comfortable and welcoming atmosphere. Breakfast is taken in the attractively decorated hallway.

Sights nearby: Kiekeberg open air museum (11 km north), Ramelsloh collegiate church (17 km southeast)

Access: Exit 42 on A 1

16 ZUM LÖWEN

Franz-Josef Otto

Marktstr. 30
37115 Duderstadt
Tel. (05527) 30 72
Fax (05527) 72630 – www.hotelzumloewen.de

Open all year • 42 rooms, including 10 with balcony, 6 non-smoking, 2 with disabled access • Restaurant with terrace: set lunch 18-25€, set dinner 19-38€; half board 18€ • Parking; dogs allowed in hotel • Indoor pool, sauna, bicycle hire

125/165 €, Breakfast included (WE: 110/145 €)

AE VISA MC

The idyllic atmosphere of Duderstadt with its array of picturesque timber-framed buildings

Why not stay in the very heart of this unique little town? The "Lion" may not be one of Duderstadt's 550-plus timber-framed houses, but together with the famous Town Hall, it is located on the delightful Marktstrasse in the middle of the pedestrianised centre. Behind a distinguished neo-Classical façade, the elegant and comfortable rooms have solid and functional furnishings. To satisfy your gastronomic needs, there is the "Alt-Duderstadt" beer-parlour, the stylish "Zum Löwen" restaurant, and a winter-garden style cafe.

Sights nearby: St Cyriakus-Kirche, Wilhelm Busch mill at Ebergötzen (13km northwest)

Access: At junction of B 247 and B 446

17 **LANDHOTEL BAUERNWALD**

Carsten Dickow

Alte Dorfstr. 8
29328 Faßberg-Müden
Tel. (05053) 9 89 90
Fax (05053) 1556
buchung@landhotel-bauernwald.de – www.bauernwald.de

Closed 3-12 Jan • 37 rooms, including 14 non-smoking • Restaurant with terrace: main course from 11€; half board 16.50-19€ • Garden, parking; dogs allowed in hotel, not in restaurant • Sauna, bicycle hire, canoe trips, carriage rides

86/105 €, Breakfast included
VISA MC

Sitting out beneath the oak trees

Together with its annexe, this lovely old farmhouse with a half-timbered and brick façade welcomes guests to the idyllic spot where two rivers meet. There is a lawn to relax on and a "heathland garden", both helping you to commune with Nature. The rooms are furnished in a variety of styles; some of them feature period pieces, while the overall ambience created is one of country-house charm with a nice balance of tradition and modernity. Fitting in beautifully with its surroundings, the rustic "Gaststuuv" with its open fire welomes you to table.

Sights nearby: Game park, Albert König Museum in Unterlüss (14km east)

Access: From Exit 45 on A 7 by B 3 towards Bergen, then via Wietzendorf, Reddingen, Reiningen and Poitzen

18 NIEMEYER'S ROMANTIK POSTHOTEL

Alexander Niemeyer

Hauptstr. 7
29328 Faßberg-Müden
Tel. (05053) 9 89 00
Fax (05053) 989064 – www.niemeyers-posthotel.de

Open all year • 36 rooms, including 14 non-smoking, 13 with air-conditioning and 6 with balcony • Restaurant with terrace: set meal 18-45€; half board 18€ • Garden, parking; dogs not allowed • Sauna, jacuzzi, solarium, bicycle hire, guided walks, kitchen parties, wine seminars

90/120 €, Breakfast included

VISA MC

The fountain beneath the romantic lime-tree in the garden

You can imagine yourself transported back to the Germany of yesteryear in this attractive timber-framed hotel on the cobbled main street of Müden. The building began life in 1871 as a stagecoach inn, and Hermann Löns, the writer whose works immortalised the world of the Lower Saxony heathlands, stayed here more than once. The hotel rooms are well-kept and elegantly furnished, and much use is made of marble in the bathrooms. There are more rooms in an annexe, the "Lührnhof", which is linked to the hotel by a lovely garden. You dine in the "Schäferstuben" which features heathland specialities and much else besides.

Sights nearby: St Laurentiuskirche, Lönsstein (2km south)

Access: From Exit 45 on A 7 towards Bergen, then via Wietzendorf, Reddingen, Reinigen and Poitzen

19 GUT SCHÖNEWORTH

Peter Göhring

Landesbrücker Str 42
21729 Freiburg (Elbe)
Tel. (04779) 9 23 50
Fax (04779) 8203 – www.gutschoeneworth.de

Open all year • 15 rooms, including 7 non-smoking and 6 with disabled access • Cafe; restaurant with terrace (closed 1 Oct to 1 Mar; Mon, Tue except for residents): main course 8.50-19€, set dinner 21-25€; half board 21€ • Children's play area, garden, parking; dogs allowed • Sauna, tennis, sunbathing lawn, bicycle hire, walks, exhibitions

80/105 €, Breakfast included

AE · Diners · VISA · MC

The apple-blossom in springtime

On the outskirts of Freiburg, this listed group of three estate buildings stands among the orchards of the "Altes Land" along the River Elbe. With their thatched roofs, they exude an authentic country charm. The comfortable bedrooms feature a variety of period or natural wood furnishings. The garden really feels more like a small park; in it you'll find a log cabin with a sauna. Some particularly lovely countryside along the wide-open landscape of the river makes a memorable day out for cyclists and experienced riders - there are stables in Freiburg.

Sights nearby: Natureum (12km west), Stade Old Town (33km south)

Access: From Exit Hohenfelde on A 23 towards Glückstadt, then by ferry across the Elbe, or from Debstedt Exit on A 27 via Bederkesa-Hemmor

20 VORBACH

Karla Godron

Johnsallee 63
20146 Hamburg
Tel. (040) 44 18 20
Fax (040) 44182888 – www.hotel-vorbach.de

Open all year • 116 rooms, including 20 non-smoking and 10 with balcony • Parking; dogs allowed • Bicycle hire, organised visits to musicals

105/150 €, Breakfast included

AE JCB VISA MC

The short distance on foot to the city centre and Alster

Hamburg's late-19th century suburb of Harvestehude is well-endowed with fine town houses and villas, among them three originally separate edifices which have been linked to form this attractive hotel. With their high ceilings and Art Nouveau detailing, the hotel's rooms speak eloquently of that elegant era, and all of them feature solid, contemporary natural wood furnishings. At the start of your day, you have a choice, not only of good things from the buffet, but of several different breakfast rooms.

Sights nearby: Communications Museum, Hamburg History Museum

Access: On side street off Rothenbaumchaussee near Hamburg Ethnographic Museum

21 **WEDINA**
Silvia Reiter

Gurlittstr. 23
20099 Hamburg
Tel. (040) 2 80 89 00
Fax (040) 2803894 – www.wedina.de

Open all year • 59 rooms, including 19 with balcony • Garden, parking; dogs not allowed • Bicycle hire, readings

105/150 €, Breakfast included (WE: 100/135 €)
AE D VISA MC

Exploring Hamburg on one of the hotel bikes

An extraordinary palette of colours awaits you here - in the form of the red, blue, yellow and green buildings on both sides of the Gurlittstrasse. Additional splashes of colour are provided by the summer garden and conservatory where breakfast is taken. The stylish rooms feature a variety of decor and fittings, including parquet floors, terracotta tiles, kitchenettes and balconies. But the establishment is rather more than than simply a place to stay. Art and literature flourish here; works by contemporary artists are on display, and as well as keeping an interestingly stocked library they also organise literary readings here.

Sights nearby: Kunsthalle art gallery, St Michael's Church

Access: Not far from the main station in a side street off "An der Alster" which runs along the east bank of the Aussenalster

22 LANDHAUS FLOTTBEK

Nils Jacobsen

Baron-Voght-Str. 179
22607 Hamburg-Flottbek
Tel. (040) 8 22 74 10
Fax (040) 82274151
n.jacobsen@landhaus-flottbek.de – www.landhaus-flottbek.de

Open all year • 25 rooms, including 1 with balcony and 1 with terrace • Bistro, restaurant with terrace: set lunch 25€, main course 9-22€ • Garden, parking; dogs allowed • Physiotherapy, cookery courses

135/155 €, Breakfast included
AE DC JCB VISA MC

The impressive wood sculptures in the nearby Ernst-Barlach-Haus

With great taste and with no expense spared, this listed 18th century farm has been turned into an unusual place to stay. The old threshing floor is now the reception area, the hayloft and the farmhouse itself feature elegant, individually designed rooms with every contemporary comfort, the stable has become a restaurant and the old eel smokery is now a bistro. The extensive garden with its fine old trees makes a perfect setting for all this. You need look no further for your country retreat!

Sights nearby: Jenisch-Haus, Altona and North German Regional Museum

Access: Exit 28 on A 7

23 ENGEL

Kathrin Engel

Niendorfer Str. 55
22529 Hamburg-Lokstedt
Tel. (040) 55 42 60
Fax (040) 55426500 – www.hotel-engel-hamburg.de

Open all year • 95 rooms • Restaurant with terrace (eve only): set meal 16-30€; half board 15€ • Garden, parking; dogs allowed in hotel, not in restaurant • Sauna, gym

113/123,50 €, Breakfast included (WE: 99 €)

AE D JCB VISA MC

Jogging in the nearby park, the Niendorfer Gehege

This purpose-built hotel in Lokstedt stands in almost rural surroundings, but is well located in relation to the city centre, which can be reached quickly and conveniently by public transport. The bedrooms mostly have furnishings in cherry-wood and mahogany, though some of them are more rustic in character. The breakfast room looks out on to greenery, and the buffet stays open for anyone who has enjoyed a lie-in. Other meals and refreshments are available in the country-style restaurant, on the outdoor terrace or in the rustic bar.

Sights nearby: Hagenbeck's Zoo, Harbour boat trip

Access: Schnelsen Exit on A 7, then by Kollaustrasse (B 447), or Stellingen Exit, then by Julius-Vosseler-Strasse and Oddernskamp

24 BELLEVUE

B. Clinging

Klütstr. 34
31787 Hameln
Tel. (05151) 9 89 10
Fax (05151) 989199 – www.hameln.de/hotels/bellevue

Open all year • 18 rooms, including 1 with balcony and 3 non-smoking • Garden, parking; dogs by arrangement

80/110 €, Breakfast included

AE, Diners, JCB, VISA, MC

Following the "Pied Piper trail" through Hamlin's lovely Old Town

Located in an attractive villa quarter only a few minutes on foot from the Old Town, this compact Art Nouveau dwelling of 1910 is now a pleasant place to spend the night, not least because of the attentive service offered. The comfortable, contemporary rooms feature lightwood furnishings. The buffet breakfast is taken either in the welcoming breakfast room or in fine weather on the terrace overlooking the garden at the back of the building. The garden is also an attractive retreat at any time of day for guests wishing to relax.

Sights nearby: Collegiate church in Fischbeck (7km northwest), Hämelschenburg (11km south)

Access: In Hamelin follow square green signs indicating "Hotel Route"

25 ALTER PACKHOF

Wilhelm Götz

Bremer Schlagd 10-14
34346 Hann. Münden
Tel. (05541) 9 88 90
Fax (05541) 988999 – www.packhof.com

Open all year • 25 rooms, including 13 non-smoking and 1 with disabled access • Cafe; restaurant (closed Jan to Mar, Mon, Sun eve): set lunch 11-15€, set dinner 20-32€; half board 17-25€ • Parking; dogs allowed • Bicycle hire, planned routes for walkers and cyclists

109/152 €, Breakfast included
VISA MC

The historic atmosphere of the Old Town with its total of more than 700 timber-framed buildings

This is a bit like the tale of the Ugly Duckling which turned into a beautiful swan. In 1837 an imposing but rather plain storage building was constructed here, incorporating part of the town wall; it is now a comfortable hotel with a very special something. With views over the valley of the river Weser, the bedrooms are decorated in elegant country-house style which feels in keeping with the age of the building. The bathrooms feature marble floors and washbasin surrounds as well as underfloor heating. There are two mini-suites with their own saunas. Gourmets will love the offerings of the pleasantly rustic restaurant and the freshly baked specialities from the patisserie.

Sights nearby: St Blasiikirche, Old Masters Gallery in Kassel Schloss (23km southwest)

Access: In northwestern corner of Old Town by confluence of Werra and Fulda

26 GUTSHOF

Edeltraud Hoffmann

Lindenstr. 5
38275 Haverlah-Steinlah
Tel. (05341) 33 84 41
Fax (05341) 338442 – www.hotelgutshof.de

Open all year • 23 rooms, including 2 non-smoking • Restaurant with terrace: set meal 18.50-32.50€; half board 18.50€ • Garden, parking; dogs allowed • Organised walks

80/101 €, Breakfast included
VISA MC

Fresh bread from the estate bakery

This quietly located old manor house promises its guests true country hospitality with a touch of refinement. The main building is an 18th century structure with a brick and timber-framed façade; it is complemented by an annexe in similar style featuring a pair of corner turrets. The individually decorated rooms with their period furnishings have a pleasantly nostalgic feel about them. The restaurant is subdivided into a number of separate dining areas and its decor - for example lace doilies - lends it something of the intimate atmosphere of a living room. And of course, no manor house would be complete without its inviting garden terrace.

Sights nearby: Rammelsberg visitor mine and museum and Goslar Old Town (20 km south)

Access: 6 km northwest of Salzgitter-Bad by B 6, turn right in Haverlah

27 LANDHAUS ARTISCHOCKE

B. Stein

Dorfstr. 30
30966 Hemmingen
Tel. (0511) 94 26 46 30
Fax (0511) 94264659 – www.artischocke.com

Open all year • 20 rooms • Restaurant with terrace (closed Mon, midday Tue-Sat): main course 17.50-23.50€ • Parking; dogs allowed

80 €, Breakfast included

AE VISA MC

The country-style cupboards used as wardrobes

This building with its exposed half-timbering on the edge of Hemmingen has long been a favourite with Hanover folk enjoying a day in the countryside. Renamed the "Artichoke" in 1999, it now offers bed as well as board. A warm and welcoming atmosphere is created in the bedrooms by the use of lime-washed furniture in solid wood. The simply furnished and rustic restaurant features pretty antiques and serves international dishes with a Mediterranean focus. When the sun shines you can eat outside in the courtyard in front of the building.

Sights nearby: Herrenhausen gardens and Lower Saxony Regional Museum in Hanover (8 km north)

Access: 8 km south of Hanover by B 3

28 ROSENHOF

G. Heinrichs

Sollingstr. 85
37603 Holzminden
Tel. (05531) 99 59 00
Fax (05531) 995915 – www.hotel-rosenhof-holzminden.de

Closed 1-6 Jan, Christmas to New Year's Eve • 11 rooms, including 1 with balcony and 5 non-smoking • Garden, parking; dogs not allowed

95/125 €, Breakfast included (WE: 88/110 €)
VISA MC

Afternoon tea or coffee on the terrace

Surrounded by the venerable trees of its delightful park, this villa extends a stylish welcome to all its guests. Contemporary works of art complement antiques as charming features of the bedrooms, and the marble bathrooms are a further highlight. Breakfast is taken in an attractive conservatory with a view of the greenery outside. In the evening, you can sit in comfort by the open fire and recover from the exertions of the day.

Sights nearby: Höxter Old Town, Fürstenberg castle museum (12km south)

Access: By B 64, B 83, or B 497

ENGEL

Sigrid Engel

Burgwedeler Str. 151
30916 Isernhagen
Tel. (0511) 97 25 60
Fax (0511) 9725646
info@hotel-engel-isernhagen.de – www.hotel-engel-isernhagen.de

Closed 1-2 Jan, Christmas to New Year's Eve • 28 rooms, including 9 with terrace and 16 non-smoking • Garden, parking; dogs allowed

77/112 €, Breakfast included

AE D VISA MC

The restful garden with its area of native planting

With its timber-framed façade the colour of the local earth, this charming place seems to have grown naturally out of the countryside. Inside there is quite a contrast, both in the main building housing the reception area and breakfast room and the peacefully located guesthouse, where bold colour schemes enhance the country-style furnishings and help create a cheerful and comfortable ambience. Friendly service and the immaculate way in which the rooms are kept make their contribution to your feeling of well-being.

Sights nearby: Marktkirche and Zoo in Hanover (14km south)

Access: From Exit 54 on A 7 via Hohenhorster Bauerschaft

30 ZUM GRÜNEN JÄGER

Claudia Kirchhoff

Itzenbütteler Waldweg 35
21266 Jesteburg-Itzenbüttel
Tel. (04181) 9 22 50
Fax (04181) 922512 – www.gruener-jaeger.com

Open all year • 14 rooms, including 7 non-smoking • Cafe-restaurant with terrace: main courses 6.50-14€; half board 15€ • Garden, parking; dogs allowed • Bicycle and canoe hire, children's riding lessons

76,50/92 €, Breakfast included
AE VISA MC

The little spring in front of the building

Tucked away on the edge of the forest, this establishment is given a refined look by the two side wings with their thatched roofs. The building dates from as long ago as 1912, but doesn't show its age! The various interiors owe their attractiveness to country-style decor with a Mediterranean touch, while the warm colour schemes in the bedrooms and the restaurant help create a welcoming ambience. In the bedrooms, natural wood or iron bedsteads are an additional special feature.

Sights nearby: Bossard art centre, Schwarze Berge big game park in Rosengarten (15km north)

Access: 3km northwest of Jesteburg towards Buchholz

31 **DER ROMANTIK-HOF**

Stefanie Bonitz-Sirpas

Ankerstr. 4
26736 Krummhörn-Greetsiel
Tel. (04926) 91 21 51
Fax (04926) 912153 – www.romantik-hof.de

Open all year • 23 rooms, including 3 with terrace, 20 non-smoking and 1 with disabled access • Restaurant with terrace, residents only (closed midday and Mon): main course from 15€; half board included in room rate • Garden, parking; dogs allowed in hotel, not in restaurant • Wellness facilities, several saunas, bicycle hire, torchlight walks

124/154 €, Breakfast included
Credit cards not accepted

The facilities of the "Mona Lisa" wellness and beauty studio

On the way out of Greetsiel towards the harbour, this newly-built establishment with its trio of prominent gables only opened in 2001. It offers a tasteful ambience together with contemporary comforts. The comfortable rooms have been designed in a refined country-house style featuring leather trimmings and harmonious colour schemes. The same style continues in the dining areas: both the elegant "Schlemmerinsel" in muted red and the cosy "Schwalbennest" in typically Frisian blue have menus featuring locally caught fish and seafood.

Sights nearby: Ludgerikirche in Norden (18km north), East Frisian Regional Museum (20km southeast)

Access: From Emden via Hinte, Jennelt and Eilsum

32 WITTHUS

Karsten Eilers

Kattrepel 7
26736 Krummhörn-Greetsiel
Tel. (04926) 9 20 00
Fax (04926) 920092 – www.witthus.de

Closed 13 Nov to 15 Dec • 16 rooms, including 9 non-smoking • Cafe; restaurant with terrace (closed Tue-Thu until 3pm in low season; Mon): set meal 23-39.90€; half board 15€ • Garden, parking; dogs not allowed

88/135 €, Breakfast included

JCB VISA MC

East Frisian tea - up here, it's not a beverage, it's a way of life!

The perfectly preserved, traffic-free fishing village of Greetsiel on the bracing East Frisian coast is a lovely holiday destination, and the intimate "White House" with its pair of annexes is just the place to make the most of it. Enjoy the best time of the year in exactly the right kind of setting: the rooms have been individually decorated and furnished with loving care and feature subtle pastel colour schemes. Breakfast is taken in the gallery of the restaurant, where changing art exhibitions are on display and on fine days there is an attractive terrace where you can dine, linger over a coffee - or learn more about the Frisian tea ceremony!

Sights nearby: Manningaburg at Pewsum (10km south), Norden tea museum (18km north)

Access: From Emden via Hinte, Jennelt and Eilsum

33 LA VILLA

Heinz-Günter Blank

Vormann-Otten-Weg 12
26465 Langeoog (Insel)
Tel. (04972) 7 77
Fax (04972) 1390 – www.hotel-lavilla.de

Closed 6-31 Jan • 9 rooms, including 1 with balcony and 1 non-smoking • Restaurant (eve only and residents only): half board 27€ • Garden; dogs by arrangement • Sauna, jacuzzi, solarium, bicycle hire

124/198 €, Breakfast included
Credit cards not accepted

The lavish fish buffet every Friday

This establishment brings off the balancing act between the elegant and the functional, the solid and the comfortable with great aplomb. The bedrooms feature stylish cherrywood furnishings, while the bathrooms are bright and welcoming with much use made of marble. If you don't want to spend your time exploring the island's sand-dunes or its 18km-long beach, you can take it easy on the roof terrace or lounge on the lawn. Then, for added warmth, there's a sauna and hot whirlpool bath, not to mention the comfortable sitting room with its open fire.

Sights nearby: Shipping museum and North Sea aquarium, dune cemetery with grave of Lale Andersen

Access: Ferry from Bensersiel (c.45 min); cars not allowed on Langeoog

34 ALTE POST

Bernd Schreder und Ingo Koernig

Kirchstr. 15
29439 Lüchow
Tel. (05841) 9 75 40
Fax (05841) 5048
www.marktplatz-luechowdannenberg.de

Open all year • 14 rooms, including 4 non-smoking • Restaurant with terrace (eve only; closed Mon): main course 11-22€ • Garden, parking; dogs allowed

76 €, Breakfast included

AE JCB VISA MC

The small-town idyll of Lüchow

In the town centre, this historic building has kept and indeed enhanced all its old-fashioned charm. The comfortable bedrooms with their exposed timbers and solid pine furnishings have a rustically refined ambience, while cheerful decor and a conglomeration of well-chosen objects help create an unusual and original atmosphere in the restaurant. The bistro-style breakfast room features an array of luxuriant plants. The courtyard where the horses were once harnessed is a real jewel, set in its lovely framework of half-timbered buildings and lavishly planted.

Sights nearby: Wendlandhof Lübeln Rundling museum (5 km west), Breese estate chapel in Bruche (12 km north)

Access: By B 493 or B 248

35 ZUM HEIDKRUG

Michael Röhm

Am Berge 5
21335 Lüneburg
Tel. (04131) 2 41 60
Fax (04131) 241620 – www.zumheidkrug.de

Closed 2 weeks in Jan, 1 week at Easter, 2 weeks in summer holidays • 7 rooms • Restaurant (closed Sun, Mon): set lunch max 20€, set dinner 36-55€; half board 20€ • Parking; dogs allowed

82/94 €, Breakfast included

Intriguing architectural details such as pointed arches and coupled niches

Dating from the second half of the 15th century, this brick-built Gothic edifice is located in the picturesque countryside of the Wasserviertel. As well as being a temple to haute cuisine, it offers its guests refined country-house style rooms with solid wood furnishings. The elegant restaurant has a traditional atmosphere, with rustic ceiling beams and red brickwork recalling the edifice's origins. Wicker chairs and candlelight create a cosy and romantic atmosphere. In summer, meals are served in the garden.

Sights nearby: St Johanniskirche, Lüne monastery (2km north)

Access: Not far from St Johanniskirche in Old Town

36 BELVEDERE AM MEER

Monika von Schlachta

Viktoriastr. 13
26548 Norderney (Insel)
Tel. (04932) 9 23 90
Fax (04932) 83590
www.hotel-belvedere.de

Closed 1 Jan to 31 Mar, 16 Oct to 31 Dec • 21 rooms, including 11 with balcony • Garden, parking; dogs not allowed • Indoor pool, sauna, steam bath, jacuzzi

145/230 €, Breakfast included
Credit cards not accepted

No two ways about it: the rooms with a sea view

Once the summer residence of the Royal Family of Hanover, the island of Nordeney still exudes the sophisticated allure of the 19th century. So too does this white villa right by the beach, which offers intimate accommodation of great charm. The rooms are all individually decorated, and some of them feature period furniture. The terraced building opposite has apartments with cooking facilities. The splendid sea views from the breakfast room will get your day off to a great start.

Sights nearby: Kurhaus and Kurpark

Access: Ferry from Norddeich (c. 1hr): car use restricted on island

37 LANDHAUS OSTERHAUS

Karl F. Osterhaus

Bramstr. 109a
49090 Osnabrück
Tel. (0541) 9 62 12 31
Fax (0541) 65820 – www.osterhaus.de

Open all year • 14 rooms, including 1 with disabled access and 4 non-smoking • Parking; dogs not allowed • Gym, tennis, bicycle hire

96/102 €, Breakfast included (WE: 90/96 €)
AE JCB VISA MC

Coffee, tea and mineral water are included in the room rate

This contemporary country house offers its guests a number of special features; the exceptionally roomy bedrooms have period furnishings, a kitchenette and extra-long (2.20 metre) beds. So you will really be able to spread yourself around! In addition, all the bathrooms are lit by daylight. For breakfast, you sit in wicker chairs at glass-topped tables in the granite-tiled reception area.

Sights nearby: City Hall with Peace Chamber, Marienkirche, Felix-Nussbaum-Haus

Access: From Autobahn Exit Osnabrück-Nord, 2km north of city centre in a side street east of Bramscher Strasse

38 TIETJEN'S HÜTTE

Erika Schmidt-Tietjen

An der Hamme 1
27711 Osterholz-Scharmbeck
Tel. (04791) 9 22 00
Fax (04791) 922036
www.tietjens-huette.de

Open all year • 9 rooms, including 5 non-smoking, 4 with balcony • Cafe; restaurant with terrace (closed Mon): set meals from 22€ • Garden, parking; dogs allowed • Painting courses, organised bicycle hire

90/103 €, Breakfast included

AE D VISA MC

A trip aboard an old peat barge, down the river and back through the years

Sited at the edge of the "Devil's Fen" on the banks of the slow-moving River Hamme, this characterful establishment seems part of the landscape and is certain to cast an instant spell on you: the overhanging thatched roof, the timber-framed façade and the idyllic location look as if they have remained unchanged for centuries. Inside there are rooms furnished in traditional, even nostalgic style, while the rustic restaurant with its hallway opening onto the fen is tastefully decorated with all kinds of atmospheric bric-a-brac. On fine summer days, make straight for the terrace by the river.

Sights nearby: St-Marien monastery church in Osterholz-Scharmbeck (3km northwest), Worpswede artists village (11km east)

Access: 3km southeast of Osterholz-Scharmbeck on Worpswede road

39 SCHÖNAU

U. Hacke

Peiner Str. 17
31228 Peine-Stederdorf
Tel. (05171) 99 80
Fax (05171) 998166 – www.hotel-schoenau.de

Open all year • 47 rooms, including 1 with balcony • Beer Stube, restaurant with terrace (closed Sun eve): main course 12.60-18€; half board from 15€ • Parking; dogs allowed

90/100 €, Breakfast included (WE: 80/90 €)
AE Diners VISA MC

We most liked

The comfortable rooms with oriel windows

A family tradition of hospitality began here in the Stederdorf part of Pein in 1915. In 1955 the original building was replaced by a new structure, which has subsequently been extended and modernised several times. It is now a stately establishment, offering accommodation ranging from the functional to the attractively elegant. The stylish restaurant where meals are served by a smartly turned-out team is decorated in welcoming colours, while the "Picture Room" has a more nostalgic and playful character.

Sights nearby: Chocolate museum, Braunschweig cathedral (26 km east)

Access: On B 444; north from Exit 52 on A 2

40 DAS WEISSE HAUS

Annette und Carsten Kindermann

Südender Str. 1
26180 Rastede
Tel. (04402) 32 43
Fax (04402) 84726
www.kindermann-weisseshaus.de

Closed 1-10 Jan • 3 rooms • Restaurant with terrace (closed Thu, midday Mon, Tue, Wed): set meal 23-44€; half board 19.50€ • Garden, parking; dogs allowed • Bicycle hire, cookery courses

79/105 €, Breakfast included
Credit cards not accepted

The restaurant "gallery" with works by local artist Nicole Hitz

This thatched house represents a dream come true for the Kindermann family, and their guests are left in no doubt about the devotion with which they run their welcoming establishment; the "White House" radiates a truly hearty family atmosphere. The bedrooms are tastefully furnished in natural woods - those on the ground floor give on to the pretty garden. Should you find the ambience so much to your liking that it becomes difficult to get up, don't worry - breakfast is served until 1pm. However, this means you will have missed one of the day's meals, which are served in the friendly, country-style restaurant or on the lovely terrace.

Sights nearby: Jaderberg Jaderpark (11 km north), Oldenburg regional museum of art and cultural history (14 km south)

Access: Exit 12 on A 29, on southern side of Rastede

41 **ALTES ZOLLHAUS**

Dieter Girnus

Hauptstr. 5
31737 Rinteln-Todenmann
Tel. (05751) 9 71 80
Fax (05751) 7761 – www.altes-zollhaus-rinteln.de

Open all year • 21 rooms, including 5 non-smoking • Restaurant with terrace: main course 12-24€; half board 17€ • Garden, parking; dogs allowed in hotel, not in restaurant • Sauna, solarium

78/113 €, Breakfast included

AE DC VISA MC

The delightful view from the terrace over Rinteln and the Weser uplands

This establishment was originally a toll house, built in 1804 under the reign of Prince Elector Wilhelm of Hessen. However, in 1816 it became a guest house, and the long tradition of hospitality was continued when it was converted into a hotel-restaurant in 1975. Guests are accommodated in attractive rooms, solidly furnished in cherrywood. Exuding traditional charm, the restaurant is subdivided by wooden pillars into a number of intimate little niches while an open fire provides welcoming warmth.

Sights nearby: Bückeburg helicopter museum (12 km north), Minden cathedral (19 km northwest)

Access: 3 km northwest of Rinteln towards Minden

42 ROMANTIK HOTEL JOSTHOF

Jörg Hansen

Am Lindenberg 1
21376 Salzhausen
Tel. (04172) 9 09 80
Fax (04172) 6225 – www.josthof.de

Closed 24 Dec • 16 rooms, including 1 with disabled access • Restaurant with terrace: set meal 32-46€ • Parking; dogs allowed

98/109 €, Breakfast included

AE JCB VISA

The choice of 250 different types of grappa and fruit brandies

Thatched timber-framed structures and an ancient church make a romantic setting for your stay here. Mentioned for the first time in 962, this inviting old farmstead consists of a group of charming buildings which have matured over the centuries. It houses bedrooms featuring comfortable, rustic furnishings - including a number of antique pieces - complemented by bright colours and fabrics. The dining areas have a delightfully intimate character, with lovely tiled stoves, timeless beams and atmospheric decor forming a harmonious background to your mealtimes. When the sun comes out, there is a garden terrace for the perfect combination of cold beer and fresh northern air.

Sights nearby: Lüneburg Heath deer park (9km west), Lüneburg Old Town (18km east)

Access: From Exit 40 on A 7 via Garlstorf and Gödenstorf

43 HOF TÜTSBERG

Bernd Rummler

29640 Schneverdingen-Tütsberg
Tel. (05199) 9 00
Fax (05199) 9050 – www.tuetsberg.de

Open all year • 23 rooms, including 7 non-smoking • Restaurant with terrace: set meal 19-38€; half board 19€ • Garden, parking; dogs allowed • Sauna, solarium, jacuzzi, massage, stables, bicycle hire, guided walks, carriage drives, wine tasting, craft evenings

99/125 €, Breakfast included

AE D VISA MC

Setting off into the blue on one of the establishment's own horses

Surounded by the Lüneburg Heath nature park, this idyllic place offers an escape from the stresses and strains of everyday life. Approached through working farm buildings, the hotel is a picturesque half-timbered place with a thatched roof. It has two separate guesthouses. Bedrooms feature furnishings in white or in natural wood: comfortable and welcoming are the words that spring to mind. The restaurant consists of three separate little dining areas, decorated in styles ranging from rustic to sophisticated. Best of all, though, is the garden, where you can find a place to sit in the dappled shade of the fine old trees.

Sights nearby: Ralf Schumacher karting centre (on A 7, 9km east), Bispingen birds of prey centre (14km southeast)

Access: From Exit 43 on A 7 towards Behringen, then Schneverdingen-Heber, turn right in Scharrl

44 GÄSTEHAUS SCHLOSS BOTHMER

Eveline Königsbauer

Alte Dorfstr. 15
29690 Schwarmstedt-Bothmer
Tel. (05071) 30 37
Fax (05071) 3039 – www.schlossbothmer.de

Open all year • 9 rooms, all with balcony or terrace, 2 non-smoking • Restaurant with terrace: set meal 26.50-46.50€; half board by arrangement • Garden, parking; dogs allowed • Riding

105/145 €, Breakfast included

AE VISA MC

The suite with sauna and open fire

Guests are not accommodated in the castle itself, which is still privately owned, but you will be just as happy in the elegant ambience of its guest-house. The rooms are comfortable and stylishly furnished - marble bathrooms come as standard - and each has its own mini-conservatory with a view over the superb park around the castle. The restaurant too has an airy conservatory, while from the bar you can see into the adjacent riding hall.

Sights nearby: Hodenhagen Serengeti Park (17km northeast), Walsrode bird park (24km north)

Access: 3km northwest of Schwarmstedt towards Ahlden-Bothmer, follow "Schloss Bothmer" signs

45 WINDMÜLLER

Kristine Specht

Kirchweg 3
21720 Steinkirchen
Tel. (04142) 8 19 80
Fax (04142) 819820 – www.hotel-windmueller.de

Open all year • 25 rooms, including 3 with balcony, 19 non-smoking and 2 with disabled access • Cafe; restaurant with terrace (closed midday Mon-Sat in winter): main course from 8€, set dinner 20-25€; half board from 12€ • Parking; dogs allowed • Bicycle hire, gym, sauna

82/92 €, Breakfast included

VISA MC

Dishes featuring beef from the establishment's own Galloway herd

The springtime sea of blossom makes an enchanting sight here in the "Altes Land" along the River Elbe downstream from Hamburg. Among the orchards, the peaceful little villages with their thatched cottages seem untouched by time. Somehow everything seems to be just as it should, especially in Steinkirchen, where this red and white timber-framed farmstead of 1746 stands behind the church. Together with its annexe, it features comfortable rooms, some with wood floors. There's even a suite with a jacuzzi. The welcoming restaurant has an open fire and atmospheric decor, while outside there is a delightful terrace beneath the pear trees.

Sights nearby: Altes Land Museum in Jork (7km southeast), Schwedenspeicher Museum in Stade (12km northwest)

Access: From B 73 between Stade and Buxtehude via Horneburg, Neuenkirchen and Mittlekirchen

BRUNNENHOF

Albert Wörner

29562 Suhlendorf-Kölau
Tel. (05820) 8 80
Fax (05820) 1777 – www.hotel-brunnenhof.de

Open all year • 43 rooms, including 4 with balcony, 3 non-smoking • Restaurant with terrace: main course 8.50-17.50€; half board 15€ • Garden, parking; dogs allowed in hotel, not in restaurant • Indoor pool, sauna, massage, wellness facilities, tennis, table tennis, badminton, bicycle hire, carriage rides, guided walks and cycle trips, paddock, trekking

42/58 €, Breakfast included

AE VISA MC

The glorious sense of space

The motto of the "Brunnenhof" might well be "Don't look a gift horse in the mouth". But it's not just equestrians who will appreciate what is on offer in this 18th century timber-framed and thatched-roofed residence, where as well as horse boxes and a riding hall there is a variety of types of accommodation. Riding lessons are available for adults and children, but even if you don't intend to saddle up, you will feel at home in both the functional bedrooms or the country-style holiday homes, and you will enjoy dining in the rustic, tiled restaurant. All around there is unspoiled countryside to explore.

Sights nearby: Suhlendorf crafts museum (2km north), Hundertwasser station at Uelzen (17km west)

Access: 2km south of Suhlendorf on B 71 between Uelzen and Salzwedel

47 LANDHAUS WALSRODE

Lieselotte Wolff

Oskar-Wolff-Str. 1
29664 Walsrode
Tel. (05161) 9 86 90
Fax (05161) 2352 – www.landhaus-walsrode.de

Closed 1-2 Jan, 15-31Dec • 19 rooms, including 1 with disabled access • Garden, parking; dogs allowed • Outdoor pool

85/155 €, Breakfast included
AE VISA MC

The twittering of the birds in the hotel garden

Guests arriving here could be forgiven for feeling like aristocrats, leaving behind the city residence to spend time relaxing on the country estate. You'll certainly live like a lord in this stylish country house, set in a lovely park planted with rhododendrons, oaks, beeches and limes. Individually decorated bedrooms, a spacious sitting room with an open fire and an elegant breakfast room with a view onto the park make a delightful setting for your stay. Add the attentive and friendly service, and the only question is - will you ever want to go back to town?

Sights nearby: Walsrode bird park (5km north), Hodenhagen Serengeti park (15km south)

Access: Exit 27 on A 27

48 KOCH

Hubert Trimpe

€€ Bahnhofstr.2
28844 Weyhe-Kirchweyhe
Tel. (04203) 8 14 70
Fax (04203) 814739 – www.hotelkoch.de

Open all year • 21 rooms, all with showers on landing • Restaurant with terrace (closed Sun eve): set lunch 8.95-19.99€, set dinner 20-32.50€; half board 24.50€ • Beer garden, garden, parking; dogs allowed • Solarium, cookery courses

68,50/74 €, Breakfast included

AE Ⓓ VISA MC

The bridal suite with its superb four-poster

On the edge of the built-up area on the road towards Bremen, this imposing courtyard building with its hipped roof dates from 1786 and was originally a coal depot. The soot has long since been swept away, though: you'll find the individually furnished rooms are neatly kept and those in the annexe have their own kitchenette. The restaurant is decorated in warm colours and offers local and international specialities. The railway runs nearby, and so the heated and part-canopied beer-garden is called the "Draisine", after those strange self-propelled wagons used by railway maintenance men.

Sights nearby: Universum Science Center in Bremen (15km north)

Access: From Exit 56 on A 1 towards Dreye, Kirchweyhe

49 **WITTINGER TOR**

Tanja Beckmann

Salzwedeler Str. 4
29378 Wittingen
Tel. (05831) 2 53 00
Fax (05831) 253010
www.wittinger-tor.de

Closed 1 Jan, 24 Dec • 16 rooms, including 1 with bathroom on landing • Restaurant with terrace (open eve only Mon-Sat, all day Sun): set lunch 10-19€, set dinner 15-25€ • Garden, parking; dogs allowed

90/100 €, Breakfast included (WE: 80/90 €)
AE VISA MC

The bathrooms lit by natural light

The "Gateway to Wittingen" is open to welcome its guests with real feeling and generosity. Sited on the edge of Wittingen where the eastern gate of the town's defences once stood, it consists of an early-20th century building and a modern extension completed in 1998. The bedrooms have contemporary, functional furnishings, while the three separate sections of the restaurant are resplendent in handsome late-19th century decor. A special touch is added by the collection of coffee-pots and musical instruments.

Sights nearby: Lüben round village (7 km north), Hankensbüttel otter sanctuary (10 km west)

Access: By B 244

50 BUCHENHOF

Jochen Semken

Ostendorfer Str. 16
27726 Worpswede
Tel. (04792) 9 33 90
Fax (04792) 933929
info@hotel-buchenhof.de – www.hotel-buchenhof.de

Open all year • 28 rooms, including 4 with balcony, 1 with disabled access and 15 non-smoking • Half board in local restaurant 18€ • Garden, parking; dogs allowed • Sauna, steam bath, solarium, bicycle hire, guided tours, punt trips

85/115 €, Breakfast included
VISA MC

A stroll to the Expressionist sculpture of the Niedersachsenstein

At the end of the 19th century a group of painters fleeing academic conventions set up an artists' colony in the striking, almost primeval landscape on the edge of the "Devil's Fen". One of their number was named Hans am Ende; in 1895, on a little wooded plot of land, he built "Buchenhof", this Art Nouveau-style villa, for himself and his wife. Since then the house has hardly changed, and thanks to its antique furnishings still conveys the atmosphere of the age in which it was built. Works by Hans am Ende can be seen everywhere, making a stay here a fascinating excursion into the glory days of the Worpswede artists colony.

Sights nearby: Barkenhoff art centre, Grosse Kunstschau gallery, Worpswede

Access: From Exit 17 on A 27 towards Ritterhude/Osterholz-Scharmbeck; on the Worpshausen/Lilienthal road in Worpswede

51 **EICHENHOF**

Dörte Köhnke

Ostendorfer Str. 13
27726 Worpswede
Tel. (04792) 26 76
Fax (04792) 4427 – www.worpswede.de/eichenhof

Open all year • 20 rooms, including 6 with disabled access and 3 non-smoking • Restaurant with terrace (eve only): set meal 33-55€ • Garden, parking; dogs allowed in hotel, not in restaurant • Health and beauty facilities with indoor pool, ayurveda, massage, bicycle hire, art walks

143/161 €, Breakfast included

VISA

Exploring the picturesque nature park

To come here is to leave the world of everyday far behind. In the middle of a splendid nature park, a 200 metre long avenue of oaks leads to a group of buildings which once formed the core of a country estate. But here in the peace and quiet of Nature there's little trace of dusty nostalgia; instead, the designers have deliberately set out to provide a stimulating contrast to the historic heritage, evident in the varied concepts for the bedrooms as well as in the restaurant - provocatively named "ARTisst" - where swags and drapes on walls and ceiling set a striking and stylishly unconventional tone.

Sights nearby: Worpswede art gallery, "Käseglocke" villa with applied arts museum

Access: From Exit 17 on A 27 towards Ritterhude/Osterholz-Scharmbeck

Nordrhein-Westfalen

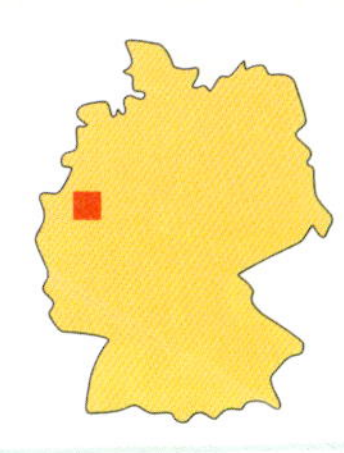

There's much more to Germany's most populous region than the great cities along the Rhine, though their superb landmarks and museums put Bonn, Cologne and Düsseldorf among the country's favourite destinations. A real feeling for living tradition attracts visitors from Germany and abroad; many of them come at Carnival time, to see how the Rhinelanders' vitality and devotion to making merry has endured over the centuries. To the north spreads the vast conurbation of the Ruhr, which has cast off its rust-belt image: nowadays an extraordinary industrial heritage mixes with the woods, lakes and parklands which penetrate into its very heart. Further north still is the tranquil Münsterland with its moated castles and manor houses, while to the east rise the cool uplands of the Sauerland, where some of the country's biggest breweries have their home. In fact, a taste for beer is shared throughout the region, with everyone staying fiercely faithful to their local brew; tell a Düsseldorfer to swap his usual glass of "Alt" for a "Kölsch", the pale, hoppy lager downed in and around Cologne, and he may decide to teach you a lesson in local pride – by buying you a drink!

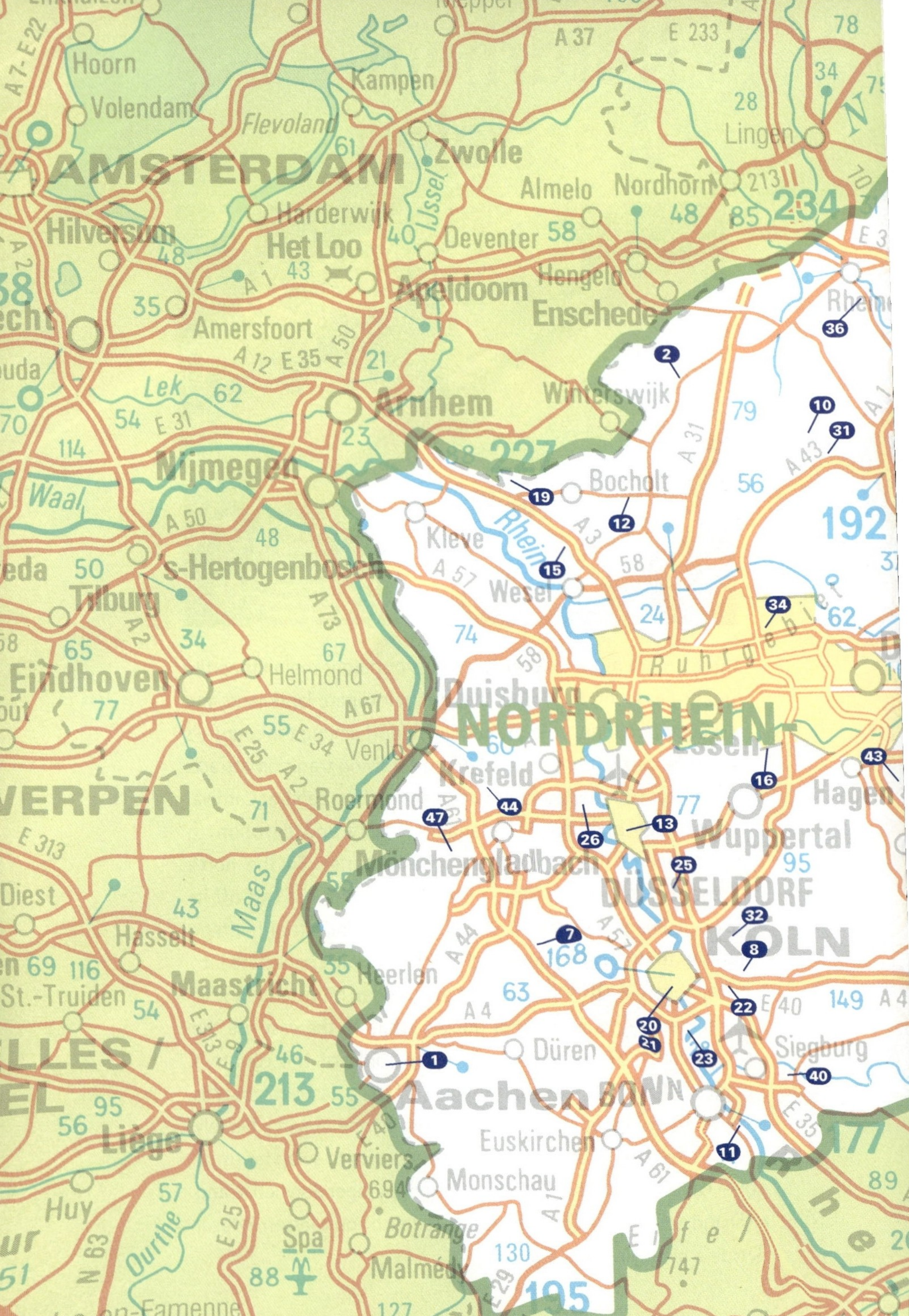

Hoorn
Volendam
Flevoland
Kampen
Zwolle
AMSTERDAM
IJssel
Almelo
Nordhorn
Lingen
234
Hilversum
Harderwijk
Het Loo
Deventer
Hengelo
Enschede
Apeldoorn
Amersfoort
Lek
Arnhem
Winterswijk
Nijmegen
227
Bocholt
Waal
Rhein
Kleve
's-Hertogenbosch
Tilburg
Wesel
Eindhoven
Helmond
Ruhrgebiet
Duisburg
NORDRHEIN-
Essen
Venlo
Krefeld
Hagen
Roermond
Wuppertal
Mönchengladbach
DÜSSELDORF
Diest
Maas
KÖLN
Hasselt
St.-Truiden
Maastricht
Heerlen
Düren
Siegburg
Aachen
213
Bonn
Liège
Verviers
Euskirchen
Monschau
Huy
Ourthe
Spa
Botrange
Eifel
Malmedy
192
177
195

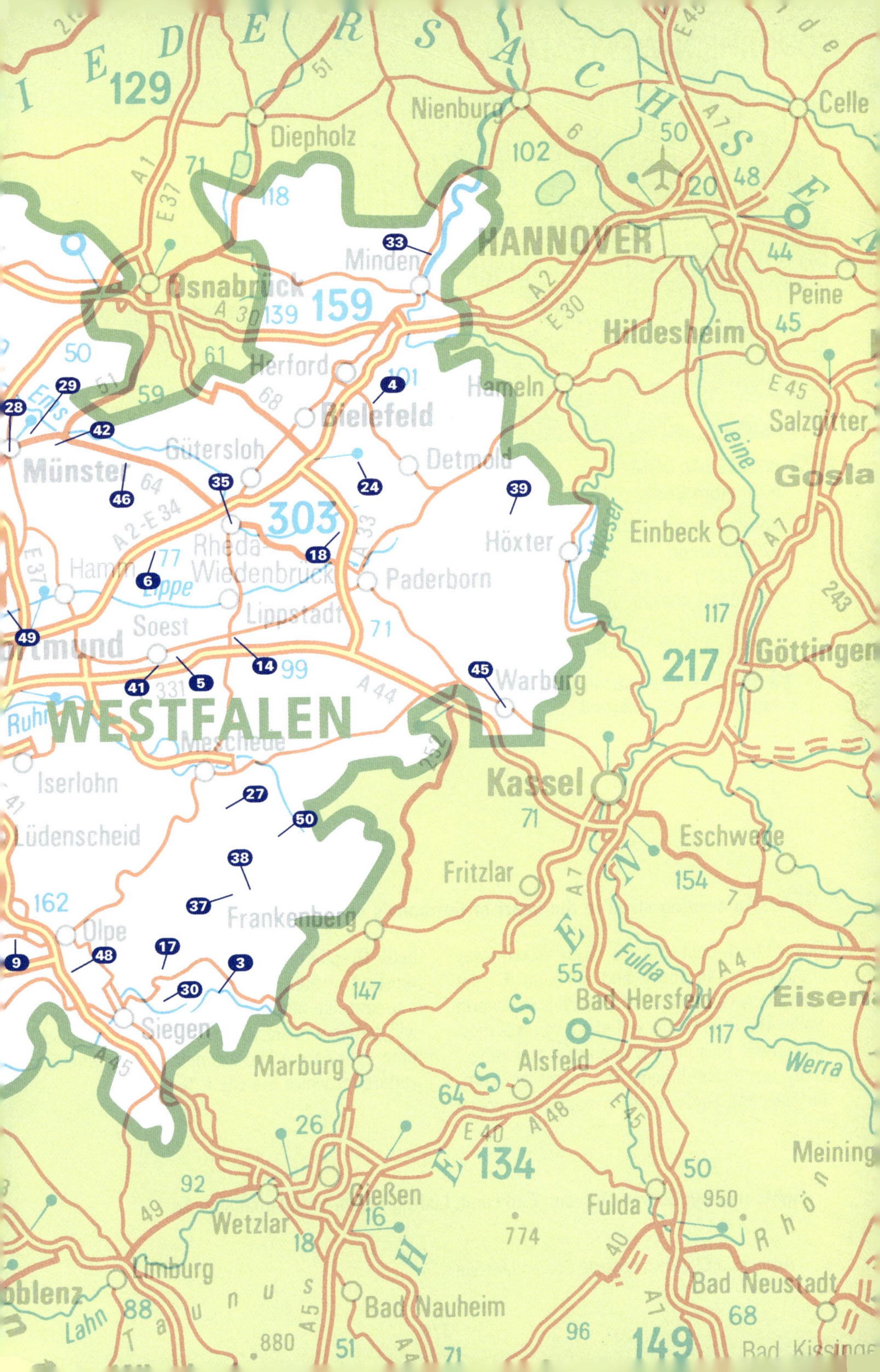

NIEDERSACHSEN
WESTFALEN
HESSEN
HANNOVER
Nienburg
Celle
Diepholz
Minden
Osnabrück
Peine
Hildesheim
Herford
Bielefeld
Hameln
Salzgitter
Münster
Gütersloh
Detmold
Gosla
Rheda-Wiedenbrück
Hamm
Höxter
Einbeck
Paderborn
Lippstadt
Soest
rtmund
Göttingen
Warburg
Meschede
Iserlohn
Kassel
Lüdenscheid
Eschwege
Fritzlar
Frankenberg
Olpe
Siegen
Bad Hersfeld
Eisen
Marburg
Alsfeld
Meining
Gießen
Fulda
Wetzlar
Limburg
oblenz
Bad Nauheim
Bad Neustadt
Bad Kissinge
Taunus
Rhön
Ems
Lippe
Ruhr
Leine
Weser
Fulda
Werra
Lahn
129
159
303
217
134
149

1 BRÜLLS AM DOM

Hannelore Brülls

Rommelsgasse 2 (Hühnermarkt)
52062 Aachen
Tel. (0241) 3 17 04
Fax (0241) 404326

Closed 21-31 Dec • 10 rooms • Dogs not allowed

95/120 €, Breakfast included
Credit cards not accepted

An evening stroll in the heart of Germany's old coronation city

This old brick-built edifice is nicely tucked away in Aachen's Old Town, and although it's not particularly easy to find, the search is well worth while. The Brüll family will make you feel most welcome in their lavishly appointed and impeccably run establishment. The rooms are comfortable and some of them boast four-poster beds. Despite these luxurious surroundings, the prospect of breakfast in the delightful, almost museum-like ambience of the breakfast rooms will certainly make you want to be up in good time - they are a fine example of the domestic culture for which the city is famous.

Sights nearby: Couven Museum, Cathedral, Ludwig Forum for International Art

Access: In Old Town opposite Couven Museum

2 HAUS IM FLÖR

F. und S. Bonato

Hörsteloe 49
48683 Ahaus-Ottenstein
Tel. (02567) 93 99
Fax (02567) 939994 – www.haus-im-floer.de

Closed 10 days in Feb, 2 weeks in the school summer holidays and around Christmas • 19 rooms • Restaurant with terrace (closed midday Sat; Mon): main course 14.50-27.50€ • Garden, parking; dogs not allowed • Bicycle hire, organised walks

80/85 €, Breakfast included

AE VISA

The rooms with a view of the beautiful little lake

This little hotel, built in classic Münsterland style, stands just outside the town, on the edge of the wood and set in glorious extensive gardens which include a pond. Enthusiastically managed and spotlessly maintained by the family who own it, the hotel itself offers guests the choice of rooms furnished in either pale-stained oak or in natural beechwood: all are extremely clean and well looked-after. In the booths and snugs of the restaurant, the dark, warm-toned wood matches the pleasantly sophisticated atmosphere.

Sights nearby: Vreden Hamaland museum (11km southwest), Ahaus moated castle (11km east)

Access: 9km west of Ahaus via Wessum and Ottenstein, then towards Alstätte

3 LAHNTAL-HOTEL

Gerhard Birkelbach

Sieg-Lahn-Str. 23
57334 Bad Laasphe-Feudingen
Tel. (02754) 12 85
Fax (02754) 1286 – www.lahntalhotel.de

Open all year • 22 rooms, all with air conditioning, including 18 with balcony and 15 non-smoking • Restaurant (closed Tues): set lunch 21.90-42.50 €, main courses from 14.80 €, half board 15 € • Garden, parking, dogs allowed only on arrangement • Bicycle hire, cooking courses, organised walks, carriage rides

98/128 €, Breakfast included

AE JCB VISA MC

The sumptuous breakfast buffet

This hospitable establishment awaits its guests on the main road through quiet little Feudingen. The bedrooms are in elegant country style, and it's obvious that great care has been taken to create harmonious colour schemes. Many of the bathrooms make use of marble. The apartments all bear the name of a native plant, and some of them have a stove and a jacuzzi. The lavishly decorated restaurant has a tastefully rustic ambience, and offers good home cooking.

Sights nearby: Panorama park Sauerland (22 km northwest)

Access: From Exit 21 on the A 45 via Siegen and Nepthen; from there continue past Deuz, Walpersdorf and Volkholz

4 **ROMANTIK HOTEL ARMINIUS**
Christof Blomeyer

Ritterstr. 2
32105 Bad Salzuflen
Tel. (05222) 36 60
Fax (05222) 366111 – www.hotelarminius.de

Open all year • 66 rooms, including 20 non-smoking • Restaurant with terrace: set lunch 21.50-39.50€, set dinner 21.50-89€; half board from 21.50€ • Parking; dogs allowed • Sauna, solarium, gym, jacuzzi, massage, organised walks, cookery courses, wine seminars

115 €, Breakfast included (WE: 92 €)
AE D VISA MC

The restaurant with its cosy nooks and crannies

There's no getting away here from the story of Arminius, the Germanic hero who smashed the legions of Roman General Varus at the Battle of the Teutoburger Forest in AD9. Even the suites are called after those loved by Hermann (to give him his German name). The whole ambience is thoroughy historic (though perhaps not quite 1st century in style), not least because the hotel consists of five delightful 16th century timber-framed buildings (together with two modern ones) in the Old Town. The stylish and spacious rooms have lime-washed furniture and some of them feature historic elements as well.

Sights nearby: Bielefeld Old Town (20 km southwest), Hermann monument (22 km southeast)

Access: Exit 29 or 31 on A 2

5 **HOF HUECK**

Volker Kirst

Im Kurpark
59505 Bad Sassendorf
Tel. (02921) 9 61 30
Fax (02921) 961350 – www.hofhueck.de

Open all year • 12 rooms, all non-smoking • Cafe; restaurant with terrace (closed Mon): set lunch 11-22.50€, set dinner 11-38€; half board 18€ • Parking; dogs not allowed • Bicycle hire

98/108 €, Breakfast included

AE D VISA MC

The good night's sleep guaranteed by the quiet location

This timber-framed 17th century structure originally stood on a site 35km away, but was then taken apart and rebuilt here in the Kurpark at Bad Sassendorf. It's an idyllic location for an inviting building of no small historic interest. The comfortable bedrooms are in a timelessly elegant style, while the restaurant, which rises up through two floors, is in typical Westphalian style, enhanced by a fine array of old farm implements. In this welcoming atmosphere you are served with choice dishes based on the cuisine of the region.

Sights nearby: Soest Old Town (6 km west), Möhne dam (17 km southwest)

Access: Exit 57 on A 45 then by B 475 and B 1

6 ALT VELLERN

Helmut Stichling

Dorfstr. 21
59269 Beckum-Vellern
Tel. (02521) 8 71 70
Fax (02521) 871758 – www.alt-vellern.de

Closed Easter, Christmas • 33 rooms, including 4 with disabled access and 8 non-smoking • Restaurant with terrace (closed Fri eve to midday Sun): set meal 15-35€; half board 15€ • Parking; dogs allowed in restaurant, not in hotel • Bicycle hire

88/150 €, Breakfast included

AE · Diners · JCB · VISA · MC

Dining in the garden restaurant on a fine day

This hospitable establishment stands on the main road through Vellern. Guests are accommodated in the main building and annexe in rooms mostly featuring cherrywood furnishings; those in the annexe are more spacious. The place is family-run with great care and attention, and guests are soon made to feel at home, not least in the welcoming dining rooms in traditional Westphalian style, with plenty of dark wood, a fireplace and choice decoration.

Sights nearby: Shrine of St Prudentia in Beckum parish church (4km southwest), Vornholz moated castle (16km north)

Access: Exit 20 on A 2; at 1st major junction in Beckum (by Autohaus) turn left into Zementstrasse, then left at next traffic lights into Oelder Strasse

7 **LANDHAUS DANIELSHOF**

Petra Brünker

Hauptstr. 3
50181 Bedburg-Kaster
Tel. (02272) 98 00
Fax (02272) 980200 – www.danielshof.de

Closed 1-8 Jan, 27-31 Dec • 39 rooms, including 3 with disabled access and 20 non-smoking • Restaurant with terrace: set lunch 16-23€, set dinner 21-28€; half board 16.50€ • Garden, parking; dogs allowed • Bicycle hire

102/112 €, Breakfast included (WE: 91/99 €)

AE ⓓ VISA MC

A trip back in time to Kaster, a remarkably preserved late-medieval town

This hotel was once part of a landed estate, and the lovely sun-trap terrace still leads out into a charming park. The listed buildings themselves actually take in part of the old town wall as well as a manor house built in 1820: no wonder, then, that an atmosphere of tradition and history really comes alive here. Most of the rooms are decorated in country style, as is the restaurant, which has a few pleasant, rustic touches to it. With plenty of country walks nearby, this is a good base for rediscovering the great outdoors.

Sights nearby: Opencast lignite mining information centre in Schloss Paffendorf (8km south), Lucien Rosengart Museum in Rath (11km east)

Access: Exit 17 on A 61

8 MALERWINKEL

Renate Krämer-Thurau

Fischbachstr. 3
51429 Bergisch Gladbach-Bensberg
Tel. (02204) 9 50 40
Fax (02204) 9504100
info@malerwinkel-hotel.de – www.malerwinkel-hotel.de

Closed 1-5 Jan, Christmas to New Year's Eve • 27 rooms, including 1 with balcony and 16 non-smoking • Garden, parking; dogs allowed • Sauna

143/168 €, Breakfast included (WE: 123/143 €)

AE D JCB VISA MC

The split-level bedroom

Considerate and genuinely friendly service will soon make you feel at home at the Malerwinkel. In actual fact, it's not really one home, but five - a row of historic half timbered houses, one of which used to be a music school and incorporates musical instruments into the decoration of the bedrooms. Tasteful décor has been well combined with hints of the original interior, particularly the exposed beams, to created a charming setting for your stay, and breakfast in the cheery atmosphere of the conservatory gets every day off to a positive start!

Sights nearby: Altenberg cathedral (12km north), Ludwig Museum in Cologne (17km west)

Access: Exit 20 on A 4; in centre of Bensberg next to Rathaus

9 RENGSER MÜHLE

Maik Vormstein

51702 Bergneustadt-Niederrengse
Tel. (02763) 9 14 50
Fax (02763) 914520
info@rengser-muehle.de – www.rengser-muehle.de

Open all year • 4 rooms • Cafe-restaurant with terrace (closed Mon, Tue): set lunch 17-20€, set dinner 30-40€ • Garden, parking; dogs allowed in restaurant, not in hotel

85 €, Breakfast included
VISA MC

Coffee enjoyed in sumptuous local style

This 19th century mill building sits in an idyllic, leafy location, with the old millstone in the garden where coffee is taken serving as a reminder of its original vocation. The place is run with great care and solicitude and you will soon be made to feel at home. The rooms are few but perfectly formed, offering comfort in cheerful country style. The restaurant is divided into three sections; careful attention to detail, wood floors, tiled stoves and decor on a seasonal theme help create a welcoming rustic ambience.

Sights nearby: Eckenhagen bird and monkey park (6 km south), Gumbala Badeland (10 km west)

Access: From Exit 17 on A 45 via Wergeringhausen and Pernze, or from Bergneustadt by B 55

10 DOMSCHENKE

Frank Groll

Markt 6
48727 Billerbeck
Tel. (02543) 9 32 00
Fax (02543) 932030 – www.domschenke-billerbeck.de

Closed 23-24 Dec • 30 rooms, including 6 with balcony • Restaurant with terrace: set lunch 11-25€, set dinner 30-40€; half board 16-24€ • Garages; dogs allowed • Bicycle hire, wine seminars on request

75/100 €, Breakfast included

AE VISA MC

Delightful dining, whatever the weather - take a seat on the terrace or in the conservatory

The two slender neo-Gothic spires of St Ludger Cathedral have kept watch over Billerbeck for over a century, but this inn was here first and has been run by the same family, and with the same enthusiasm, for over 125 years. The original building and its clapboard-fronted neighbour provide sound, comfortable rooms, furnished in wood and decorated either in good, old-fashioned Münsterland style or with a dainty and elegant touch - some rooms have pretty canopy beds. The restaurant combines a similar range of styles, from the rustic bar and old cartwheels to a touch of Mediterranean design: the cuisine, however, stays true to its roots, with plenty of local Münsterland flavour to it.

Sights nearby: Schloss Darfeld (6km north), Schloss Hülsoff moated castle (17km east)

Access: From Exit 4 on A 43 via Nottuln

11 AM HOHENZOLLERNPLATZ

Doris Grube

Plittersdorfer Str. 54-56
53173 Bonn-Bad Godesberg
Tel. (0228) 95 75 90
Fax (0228) 9575929 – www.akzent.de/bonn

Closed 24-31 Dec • 20 rooms, including 3 with balcony • Light meals for residents • Garden; dogs allowed • Sauna, solarium

95/160 €, Breakfast included (WE: 85/160 €)

AE JCB VISA

Teatime in the garden, where the waffle stand is sure to tempt you with its enticing aromas

In a quiet residential district of Bad Godesberg, these two linked Art Nouveau villas are protected as listed buildings. The bedrooms have individually designed lightwood furnishings, and each bears the name of the artist whose work is featured. Sofas and couches enhance the comfortable atmosphere. Breakfast is taken in separate smoking or non-smoking rooms, both of which enjoy a pretty view of the leafy setting.

Sights nearby: Godesburg, Museum of Contemporary History, Bonn museum of art

Access: Roughly opposite the Godesburg in Bad Godesberg, turn northeast off B 9 (Bonner Strasse) into Plittersdorfer Strasse towards the Rhine

12 LANDHAUS GRÜNEKLEE

Tatjana Grüneklee

Rhedebrügger Str. 16
46325 Borken-Rhedebrügge
Tel. (02872) 18 18
Fax (02872) 2716
info@landhaus-grueneklee.de – www.landhaus-grueneklee.de

Closed fortnight in Jan, fortnight in Oct • 5 rooms, including 2 with balcony • Cafe; restaurant with terrace (closed Mon, Tue, midday Wed-Sat): main course 10-21€, set dinner 25-35€; half board 14.50€ • Garden, parking; dogs allowed • Bicycle hire

60/70 €, Breakfast included

AE VISA MC

The tasty home-made cakes

Tired of the stress of city life? There is another way - a country house surrounded by woods and meadows, where you can truly experience Westphalian hospitality. The rooms are furnished with rustic country style furniture, enhancing an already cosy atmosphere. The lounges also have their own charm, none more than the traditional farmhouse parlour: the nostalgic touches to the design transport you back to ‘good old days’ of country living. In addition to this, the restaurant area has been decorated in bright and friendly Mediterranean colours and when the sun appears there is a very inviting terrace for your relaxation.

Sights nearby: Gemen moated castle (8km east), Raesfeld moated castle (9km southeast)

Access: 6km west of Borken by B 67 towards Bocholt; turn left in Rhedebrügge

13 ORANGERIE

Petra Wenske

Bäckergasse 1
40213 Düsseldorf
Tel. (0211) 86 68 00
Fax (0211) 8668099 – www.hotel-orangerie-mcs.de

Open all year • 27 rooms, including 5 non-smoking • Dogs not allowed • Bicycle hire, personal fitness trainer

126/180 €, Breakfast included (WE: 100 €)

AE, Diners, VISA, MC

The distinguished architectural surroundings of palace, church and orangery

This fine neo-Classical edifice stands between the Rhine promenade and the sophisticated Königsallee with its elegant shops. It's also only a stone's throw to what is called "the world's longest bar", the countless pubs and other establishments of Düssseldorf's Old Town. Thanks to the traffic-calming measures you can enjoy the advantages of a central location plus peace and quiet. In contrast to the building's external appearance, the contemporary design of the interior is characterised by clear lines and cool elegance. The breakfast room fits into this concept too, giving a stylish start to your day.

Sights nearby: Hetjens Museum, museum kunst palast

Access: In the heart of Düsseldorf's Old Town south of the Alter Hafen (Old Harbour)

14 **SCHLOSSHOTEL**
Heidrun Feuerhahn

Schlossallee 14
59597 Erwitte
Tel. (02943) 9 76 00
Fax (02943) 486445 – www.schlosshotel-erwitte.de

Closed between the 23-25 December • 20 rooms, including 1 with disabled access • Café-restaurant with terrace: set lunch 12-20 €, set dinner 18-30 €, half pension 15 € • Garden, parking; dogs allowed • Bicycle hire, exhibitions, concerts

90/110 €, Breakfast included
AE VISA MC

The changing art exhibitions

The romantic ambience of this 17th century moated castle in Weser Renaissance style makes it a favourite for honeymooners, but its appeal is far from being limited to newly-weds. The comfortable accommodation features lime-washed furnishings in natural wood; the suites are festively elegant, the ordinary rooms a little plainer but equally attractive. Some of the bathrooms have grey marble tiles. There's an authentically historic atmosphere in the vaulted cellars which house the tastefully rustic restaurant.

Sights nearby: Old town Soest (17 km west); Bilsteinhöhle Warstein (22 km south)

Access: From Exit 58 of the A 44

15 ROMANTIK HOTEL HAUS ELMER

René Nicke

An der Klosterkirche 12
46499 Hamminkeln-Marienthal
Tel. (02856) 91 10
Fax (02856) 91170 – www.romantikhotels.com/hamminkeln

Open all year • 30 rooms, all non-smoking • Cafe; restaurant with terrace: set lunch 15-25€, set dinner 17-30€; half board 25€ • Garden, parking; dogs allowed • Bicycle hire, cookery courses, cultural evenings

102,50/155 €, Breakfast included

AE VISA

Bread and cakes from the establishment's own bakery

This old monastery building offers its guests a wide choice of types of accommodation, and you are sure to find something to suit. There are rooms in elegant traditional style featuring period furnishings, others with exposed timbers and a more rustic but nevertheless refined character, and still others of modern design with clean, contemporary lines. The bathrooms are lavishly equipped. The restaurant has a lovely country-style atmosphere and extends outside onto a beautiful terrace.

Sights nearby: Schloss Raesfeld (10 km northeast), Prussia Museum in Wesel (14 km southwest)

Access: From Exit 6 on A 3 towards Haltern, then towards Borken/Bocholt

16 ZUM HACKSTÜCK

Stefan Hänseler, Harald Hagenbruch

Hackstückstr. 123
45527 Hattingen-Bredenscheid
Tel. (02324) 9 06 60
Fax (02324) 906655 – www.hackstueck.de

Open all year • 23 rooms, including 5 non-smoking • Restaurant with terrace (closed Tue): set dinner 28-95€, main course 13-24€ • Garden, parking; dogs allowed

103/108 €, Breakfast included

AE VISA MC

An evening meal on the garden terrace, under the spreading branches of the lime tree.

Are you yearning to escape the stress of everyday life or the hustle and bustle of the city? This could be just the change you're looking for. The house is situated in the midst of a spacious park with beautiful waterlily ponds: the idyllc calm is wonderfully soothing, and the pleasant atmosphere created by the friendly service does the rest. The upkeep of the rooms is first class, ensuring that the bright wood and country-style décor is always seen at its best, and there's a special treat for true romantics: the wedding suite comes complete with its very own four-poster bed and whirlpool.

Sights nearby: German Mining Museum and Railway Museum in Bochum (15km north)

Access: Exit 22 on A 43, c 6km towards Hattingen then turn left into Johannes-Segener-Strasse and continue for 2km

17 STEUBERS SIEBELNHOF

Erich W. Steuber

Vormwalder Str. 56
57271 Hilchenbach-Vormwald
Tel. (02733) 8 94 30
Fax (02733) 7006 – www.steubers-siebelnhof.de

Open all year • 42 rooms, including 19 with balcony, 5 non-smoking and 5 with disabled access • Restaurant with terrace: set lunch 14-28€, set dinner 36-65€; half board 15€ • Garden, parking; dogs allowed • Swimming pool, gym, sauna, bicycle hire, cookery courses, organised walks

90/180 €, Breakfast included (WE: 65/148 €)
AE JCB VISA

The well-equipped leisure area, a real boon for relaxation

This historic inn on the outskirts of Vormwald has acquired a modern extension in the shape of the “Residenz La Villa”. Here you will find tasteful, elegant rooms with parquet floors and traditional cherrywood furnishings, all of them with a loggia affording a view of the uplands of the Rothaargebirge. Some of the bathrooms have an exceptional amenity in the form of a jacuzzi. The rooms in the guesthouse are simpler but correspondingly less expensive. Refined regional cooking is a feature of the rustic dining areas with their attractive wood panelling.

Sights nearby: Siegerland museum and Museum of contemporary art in Siegen (20km southwest)

Access: From Exit 19 or 20 on A 45 via Kreuztal, then via Hilchenbach by B 508; Vormwald is c 2km from here, still on B 508

18 GASTHOF BRINK

Kirsten Brink

Allee 38
33161 Hövelhof
Tel. (05257) 32 23
Fax (05257) 932937

Closed 2 weeks early Jan, 3 weeks in summer holidays • 9 rooms, including 2 with balcony and 2 non-smoking • Restaurant with terrace (eve only, closed Mon): set meal 49-65€ • Parking; dogs allowed in hotel, not in restaurant • Cookery courses

65/85 €, Breakfast included
Credit cards not accepted

A walk to the source of the River Ems

This welcoming establishment built in white brick stands in the middle of Hövelhof, the home of the Senner, Germany's oldest breed of horse. You will be pleased by the friendly reception and the care taken to make guests feel at home. Accommodation is in well kept, contemporary rooms with mahogany furnishings. In the restaurant, which has the character of a cosy living-room, you will appreciate the attentive service and well-considered advice on what to choose from the tradtional menu.

Sights nearby: Safari and Hollywood Park (8km north), Cathedral and Heinz Nixdorf Museums Forum in Paderborn (15km south)

Access: Exit 23 or 24 on A 33

19 **PARKHOTEL WASSERBURG ANHOLT**

J. u. P. Brune

Klever Straße
46419 Isselburg-Anholt
Tel. (02874) 45 90
Fax (02874) 4035 – www.parkhotel-wasserburg-anholt.de

Closed 24 Dec • 33 rooms • Restaurant with terrace (closed midday Tue-Sat, Sun and Mon): main course from 16€, set dinner 39-70€; half board 31€ • Garden, parking; dogs allowed in hotel, not in restaurant • Bicycles, castle park, museum, golf course, cookery and flower arranging courses, organised walks and cycle tours

125/265 €, Breakfast included (WE: 135/265 €)
AE D VISA MC

The noble zu Salm family's art collection: their masterpieces by Rembrandt, Murillo and Holbein are now in the museum

The awe-inspiring Wasserburg, originally dating back to the 12th century, was rebuilt as a Baroque stately home around 1700. Surrounded by a glorious park, the rooms can only be described as incredibly luxurious, decorated with steady but impeccably sure sense of good taste. The deep leather armchairs are an invitation to relax in the fireside warmth of the lounge, before making the difficult choice between the two restaurants: there's the Castle dining room, its impressive chandeliers lending a touch of classic, even aristocratic elegance, and the Pavillion with a glass façade and an enchanting terrace with views across the water.

Sights nearby: Huis Bergh near s'Heerenberg (16km west), Westphalian Industry and Textile Museum in Bocholt (17km east)

Access: Exit 4 on A 3; 3km northwest of Isselburg

20 CLASSIC HOTEL HARMONIE

Claudia Mewaldt

Ursulaplatz 13
50668 Köln
Tel. (0221) 1 65 70
Fax (0221) 1657200
harmonie@classic-hotels.com – www.classic-hotel-harmonie.de

Open all year • 72 rooms, including 55 with air conditioning, 20 non-smoking and 2 with disabled access • Garden, parking; dogs allowed

95/250 €, Breakfast included (WE: 70/115 €)

AE D JCB VISA MC

The leafy roof-terrace with a view over the town

This stylish town-house offers a whole range of amenities to help make your stay in the cathedral city a pleasant one. Thanks to its central location, the important sights are within easy walking distance. When you have completed your exploration of the urban attractions you can relax in a bedroom tastefully furnished and decorated in a timelessly elegant style. The rooms are even more inviting on a hot summer's day, when you will really appreciate the benefits of the air-conditioning. And finally, the hotel bar makes an excellent spot to round off the day with a cocktail of your choice.

Sights nearby: St Ursula's Church, Ludwig Museum, Romano-Germanic Museum

Access: In central Cologne opposite St Ursula's Church northwest of the main station

21 VIKTORIA

Herr Thäns

Worringer Str. 23
50668 Köln
Tel. (0221) 9 73 17 20
Fax (0221) 727067
hotel@hotelviktoria.com – www.hotelviktoria.com

Closed 1-2 Jan, Easter, Christmas • 47 rooms, including 20 non-smoking • Parking; dogs not allowed

113/230 €, Breakfast included (WE: 90/230 €)

AE DC VISA MC

The filigree Art Nouveau banisters

This neo-Classical building with Art Nouveau trimmings once housed a museum of musical history, and something of the spirit of this previous vocation still seems to linger. It's a real architectural jewel, its distinction enhanced by ceiling paintings, stucco-work and marble-clad walls. The bedrooms are individually furnished and decorated in an elegantly traditional style, and the breakfast room is graced by changing exhibitions of contemporary art. Everywhere you look there's a symphony of delightful features and details to discover.

Sights nearby: Cathedral, Wallraf Richartz Museum Fondation Corboud, Zoo

Access: In a side street off Rhine embankment road north of cathedral

22 **GUT WISTORFS**

Jochen Kinne

Olpener Str. 845
51109 Köln-Brück
Tel. (0221) 8 80 47 90
Fax (0221) 88047910
info@gut-wistorfs.de – www.gut-wistorfs.de

Open all year • 14 rooms, all non-smoking, 3 with disabled access • Restaurant with terrace (closed Mon): set lunch 9.90-39.80€, set dinner 39.80-84€ • Parking; dogs allowed • Cookery courses, wine seminars

105/176 €, Breakfast included (WE: 90/110 €)

AE VISA MC

Home-baked cakes for breakfast

This 18th century estate has successfully managed to preserve its original charm down the years. The first thing you see from the street is its fine shingle-clad façade, then its cobbled inner courtyard, surrounded by half-timbering. It's the perfect place to sit in the glorious sunshine whilst enjoying something to eat or a leisurely afternoon coffee. The estate bar comes highly recommended when in search of a quick drink or even somewhere to settle in for the evening. The design of the rooms has a likeable simplicity to it; the tiled floors and solid natural wood furniture give them a trim, unfussy feel.

Sights nearby: Museum of East Asian Art and Diocesan Museum in Cologne (11km west)

Access: From Mehrheim-Brück Exit on A 4 east of Cologne towards centre of Brück

23 FALDERHOF

Rudolf Peer

Falderstr. 29
50999 Köln-Sürth
Tel. (02236) 96 69 90
Fax (02236) 966998
info@falderhof.de – www.falderhof.de

Closed 1-3 Jan, 23-31 Dec • 33 rooms, including 17 non-smoking • Restaurant with terrace (closed midday Sat; Mon Oct to Apr): set lunch 13.50-17.50€, set dinner 29.80-38.50€; half board 22€ • Garden, parking; dogs allowed • Bicycle hire, wine tastings, whisky tastings, grill parties

115 €, Breakfast included (WE: 100 €)
AE D VISA MC

The rural idyll of the garden terrace

This is one of the oldest-maintained properties in the Cologne region - first recorded right back at the beginning of the 13th century - but it seemed doomed to demolition until an artist by the name of Rudolf Peer came to its rescue, dedicating himself to the job of restoring the old estate. Despite the overhaul he has managed to preserve the charm of the original building. The rooms are peaceful - all face the courtyard or the garden - and some are decorated with antiques and works of various artists, most notably Peer's. In the oldest part of the building you will find the 'Altes Fachwerkhaus' restaurant, which has been lovingly decorated and has a very cosy atmosphere.

Sights nearby: Applied Arts Museum in Cologne (10 km north), Schloss Augustusburg in Brühl (12 km southwest)

Access: From south Köln-Godorf Exit on A 555, from north Rodenkirchen/Sürth/Rondorf Exit

24 HAUS BERKENKAMP

Fritz Berkenkamp

Im Heßkamp 50
32791 Lage-Stapelage
Tel. (05232) 7 11 78
Fax (05232) 961033 – www.haus-berkenkamp.de

Closed from 1st to the 19th October • 20 rooms, including 1 with disabled access and 18 with balcony • Half board possible • Garden, parking, dogs not allowed • Cosmetic treatments, massages, sauna, bicycle hire

62/66 €, Breakfast included
Credit cards not accepted

Fresh products from the establishment's own butchery and orchard

If you have ever felt the need for somewhere secluded where you could get away completely from everyday cares and worries, this could be the place for you. Haus Berkenkamp is an old farmstead of 1849, tucked away on its own in a quiet location. Its two guesthouses offer an attractive and comfortable ambience, with much use of wood in the immaculately-kept rooms. The extensive, park-like garden and a fallow deer enclosure enhance the place's attractiveness, particularly for families.

Sights nearby: Hermanns monument (10 km south) ; Westphalian open-air museum Detmold (11 km east) ; Safari- and Hollywood-Park (15 km southwest)

Access: From Exit 22 on the A 33 via Stukenbrock, Augustdorf and Hörste; from Stapelage half way to Billinghausen

25 **ROMANTIK HOTEL GRAVENBERG**
Frank Lohmann

Elberfelder Str. 45
40764 Langenfeld
Tel. (02173) 9 22 00
Fax (02173) 22777 – www.gravenberg.de

Closed between 1 -5 January, Christmas to New Year • 48 rooms, including 4 with balcony and 13 non-smoking • Forest café, restaurant with terrace (closed Sun evening, Mon noon) ; set meal 23.50-43.50 €, half board 28 € • Garden, parking, dogs allowed • Health and beauty facilities, bicycle hire

135/208 €, Breakfast included
AE D VISA MC

A glass or three in the wine-cellar

This country hotel is conveniently located on the main road between Langenfeld and Solingen at the point where the uplands of the Bergisches Land give way to the Rhineland. The surrounding area is a paradise for walkers, and right next door there is a fascinating fallow deer enclosure. The hotel itself offers friendly hospitality together with rooms in a variety of styles, some playfully romantic, others comfortably rustic. Stylish wellness and beauty facilities, an inviting garden, and an elegant country-style restaurant complete the place's attractions.

Sights nearby: Solingen metalwork museum (11 km northeast); Neanderthal museum (15 km north)

Access: From Exit 20 of the A 3 continue in the direction of Solingen

26 GÄSTEHAUS MEERERBUSCH

Beate Stöhr

Hindenburgstr. 4
40667 Meerbusch-Büderich
Tel. (02132) 93 34 00
Fax (02132) 933429
www.gaestehaus-meerbusch.de

Closed 1-4 Jan • 16 rooms, including 4 non-smoking • Garden, parking; dogs allowed

99/144 €, Breakfast included

AE VISA MC

Breakfast is served communally on at a large table.

Even if you're sure you've crossed the Channel, you may wonder if you've come quite as far as you think. The husband and wife team who own the inn have decorated the interior with more than a nod to old-English country house styling, even if a touch of Britishness is the last thing you'd expect from the outside. There's a simple enough reason behind it all: the man of the house is English and his wife is an antiques dealer, which explains their excellent taste in English antiques! A delightfully unusual address, made even more special by its regularly changing art exhibitions.

Sights nearby: Hofgarten and Schloss Jägerhof with Goethe Museum in Düsseldorf (11km east), Neuss Minster (11km south)

Access: Exit 16 on A 57, or Exit 28 on A 44; on a side road off B 9 on way into town

27 LANDHOTEL DONNER

Georg Donner

Zur alten Schmiede 5
59872 Meschede-Remblinghausen
Tel. (0291) 59 27 00
Fax (0291) 5927010 – www.landhotel-donner.de

Closed mid to late Jan • 14 rooms • Restaurant with terrace (closed Wed, but open to residents 6pm-7.30pm): set lunch 16.50-25€, main course 8.70-22.50€; half board 14€ • Parking; dogs allowed in hotel, not in restaurant • Bicycle hire

70/74 €, Breakfast included
VISA MC

The attractive terrace with a view of the church

Founded in 1860 as a business establishment, this property is now a pleasant country hotel. It's ideal not just for those wanting to explore the surrounding countryside on foot, but for anyone in search of peaceful surroundings in which to really relax. The rooms are decorated and furnished in solid country style and together with the friendly and competent service help create a pleasant setting for your stay. The tasteful restaurant too has a welcoming country air.

Sights nearby: Hennesee (2 km west), Ramsbeck ore mining museum (13 km east), Fort Fun adventure park (16 km east)

Access: Exit 70 on A 445; 6 km south of Meschede

28 SCHLOSS WILKINGHEGE

Lubert und Rembert Winnecken

Steinfurter Str. 374 (B 54)
48159 Münster (Westfalen)
Tel. (0251) 14 42 70
Fax (0251) 212898 – www.schloss-wilkinghege.de

Closed 24-25 Dec • 35 rooms, including 3 with disabled access • Cafe-restaurant with terrace: set meal 39-72€ • Garden, parking; dogs allowed in hotel, not in restaurant • Reduced fees for hotel guests on adjoining golf course

140/305 €, Breakfast included

AE VISA

Breakfasting beneath the vaults of the castle cellars

Dreams you may have had of passing the night in a princely residence can be fulfilled in this moated castle not far from the old city of Münster. Schloss Wilkinghege was first mentioned in the 14th century; it offers its guests classically elegant rooms with fine furnishings together with lavishly equipped bathrooms - some with a jacuzzi. The stylish restaurant has red and gold wall-coverings and glittering chandeliers. Outside extends a glorious tract of parkland, while inside, attentive spirits cater for your every need.

Sights nearby: Münster Old Town (3 km southeast), Mühlenhof open air museum (4 km south), Burg Hülsoff moated castle (10 km west)

Access: From Exit 77 on A 1 by B 54 towards Münster

29 ROMANTIK HOTEL HOF ZUR LINDE

Otto Löfken

Handorfer Werseufer 1
48157 Münster-Handorf
Tel. (0251) 3 27 50
Fax (0251) 328209 – www.hof-zur-linde.de

Closed 23-25 Dec • 47 rooms, including 14 with balcony and 8 non-smoking • Restaurant with terrace; set lunch 25.50-43.50 €, set dinner 43.50-65.50 €; half pension 25 € • Garden, parking, dogs allowed in restaurant, not in hotel • Sauna, solarium, steam bath, fitness room, bicycle hire

122/141 €, Breakfast included

AE D VISA MC

Slightly incongruous so far inland, the beach chairs are nevertheless very tempting

The foundation stone of this establishment was laid as long ago as 1648, the year in which the Peace of Westphalia brought the Thirty Years War to an end. There's an appealing air of history about the place, while its location on the banks of the Werse is another plus. Inside, exposed timbers add to the allure of the main building, while the rooms here and in the guesthouse are decorated and furnished in a romantically rustic country style and are sure to please. Authenticity combines with elegance in the attractive ambience of the restaurant, where an open fire provides welcome warmth.

Sights nearby: Westphlian country museum for art and cultural history in Münster (7 km southwest) ; port of registry museum Münsterland in Telgte (8 km east)

Access: 7 km north of Münster via the B 51 in the direction of Telgte/Warendorf

30 FORSTHAUS LAHNQUELLE

Eckhard Sinning

Lahnhof 1
57250 Netphen-Lahnhof
Tel. (02737) 2 41
Fax (02737) 243 – www.forsthaus-lahnquelle.de

Open all year • 23 rooms, including 10 non-smoking and 9 with balcony • Cafe; restaurant with terrace: main course 8-22€ • Garden, parking; dogs allowed • Sauna, steam bath, solarium, bicycle hire, cookery seminars, guided walks, treks

85/95 €, Breakfast included

VISA MC

Freshly caught trout straight from the establishment's own pond

Here among the fields and meadows around the source of the River Lahn high up in the hills of the Rothaargebirge you can almost hear the silence. Your accommodation is in comfortable, country-style rooms with furnishings in natural wood. The establishment is run along lines inspired by the unspoiled landscape all around; the welcoming restaurant for example specialises in dishes made from local and seasonal ingredients.

Sights nearby: Rothaarsteig long-distance trail

Access: Exit 23 on A 45 via Rudersdorf and Gernsdorf, right in Werthenbach towards Hainchen; just before the Hainchen place-name sign, left towards Lahnho

31 GASTHAUS STEVERTAL

Ulrike und Dieter Elfers

Stevern 36
48301 Nottuln-Stevern
Tel. (02502) 9 40 10
Fax (02502) 940149 – www.gasthaus-stevertal.de

Closed 1 Jan, 24-26 Dec • 12 rooms • Restaurant with terrace: main course 8-20€, set dinner 25-36€ • Garden, parking; dogs allowed • Bicycle hire, cookery courses, wine tasting

75 €, Breakfast included
Credit cards not accepted

The appetizing smoked hams on display

This authentically Westphalian establishment of 1911 has been run by four generations of the Elfers family. Sausages and hams come from their own butchery, and bread is baked here too. The emblem of the house however is the trout, which is brought to the rustic restaurant straight from the pond. Regional tradition doesn't stop at the table; the bedrooms too are designed and decorated in an attractive country style and feature furnishings in solid natural wood.

Sights nearby: Burg Hülsoff moated castle (12 km northeast), Picasso graphic museum in Münster (20 km east)

Access: From Exit 4 on A 43 via Nottuln and then towards Schapdetten

32 ZUR POST

Alexander Wilbrand

Altenberger-Dom-Str. 23
51519 Odenthal
Tel. (02202) 97 77 80
Fax (02202) 9777849 – www.hotel-restaurant-zur-post.de

Closed 1 week in Jan, 1 week during North-Rhine Westphalia autumn holidays • 16 rooms, including 7 non-smoking • Restaurant with terrace (closed Mon): set lunch 25-29€, set dinner 55-85€; half board 24€ • Parking; dogs allowed in hotel, not in restaurant

125/150 €, Breakfast included

AE VISA

The traditional local waffles freshly served up on Sundays and holidays

This hospitable establishment consists of an historic inn with hung tiles of slate and a newer hotel building. The spacious and comfortable bedrooms in a timelessly elegant style feature cherrywood or lime-washed furnishings, while the elegantly rustic dining areas are in the style typical of the Bergisches Land, with panelled walls and tiled stoves. The gourmet cuisine is outstanding, though if you fancy something simpler, there is an alternative in the shape of the bistro-style “Postschänke”.

Sights nearby: Altenberg cathedral (3km north), Ludwig museum in Cologne (17km southwest)

Access: From Exit 24 on A 3 via Leverkusen and Schildgen

33 ROMANTIK HOTEL SCHLOSS PETERSHAGEN

Herr Hestermann

32469 Petershagen
Tel. (05707) 9 31 30
Fax (05707) 931345 – www.schloss-petershagen.com

Closed late Jan to early Feb • 15 rooms • Restaurant with terrace: set meal 39.50-53.50€ • Garden, parking; dogs allowed • Tennis, outdoor pool, bicycle hire, cookery courses, castle tours

128/145 €, Breakfast included

AE D VISA MC

A medieval banquet in what used to be the castle kitchens

There's so much to discover here at the 14th century Schloss Petershagen that it should really be called a museum with a hotel attached. Everywhere there are original paintings and graphic works depicting the history of the castle and the area around. The rooms are stylish and attractive and feature period furnishings, and some of them even have four-poster beds. From the elegantly traditional restaurant there is an uninterrupted view of the idyllic landscape of the Weser valley, while the castle's romantic park is ideal for a relaxing stroll.

Sights nearby: Minden cathedral (10 km south), potts park (16 km south)

Access: From A 2 via Minden and B 61

34 PARKHOTEL ENGELSBURG

Peter Berkelmann

Augustinessenstr. 10
45657 Recklinghausen
Tel. (02361) 20 10
Fax (02361) 201120 – www.parkhotel-engelsburg.de

Closed 1-2 Jan • 69 rooms, including 7 with balcony, 2 with disabled access and 16 non-smoking • Restaurant with terrace (closed Sun eve): set meal 16-50€; half board 22€ • Garden, parking; dogs allowed • Sauna, steam bath

129/228 €, Breakfast included (WE: 100/176 €)

AE DC JCB VISA MC

Soaking up the sun on the roof terrace

This princely property of 1701 stands at the western end of the town's historic core. A stay here enables you to enjoy the refined lifestyle of a bygone age without having to forego modern comforts and conveniences. The spacious bedrooms are tastefully decorated and furnished in elegant English style, and are ideally complemented by timelessly designed bathrooms featuring much use of marble. The restaurant matches the rooms in its classic stylishness, and it is here that breakfast is taken.

Sights nearby: Icon museum, Heinrichenburg boat lift in Waltrop (16 km east)

Access: From Recklinghausen-Herten Exit on A 43 by Hertener Strasse into town, then Herzogswall

35 ROMANTIK HOTEL RATSKELLER

Peter Surmann

Markt 11 (Eingang auch Lange Straße)
33378 Rheda-Wiedenbrück
Tel. (05242) 92 10
Fax (05242) 921100
ratskeller@romantikhotels.com – www.romantikhotels.com/rheda-wiedenbrueck

Closed 1st week in Jan, 23-25 Dec • 33 rooms, including 1 with balcony and 13 non-smoking • Restaurant with terrace: set dinner 36.50-58€, main course 17.20-23.20€; half board 25€ • Parking; dogs allowed • Sauna, solarium, jacuzzi, town tours, bicycle hire, balloon trips

105/142 €, Breakfast included

AE JCB VISA

The idyllic terrace in front of the building

Guests have been accommodated here since 1560, and the present hotel shows traces of no fewer than five building periods. There's much to marvel at, outside as well as in; just studying the details on the picturesque façade could keep you busy for hours. Because of the varied nature of the building, the rooms come in diverse shapes and sizes, some of them featuring strikingly exposed timbers. The style is rustic, but in a refined way. The dining areas too evoke the place's long history, with massive oak beams and a charming decorative scheme. You are left in no doubt that you are in the very heart of historic Wiedenbrück.

Sights nearby: Rheda moated castle, Shrine of St Prudentia in Beckum parish church (23 km southwest)

Access: Exit 23 on A 2; in centre of Wiedenbrück

36 ALTES GASTHAUS BORCHARDING

Helga und Josef Borcharding

€€ Alte Bahnhofstr. 13
48432 Rheine-Mesum
Tel. (05975) 12 70
Fax (05975) 3507
www.altes-gasthaus-borcharding.de

Open all year • 9 rooms, including 2 with balcony • Restaurant with terrace (closed Thu, midday Fri and Sat): set meal 12-42€; half board 15€ • Garden, parking; dogs allowed • Bicycle hire, cookery courses, wine seminars

63/90 €, Breakfast included

AE DC JCB VISA MC

The extraordinary conglomeration of decorative objects in the dining areas

In the hands of the Borcharding family since 1712, this traditional inn combines Westphalian cosiness with modern comfort. The bedrooms, most of which are in the new building of 1990, are distinguished by their tasteful decor and furnishings; lovely brass bedsteads and lavishly equipped marble bathrooms help create a stylish ambience. The dining areas exude an authentically rustic atmosphere, while by contrast the modern glass-roofed atrium adds an exotic note.

Sights nearby: Naturzoo and Bentlage monastery in Rheine (7 km northwest)

Access: 7 km southeast of Rheine by B 481 towards Münster

37 SCHÄFERHOF

Rudolf Grobbel

Jagdhaus 21
57392 Schmallenberg-Jagdhaus
Tel. (02972) 4 73 34
Fax (02972) 47336 – www.schaeferhof.com

Closed 21/2 weeks between Carnival and Easter, 10 days late Nov • 8 rooms, including 6 with balcony • Restaurant with terrace (closed Tue): set meal 12-25€; half board 12€ • Garden, parking, wine cellar; dogs allowed • Sauna, bicycle hire, guided walks

60/82 €, Breakfast included
Credit cards not accepted

The rustic chalet available for stays of three nights or more

In its idyllically leafy setting, this old farmstead exudes great charm, all the more appealing because it is utterly authentic. This is the place to come if you are hoping to stay in the bosom of Nature. From here there are any number of attractive walks through the woods and meadows of the Sauerland, all the more enjoyable because the hotel will arrange to take you out and pick you up again. Back in your lodgings, you will find attractive country-style bedrooms with furnishings in natural wood, along with a restaurant with a menu supplemented by daily specials communicated to you verbally.

Sights nearby: Fortified church of St Cyriakus in Berghausen (14 km north), castle in Bad Berleburg (19 km southeast)

Access: 7 km south of Schmallenberg by B 236, turn left in Fleckenberg

38 GASTHOF SCHÜTTE

Karl-Anton Schütte

Eggeweg 2 (near the B 236)
57392 Schmallenberg-Oberkirchen
Tel. (02975) 8 20
Fax (02975) 82522 – www.gasthof-schuette.de

Closed 27 Nov to 26 Dec • 64 rooms, including 21 with balcony and 2 with disabled access • Cafe-restaurant with terrace: set lunch 10-20€, set dinner 40-54€; half board 19€ • Garden, parking; dogs allowed in restaurant, not in hotel • Indoor pool, outdoor pool, sauna, billiards, bicycle hire

106/214 €, Breakfast included

AE D VISA MC

Sitting by the open fire in the charming hallway

This timber-framed farmstead of 1774 with its various outbuildings in similar style is an ideal place for a countryside stay. The comfortable bedrooms are furnished in a variety of distinctive ways. The low ceilings in the main building add lots of character to the decorative schemes in elegant country style. Also in the main building, the restaurant features exposed ceiling beams and is in an equally appealing rustic style. For relaxation, there are outdoor and indoor pools as well as an idyllic garden.

Sights nearby: Grafschaft monastery (5 km west), Kahler Asten (12 km east)

Access: 8 km east of Schmallenberg by B 236

39 SCHWALENBERGER MALKASTEN

Claus-Jürgen Kotzenberg

Neue Torstr. 1
32816 Schwalenberg
Tel. (05284) 9 80 60
Fax (05284) 980666 – www.schwalenberger-malkasten.de

Closed 2 Jan to 15 Feb • 44 rooms, including 10 with balcony • Beer Stube, restaurant with terrace: set lunch 16€, main course 7.50-16.50€; half board 13€ • Garden, parking; dogs allowed in restaurant, not in hotel • Sauna

62/84 €, Breakfast included

VISA

The welcoming atmosphere in the cosily authentic beer parlour

The name of this establishment means "paint-box" and there's no denying that lots of painting has gone on in this timber-framed edifice on the edge of the Old Town. Part of its façade was embellished with an array of colourful figures, walls and doors are charmingly decorated and furniture too is enhanced with a variety of pretty motifs. All this adds to the welcoming, rustic ambience of bedrooms, restaurant and cafe in a delightfully decorative way. The colours and the cheerful folksy pictures are sure to give you lots of pleasure.

Sights nearby: Bad Pyrmont Kurpark (20 km north), Corvey monastery church in Höxter (23 km southeast)

Access: By B 239 between Detmold and Höxter

40 KLOSTERHOF SELIGENTHAL

Andreas Behner

Zum Klosterhof 1
53721 Siegburg-Seligenthal
Tel. (02242) 87 47 87
Fax (02242) 874789 – www.klosterhof-seligenthal.de

Open all year • 12 rooms • Restaurant with terrace: main course 15-21€, set dinner 29-38€; half board 24.50€ • Garden, parking; dogs allowed in restaurant, not in hotel

100/120 €, Breakfast included

AE D VISA MC

Sunday brunch

In a pleasantly quiet location close to the Wahnbach reservoir, this hotel-restaurant occupies what used to be a monastery. Visible from some distance away, the church's ridge-turret is quite a landmark. The comfortable rooms have furnishings in light beechwood, and those on the attic floor feature exposed beams, lending them an attractively rustic character. The hotel is separate from the elegant country-style restaurant, which is housed in a long and low timber-framed structure with a fine timber ceiling and a conservatory.

Sights nearby: Siegburg Benedictine abbey (5km west), Rhineland regional museum in Bonn (17km southwest)

Access: From Exit 31 on A 3 by B 484 towards Siegburg, in 500 metres turn on to B 56 towards Much; follow signs to Seligenthal from Stallberg

PILGRIM-HAUS

Friedrich-Hans Andernach

Jakobistr. 75
59494 Soest
Tel. (02921) 18 28
Fax (02921) 12131 – www.pilgrimhaus.de

Closed 24-31 Dec • 10 rooms • Restaurant with beer garden (closed Tue; midday Mon-Fri): set lunch (Sat, Sun, public holidays) 12-17.50€, main course 10.50-18.80€ • Garden, parking; dogs allowed

85/95 €, Breakfast included

JCB VISA MC

The home-made herb liqueur

This establishment was dispensing hospitality as long ago as the early 14th century, when it welcomed pilgrims on their way to Santiago de Compostela. Those early days are commemmorated every year on 25th July, the saint's day of St James, when a particularly fine wine is put on the table. Despite its long past, the inn shows few signs of ageing. The rooms are solidly furnished in pale wood and the dining areas exude a delightfully nostalgic charm, due not least to the array of pictures and other objects assembled by the previous owners.

Sights nearby: St Patroclus Cathedral, Wiesenkirche, Hohnekirche

Access: By the Jakobi Gate in the southwestern corner of the Old Town

42 HEIDEHOTEL WALDHÜTTE

M. Krabbe

Im Klatenberg 19
48291 Telgte
Tel. (02504) 92 00
Fax (02504) 920140 – www.heidehotel-waldhuette.de

Closed 3-8 Jan • 33 rooms, including 5 with balcony • Restaurant with terrace: set meal 32-39.50€; half board on request • Garden, parking; dogs allowed • Sauna, solarium, gym, bicycle hire

108/115 €, Breakfast included

AE VISA MC

The glorious flowering of the rhododendrons in springtime

This green oasis of a country hotel on the edge of the forest has evolved from what was just a simple inn patronised by day-trippers. The location is idyllic, with a garden terrace extending out in a park-like landscape with a deer enclosure, aviaries, and a pond. Inside, the bedrooms are in Old German style, but their attractively rustic character does not mean that you will have to do without modern comforts. The restaurant is in the same style, with a fine fireplace helping to reinforce the cosy atmosphere.

Sights nearby: Heimathaus museum of the Münsterland in Telgte (3 km southwest), Town Hall with Peace Chamber in Münster (15 km west)

Access: 3 km northeast of Telgte by B 51 towards Osnabrück

43 SCHLOSS HOTEL HOLZRICHTER

Werner Holzrichter

Hohenlimburger Str. 15
58769 Veserde-Wiblingwerde
Tel. (02334) 92 99 60
Fax (02334) 1515 – www.hotel-holzrichter.de

Closed 3 weeks in summer holidays, Christmas • 30 rooms, all non-smoking, 26 with balcony and 1 with disabled access • Restaurant with terrace (closed Thu; eve only Mon, Tue, Wed, Fri): main course 11.90-21.90€; half board 22.50€ • Garden, parking; dogs by arrangement • Wellness facilities, skittles, archery, carriage drives, organised walks

128/160 €, Breakfast included

AE VISA MC

The festive Kaisersaal which also serves as a registry office

In the triangle bounded by the towns of Hagen, Iserlohn and Lüdenscheid, this well-established property stands on a rise commanding a fine view over the surrounding area. With its delightful half-timbered towers, it makes a striking first impression. Inside, the elegant country-style bedrooms feature attractive wood furnishings. The stylish restaurant too makes lavish use of wood; together with the attentive service, this creates a warm and welcoming atmosphere.

Sights nearby: Schloss Hohenlimburg (4 km northwest), Westphalian open air museum at Hagen (12 km west)

Access: From Exit 13 on A 45 via Wiblingwerde, then 3 km northwest towards Hohenlimburg

44 ALTE VILLA LING - JOSEFINE

Thomas Teigelkamp

Hindenburgstr. 34
41749 Viersen-Süchteln
Tel. (02162) 97 01 50
Fax (02162) 9701510 – www.alte-villa-ling.de

Closed 23-24 Dec • 7 rooms, all non-smoking • Restaurant with beer garden (closed Mon, Tue, midday Sat): main course 16-28€ • Garden, parking; dogs allowed in restaurant, not in hotel

100/130 €, Breakfast included
VISA MC

Sitting in the summer beer garden beneath the ancient trees

This Art Nouveau villa of 1899 has a well-deserved reputation for pampering its guests. The splendid hall and some of the rooms still exude the stylish spirit of the era in which it was built. The other rooms too provide spacious and well-equipped accommodation. Outstanding traditional cuisine characterises the festively elegant "Josephine" restaurant, named after the wife of the villa's original owner. Breakfast is taken in the panelled "Gaststube", which is simpler and rather more rustic in style.

Sights nearby: Abteiberg town museum in Mönchengladbach (17 km southeast), gardens of Castle Arcen in Venlo (19 km northwest)

Access: Exit 6 on A 61

45 ROMANTIK HOTEL ALT WARBURG

Hermann Fritz

Kalandstr. 11
34414 Warburg
Tel. (05641) 7 89 80
Fax (05641) 789815 – www.romantikhotel-alt-warburg.de

Open all year • 20 rooms, including 2 non-smoking • Restaurant with terrace (closed Sun, midday Sat): set meal 44-57€; half board 24€ • Parking; dogs allowed • Skittles, cookery course, town tours

110 €, Breakfast included

AE DC JCB VISA MC

A stroll among the picturesque old timber-framed buildings of Warburg

Together with the guesthouse opposite, this smartly restored half-timbered building of 1540 stands by the church close to the market square, and offers its guests rooms in a timeless style. Some of those in the historic main building feature exposed beams. At breakfast-time, it's fun to sit in the raised section of the restaurant. The restaurant itself is most attractive, with a wood ceiling and stylish dark timberwork.

Sights nearby: Desenberg (4 km northeast), Schloss Wilhelmsthal (24 km southeast)

Access: From Exit 65 on A 44 follow hotel signs in Warburg

46 IM ENGEL

Gerhard Leve

Brünebrede 33-37
48231 Warendorf
Tel. (02581) 9 30 20
Fax (02581) 62726 – www.hotel-im-engel.de

Open all year • 22 rooms, all non-smoking, 15 with air conditioning, 5 with disabled access, 2 with balcony • Restaurant with terrace (closed Sun): set meal 19.50-49€; half board 20€ • Garden, parking; dogs allowed • Sauna, gym, bicycle hire, organised cycle tours and walks, cookery courses, wine seminars

85/125 €, Breakfast included

AE VISA MC

The angel motif which crops up throughout the building

Two things make this establishment quite outstanding. The first is the fact that it has been in the hands of the Leve family since 1692 - though the property itself actually dates from 1545. The second is the amazing range of wines on offer, which, thanks to the adjacent shop, you can take home with you as well. The rustic dining areas in authentically Old German style make an ideal setting for judicious tasting before you make your choice, after which you can wend your way to your elegant and comfortable room with its cherrywood furnishings.

Sights nearby: Warendorf Stallion Parade (Sep/Oct), Heimathaus museum of the Münsterland in Telgte (15 km west)

Access: In Warendorf Old Town; by B 64 and Freckenhorst Gate

47 MOLZMÜHLE

Brigitte Hoyer

Im Bollenberg 41
41844 Wegberg-Rickelrath
Tel. (02434) 9 97 70
Fax (02434) 25723 – www.molzmuehle.de

Open all year • 9 rooms • Restaurant with terrace (closed Mon, Tue): set lunch 15-24.50€, set dinner 22-42.50€; half board 20€ • Garden, parking; dogs allowed • Swimming pool, sauna, bicycle hire, exhibitions, readings

100/140 €, Breakfast included

AE DC VISA MC

Sitting out in the secluded courtyard

What is it about old mills that make them so alluring? Could it be their location by the water, especially when the setting is as attractively leafy as it is here? Or perhaps it's the massive scale of machinery and waterwheel which contrasts so sharply with the delicacy of the powdery product. Here in the restaurant, the old waterwheel and the millstones are on display, though what is produced here is no longer flour, but cuisine of exceptional quality. The rooms too are exceptional, each with an individual character, while some of them feature antique pieces. Altogether, the old mill is a comfortable and distinctive place to stay.

Sights nearby: Minster and Schloss Rheydt in Mönchengladbach (19 km east)

Access: Exit 4 on A 52

48 LANDHAUS BERGHOF

Ulrich Stracke

57482 Wenden
Tel. (02762) 50 88
Fax (02762) 3708
www.landhaus-berghof.de

Open all year • 15 rooms, including 4 with balcony • Cafe-restaurant with terrace (closed Mon): set lunch 12.50-21€, main course 7.50-19.50€; half board 15€ • Garden, parking; dogs not allowed • Skittles

84 €, Breakfast included

AE D VISA MC

The terrace looking out onto a lovely woodland clearing

On the woodland edge, this inviting country hotel extends a friendly welcome to its guests and provides them with attentive, personal service. It's an ideal place to relax and let yourself be pampered. The rooms feature solid wood furnishings, and the bathrooms make lavish use of marble; elegance and comfort are the watchwords here. The country-style restaurant offers hearty plain food.

Sights nearby: Biggesee (20 km north)

Access: 2 km south of Wenden on the road to Hünsborn

49 **BAUMHOVE HOTEL AM MARKT**

Familie Baumhove

Markt 2
59368 Werne
Tel. (02389) 98 95 90
Fax (02389) 98959120 – www.baumhove.de

Open all year • 17 rooms, 3 with showers on landing • Restaurant with terrace (closed Sun eve): set meal 25-30€; half board 17.50€ • Dogs allowed • Bicycle hire, town walks by torchlight

77/79 €, Breakfast included (WE: 72/74 €)

AE JCB VISA

The saline spa just a short walk away

The Baumhove family have been dispensing hospitality for over 500 years in this listed timber-framed building right by the market square. The stylishly furnished rooms exude a sense of the building's long history - it was mentioned in documents in 1484 - but at its heart is the restaurant that rises through two storeys from the old threshing floor. Here, the lavish but sensitive use of wood helps create an atmosphere of appealing authenticity.

Sights nearby: Vischering moated castle (22 km northwest), Westfalenpark in Dortmund (24 km southwest)

Access: Exit 80 or 81 on A 1; in Werne follow green and white "Hotelroute" signs

50 BERGHOTEL ASTENKRONE

Jörg Templin

Astenstr. 24
59955 Winterberg-Altastenberg
Tel. (02981) 80 90
Fax (02981) 809198
berghotel@astenkrone.de – www.astenkrone.de

Open all year • 39 rooms, including 16 with balcony, 1 with disabled access and 4 non-smoking • Restaurant with terrace: set meal 29-50€; half board from 29€ • Garden, parking; dogs by arrangement • Wellness facilities including indoor pool and sauna, skittles, billiard room, bicycle hire, organised walks

120/165 €, Breakfast included

VISA MC

The lavish and imaginatively designed wellness facilities

800 metres up at the foot of the Kahler Asten, the highest summit in the Sauerland, this long-established country hotel welcomes its guests at any time of the year, its slate-hung walls well able to stand up to anything the weather might throw at it. Inside, the tasteful, country-style bedrooms feature harmonious colour schmes - continued in the bathrooms - as well as fine fabrics, all helping to create an inviting and comfortable atmosphere. Tasteful wood panelling contributes to the pleasant ambience in both the elegant “Kronenrestaurant” and the more rustic “Kronenstube”.

Sights nearby: Kahler Asten, castle in Bad Berleburg (23 km southwest)

Access: 5 km west of Winterberg by B 236 towards Schmallenberg

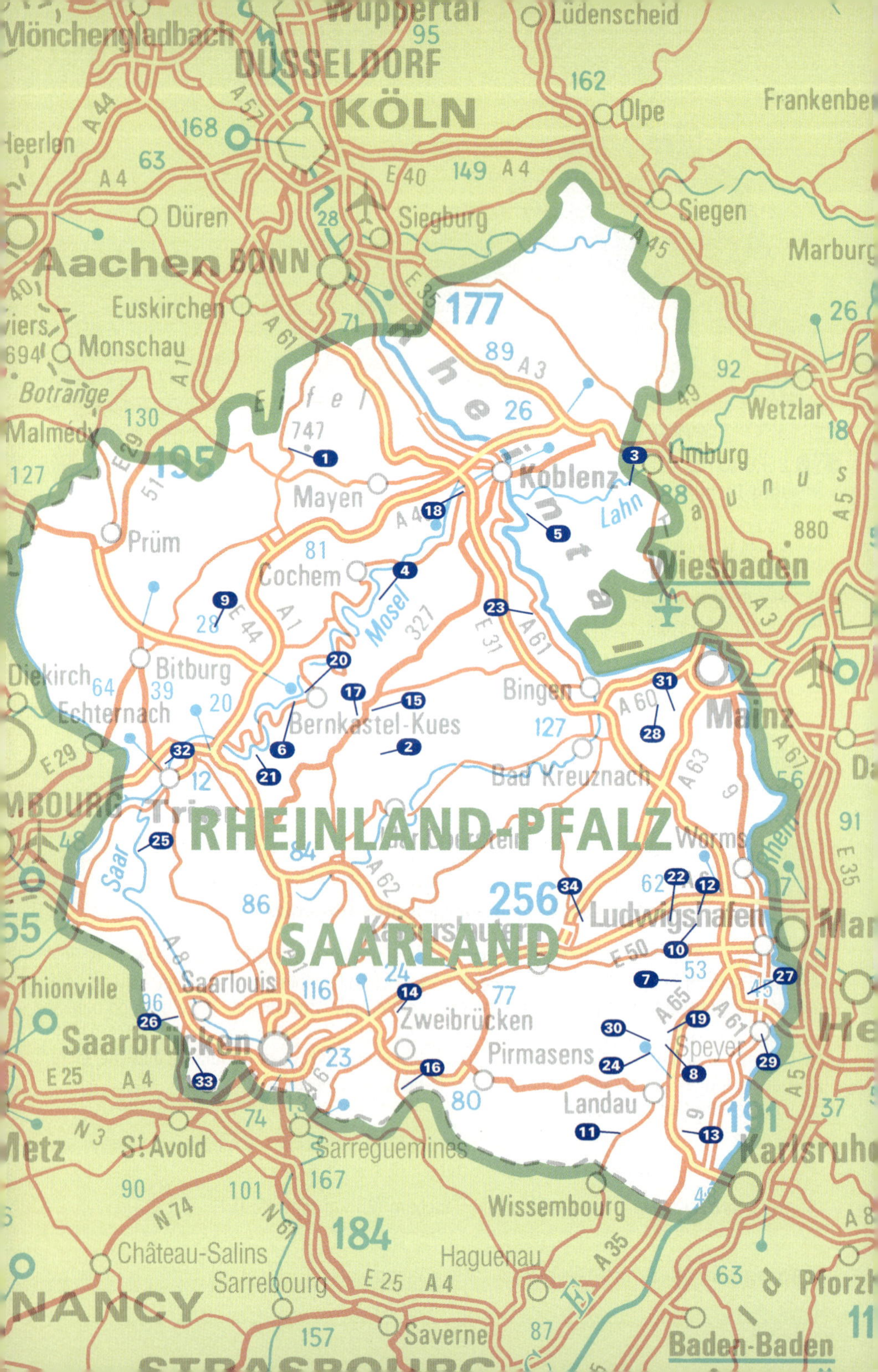

RHEINLAND-PFALZ
SAARLAND
Mönchengladbach
Wuppertal
Lüdenscheid
DÜSSELDORF
KÖLN
Olpe
Frankenberg
Heerlen
Düren
Siegburg
Siegen
Marburg
Aachen
BONN
Euskirchen
Monschau
Botrange
Malmédy
Eifel
Mayen
Koblenz
Limburg
Wetzlar
Lahn
Taunus
Prüm
Cochem
Mosel
Rheintal
Wiesbaden
Bitburg
Bingen
Mainz
Diekirch
Echternach
Bernkastel-Kues
Bad Kreuznach
Trier
Idar-Oberstein
Worms
Saar
Ludwigshafen
Kaiserslautern
Thionville
Saarlouis
Zweibrücken
Pirmasens
Speyer
Saarbrücken
Landau
Metz
St. Avold
Sarreguemines
Karlsruhe
Wissembourg
Château-Salins
Haguenau
Sarrebourg
NANCY
Saverne
Pforzheim
Baden-Baden
STRASBOURG

Rheinland-Pfalz/ Saarland

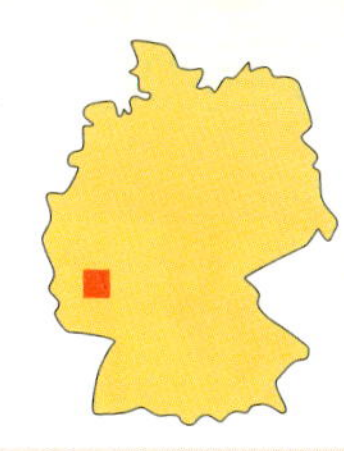

The Rhineland-Palatinate and the Saarland have always been a frontier region, where cultures have met and mixed.The Romans left the mighty Porta Nigra in Trier as their legacy, long before the glorious cathedrals at Speyer, Worms and Mainz marked the heartland of the new Holy Roman Empire. After the French Revolution, Koblenz became the capital of a French *département*, and the Saarland was a point of bitter contention even in living memory. Today's frontiers are peacefully permeable; cultural and other exchanges with France are part of everyday life, and the locals have kept their ability to enjoy the simple pleasures. Chief among these is their world-famous wine; the vines grow in abundance along the German Wine Road, in the Rhinehessen area between Mainz and Worms, and on the banks of the Mosel, Saar and Ruwer. Above them rise wonderful wooded heights, a paradise for walkers; the Palatinate Forest merges seamlessly with the Vosges in France, while the Eifel features a series of strange, enchanting volcanic lakes, the *Maare*. The region's most famous landscape, however, is the Rhine gorge, with its Loreley rock from which the mermaid sang her seductive song.

1 LANDHAUS SONNENHOF

Rosemarie Bell

Auf dem Hirzenstein 1
53518 Adenau
Tel. (02691) 9 22 70
Fax (02691) 8664
info@sonnenhof-adenau.de – www.sonnenhof-adenau.de

Open all year • 37 rooms, including 32 with balcony, 4 with disabled access and 11 non-smoking • Restaurant with terrace: set meal 21.50-49€; half board 21.50€ • Garden, parking; dogs allowed • Wellness and beauty facilities including sauna and gym, skittles, table tennis, bicycle hire, nordic walking, walks by torchlight, herb and mushroom walks, survival training

100/155 €, Breakfast included
VISA MC

The stables next door mean you can even bring your horse on holiday with you!

Situated on a slope overlooking the village, this country-house is located in a peaceful spot which, as the name suggests, always seems to catch the best of the sun. Behind its balcony façade you'll discover country style rooms, most laid out on a spacious scale, and a restaurant, fitted out in pale wood, with its own stove. Warm water is provided by the solar-panels - the owners are clearly keen to do their bit for the environment. There's a children's play area right by the house and the nearest small town - with its indoor and outdoor swimming pools as well as a historic marketplace - is only 10 minutes journey from the hotel.

Sights nearby: Hohe Acht (4 km east), Nürburgring (8 km south)

Access: Exit 2 on A 48 then B 257 or Exit 33 on A 61 then B 412

2 HARFENMÜHLE

Marco Koch

55758 Asbacherhütte
Tel. (06786) 13 04
Fax (06786) 1323 – www.harfenmuehle.de

Open all year • 4 rooms • Restaurants with terrace: Harfenmühle (closed Mon, Tue except public holidays): set meal 37-55€; Mühlenstube (closed Mon Sept to before Easter except before and on public holidays): main course 7.50-15.50€; half board 8.50€ • Garden, parking; dogs not allowed • Sauna, solarium, natural pool, tennis, table tennis, boule

57 €, Breakfast 8 €
Credit cards not accepted

The range of recreational activities available directly on site

With the details on its façade picked out in light blue, this idyllic property stands just outside the village. Its contemporary country-style rooms are located in a flat-roofed building in the garden. A shared kitchen is available on demand, though in fact everything needed is already provided for; the "Harfenmühle" restaurant in the old barn offers superior cuisine in its pleasing Mediterranean-style ambience with dark beams, an open fireplace and wicker seating. Alternatively you can eat in the more rustic ambience of the "Mühlenstube", which offers a more limited choice of plain but satisfying fare.

Sights nearby: German Museum of Precious Stones and Felsenkirche in Idar-Oberstein (16 km south)

Access: 3 km east of Kempfeld towards Herrstein

3 LANDHOTEL ZUM BÄREN

Walter Buggle

Bahnhofstr. 24
65558 Balduinstein
Tel. (06432) 80 07 80
Fax (06432) 8007820 – www.landhotel-zum-baeren.de

Closed 3 1/2 weeks after Ash Wednesday • 10 rooms • Restaurant with terrace (closed Tue): set meal 56-86€ • Garden, parking; dogs allowed in hotel, not in restaurant

105/157 €, Breakfast included
AE VISA MC

Relaxing in the cool shade of the terrace

Located directly on the Lahn, this house has a great tradition of welcoming visitors: in the course of its long history it has served as a posting halt and tow station, but since 1827 the estate has been owned by a family and the cosy atmosphere has as much to do with a natural but well-practiced hospitality as with the brightly furnished, country-style rooms. It is not only the first class service that will ensure a pleasant stay, but also the tasteful colours of the interior and its inviting three piece suites. There are also a few culinary pleasures waiting in the 'Library' restaurant. However if you are in search of something more simple and traditional, then try the wine tavern.

Sights nearby: Schaumburg, Limburg cathedral (9km northeast)

Access: From Exit 42 on A 3 via Limburg and Diez

4 HAUS LIPMANN

Marion Thölén-Lipmann

Marktplatz 3
56814 Beilstein
Tel. (02673) 15 73
Fax (02673) 1521 – www.hotel-haus-lipmann.de

Closed 1 Jan to 30 Mar, 1 Nov to 31 Dec • 5 rooms • Cafe-restaurant with terrace: set lunch 9.50-15€, set dinner 18-23€; half board 13€ • Dogs allowed

85/90 €, Breakfast included
Credit cards not accepted

Watching the sun go down from the lovely terrace overlooking the river

The property of Prince Metternich, Chancellor of Austria in Hapsburg times, this building passed into the ownership of the Lipmann family as long ago as 1795 and it is they who have run it ever since. Just its location in picturesque Beilstein an der Mosel makes it something special, but more than anything else, it is the historic ambience with which it is suffused that makes it almost unique; some of the elegant bedrooms have antique furnishings, while you can choose to dine either in the wood-panelled Stube or the Knights Hall with its romantically medieval atmosphere.

Sights nearby: Marienburg (22 km south) ; Burg Eltz (25 km northeast)

Access: From exit 4 on the A 48 via Cochem

5 **ZUM WEISSEN SCHWANEN**
Karolin König-Kunz

Brunnenstr. 4
56338 Braubach
Tel. (02627) 98 20
Fax (02627) 8802 – www.zum-weissen-schwanen.de

Open all year • 20 rooms, including 1 with disabled access and 10 non-smoking • Restaurant with terrace (closed Wed, midday Sun): set lunch 12-25€, set dinner 25-45€; half board 20€; brasserie (closed Sat, eve Sun) • Garden, parking; dogs allowed • Bicycle hire, organised walks, exhibitions, cookery courses, wine seminars

85/95 €, Breakfast included
AE JCB VISA

Visiting the Marksburg which keeps watch over Braubach

This address began as three historical buildings set against the old city wall: the traditional pub, first mentioned in 1693, the town mill, built in the 14th century but still with a working mill-wheel, and the old vintners' house. Old timbers, inside and out, and relics from down the centuries, like spinning wheels and pine bedsteads, all add to the character: it's a trip back in time, but not one without modern facilities, you'll be pleased to hear! The historical atmosphere is just as strong in the lounge and the old kitchen, which provides a truly traditional setting at mealtimes.

Sights nearby: Burg Lahneck (5 km northwest), Deutsches Eck in Koblenz (14 km north)

Access: On right bank of Rhine south of Koblenz by B 42

6 BRAUNEBERGER HOF

Hilde Conrad

Moselweinstr. 136
54472 Brauneberg
Tel. (06534) 14 00
Fax (06534) 1401 – www.mosel-erlebnis.de

Closed mid-Jan to Feb, 24 Dec • 16 rooms, including 8 with balcony and 1 non-smoking • Cafe; restaurant with terrace (closed Thu and midday except May to Nov: light lunch): main course from 11.50€, set dinner 18.50-55€; half board 18.50€ • Parking; dogs by arrangement • Wine seminars, bicycle hire, walks with picnic provided, exhibitions

68/85 €, Breakfast included

VISA MC

Candle-lit gourmet evenings in the vaulted cellar

Guests of the Brauneberger Hof are housed either in an 18th century timber-framed building or in an adjacent modern structure. The design and decor of the bedrooms corresponds to the character of the buildings; you have the choice between nostalgic atmosphere and timeless elegance. Among the delicacies proferred in the rustic restaurant - which has many a cosy niche - are Riesling wines from the patron's own vineyard, the history of which goes back to 1558. Completing the attractive picture, at the rear of the building is an idyllic garden with a little pool.

Sights nearby: St Nikolaus-Hospital in Kues (9km east), Burg Landshut (12 km east)

Access: From Exit 127 on A 1 towards Bernkastel-Kues

7 DEIDESHEIMER HOF

Artur Hahn

Am Marktplatz 1
67146 Deidesheim
Tel. (06326) 9 68 70
Fax (06326) 7685 – www.deidesheimerhof.de

Closed 1 week Jan • 28 rooms, including 10 with air conditioning and 10 non-smoking • Restaurants with terrace: St Urban: set meal 31-43€; Schwarzer Hahn (eve only, closed Sun, Mon): set meal 70-100€; half board 20€ • Garden; dogs allowed • Bicycle hire, organised walks, cookery courses, wine seminars

120/190 €, Breakfast 12 €

AE JCB VISA

The photo gallery of all the famous guests who've stayed here over the years

The epitome of Rhineland hospitality. This group of historic buildings in the village centre of Deidesheim includes a number of tastefully furnished rooms, their fine fabrics and warm colours creating an elegant and homely ambience. The bathrooms continue in the same vein, stylishly furnished with granite in some areas and marble in others. The Deidesheimer Hof's greatest claim to fame is its old regular, the former Chancellor of Germany Helmut Kohl, who gave many a state visitor, including Margaret Thatcher and Ronald Reagan, an insight into his native Rhineland by serving them the legendary dish Saumagen. You can try it too, though some might say it's an acquired taste!...

Sights nearby: Hambach castle (12 km south), Holiday Park (17 km southeast)

Access: From Exit 11 on A 65 by B 271

8 SCHLOSS EDESHEIM

Andreas Lorenz

Luitpoldstr. 9
67483 Edesheim
Tel. (06323) 9 42 40
Fax (06323) 942411 – www.schloss-edesheim.de

Closed 3-9 Jan, from 24 Dec by arrangement • 36 rooms, including 8 with balcony • Restaurant with terrace: set lunch max 23€, set dinner 44-64€; half board 30€ • Garden, parking; dogs allowed in hotel, not in restaurant • Sauna, massage and ayurveda, bicycle hire

133/150 €, Breakfast included

AE, DC, VISA, MC

The performances on the open-air stage every July and August

It's not only romantics who succumb to the ineffable feelings of love here. Surrounded by a moat, five acres of parkland and sun-drenched vineyards, this stately castle was once owned by the powerful Prince-bishops of Speyer. It's not only the setting and the history that impress, however. The rooms themselves are definitely a cut above the ordinary: some are equipped with Biedermeier furniture and marble bathrooms, while the modern suites are decorated in a palette of sunny colours. The restaurant has a delightful terrace and the chef's very own Mediterranean creations taste even better in the open air on a warm summer night.

Sights nearby: Schloss Villa Ludwigshöhe (6 km west), Landau Zoo (9 km south)

Access: From Exit 14 on A 65 via Edenkoben

9 **MOLITORS MÜHLE**

Michael Molitor

54533 Eisenschmitt-Eichelhütte
Tel. (06567) 96 60
Fax (06567) 966100 – www.molitor.com

Closed 8 Jan to 4 Feb • 28 rooms, including 14 with balcony and 15 non-smoking • Restaurant with terrace: set lunch 15-30€, set dinner 15-39€; half board 18€ • Playground, garden, parking; dogs allowed • Wellness and beauty facilities, tennis, bicycle hire, canoe trips, wine seminars, guided walks with picnic

98/140 €, Breakfast included

VISA MC

Guaranteed quality: home-made cakes and jams as well as wine and spirits from the establishment's own vineyards

This charmingly isolated spot among woods and meadows could hardly be bettered if it's real relaxation you are looking for. The idyllic ambience is further enhanced by three little lakes, which you can explore by rowing boat. Each of the elegant country-style bedrooms has an individual character and all feature period furnishings; they make a stylish and comfortable setting for your stay. Meals are served either in a cosy dining room with a fireplace or in the conservatory extension, which, like the terrace, has a view of the water.

Sights nearby: Himmerod monastery (2 km east), Manderscheid volcanic lakes museum (12 km northeast)

Access: Exit 8 on A 60 or Exit 122 on A 1 then via Manderscheid

10 **LUTHER**

Gisela Luther

Hauptstr. 29
67251 Freinsheim
Tel. (06353) 9 34 80
Fax (06353) 934845 – www.luther-freinsheim.de

Closed Feb, Christmas week • 14 rooms, including 8 non-smoking • Restaurant with terrace (closed midday Mon-Sat, all day Sun): main course 22-30€, set dinner 75€ • Garden, parking; dogs not allowed

90/130 €, Breakfast included

AE VISA MC

Sitting out in fine weather in the charming cobbled courtyard

Despite the name, these two buildings in the centre of Freinsheim have nothing to do with the great reformer. Firstly, they date from the time of the Baroque, and secondly the name is that of the establishment's chef, who pampers his guests with contemporary French cuisine. Meals are served in the Mediterranean elegance of a subtly-lit vaulted chamber divided by pillars. Accommodation is in stylishly comfortable rooms with cherrywood furnishings.

Sights nearby: Burg Neuleiningen (9 km northwest), Limburg monastery ruins (11 km southwest)

Access: From Exit 19 on A 6 via Herxheim or Maxdorf Exit on A 650

11 ZUM LAM

Sven-Erik Ball

Winzergasse 37
76889 Gleiszellen-Gleishorbach
Tel. (06343) 93 92 12
Fax (06343) 939213 – www.zum-lam.de

Closed 10 Jan to 2 Feb • 11 rooms • Restaurant with terrace (closed Wed, eve only Mon-Fri Nov to Mar): set meal 11.50-18.50€; half board 11€ • Garden, parking; dogs allowed • Organised walks, wine tasting

75/85 €, Breakfast included

AE MC

Savouring a sundowner on the garden terrace

This venerable 18th century timber-framed building stands on an idyllic lane in the wine village of Gleiszellen, where vines are trained high overhead and the only sound is that of water splashing in the fountains. The interior is just as charming, with exposed beams and stonework helping to create a cheerfully rustic atmosphere in both bedrooms and dining areas. The comfortable ambience is further enhanced by attractive furnishings in light natural wood - bog-oak in the annexe.

Sights nearby: Silz deer park (10 km west), Old Town in Wissembourg, France (14 km south), Landau Zoo (16 km northeast), Trifels (17 km northwest)

Access: From Exit 20 on A 65 via Bad Bergzabern

12 RESTAURANT GEBR. MEURER

H. und W. Meurer

Hauptstr. 67
67229 Großkarlbach
Tel. (06238) 6 78
Fax (06238) 1007 – www.restaurant-meurer.de

Open all year • 15 rooms, all non-smoking • Cafe, restaurant with terrace (eve only): set meal 43.50-55€ • Garden, parking; dogs by arrangement

112/125 €, Breakfast included

AE VISA MC

Coffee and cakes in the hall or on the terrace: weekends from 2pm

Stepping out into the garden here is like being suddenly transported to Tuscany. Tall cypresses, luxuriant Mediterranean vegetation and a little Classical pavilion with a red-tiled roof complete the illusion. The rooms too are tastefully furnished and decorated in a relaxed, Italian country style, while the bathrooms feature a lavish use of marble. Consisting of a number of separate dining areas, the restaurant is in a welcoming, rustic style, partly vaulted and partly with wood panelling. When the sun shines you will be unable to resist the attractions of the lovely outside terrace.

Sights nearby: Limburg monastery ruins (12 km south), Cathedral and Heylshof Museum in Worms (18 km northeast)

Access: From Exit 19 on A 6 via Kirchheim

13 **KRONE**

Karl Kuntz

Hauptstr. 62
76863 Herxheim-Hayna
Tel. (07276) 50 80
Fax (07276) 50814 – www.hotelkrone.de

Closed from 24-26 December • 52 rooms, 50 with balcony, 35 non-smoking • Restaurant with terrace ; "Zur Krone" (evenings only; closed Mon, Tues) set meals 77-88 €; "Pfälzer Stube" set meals 33-52 €; half board 24 € • Garden, parking, dogs allowed on arrangement • Indoor swimming pool, sauna, steam bath, tennis, bicycle hire, guided walks and cycle tours, carriage drives

124/160 €, Breakfast included

AE VISA MC

An evening stroll through the picturesque village streets

Let yourself be properly spoilt for once: everyone is treated like royalty here! Timelessly elegant rooms are alluringly furnished with a lot of love; the fine attention to detail - from the well cared-for antiques to the flower arrangements - certainly shows them at their best. If you feel like a more active break, try a game of tennis or even a more strenuous cycling tour, topped off with an hour of relaxation in the indoor swimming pool and sauna. Your every culinary desire is looked after by the chef, who'll prepare a few imaginative dishes while you sit in the cosy, wood-panelled dining room.

Sights nearby: Landau collegiate church (15 km northwest), Madenburg (20 km northwest), Baden regional museum in Karlsruhe (25 km southeast)

Access: Exit 20 on A 65; in Hayna

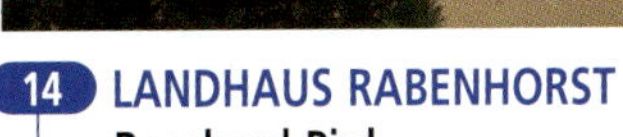

14 LANDHAUS RABENHORST

Bernhard Pinl

Kraepelinstr. 60
66424 Homburg/Saar
Tel. (06841) 9 33 00
Fax (06841) 933030 – www.hotel-rabenhorst.de

Closed 1-2 Jan, 27-31 Dec • 22 rooms, including 3 with balcony and 11 non-smoking • Restaurant with terrace: set meal 29-49€; half board 18€ • Garden, parking; dogs allowed • Bicycle hire

99/140 €, Breakfast included (WE: 95/135 €)

JCB VISA MC

The idyllic terrace looking out over the trees

Since the Pinl family took it over, what was once a woodland inn frequented by day trippers has been turned into an attractive country hotel. The lady of the house herself was responsible for the tasteful design and layout of the bedrooms, which are cheerful and comfortable. A careful choice of materials has helped to create an inviting ambience, both here and in the stylish dining areas, where you can choose between a traditional country-style restaurant and the more rustic "Karlsbergstube" where light meals are served.

Sights nearby: Schlossberg caves, Schwarzenacker Roman museum (4 km south)

Access: Exit 30 on A 8 or Exit 9 on A 6; in eastern part of Homburg, follow signs towards Universitätsklinik and Waldstadion

15 HISTORISCHE SCHLOSSMÜHLE

A. und R. Liller

55483 Horbruch
Tel. (06543) 40 41
Fax (06543) 3178
info@historische-schlossmuehle.de

Closed fortnight in Jan • 18 rooms, all non-smoking, 1 with balcony • Restaurant with terrace (closed Mon): set lunch 30-35€, set dinner 42-70€; half board 35€ • Garden, parking; dogs not allowed • Exhibitions, meadowland herb courses

120/160 €, Breakfast included
VISA MC

The "Frog-King" fountain in front of the building

This fine old mill is ideal for anyone hoping to escape the tiresome routines of everyday life and immerse themselves in the welcoming embrace of unspoiled countryside. Deep in the heart of the lovely Hunsrück uplands, the 17th century building offers tasteful accommodation in which great care has been taken with every detail, and where curtains, carpets and choice items of furniture give every room a distinctive character. The bathrooms feature splendid old-fashioned free-standing tubs. There is a library with an open fire crackling in the grate, and a garden with an idyllic pond. A stay here will soon recharge those batteries!

Sights nearby: Belginum archeology park (5 km north), Schmidtburg near Bundenbach (14 km southeast), St Nikolaus Hospital in Kues (19 km west)

Access: By Hunsrück High Road (Hunsrückhöhenstrasse B 327)

16 KLOSTER HORNBACH

Christiane Lösch

Im Klosterbezirk
66500 Hornbach
Tel. (06338) 91 01 00
Fax (06338) 9101099 – www.kloster-hornbach.de

Open all year • 28 rooms, including 22 non-smoking and 1 with balcony • Restaurant with terrace (closed Mon): main course from 17€, set meal 35-55€; half board 36€ • Garden, parking; dogs allowed in hotel, not in restaurant • Bicycle hire, sauna, steam bath, herb garden, art exhibitions, readings

147/150 €, Breakfast included

AE VISA

The exceptionally luxurious facilities of the "Bade Lust" pool and wellness area

An up-to-date hotel has been inserted with great taste and sensitivity into the walls of this old monastery, parts of which go back to the 8th century. The comfortable rooms come in a choice of four styles, Shaker, Ethno, Asian and Mediterranean, each of which features carefully selected natural materials and inventive colour schemes. Fascinating contrasts are thereby created within the setting of the monastery's venerable walls. Atmospheric old vaults enhance the romantic ambience of the restaurant.

Sights nearby: "Europas Rosengarten" park in Zweibrücken (11 km north), Citadel in Bitche, France (20 km south)

Access: Exit 33 on A 8

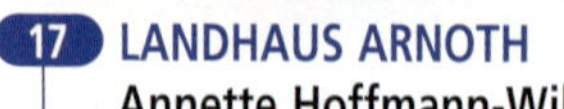

17 LANDHAUS ARNOTH

Annette Hoffmann-Wild

Auf dem Pütz
54483 Kleinich
Tel. (06536) 9 39 90
Fax (06536) 1217 – www.landhaus-arnoth.de

Open all year • 16 rooms • Restaurant with terrace (closed Mon, Tue, midday Wed to Sat): main course 7.50-17€, set dinner 17.50-36.50€; half board 15€ • Garden, parking; dogs not allowed • Bicycle hire, sauna, gym, wine tasting, organised walks

75/95 €, Breakfast included

VISA MC

The cosy old library

This establishment in the middle of Kleinich consists of a slate-hung late 19th century villa and two guesthouses. Some of the bedrooms have kept the dreamy atmosphere of a bygone age, while others feature outstandingly lively colour schemes. Everywhere, not just on the staircase, numerous pictures lend a personal, individual touch to the overall ambience. Equally attractive is the pleasantly intimate restaurant, where you will feel as if you are dining with friends. You are sure to take away happy memories of your stay here.

Sights nearby: St Nikolaus Hospital in Kues (16 km west), Marienburg monastery (22 km north)

Access: By Hunsrück High Road (Hunsrückhöhenstrasse B 327)

18 ALTE MÜHLE THOMAS HÖRETH

Gudrun Höreth

Mühlental 17
56330 Kobern
Tel. (02607) 64 74
Fax (02607) 6848 – www.thomas-hoereth.de

Closed 23-24 Dec • 10 rooms, including 8 non-smoking, 1 with balcony, plus 2 suites • Restaurant with terrace (closed midday Mon-Fri): set dinner 60€, main course 14-30€ • Parking; dogs allowed • Wine tasting, bicycle hire, organised walks

145/160 €, Breakfast included

JCB VISA MC

The mill garden in full bloom

There is a certain magic surrounding this house and wine growing estate that will undoubtedly win you over - you can almost feel the sense of history surrounding it. A fairytale mill from the 11th century and its adjacent building, not to mention the gently splashing millstream and an idyllic garden could prompt even the most pragmatic person to explore their romantic side. In the house itself, the original exposed stone shows through here and there, combining surprisingly well with carefully chosen furnishings and a lively décor. Underfloor heating keeps the chill out of the rooms on even the coldest morning, but the friendly, family atmosphere provides a special warmth of its own.

Sights nearby: Koblenz Old Town (18 km north), Maria Laach monastery (23 km northwest)

Access: Exit 8 on A 48

19 **WALDHAUS WILHELM**
Günter Wilhelm

Kalmithöhenstr. 6
67487 Maikammer
Tel. (06321) 5 80 44
Fax (06321) 58564 – www.waldhaus-wilhelm.de

Open all year • 22 rooms, including 2 with balcony • Restaurant with terrace (closed Mon): set meal 15-45€; half board 17€ • Garden, parking; dogs by arrangement • Woodland and herb walks, wine seminars

34/42 €, Breakfast included
AE VISA

The view of kitchen activity through the big window in the foyer

This welcoming timber-framed building stands in woodland at the foot of the Kalmit, at 673 metres the highest summit in the Pfälzer Wald. It's a quiet and peaceful spot, with endless possiblities for walkers. Acommodation is in comfortable rooms with solid, rustic furnishings, with fine carpets and fabrics lending an extra touch of quality. You dine in an elegant country-style restaurant, or in fine weather on the terrace, with its woodland views and resin-scented breezes.

Sights nearby: Kalmit, Neustadt an der Weinstrasse Old Town (8km north), Schloss Villa Ludwigshöhe (9 km southwest)

Access: Exit 13 or 14 on A 65; 2.5 km west of Maikammer towards Kalmit

20 WEINROMANTIKHOTEL RICHTERSHOF

Armin Hoeck

Hauptstr. 81-83
54486 Mülheim (Mosel)
Tel. (06534) 94 80
Fax (06534) 948100 – www.weinromantikhotel.de

Closed 24th of December • 44 rooms, including 2 with disabled access and 13 non-smoking • Restaurant with terrace (evenings only, except Sun and on bank holidays); set meals 34-85 €; half board 25 € • Garden, parking; dogs allowed in hotel, not in restaurant • Health and beauty facilities, bicycle hire, cooking courses, wine seminars, organised walks

120/150 €, Breakfast included
VISA MC

The breakfast buffet set out in an original butcher's shop of 1911

This wine-growing establishment combines old and new with great success. In its lovely parkland setting, the historic building fabric has been extended with great taste and sensitivity to provide accommodation catering for every need. Elegant, individually designed bedrooms, attractive wellness and beauty facilities, a stylish traditional restaurant with Rosenthal porcelain, a conservatory cafe and a bistro-bar with a fireplace and a terrace overlooking a pond - everything is calculated to give guests a luxurious and relaxing stay.

Sights nearby: Bernkastel-Kues Mosel wine museum (6km east), Burg Landshut (9 km east)

Access: From Exit 127 on A 1 towards Bernkastel-Kues

21 LANDHAUS ST. URBAN

Ruth und Harald Rüssel

Büdlicherbrück 1
54426 Naurath/Wald
Tel. (06509) 9 14 00
Fax (06509) 914040 – www.landhaus-st-urban.de

Open all year • 16 rooms • Restaurant with terrace (closed Tue, Wed): set lunch 65-85€, set dinner 75-95€; half board 40€ • Garden, parking; dogs allowed • Bicycle hire, cookery courses, wine tasting in own winery

95/160 €, Breakfast included

AE VISA MC

The freshly-baked sourdough bread straight from the oven

Named after the patron saint of wine-growers, this old mill is picturesquely located in the valley of the Dhron. As well as the peace and quiet of the place, you will appreciate the rooms furnished and decorated in attractive French country style, to say nothing of the outstanding cuisine. Classic French dishes are attentively served in the bright and welcoming restaurant with its contemporary design features. On fine days, it's a wonderful experience to dine on the terrace overlooking the idyllic millpond.

Sights nearby: Porta Nigra, Basilica, Episcopal Museum in Trier (26 km west)

Access: Exit 131 on A 1

22 ALTE PFARREY

Susanne und Utz Ueberschaer

Untergasse 54
67271 Neuleiningen
Tel. (06359) 8 60 66
Fax (06359) 86060
www.altepfarrey.de

Open all year • 9 rooms, including 3 with balcony • Restaurant with terrace (closed Mon, Tue): set lunch 27-78€, set dinner 58-78€; half board 30€ • Garden; dogs allowed

95/150 €, Breakfast included

VISA MC

The attractive atmosphere, underlined by the many charming details and attentive service

This little treasure of a place is tucked away among the crooked lanes and alleyways of Neuleinigen's castle hill. The front of the building with its picturesque corner turrets is bedecked with plants, while inside, the rooms, each with its own character, have been designed and decorated with sure taste. Here and there, ancient stonework and massive timbers form a most attractive symbiosis with the stylish furnishings. Equally enchanting is the classically elegant restaurant with its attractive conservatory.

Sights nearby: Castle, Cathedral, Jewish Cemetery and Niebelungen Museum in Worms (23 km northeast)

Access: From Exit 19 on A 6 via Grünstadt and Sausenheim

23 WEINHAUS WEILER

Familie Klaus Weiler

Marktplatz 4
55430 Oberwesel
Tel. (06744) 70 03
Fax (06744) 930520 – www.weinhaus-weiler.com

Closed 31 Jan to 3 Mar • 10 rooms, including 1 with balcony and 4 non-smoking • Restaurant with terrace (closed Thu Nov to Apr): set meal 24-26€; half board 17€ • Parking; dogs allowed

65/95 €, Breakfast included

AE JCB VISA MC

The Christmas market held right in front of the building

This trim half-timbered building of 1552 stands on the historic market square in the middle of Oberwesel. You have a choice of rooms furnished and decorated in a variety of ways. Some are in a romantic country style, others are more modern, while still others feature dark farmhouse-style furnishings or are decorated in a tasteful, timeless manner. consisting of a number of little dining rooms in traditional style, the restaurant has a menu which is changed monthly, along with a list of recommended wines.

Sights nearby: Liebfrauenkirche, steamer trips on Rhine

Access: Exit 44 on A 61

24 WEINSTUBE WALDKIRCH

Dorothea Waldkirch

Weinstr. 53
76835 Rhodt unter Rietburg
Tel. (06323) 70 53
Fax (06323) 81137

Open all year • 15 rooms • Weinstube with terrace (closed Thu): main course 6-12€ • Garden, parking; dogs allowed • Bicycle hire, wine tasting

70 €, Breakfast included
VISA MC

The charming breakfast room in the old press-house

Entered through a sculpted sandstone archway, this welcoming courtyard building is one of the many idyllic vintner's dwellings in the wine village of Rhodt, the whole of which is a conservation area. The immaculately kept rooms feature furnishings in light wood, while exposed beams emphasize the establishment's rustic character. Wine is sampled in the old wash-house, which is distinguished by two really unusual features: firstly a pear tree which has managed to grow through the wall in search of the light, and secondly the glass-covered table from which you can peer down at the water at the bottom of the eight-metre well.

Sights nearby: Schloss Villa Ludwigshöhe, museum of wine and local history in Edenkoben (2 km north), Hambach castle (9km north)

Access: From Exit 14 on A 65 via Edenkoben

25 VILLA KELLER

W. Müntnich

Brückenstr. 1
54439 Saarburg
Tel. (06581) 9 29 10
Fax (06581) 6695 – www.villa-keller.de

Closed 1-30 Jan • 11 rooms, all non-smoking, 1 with balcony • Restaurant with terrace (closed Mon, midday Tue): set lunch 20-25€, set dinner 27-35€; half board 20€ • Garden, parking; dogs allowed • Literary evenings Oct to Mar

90/100 €, Breakfast included

AE DC VISA MC

A stroll through the medieval lanes of old Saarburg

This charming gentleman's residence of 1801 on the banks of the River Saar stands directly opposite the castle hill. Guests are accommodated in elegant rooms with tasteful walnut furnishings. Those on the first floor have retained their original parquet floors, while those above are fully carpeted. The traditional restaurant has overtones of country-house style, and features a striking tiled stove with filigree decoration. As an alternative, there is the cosy "Wirtshaus"with its pleasant beer garden.

Sights nearby: Amüseum, Roman villa in Nennig (20 km southwest)

Access: From Exit 132 on A 62 by B 407

26 ALTES PFARRHAUS BEAUMARAIS

Jürgen Trampert

Hauptstr. 2
66740 Saarlouis-Beaumarais
Tel. (06831) 96 56 70
Fax (06831) 965671 – www.restaurant-trampert.de

Open all year • 37 rooms, including 4 with disabled access and 5 non-smoking • Restaurant with terrace (closed midday Sat to midday Mon): set meal 18.50-46€; half board by arrangment • Garden, parking; dogs allowed • Private views, cabaret, jazz events, wine, cigar and piano evenings

78/134 €, Breakfast included (WE: 70,20/120,60 €)

AE VISA

The ivy-clad courtyard and beer garden with live music

This property was originally built as a summer residence for Baroness von Salis, before serving for many years as a rectory. It is now a hotel with a most attractive historic ambience and elegant rooms featuring many choice antique pieces. Thanks not least to its rough stone walls, an authentic atmosphere permeates the “Hofhaus” brasserie, which is also used for private views and artistic events. By contrast, the “Trampert” restaurant has more of the ambience of an elegant bistro, its red leather benches and big mirrors a reminder that France is not very far away.

Sights nearby: Fortifications in Saarlouis (3 km southeast), Völklinger Hütte World Heritage steelworks (15 km southeast)

Access: From Exit 2 on A 620 towards Wallerfangen

27 **SALISCHER HOF**

Karsten Möller

Burgstr. 12
67105 Schifferstadt
Tel. (06235) 93 10
Fax (06235) 931200
info@salischer-hof.de – www.salischer-hof.de

Closed between 1st and 15th Jan. • 24 rooms, including 1 with disabled access • Restaurant with terrace (closed Sat noon, Sun); set lunch 17-29 €, set dinner 38-49 € • Garden, parking; dogs allowed • Cooking courses, food and local wine evenings

95 €, Breakfast included

AE JCB VISA MC

The restaurant's tempting special offerings

In the heart of Schifferstadt, not far from the Town Hall, this establishment of 1732 offers its guests comfortably appointed rooms in three partly timber-framed buildings. Furnishings in pale wood and rattan lend a timeless air, in contrast to the historic setting. The bathrooms feature lavish use of marble. On two levels in the old barn, the restaurant surrounds diners with a cheerful, contemporary country house ambience.

Sights nearby: Cathedral, Technology museum, Palatinate historical museum in Speyer (9 km southeast), Wilhelm Hack Museum in Ludwigshafen (13 km north)

Access: Exit 62 on A 61

28 ZUM ALTEN WEINKELLER

Familie Immerheiser

Schulstr. 6
55270 Schwabenheim
Tel. (06130) 94 18 00
Fax (06130) 9418080 – www.immerheiser-wein.de

Open all year • 11 rooms, including 4 non-smoking • Restaurant with terrace: set dinner 30-49€, main course 15-24€ • Garden, parking; dogs allowed • Bicycle hire, wine tasting, vineyard walks and picnics

70/82 €, Breakfast included

VISA MC

The ornamental pool as seen from the garden terrace

This is the place to immerse yourself in the cult of the vine! Naturally enough, most of the wine consumed here will be the Riesling or Pinot Gris from the establishment's own vineyard; it is best savoured in the cheerful setting of the rustic restaurant, where old timbers and stone walls help create a pleasantly rustic atmosphere. The attractive country-style bedrooms feature solid furnishings in pale wood. Even more romantic, complete with iron four-poster beds, are the three Tuscan-style rooms in the stone-built annexe.

Sights nearby: Mainz cathedral (22 km northeast), Burg Klopp in Bingen (22 km west)

Access: From Exit 16 on A 60 via Ingelheim or from Exit 4 on A 63 via Stadecken-Elsheim

29 DOMHOF

Ralf Schmitt

Bauhof 3
67346 Speyer
Tel. (06232) 1 32 90
Fax (06232) 132990 – www.domhof.de

Open all year • 49 rooms, including 26 non-smoking and 1 with disabled access • Restaurant with beer garden: main course 6-15€; half board 16€ • Parking; dogs allowed

112/122 €, Breakfast included (WE: 106 €)
AE VISA MC

Watching the shipping on the busy Rhine from one of the inviting benches on the riverside promenade

With deep historic roots, this was once the place where kings and kaisers stayed and where the highest court of the Holy Roman Empire had its seat. The present hotel occupies buildings which were erected in the years following the terrible fire of 1689 that affected the whole town. The comfortable rooms are solidly furnished with period pieces or in oak. Since 1988 the establishment has had its own microbrewery, with a lovely beer garden in the courtyard, which also serves as breakfast room in good weather.

Sights nearby: Cathedral, Museum of technology, Historical museum of the Palatinate, Jewish ceremonial bath

Access: In city centre, nearly opposite cathedral

30 DAS LANDHOTEL WEINGUT GERNERT

Astrid Gernert

Maikammerer Str. 39
67487 St. Martin
Tel. (06323) 9 41 80
Fax (06323) 941840 – www.das-landhotel.com

Closed 15-31 Jan • 16 rooms, including 9 with balcony and 8 non-smoking • Straußwirtschaft: bar serving local wines and light snacks • Garden, parking; dogs by arrangement

96 €, Breakfast included
Credit cards not accepted

Strolling through the lanes and alleyways of idyllic old St Martin

At the foot of the vineyards, this establishment is in the very heart of the southern Palatinate, where the mild climate allows figs, almonds and even lemons to flourish. Guests are accommodated in rooms in Mediterranean country style, featuring lime-washed pine furniture and terracotta tiles. And because the property has its own vineyard, the benevolent spirit of Bacchus presides over the proceedings; even the minibar in your room has a special compartment for red wine, and the establishment's vaulted cellar of 1851 makes an ideal setting in which to raise your glass to the jovial god of wine.

Sights nearby: Schloss Villa Ludwigshöhe (7 km south), Holiday Park (20 km east)

Access: From Exit 14 on A 65 via Edenkoben

31 CHRISTIAN GARTENHOTEL

Ariane Kersten

Christian-Reichert-Str. 3-5
55271 Stadecken-Elsheim
Tel. (06136) 9 16 50
Fax (06136) 916555 – www.christian-gartenhotel.de

Open all year • 22 rooms, including 3 with balcony, 3 with terrace, 1 with disabled access and 10 non-smoking • Restaurant with terrace (eve only): set meal 18-42€; half board 18-26€ • Garden, parking; dogs allowed in hotel, not in restaurant • Indoor pool, sauna, massage, cosmetic treatments, gym, boule, audio library, bicycle hire, carriage drives, wine tasting

92/110 €, Breakfast included

AE JCB VISA

The view from the elegant breakfast room, a great start to the day

This stylish hotel stands on the outskirts of Mainz at the point where the houses end and the vineyards begin. In its own little park, it offers lavishly furnished and decorated rooms in tasteful country style. Carefully considered colour schemes lend the interiors an almost Mediterranean air, so it hardly comes as a surprise to be invited to take a glass of wine in the garden and to try your luck at a game of boule.

Sights nearby: Stefanskirche (with stained glass by Chagall) and Gutenberg museum in Mainz (13 km northeast)

Access: Exit 4 on A 63

32 VILLA HÜGEL

Claus Schütt

Bernhardstr. 14
54295 Trier
Tel. (0651) 3 30 66
Fax (0651) 37958 – www.hotel-villa-huegel.de

Open all year • 34 rooms, including 2 with balcony and 1 with terrace • Restaurant with terrace (dinner only; closed Fri to Sun): main course 16-22€ • Garden, parking; dogs allowed in hotel, not in restaurant • Indoor pool, sauna, jacuzzi, bicycle hire

99/138 €, Breakfast included

AE ⓓ JCB VISA MC

Being able to relax completely thanks to the super-competent management and friendly service

Dating from 1914, the Villa Hügel enjoys an elevated position to the south of Trier with fine views over the city in its setting. The attractiveness of the place is further enhanced by the pretty gardens and the fine Art Nouveau architecture of the building. The elegant rooms feature a variety of furnishings, but everywhere there is an enchantingly bright and stylish atmosphere. On fine days, it's a special treat to take breakfast on the superb panoramic terrace.

Sights nearby: Porta Nigra, Rhineland museum, Imperial baths, Amphitheatre, Karl Marx birthplace

Access: In southern part of Old Town, close to "ERA" (Europäische Rechtsakademie)

33 LINSLERHOF

Nicola Flierl

66802 Überherrn
Tel. (06836) 80 70
Fax (06836) 80717 – www.linslerhof.de

Open all year • 60 rooms • Restaurant with terrace: set meal 24.50€, main course 10.50-26.50€; half board from 23.50€ • Garden, parking; dogs allowed • Wet and dry saunas, jacuzzis, massage, firing range and instruction, bicycle hire, cookery courses

117/140 €, Breakfast included

AE VISA MC

The shop where you can buy estate products to take home with you

Together with its chapel and various outbuildings, this property on the outskirts of Uberherrn almost amounts to a village in its own right and it's certainly a place where you can emjoy country life to the full. The rooms are tastefully furnished in English country style, while the inviting restaurant offers dishes based on local game or on ingredients grown on the estate. And while we're on the subject of game: not only do antlers feature prominently in the decor, but the establishment has its own, very modern shooting range and in fact adjoins a marksman's school for would-be hunters. Keen riders should note that there are stables as well.

Sights nearby: Völkinger Hütte World Heritage steelworks (16 km east), Niederaltdorf dripstone caves (18 km north)

Access: Exit 3 on A 8; turn left in Altfortweiler and follow sign; the hotel is 2 km east of Überherrn

34 WARTENBERGER MÜHLE

Martin Scharff

Schloßberg 16
67681 Wartenberg-Rohrbach
Tel. (06302) 9 23 40
Fax (06302) 923434 – www.wartenberger-muehlenhof.de

Open all year • 14 rooms, all with balcony, 12 with air conditioning • Restaurant with terrace (closed Mon, Tue): set lunch 23-29€, set dinner 59-84€; bistro: set meal 19.50-29.50€ • Garden, parking; dogs not allowed • Courses on cookery, herbs, wine and cheese

79/115 €, Breakfast included

AE VISA

The wonderful garden terrace with a view of the Lohnsbach valley and the fine herb and vegetable garden

This 16th century courtyard farm has been turned into an unusual country hotel under the expert direction of architectural professor Horst Ermel. The rooms are furnished with works by local artists. Modern art, the carefully thought-out decor and the historic setting make a perfect combination. Refined contemporary cuisine is served in what used to be the stables, a lovely vaulted space divided up by stone columns. The stylish "Bistro-Vinothek", featuring an exposed tiled ceiling, is more informal.

Sights nearby: Otterberg abbey church (9 km west), Pfalzgalerie in Kaiserslautern (14 km southwest)

Access: Exit 14 on A 63 or Exit 17 on A 6

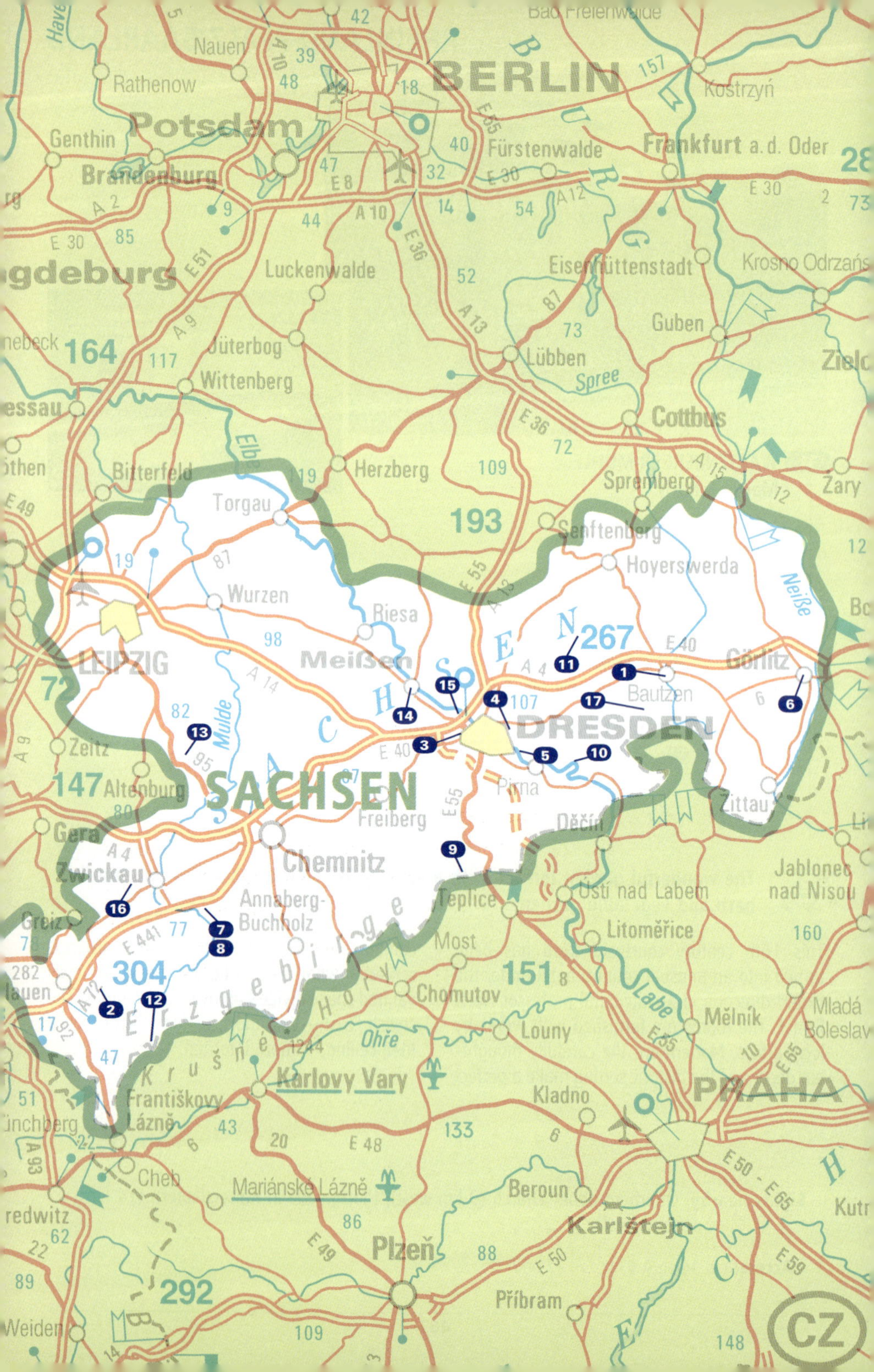

BERLIN
Nauen
Rathenow
Potsdam
Genthin
Brandenburg
Kostrzyń
Frankfurt a.d. Oder
Fürstenwalde
Luckenwalde
Eisenhüttenstadt
Krosno Odrzańskie
Guben
Jüterbog
Wittenberg
Lübben
Spree
Cottbus
Bitterfeld
Herzberg
Spremberg
Żary
Torgau
Senftenberg
Hoyerswerda
Neiße
Wurzen
Riesa
Meißen
LEIPZIG
Görlitz
Bautzen
DRESDEN
Mulde
Zeitz
Altenburg
SACHSEN
Freiberg
Pirna
Zittau
Gera
Chemnitz
Děčín
Zwickau
Annaberg-Buchholz
Teplice
Ústí nad Labem
Jablonec nad Nisou
Greiz
Litoměřice
Most
Chomutov
Louny
Labe
Mělník
Mladá Boleslav
Ohře
Karlovy Vary
PRAHA
Františkovy Lázně
Kladno
Cheb
Mariánské Lázně
Beroun
Karlštejn
Plzeň
Příbram
Weiden
CZ

Sachsen

The jewel of Saxony is, of course, its capital Dresden, justly named "Florence on the Elbe". Despite its near-total destruction in the Second World War, this lovely city has kept its unique charm, while decades of patient work have restored much of its Baroque glory. Downstream from Dresden stands Meissen, where visitors come to learn the secrets of the world-famous porcelain still manufactured here. Just as fascinating is historic Leipzig, once home to Bach and Mendelssohn, with its warren of shopping arcades and the cellar bar where Faust once caroused with his tempter Mephistopheles. On the outskirts, a man-made memorial mountain recalls victory over Napoleon's armies in the Battle of the Nations while, in the town itself, there are many memories of 1989, when Leipzig's citizens led the peaceful protests which brought down the GDR. Beyond Saxony's cities, you'll discover unspoiled countryside by the mile, especially along the Czech border to the south. The mountains of the Erzgebirge harbour many a venerable tradition, while the bizarre sandstone formations of "Saxon Switzerland" are a stunning backdrop for hikes and cycle rides, and a real challenge for climbers.

SCHLOSS-SCHÄNKE

David Rösner

Burgplatz 5
02625 Bautzen
Tel. (03591) 30 49
Fax (03591) 490198
david roesner@web.de – www.schloss-schaenke.net

Open all year • 11 rooms, including 1 with small terrace • Restaurant with terrace (closed midday Mon-Fri): set meal 20-25€ • Parking; dogs allowed • Bicycle hire, organised walks, exhibitions, wine seminars

66/99 €, Breakfast included

AE · Diners · JCB · VISA · MC

The romantic room in the mill tower 50 metres away

Guests are made heartily welcome here in the heart of Bautzen's Old Town, with a basket of fruit, mineral water, juice and a digestif provided in every bedroom. The bedrooms themselves are furnished in natural wood or with painted country-style items. Divided into several separate spaces, the restaurant will enchant you with its vaulted ceilings, wood panelling and its atmospheric decor, which includes an array of weaponry in the "Knights' Parlour".

Sights nearby: Cathedral, Alte Wasserkunst water tower, Sorbian Museum

Access: In Old Town near Ortenburg

2 LANDHAUS MARIENSTEIN

Frank Straubel

Thomas-Müntzer-Str. 9
08239 Bergen (Vogtland)
Tel. (037463) 85 10
Fax (037463) 851109 – www.landhaus-marienstein.de

Open all year • 13 rooms, including 2 non-smoking • Restaurant with terrace (closed midday Mon-Fri): set meal 19-42€; half board 15€ • Parking; dogs allowed • Sauna, steam bath, massage, bicycle hire, carriage drives, cookery courses

99 €, Breakfast included (WE: 89 €)

AE VISA MC

Watching sunrise from the terrace

It's difficult to believe that this lovely timber-framed structure was only built in 1934. However that may be, the location was certainly well chosen; here above Bergen on the edge of the forest you can really appreciate the peace and quiet of the unspoiled surroundings, to say nothing of the panoramic view over the countryside of the Vogtland. Restaurant and bedrooms are in a refined country style, and each bedroom has been tastefully decorated to lend it an individual character. The "Cigar Room" is particularly stylish; here you can settle down in a well-upholstered armchair with a good book, have a game of chess, or enjoy a glass of wine or a good cigar.

Sights nearby: Plauener Spitze embroidery works in Plauen (13 km west), Drachenhöhle caves in Syrau (20 km northwest)

Access: From Exit 7 on A 72 towards Auerbach via Mechelgrün

3 ROMANTIK HOTEL PATTIS

Michael Pattis

Merbitzer Str. 53
01157 Dresden-Briesnitz
Tel. (0351) 4 25 50
Fax (0351) 4255255 – www.pattis.de

Open all year • 46 rooms, including 6 with balcony or terrace, 1 with disabled access and 13 non-smoking • Restaurants with terrace: Gourmet (closed Sun, Mon, midday): set meal 63-83€; Vitalis: set meal 25-30€; half board 25-72€ • Garden, parking; dogs allowed • Health and beauty facilities including sauna and massage, bicycle hire, organised excursions

135/315 €, Breakfast included (WE: 150/350 €)

AE D VISA MC

Splashing around in the old-fashioned bathtubs

If you are looking for a relaxing stay, hanker after comfort and would not object to being shamelessly pampered, this could be the place for you. The bedrooms are tastefully decorated and furnished in stylish dark wood, the wellness and beauty facilities offer all kinds of delightful experiences, from ayurveda to treatment with volcanic earth, there is an idyllic park behind the hotel, and the gourmet restaurant serves exquisite food on Meissen porcelain. We could go on...

Sights nearby: Zwinger, Schloss Moritzburg (15km north)

Access: In a side road off Meissner Landstrasse (B 6) northeast of city centre

4 SCHLOSS ECKBERG

Hans-Joachim Herrmann

Bautzner Str. 134
01099 Dresden-Loschwitz
Tel. (0351) 8 09 90
Fax (0351) 8099199
email@schloss-eckberg.de – www.schloss-eckberg.de

Open all year • 17 rooms in the castle, all with air conditioning; 67 rooms in the Kavaliershaus • Restaurant with terrace: set lunch 20€, set dinner 38-63€; half board 25€ • Garden, parking; dogs allowed in hotel, not in restaurant • Wellness and beauty facilities, bicycle hire, test drives in luxury limousines, wine seminars

135/235 €, Breakfast included

AE D JCB VISA MC

The view over Dresden from the castle terrace

Who didn't as a child dream of living in a castle? The fantasy can become reality here, at least for the length of your stay in Schloss Eckberg, a Tudor-style castle built high above the River Elbe in 1860. Fit for a prince, the rooms are tasteful and elegant creations by the Italian designer Danilo Silvestrin, featuring silk hangings, antique furnishings, and marble bathrooms. In the extensive, romantic park, the "Kavaliershaus" offers somewhat plainer accommodation, which is nevertheless just as well-kept.

Sights nearby: Hofkirche, Pfunds Dairy, German Hygiene Museum

Access: On B 6 from centre towards Bautzen

5 **SCHLOSS HOTEL PILLNITZ**

Georg Zepp

August-Böckstiegel-Str. 10
01326 Dresden-Pillnitz
Tel. (0351) 2 61 40
Fax (0351) 2614400 – www.schlosshotel-pillnitz.de

Open all year • 42 rooms, including 20 non-smoking • Restaurant with terrace (closed Sun): main course 18-25€, set dinner 35-55€; half board 30€ • Garden, parking; dogs allowed in hotel, not in restaurant • Bicycle hire, organised walks, cookery courses, wine seminars, exhibitions, golf, help with cultural visits

125/205 €, Breakfast included

AE JCB VISA MC

The castle's landing-stage for the pleasure steamers on their way between Dresden and Saxon Switzerland

Still dispensing hospitality today, albeit in a rather different style, this establishment occupies what was once the castle tavern of lovely Schloss Pillnitz on the banks of the River Elbe. Accommodation is in spacious and comfortable rooms with furnishings in cheerful country-house style. If you are looking for something really special, there are 3 suites, two of them with water-beds. The restaurant is stylishly rustic and of course the outside terrace benefits enormously from the wonderful, historic setting.

Sights nearby: Schloss Pillnitz, Semper Opera House, Bastei rocks (16km east)

Access: 13km southeast of Dresden city centre by Pillnitzer Landstrasse along north bank of River Elbe

6 ROMANTIK HOTEL TUCHMACHER

Helmut Wilzbach

Peterstr. 8
02826 Görlitz
Tel. (03581) 4 73 10
Fax (03581) 473179 – www.tuchmacher.de

Closed 1-3 Jan, 18-21 Dec • 30 rooms, including 18 non-smoking • Restaurant with terrace (closed midday Mon): set meal 15-59€; half board 15€ • Garden, parking; dogs allowed • Gym and wellness facilities, bicycle hire

109/149 €, Breakfast included

AE Ⓓ VISA MC

The delightful little bar beneath ancient vaults

The old cloth town of Görlitz was largely spared from destruction in the second world war, and its heritage of more than 3500 listed buildings is well worth seeing. This hotel is one of the town's finest edifices, made up of what were once three separate buildings dating from Renaissance times. Lovely doors and windows speak eloquently of those days. Amongst other features, the interior has preserved beautifully painted timber ceilings of the Baroque era. This all makes a striking setting which has been enhanced by elegant decor and furnishings in traditional style. You are sure to appreciate the stylish historical ambience in both bedrooms and restaurant.

Sights nearby: St Marienthal monastery (15km south)

Access: In Old Town, close to River Neisse and Peterskirche

7 ROMANTIK HOTEL JAGDHAUS WALDIDYLL

Hertha Sellmair und Andrea J. Kahl

Talstr. 1
08118 Hartenstein
Tel. (037605) 8 40
Fax (037605) 84444 – www.romantikhotels.com/hartenstein

Open all year • 28 rooms, including 7 with balcony and 8 non-smoking • Restaurant with terrace: set lunch 18-22.80€, set dinner 22.50-54€; half board 22€ • Garden, parking; dogs allowed in hotel, not in restaurant • Health and beauty spa on edge of forest: sauna, jacuzzis, steam bath, solarium, fitness equipment, massage and cosmetic treatments; carriage drives

105/129 €, Breakfast included (WE: 119/129 €)

AE ⓓ JCB VISA MC

The bathtub with the gilt swan-shaped taps in the honeymoon suite

In its woodland setting, this steep-gabled edifice in typical local style was originally built as a miners' holiday home. However, any idea that the accommodation provided might be spartan in character soon proves unfounded; the rooms have been decorated with loving attention to detail in English country-house style. The peaceful terrace, the pool in its clearing, and the wellness facilities in their own building make their own contribution to a relaxed and pleasant stay.

Sights nearby: Museum of miners' folk art in Schneeberg (10 km south), Robert Schumann's birthplace in Zwickau (16 km northwest)

Access: Exit 12 on A 72 or Exit 11 via Wildenfels

8 SCHLOSS WOLFSBRUNN

Karl-Ludwig Leonhardt

Stein 8
08118 Hartenstein
Tel. (037605) 7 60
Fax (037605) 76299
wolfsbrunn@t-online.de – www.schloss-wolfsbrunn.de

Open all year • 24 rooms, including 4 with balcony and 11 non-smoking • Restaurant with terrace (closed midday Mon-Sat); set dinner 25-50€, main course 12-30€; half board 25€ • Garden, parking; dogs allowed in hotel, not in restaurant • Cosmetic treatments, massage, sauna, steam bath, tennis, bicycle hire

145/175 €, Breakfast included

AE VISA

Game, set and match on the private tennis court

In 1912 a local businessman fulfilled his dreams by building himself a castle in Art Nouveau style, set in a spacious park. Today, as a guest in what is now a hotel, you can share his dreams. The bedrooms are mainly furnished in period pieces - some of them real originals. For dining you have a choice of restaurant - tastefully elegant and with a conservatory on the ground floor, gently rustic in the castle cellars - while drinks are taken in the castle bar.

Sights nearby: Aue Zoo (10km south), Zwickau cathedral (16km northwest)

Access: From Exit 11 or 12 on A 72 via Wildenfels

9 ALTES ZOLLHAUS

Frau Gronowsky

€€ Altenberger Str. 7
01776 Hermsdorf-Neuhermsdorf
Tel. (035057) 5 40
Fax (035057) 54240 – www.landhotel-altes-zollhaus.de

Open all year • 41 rooms, all non-smoking • Restaurant with terrace: main course from 5.20€; half board 13€ • Garden, parking; dogs allowed • Sauna, solarium, jacuzzi, gym, bicycle hire, ski equipment hire

59/89 €, Breakfast included

AE D JCB VISA MC

The snow sculptures created early in the New Year during the "art of snow" competition

This spot in the eastern Erzgebirge uplands was once the site of the customs post on the border between Saxony and Bohemia. The long timber-framed building is now an attractive rural hotel, offering accommodation in solid and comfortably furnished country-style rooms. You dine either beneath the vaults of the "Käsestube", where the accent is on fondue, or in the "Kreuzgewölbe" restaurant which features lovely arches built in brick. If you fancy working off superflous calories gained in this way, there are any number of footpaths inviting you to explore the unspoiled countryside stretching out along the border with the Czech Republic.

Sights nearby: Altenberg mining museum (14km east), "Vereinigt Zwitterfeld zu Zinnwald" visitor mine (18km east)

Access: From B 171 via Frauenstein or from B 170 via Altenberg, then towards Rehefeld-Neuhermsdorf

10 LUK - DAS KLEINE LANDHOTEL

Dieter Sennewald

Basteiweg 12
01848 Hohnstein-Rathewalde
Tel. (035975) 8 00 13
Fax (035975) 80014 – www.luk-landhotel.de

Open all year • 8 rooms, all with balcony and all non-smoking • Restaurant (eve only, residents only): set meal 24€ • Garden, parking; dogs allowed in hotel, not in restaurant • Table tennis, boule, bicycle hire, organised walks

77/87 €, Breakfast included
Credit cards not accepted

A walk to the Bastei rocks with their enchanting views over Saxon Switzerland

In its quiet and peaceful location, this dazzling white building makes a bright and welcoming impression when seen from outside. Once inside, the reception is more than friendly; your welfare and comfort enjoy top priority, and so the individually styled rooms feature mostly natural materials like wool and cotton as well as natural colour schemes. To start the day, breakfast in the light and airy breakfast room consists mostly of organic products of various kinds. In the evening, you can enjoy a glass of wine by the open fire.

Sights nearby: Schloss Pillnitz (15 km west), Fort Königstein (16 km south)

Access: 13 km east of Pirna via Lohmen

11 VILLA WEISSE

Mathias Weinhart

Poststr. 17
01917 Kamenz
Tel. (03578) 37 84 70
Fax (03578) 3784730 – www.kamenz.de/gaeste/villa-weisse

Open all year • 14 rooms, including 1 with balcony, 1 with disabled access and 5 non-smoking • Cafe (Sat, Sun, public holidays 2pm-6pm) • Garden, parking; dogs allowed • Bicycle hire

66/77 €, Breakfast included

AE VISA MC

Breakfast in the adjacent cafe-restaurant with its view of the park

This establishment occupies the villa of Wilhelm Weisse, the one-time parks director of Kamenz, whose work beautified the town and now forms part of its heritage. The neighbouring park, which he designed as a "tree nursery for private and professional use", still fascinates as an oasis of luxuriant greenery, while his Hutberg park attracts thousands with its rhododendron and azalea displays around Whitsuntide. The walls of the comfortable rooms are hung with botanical illustrations and with portraits of figures connected with the history of the villa.

Sights nearby: Lessing Museum, St Marienstern monastery (7km southeast)

Access: From Exit 87 on A 4 via Rauschwitz, Elstra and Prietitz; near station in Kamenz

12 BERGGASTHAUS SCHÖNE AUSSICHT

Heiko Nickel

Aschbergstr. 19
08248 Klingenthal
Tel. (037467) 2 02 81
Fax (037467) 20298 – www.gast-in-klingenthal.de

Open all year • 5 rooms • Restaurant with terrace: main course 7.50-12.10€; half board 8€ • Parking; dogs allowed

43/59 €, Breakfast included
Credit cards not accepted

Sociable winter evenings over mulled wine

Words can hardly do justice to the wonderful panorama from this spot almost 900 metres above sea level overlooking the upland resort of Klingenthal close to the border with the Czech Republic. To the south, the view extends to the heights of the far-off Fichtelgebirge in Franconia. The "Schöne Aussicht" ("Lovely View") is a real mountain establishment, unpretentious but by no means lacking in charm. Limited in number, the bedrooms have been decorated and furnished with loving care in a nostalgic style, and the dining rooms too are pleasingly authentic. The place is ideal as a base for long summer walks or for cross-country explorations of the unspoiled mountain landscape in winter.

Sights nearby: "Zum Friedensfürsten" circular church, Music and Winter Sports Museum

Access: From Exit 6 on A 72 via Ölsnitz and Schöneck, or from Exit 9 via Auerbach

13 ELISENHOF

A. Fichtner

Terpitz 27
04655 Kohren-Sahlis
Tel. (034344) 6 14 39
Fax (034344) 62815 – www.hotel-elisenhof.de

Closed fortnight in Jan • 8 rooms, all with balcony • Restaurant with terrace: main course 4-13€ • Garden, parking: dogs allowed

65 €, Breakfast included

VISA MC

Not just for newly-weds, the bridal suite with its four-poster

If you fancy a country holiday among fields and meadows in the unspoiled heart of Mother Nature, this is the place for you. In 1992 a new hotel building was added to this farm of 1855 which is laid out around a courtyard. It offers comfortable and well-kept country-style rooms with furnishings in pale untreated firwood. The welcoming restaurant serves plain but hearty fare in a rustic setting with plenty of wood panelling; many of the dishes are prepared with ingredients from the family-owned farm.

Sights nearby: Kohren-Salis pottery museum (2 km west), Lindenau museum in Altenburg (17 km west)

Access: In Terpitz 2 km east of Kohren-Salis; by B 95 via Dolsenhain and Gnandstein

14 BURGKELLER

Claus Scholze und Mara Neumann

Domplatz 11
01662 Meißen
Tel. (03521) 4 14 00
Fax (03521) 41404 – www.meissen-hotel.com

Open all year • 10 rooms, including 2 with balcony • Cafe; restaurant with terrace: main course from 4.10€, set meal 16-55€; half board 14€ • Garden, parking; dogs allowed • Bowling, bicycle hire, town tours, wine tasting

115/160 €, Breakfast included
AE VISA MC

The "Benno" wine bar, an attractive addition to the arrangements for wining and dining

First opened in 1881, this hotel stands high above the River Elbe, perfectly integrated into the prominent group of buildings clustered atop Meissen's Burgberg. The comfortable bedrooms are in an elegant, timeless style. The building is on the sunny side of the citadel, and many of its rooms provide a grandiose view over the town. The view can also be enjoyed from the "Böttgerstube" restaurant and, even better, on fine days from the very popular terrace. It is even shared by the "Viennese Cafe", attractively decorated in pastel tones, where you can sit and sample the home-made cakes and pastries.

Sights nearby: Cathedral, Albrechtsburg, State Porcelain Manufactory

Access: By cathedral on the Burgberg

15 SORGENFREI

Jutta Steiner-Hanson

Augustusweg 48
01445 Radebeul
Tel. (0351) 8 93 33 30
Fax (0351) 8933355 – www.hotel-sorgenfrei.de

Open all year • 14 rooms, including 1 with disabled access and 10 non-smoking • Restaurant with terrace (from 2pm Mon-Fri, from noon Sat, Sun and public holidays): set lunch 19.50-38€, set dinner 31-58€; half board 30€ • Garden, parking; dogs allowed • Bicycle hire, choice of guided tours

128/145 €, Breakfast included

AE JCB VISA MC

The enchanting French-style park

Built between 1783 and 1789 in a transitional style between Rococo and neo-Classical, this delightful gentleman's residence stands in the middle of a wine-growing estate. Many original features have been retained, among them wall-paintings in the bedrooms and the sandstone floor in the entrance (now with sensitively inserted underfloor heating!). The decor and furnishing of the bedrooms has been carried out with great care in the spirit of the late 18th century, supplemented however by every modern comfort. You are sure to enjoy your trip back in time, not least when dining in the venerable ambience of the garden room with its stucco ceiling and crystal chandeliers.

Sights nearby: Old Masters gallery in Dresden (7 km southeast), Schloss Moritzburg (10 km north), Meissen citadel (16 km west)

Access: From Exit 89 on A 4 towards Moritzburg

16 IN DER MÜHLE

Ralph Decker

Mühlenweg 1
08432 Steinpleis bei Zwickau
Tel. (03761) 18 88 80
Fax (03761) 58307 – www.hotel-indermuehle.de

Open all year • 21 rooms, including 5 non-smoking • Restaurant with terrace (open 2pm-midnight, closed Fri): set meal 12-18.50€; half board 10-15€ • Garden, parking; dogs allowed • Bicycle hire

55/65 €, Breakfast included (WE: 55 €)

VISA MC

The lovely terrace with its unobstructed view of the surrounding landscape

In its idyllic countryside setting, this old mill kept on working right up to 1992, though latterly it used turbines rather than the mill-wheel. Despite everything, it has kept its authentic character, with materials salvaged from the old building used in a very effective way to enhance the ambience of the hotel. So for example the timber used in the reception area and bar comes from the old grain silos. The bedrooms are in simple country style, plain but perfectly comfortable. The rustic restaurant is in similar style, again with lots of nicely integrated bits and pieces from the old mill.

Sights nearby: Cathedral and “Augæst Horch” motor museum in Zwickau (8km east)

Access: 8km west of Zwickau town centre by Werdauer Strasse (B 175), turning off on to Marienthaler Strasse which leads to Steinpleiser Strasse

17 ERBGERICHT TAUTEWALDE

Kerstin Mickan

Tautewalde 61
02681 Wilthen-Tautewalde
Tel. (03592) 3 83 00
Fax (03592) 383299 – www.tautewalde.de

Open all year • 32 rooms, including 2 with disabled access and 15 non-smoking • Restaurant with terrace (closed fortnight in Feb): set meal 27-48€; half board 22€ • Garden, parking; dogs allowed in hotel, not in restaurant • Sauna, steam bath, solarium, tennis, table tennis, bicycle hire, organised walks, herb cookery courses, seminar on "Foolproof food"

89 €, Breakfast included

AE D VISA MC

The fascinating view into the kitchens

This venerable, bright red inn stands on the main road in the peaceful village of Tautewald at the foot of the Upper Lusatian highlands. Accommodation is in a new, purpose-built structure to the rear, in neat rooms with solid wood furnishings and attractive leafy views. The use of colourful fabrics makes a striking contrast with the timeless elegance of the furniture. Meals are served in the pleasant country-style restaurant or in the inviting beer garden.

Sights nearby: Bautzen Old Town (14 km north), Kleinwelka dinosaur park (18 km north)

Access: From B 96 via Wilthen towards Neukirch

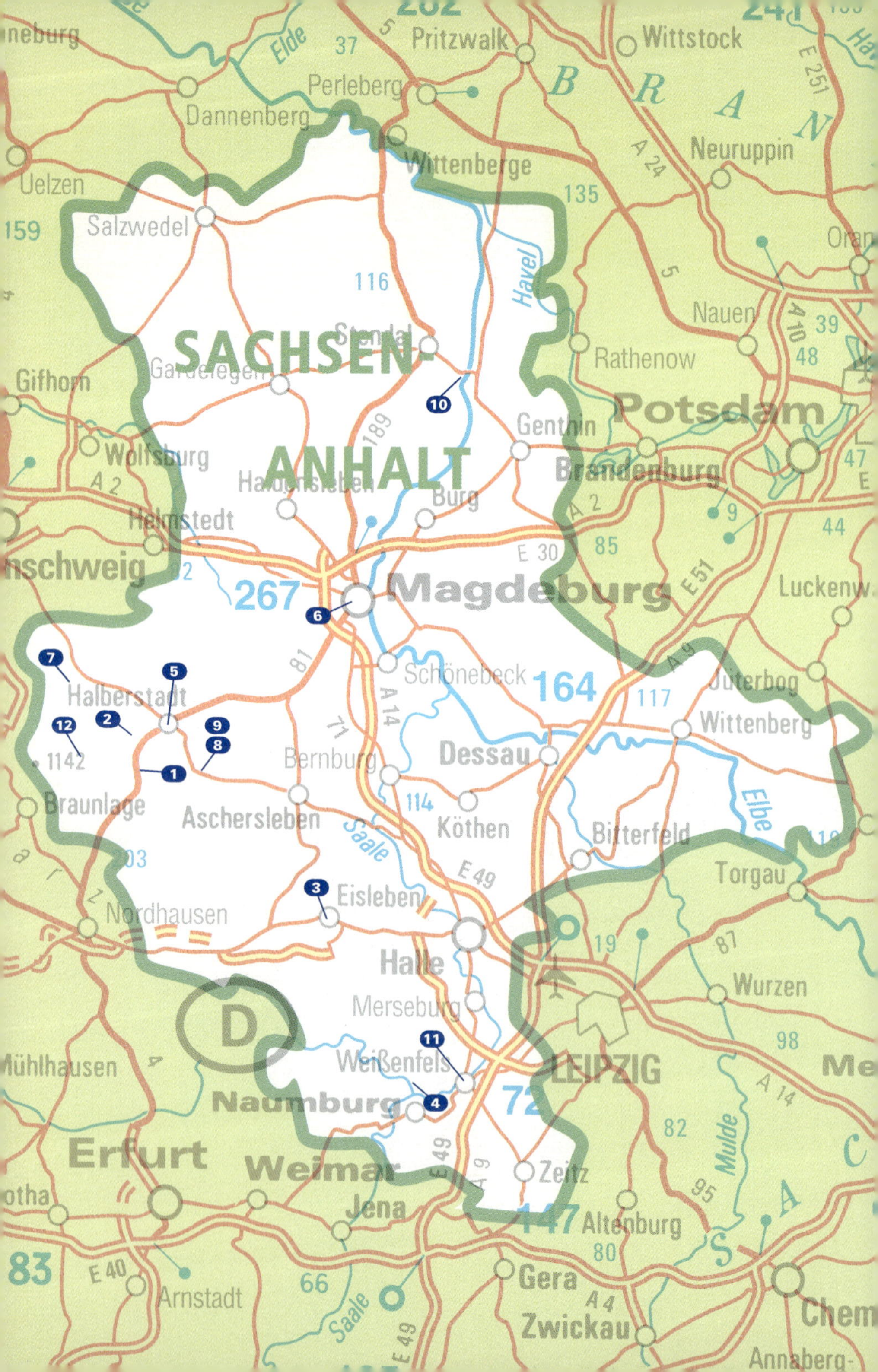

SACHSEN-
ANHALT
Salzwedel
Stendal
Gardelegen
Genthin
Haldensleben
Burg
Magdeburg
Helmstedt
Halberstadt
Schönebeck
Bernburg
Dessau
Wittenberg
Köthen
Aschersleben
Bitterfeld
Braunlage
Eisleben
Halle
Merseburg
Weißenfels
Naumburg
Zeitz
Nordhausen
Wittenberge
Perleberg
Pritzwalk
Wittstock
Neuruppin
Dannenberg
Uelzen
Gifhorn
Wolfsburg
nschweig
Rathenow
Nauen
Potsdam
Brandenburg
Luckenw.
Jüterbog
Torgau
Wurzen
LEIPZIG
Erfurt
Weimar
Jena
Gera
Altenburg
Zwickau
Arnstadt
Mühlhausen
otha
Chem
Annaberg-
neburg
Oran
Elde
Havel
Saale
Elbe
Mulde
D
1142
267
164
72
147
135
116
159
117
114
85
44
47
39
48
9
19
87
98
82
95
80
66
83
37
189
81
71
A 2
A 9
A 10
A 14
A 24
A 4
E 30
E 49
E 51
E 40
E 251
B R A N
S A C
1
2
3
4
5
6
7
8
9
10
11
12

Sachsen-Anhalt

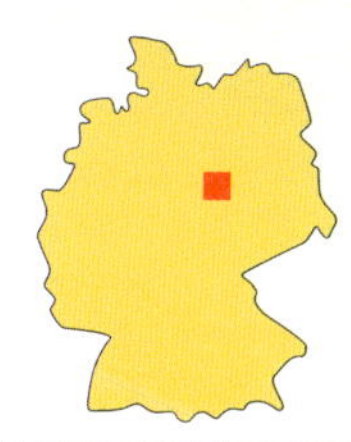

Although at the geographical heart of Germany, Saxony-Anhalt remains one of the country's best-kept secrets. Even many Germans are unaware that the region is richer in World Heritage Sites than any other in the country. They range from medieval half-timbered Quedlinburg, through the little Lutheran cities of Eisleben and Wittenberg, to Dessau, home of the Bauhaus and the "garden realm" of Wörlitz, a glorious landscape of parks and palaces. Elsewhere, there's Handel's native Halle and the cathedral city of Magdeburg, once renowned as the Pearl of Europe. The countryside is threaded by a "Blue Band" of lakes and waterways, which offer a new way of discovering the region's treasures, among them the great churches of the Romanesque Road. Hikers will want to conquer the splendid forested uplands of the Harz, especially the legendary Brocken, the highest point in the northern half of Germany, although the summit can also be reached by a spectacular steam train ride. Wine-lovers are in for a special treat too; the little-known Saale-Unstrut region produces delicate and distinctive wines, celebrated and enjoyed in local "Weinfeste" at harvest time.

1 VIKTORIA LUISE

Andrea Heres

Hasselfelder Str. 8
38889 Blankenburg
Tel. (03944) 9 11 70
Fax (03944) 911717
info@viktoria-luise.de – www.viktoria-luise.de

Open all year • 15 rooms, including 2 with balcony and 1 with disabled access • Restaurant and wine cellar with terrace (from 6.30pm; lunch by arrangement): set meals 21-31€; half board 18€; coffee and cakes from 2pm • Garden, parking, dogs allowed in hotel, not in restaurant • Sauna, sanarium, massage by arrangement, bicycle hire

112/133 €, Breakfast included

AE VISA MC

The authentic, atmospheric wine cellar with its rugged stone walls

Looking like something out of a picture postcard, this late-19th century brick-built villa crowned by an array of little turrets stands on a wooded slope above the town. There are fine views of the surrounding woods and of Blankenburg with its castle. The well thought-out design and layout of the interior has been implemented with impeccable taste; the bedrooms have an aristocratic air, with Italian period furnishings and varied colour schemes. The view from conservatory or terrace can be savoured at breakfast-time, or in the afternoon to the accompaniment of coffee and home-made cakes.

Sights nearby: Baroque castle gardens, Rübeland caves (8km southeast), Rosstrappe viewpoint (9km southeast)

Access: At junction of B 6 and B 81 between Wernigerode and Quedlinburg; on the road to Thale on the way out of Blankenburg

2 SCHLOSSVILLA

André Diezel

Schlossstr. 15
38895 Derenburg
Tel. (039453) 67 80
Fax (039453) 67850 – www.schlossvilla.de

Open all year • 15 rooms, including 1 with balcony • Cafe; restaurant with terrace: main course 8.80-14.30€; half board 8-12.50€ • Garden, parking; dogs allowed • Bicycle hire, guided mountain-bike tours

75/92 €, Breakfast included

VISA MC

The idyllic garden pool

With half-timbering, stepped gables and a little tower, as well as a few Art Nouveau touches, this early-20th century villa looks like something out of a fairy tale.The reception hall with its stylish use of wood still exudes the elegant atmosphere of a century ago, while the comfortable bedrooms are somewhat more sober in character, with contemporary cherrywood furnishings and (in some of them) views of the garden, which is enchantingly laid out like a little English-style park. You can appreciate it best of all from the terrace to the rear of the building.

Sights nearby: Halberstadt cathedral (11km east), Wernigerode Old Town (12km southwest)

Access: Coming from Halberstadt by B 81 continue towards Wernigerode; at start of built-up area of Derenburg

3 GRAF VON MANSFELD

Frau Gödecke

Markt 56
06295 Eisleben (Lutherstadt)
Tel. (03475) 25 07 22
Fax (03475) 250723 – www.hotel-eisleben.de

Open all year • 50 rooms, including 25 non-smoking • Restaurant with terrace: set meal 14.50-18.50€; half board 14.50€ • Garden, parking; dogs allowed • Town tours

80 €, Breakfast included

VISA MC

The excellent central location on the market square with its Luther monument

Born here in Eisleben, Martin Luther would have been familiar with this edifice, which was built in the 15th century as the town residence of Count von Mansfeld. It has been lavishly restored, and now welcomes its guests with individually styled and tastefully furnished rooms. Attractive, fresh fabrics and elegant period furnishings help create a comfortable and welcoming atmosphere, enhanced in places by the retention of the original tiled floors. You dine in the restaurant beneath venerable vaults, and breakfast is taken in an attractive extension built like a conservatory.

Sights nearby: Luther monuments in Eisleben Old Town including birthplace and house where he died

Access: In Old Town next to town hall

4 UNSTRUTTAL

Jan Kannetzky

Markt 11
06632 Freyburg (Unstrut)
Tel. (034464) 70 70
Fax (034464) 70741 – www.unstruttal.info

Open all year • 17 rooms • Restaurant with terrace: main course 7.90-20€; half board 14.50€ • Parking; dogs allowed

79 €, Breakfast included

VISA MC

The courtyard statue of Pomona, goddess of fruit and wine

This pretty establishment with its tiny dormers is located in the heart of the little wine town of Freyburg. Guests have been made welcome here since 1653, and there are any number of fascinating historical details such as the vaulting in the restaurant, the Renaissance-style spiral staircase tower and the 10.50-metre-deep well. The charming bedrooms feature attractive dark-wood rustic-style furnishings. On fine days it's a pleasure to sit beneath the vines in the lovely courtyard. For special occasions, there are two vaulted cellars with rugged stone walls.

Sights nearby: St Marien Stadtkirche, Neuenburg castle, Naumburg cathedral (7km southeast)

Access: On Marktplatz in centre of Old Town

5 HALBERSTÄDTER HOF

Frau Zimmermann

Trillgasse 10
38820 Halberstadt
Tel. (03941) 2 70 80
Fax (03941) 26189 – www.hotel-halberstaedter-hof.de

Open all year • 23 rooms, including 1 with balcony • Restaurant with beer garden (closed Sun eve 1 Jan to 28 Feb): set meal 18.50-25€; half board from 12€ • Garden, parking; dogs allowed

89/98 €, Breakfast included

AE JCB VISA MC

The bedrooms in the 12th century Romanesque tower

Built as a bailiff's residence in the 16th century, this delightfully ramshackle edifice has kept all its venerable charm. Subsequently used as an orphanage, since 1991 the property has functioned as a hotel and restaurant. Exposed timbers make a delightful contrast to the cool contemporary decor and furnishings of the bedrooms, while dark beams and exposed stonework help create a welcoming atmosphere in the restaurant. In summer you can make yourself comfortable in the attractive courtyard.

Sights nearby: Cathedral, Liebfrauenkirche

Access: In Old Town; follow green signs

6 RESIDENZ JOOP

Familie Joop

Jean-Burger-Str. 16
39112 Magdeburg
Tel. (0391) 6 26 20
Fax (0391) 6262100 – www.residenzjoop.de

Open all year • 25 rooms, including 20 non-smoking and 1 with balcony • Garden, parking; dogs not allowed • Bicycle hire

104/154 €, Breakfast included (WE: 82/102 €)

AE JCB VISA MC

The peaceful little garden

No-one could fail to be impressed by the very special character of this privately owned and impeccably-run hotel. In Magdeburg's prestigious villa quarter just south of the city centre, the lovely early-20th century residence housed the Swedish consulate until the Second World War. The then consul was the grandfather of the present owner, to whom the building was restituted in 1991 following the fall of the GDR. The Joop family decided to convert it into a hotel: their choice of cream-coloured furnishings in the bedrooms is beautifully complemented by pastel colour schemes, while the breakfast room with its crystal chandeliers has a delightfully festive ambience.

Sights nearby: Magdeburg cathedral, monastery of Unser Lieben Frauen, Elbauen park

Access: From Magdeburg-Zentrum Exit on A 2 or Magdeburg-Sudenburg Exit on A 14, turn off Magdeburg ring road at Uni-Klimikum or Zentrum-Süd Exit

7 **BRAUNER HIRSCH**

R. Haarnagel

Stephanikirchgasse 1
38835 Osterwieck
Tel. (039421) 79 50
Fax (039421) 79599
hotel-braunerhirsch@t-online.de – www.hotel-braunerhirsch.de

Closed 24 Dec • 24 rooms, including 12 non-smoking • Restaurant with terrace: main course 8.50-12.80€; half board 12€ • Parking; dogs allowed • Sauna, skittles

80 €, Breakfast included (WE: 76 €)
VISA MC

The courtyard with its intimate nooks and crannies

This striking 18th century building makes a special contribution to the picturesque townscape of the little half-timbered town of Osterwieck. Guests were already being received here in 1828, but the interior has been largely rebuilt, so that only here and there are fragments of the original structure to be seen, for example the barrel-vaults of the wine cellar or the exposed timbers in some of the bedrooms. These are comfortably equipped with timeless furnishings in natural wood. The restaurant on the first floor, where breakfast is taken, features much use of pale wood, giving a pleasantly rustic atmosphere.

Sights nearby: Stephanikirche, Old Town of Wernigerode (22km south)

Access: In Old Town near Stephanikirche

8 ROMANTIK HOTEL AM BRÜHL

Ursula Schmidt

Billungstr. 11
06484 Quedlinburg
Tel. (03946) 9 61 80
Fax (03946) 9618246 – www.hotelambruehl.de

Open all year • 46 rooms, including 1 with disabled access and 30 non-smoking • Restaurant (eve only): set meal 25-40€; half board 25€ • Garden, parking; dogs not allowed • Sauna, solarium, cookery courses

100/135 €, Breakfast included

AE VISA MC

Relaxing in the courtyard

This listed residence offers refined accommodation in an historic setting. Stone walls and exposed timbers have been combined with tasteful decor and furnishings to create a lovely country-style ambience. Many of the rooms feature enchantingly subtle pastel colour schemes. The sun streams into the light and airy breakfast room, while other meals are taken in the rustic “Weinstube” restaurant. Enjoy a peaceful end to your day in the cosy atmosphere of the hotel hallway with its open fire.

Sights nearby: Schloss museum, Gernrode collegiate church (7km south)

Access: In southern part of Old Town of Quedlinburg, in street off ring road

9 ROMANTIK HOTEL THEOPHANO

Gabriele Vester

Markt 14
06484 Quedlinburg
Tel. (03946) 9 63 00
Fax (03946) 963036 – www.hoteltheophano.de

Open all year • 22 rooms, including 1 with balcony and 12 non-smoking • Cafe (closed Tue Apr to Dec), restaurant with terrace (eve only, closed Sun Apr-Oct, closed Sun, Mon Nov to Mar): set meal 25-40€; half board 25€ • Parking; dogs allowed in hotel, not in restaurant • Bicycle hire; craft courses Jan to Mar

98/120 €, Breakfast included

AE JCB VISA MC

The elegant ground-floor cafe looking out into the square

Consisting of several 17th century buildings, this is a most delightful place to stay, a labyrinth of unexpected nooks and crannies, steps, stairs and landings. The elegant bedrooms have been furnished with sure taste, with harmonious use made of lively colours and lovely materials. The result is a comfortable, romantic ambience. The cellar restaurant with its rustic brick vaulting is particularly enchanting.

Sights nearby: St Servatius collegiate church, Rosstrappe viewpoint (12 km southwest)

Access: On historic market square in heart of Old Town

10 SCHLOSS TANGERMÜNDE

M. Busse

Amt 1
39590 Tangermünde
Tel. (039322) 73 73
Fax (039322) 73773 – www.schloss-tangermuende.de

Open all year • 24 rooms, including 2 non-smoking • Cafe-restaurant with terrace (hot meals all day Sat, Sun, from 5.30pm Mon-Fri): set meals 15-32.60€; half board 16€ • Garden, parking; dogs allowed • Cosmetic treatments, sauna, steam bath, sunbathing lawn, bicycle hire, town tours, guided walks

87/128 €, Breakfast included

AE D VISA MC

The commanding prospect from this elevated viewpoint

A stronghold was first mentioned here in 1003. In the reign of Emperor Charles IV a mighty castle was constructed, which was destroyed by a Swedish army in 1640. At the end of the 17th century, Prince-Elector Frederick III ordered the construction of an "Amtshaus" on the formidable defensive walls, using surviving fragments of the original building. This edifice still stands, high above the River Elbe, looking enchantingly like a real castle. Bedrooms as well as restaurant are in a tasteful traditional style, providing a stylish and dignified setting for your stay.

Sights nearby: Jerichow Premonstratensian monastery (9km southeast), Stendal cathedral (10km northwest), Wischer woodland spa (19km north)

Access: On River Elbe, 10km southwest of Stendal

11 JÄGERHOF

Uwe Weigelt

Nikolaistr. 51
06667 Weißenfels
Tel. (03443) 33 40
Fax (03443) 334100 – www.jaegerhof-weissenfels.de

Open all year • 35 rooms, including 3 with balcony and 15 non-smoking • Restaurant with terrace: set lunch 6.66-69€, set dinner 19.99-69€; half board 10-20€ • Parking; dogs allowed • Bicycle hire, boat hire and organised boat trips

70/90 €, Breakfast included

AE VISA MC

The appetising and inexpensive Sunday brunch

Many of the rooms here are quite small, but this is more than compensated for by the historic ambience and the intimate atmosphere of the building, for which records go back as far as the 15th century. Behind the plant-covered façade of the stately courtyard farmstead, the often decidedly irregular rooms charm with their exposed timbers, lightwood furnishings and rustic atmosphere. You dine in a similarly homely ambience, whether in the "Zum Fasan" restaurant or beneath the attractively illuminated vaults of the wine cellar.

Sights nearby: Cathedral and castle in Merseburg (14 km north), Naumburg cathedral (17 km southwest)

Access: Exit 20 on A 9; by the Schwedenstein roundabout on the southwestern corner of the centre of Weissenfels

12 **JOHANNISHOF**
Familie Herlemann

Pfarrstr. 25
38855 Wernigerode
Tel. (03943) 9 49 40
Fax (03943) 949449 – www.hotel-johannishof.de

Open all year • 25 rooms, including 22 non-smoking and 1 with balcony • Parking; dogs not allowed

70 €, Breakfast included
VISA MC

The cosy atmosphere in the panelled breakfast room

This country residence with its green and white façade makes a welcoming impression. Its comfortable bedrooms are equally inviting, with charming furnishings in natural wood and carefully colour-coordinated bedspreads and curtains. Impeccably run, the Johannishof is sure to make your stay a pleasurable and relaxing one. It is an ideal base for explorations on foot of the picturesque Old Town of Wernigerode, as well as for excursions into the unspoiled landscapes of the Harz mountains.

Sights nearby: Schloss, caves at Rübeland (15km south), Halberstadt cathedral (21km east)

Access: On northern fringe of Old Town

Ribe
Kolding
Haderslev
Assens
Fyn
Nyborg
Fåborg
Svendborg
Åbenrå
Als
Sønderborg
Tønder
Rømø
Rudkøbing
Langeland
Bagenkop
Ærø
Föhr
Niebüll
Flensburg
Schleswig
Husum
Kiel
Rendsburg
Oldenburg
Plön
Neustadt
Puttgarden
Lolland
Inseln
SCHLESWIG-
HOLSTEIN
Heide
Neumünster
Itzehoe
Bad Segeberg
Travemünde
Lübeck
Ratzeburg
Cuxhaven
Elmshorn
HAMBURG
Bremerhaven
Stade
Bremervörde
Lauenburg
Boizenburg
Lüneburg
BREMEN
Rotenburg
Soltau
Verden
Uelzen
Weser
Elbe
Harwich
Oslo
Göteborg
St.Peterburg
Klaipeda
Lüneburger Heide
236
302
233
105
147

Schleswig-Holstein

The character of Schleswig-Holstein is formed by two seas, each with a very different coastline. The sun rises over the Baltic shore, where low cliffs line the coast and narrow fjords reach far inland; on one of them stands the regional capital, Kiel, world-famous for its week-long regatta and its naval traditions. Facing the North Sea are the beaches and dunes of the North Frisian islands, set among the tidal flats of the vast Wattenmeer. Huddled low against the wind, thatched houses are reminders of the hard life of times past, but the living is much easier today, notably on the fashionable holiday island of Sylt. Away from the coast, the low landscape has a peaceful, almost meditative atmosphere; miles of hedges parcelling the countryside into a neat patchwork beneath immense skies. There's more variety in the *Holsteinische Schweiz*, Holstein's highest if hardly alpine land, with lovely lakes set in gentle wooded hills, but the region's greatest treasure is the medieval port of Lübeck, now protected by UNESCO World Heritage status. Visitors flock to admire its superb red-brick buildings, but also to taste the city's most mouth-watering export, Lübeck marzipan.

1 **SEEHOTEL TÖPFERHAUS**

Gert Thies-Lembcke

Am See
24791 Alt-Duvenstedt
Tel. (04338) 9 97 10
Fax (04338) 997171
info@toepferhaus.com – www.toepferhaus.com

Open all year • 46 rooms, including 13 with balcony, 1 with disabled access and 23 non-smoking • Restaurants with terrace: Töpferhaus (closed Sun, Mon): set meal 52-78€; Pesel: set meal 24.50€; half board 24.50€ • Garden, parking; dogs allowed • Bathing lake, sunbathing lawn, bicycle hire, Nordic walking, art exhibitions

130/165 €, Breakfast included

AE Diners VISA MC

The bronze sculptures to be found everywhere in the building

What could be lovelier than to stay on the banks of an idyllic lake? Should you agree, you will find your dreams fulfilled here. The location is particularly picturesque, and the rooms with a balcony or terrace overlookingthe Bistensee will allow you to drink in the view to your heart's content. The rooms themselves are solidly furnished in country style. Naturally enough, the restaurant - where the crockery comes from the Royal Porcelain Manufactury in Berlin - has its own terrace. As well as enjoying the establishment's excellent cuisine, you can also sit out here for your afternoon coffee and cakes.

Sights nearby: Rendsburg railway bridge (12 km south), Schloss Gottorf in Schleswig (23 km northwest)

Access: Exit 8 on A 7; in Holzburg follow signs towards Alt-Duvenstedt

2 UAL ÖÖMRANG WIARTSHÜS

Ute Decker

Bräätlun 4
25946 Norddorf
Tel. (04682) 8 36
Fax (04682) 1432
www.deramrumer.de

Closed 10 Jan to 21 Feb, 19-27 Dec • 12 rooms • Restaurant with terrace (closed Tue, midday Wed in winter): set meals 18-26€; half board 16€ • Garden, parking; dogs allowed • Sauna

102 €, Breakfast included
Credit cards not accepted

The home-made jams for breakfast

This friendly little hotel, ideally situated in a peaceful location, is a charming old Frisian farmstead, picture-perfect from its thatched roof to its natural wood furniture. Typically thoughtful touches include making sure that guests have water, fruit and something sweet waiting for them when they arrive. The pretty garden looks out to sea, as do a few of the rooms, but there's a no less typical North German sight in the wonderfully inviting 'Seemannstube': blue-and-white painted wood, old tiles and a few other inimitably local details make for a very cosy atmosphere.

Sights nearby: Esenhugh, mud-flat walks to Föhr

Access: Ferry from Dagebüll (c. 2hr); book cars in advance with Wyker Dampfschiffsreederei GmbH in Wyk auf Föhr (Tel: 0180 5080140

3 FÜRST BISMARCK MÜHLE

C.-H. Szaggars

Mühlenweg 3
21521 Aumühle
Tel. (04104) 20 28
Fax (04104) 1200 – www.bismarckmuehle.de

Open all year • 7 rooms, including 1 with balcony • Restaurant with terrace (closed Wed): set meal 23-58€ • Garden, parking; dogs allowed

98 €, Breakfast included
VISA MC

The authentic "Iron Chancellor" memorabilia in the Bismarck Room and Bar

Just off the main road, this old mill has a lovely location by a little lake. Travellers could be served with a drink here as long ago as 1350, but the place only really gained its historic significance in 1871 when it was purchased by Chancellor Otto von Bismarck. The rooms feature period furnishings and offer fine views over the millpond and the surrounding woodland. The traditions of 600 years ago are continued in the rustic restaurant and on the idyllic terrace, where as well as international dishes you can enjoy cakes from the establishment's own bakery.

Sights nearby: Aumühle locoshed preserved railway, Bismarck Museum and Mausoleum in Friedrichsruh (3km northeast)

Access: From Exit 5 on A 25 via Reinbeck and Wohltorf, or from Exit 5 on A 24 via Grande and Friedrichsruh

4 WEISSER HOF

Familie Heusser-Schmieder

Voßstr. 45
23714 Bad Malente-Gremsmühlen
Tel. (04523) 9 92 50
Fax (04523) 6899 – www.weisserhof.de

Open all year • 18 rooms, including 15 with balcony and 5 non-smoking • Cafe; restaurant with terrace: set meal 27-37.50€; half board 20€ • Garden, parking; dogs allowed • Swimming pool, sauna, gym, wellness facilities, walking and cycle tours

125/150 €, Breakfast included
VISA MC

The artificially created wetland habitat in the garden

Consisting of three buildings whose facades and even roofs are white, this establishment lives up to its name, “White Homestead”. The stylishness of the exterior is continued inside, where the comfortable bedrooms are furnished and decorated in a variety of ways, all tasteful. In addition, there are lavish wellness facilities, a leafy interior courtyard, and a lovely, extensive garden area, all helping to guarantee a pleasant and relaxing stay.

Sights nearby: Eutin Old Town (7km southeast), Hansa Park (23km southeast)

Access: From Exit 15 on A 1 via Eutin; from Eutin on the edge of the built-up area of Malente

5 ANDRESEN'S GASTHOF

Elke Andresen

Dörpstraat 63 (B 5)
25842 Bargum
Tel. (04672) 10 98
Fax (04672) 1099 – www.andresensgasthof.de

Closed 2 weeks in Jan, 2 weeks in Feb, 1 week in Sep • 5 rooms, all non-smoking • Restaurant (closed Mon-Tue, eve only Wed-Thu): set meal 39-79€ • Garden, parking; dogs allowed • Cookery courses

100 €, Breakfast included

The idyllic garden and pool

Welcoming its guests on the outskirts of Bargum, this brick building beneath its colour-coordinated hipped roof is a typical example of the vernacular architecture of this part of the world. The interiors are harmonious too, with loving attention paid to every detail; the bedrooms feature solid furnishings in natural wood. The restaurant, where diners are pampered with fine traditional cuisine, has three sections; two little dining rooms in typical Frisian style and another with alcoves and lovely Delft tiling. Pictures, flowers, and a variety of decorative objects further enhance the stylish and welcoming ambience.

Sights nearby: Frisia museum in Niebüll (15 km northwest), Emil Nolde Museum in Seebüll (29 km northwest)

Access: North of Husum by B 5

6 STRAUERS HOTEL AM SEE

Familie Strauer

Gerolddamm 2
23715 Bosau
Tel. (04527) 99 40
Fax (04527) 994111 – www.strauer.de

Closed Jan and Feb • 30 rooms, all with balcony or terrace, 2 non-smoking • Cafe; restaurant with terrace (closed Mon eve): set lunch 18.50-23€, set dinner 18-23€; half board 16€ • Garden, parking; dogs allowed • Swimming pool, bathing place on lake, sauna, massage, cosmetic treatments, medicinal baths

112/134 €, Breakfast included

JCB MC

The indoor swimming pool which leads out into the garden

Here, on the east bank of the Great Ploener Lake, relaxation and serenity are guaranteed. Tasteful and stylish rooms await your visit and spacious suites with their very own kitchenettes can be found in the neigbouring house. The hotel is further enhanced by the stunning location and its very own bathing platform and landing stage. You can relax in total comfort and enjoy the fantastic views from the shoreline from one of the loungers and wicker beach chairs set out on the lakeshore. Even at the dawn of every new day you don't have to miss out, with the hotel providing breakfast on the terrace or in the conservatory overlooking the water.

Sights nearby: Evangelical church, Eutin Old Town (17km east)

Access: From B 76 between Eutin and Plön via Bösdorf

7 VOSS-HAUS

Lars Ruländer

Vossplatz 6
23701 Eutin
Tel. (04521) 4 01 60
Fax (04521) 401620 – www.vosshauseutin.de

Open all year • 12 rooms • Restaurant with terrace (closed all of Feb, every Mon): main course 6.50-21.50€; half board 15€ • Garden, parking; dogs allowed • Bicycle hire, wine seminars

90 €, Breakfast included

VISA MC

A morning spent strolling through the streets of the lovely old town

This historic house in the town centre is named after Johann Heinrich Voss, best remembered for completing his translations of Homer's Iliad and Virgil's Aeneid here over 200 years ago, and inspiring literary Germany in its own Classical period. Looking around the stylishly furnished foyer, it still feels very true to the time; the comforts are rather grander than anything the great man of letters would have been used to, but there's a classically elegant look to the cherry-red wood panelling and black leather seats. As for the comfortable rooms, they are fitted out in natural wood. Behind the house, a leafy terrace and garden runs down to the shore of the Eutiner See.

Sights nearby: Michaeliskirche, Eutin Festival (Jul-Aug), Hansa Park (16km southeast), Timmendorfer Strand Sea Life Center (22km southeast)

Access: Eutin Exit on A 1, in Eutin follow signs towards Malente

8 LANDHAUS LAURA

Jörn Sternhagen

Buurnstrat 49
25938 Oevenum
Tel. (04681) 5 97 90
Fax (04681) 597935 – www.landhaus-laura-foehr.de

Closed 9 Jan to 3 Feb • 15 rooms, including 2 non-smoking • Restaurant with terrace (closed Mon and midday Wed-Thu in winter, Tue): main course 14-19.80€, set dinner 28-45€ • Garden, parking; dogs allowed in hotel, not in restaurant • Sauna, solarium, gym equipment, organised mudflat walks, wine tastings, readings, herb seminars

110/150 €, Breakfast included
VISA

A walk round the bustling 'Wochenmarkt': it's market day every Thursday morning from May to September

What do you hope for from your holidays? Heavenly images come to mind: perhaps a green island surrounded by the big skies and long horizons of the Wattenmeer; over ten miles of glorious golden beaches and the refreshing breeze coming off the North Sea? You've come to the right place. This converted North German farmhouse, dating back over 300 years, is just as you'd imagine it: redbrick walls holding up a characterful thatched roof, a pretty courtyard garden and rooms, some furnished with antiques, which range from homely and traditionally rural to quirkily romantic. Frisian rustic character shines through in the restaurant as well, right down to the original stone floor.

Sights nearby: Frisia Museum in Wyk, St Nikolai-Kirche in Boldixum

Access: By ferry from Dagebüll (c 45 min); book cars in advance, Wyker Dampfschiffsreederei GmbH in Wyk auf Föhr (tel: 01805080140)

9 HOLLÄNDISCHE STUBE

Klaus-Peter Willhöft

Am Mittelburgwall 22-26
25840 Friedrichstadt
Tel. (04881) 9 39 00
Fax (04881) 939022 – www.hollaendischestube.de

Open all year • 9 rooms, including 1 with balcony • Cafe-restaurant with terrace (closed Nov to Feb, Mon, Tue): set meal 25-31€; half board 16€ • Garden; dogs allowed • Bicycle hire

75/95 €, Breakfast included

AE VISA

The view from the garden cafe over the picturesque market square

The little town of Friedrichsstadt was founded in 1621 for religious refugees from Holland, and the typical Dutch features of stepped gables and rectilinear canals make for an unusual townscape in this part of the world. Close to the market square on Mittelburggraben, this building dates from those days. Its interiors are a real jewel, faithfully restored in the style of the Dutch Baroque, with wall-hangings, tiles, and panelling helping to create an authentically traditional ambience. The bedrooms (in the annexe) are stylish and comfortable, with a number of well-chosen antique pieces

Sights nearby: Ludwig Nissen Haus North Frisian Museum (15km north), Eider flood barrier (20km south)

Access: West of Rendsburg by B 202

10 OLE LIESE

Tina Schulz

24321 Gut Panker
Tel. (04381) 9 06 90
Fax (04381) 9069200 – www.ole-liese.de

Closed 2 weeks Jan, 1st 3 weeks in Nov • 20 rooms • Restaurant with terrace (From Whitsun to end Oct : closed Mon, Tue lunchtime; Nov to Whitsun Mon, Tue, Wed lunchtime): set lunch 25-35€, set dinner 34-70€ • Sauna, lounge/library with open fireplace

110/140 €, Breakfast included
Credit cards not accepted

Changing art exhibitions on the Panker estate

This brick-built establishment forms part of the venerable Panker estate idyllically located among the hills and lakes of "Holstein Switzerland". It owes its name to a horse belonging to Prince Hessenstein which was looked after in old age by the then landlord. It's a lovely place to stay, thanks to the peace and quiet and the romantic atmosphere. The rooms in the main building and the guesthouse are elegantly furnished and decorated in contemporary country style, with warm colour schemes, wood floors, and much use of marble in the bathrooms helping to create an ambience of refined relaxation. The restaurant too is most attractive, with rustically festive decor and fittings.

Sights nearby: Hohwachter Bay (5km northeast)

Access: 5km north of Lütjenburg (at junction of B 202 and B 430) towards Schönberg

11 ROMANTIK HOTEL ALTES GYMNASIUM

Stephan Schütt

Süderstr. 2-10
25813 Husum
Tel. (04841) 83 30
Fax (04841) 83312 – www.altes-gymnasium.de

Open all year • 72 rooms, all with air conditioning, 37 with balcony, 3 with disabled access and 34 non-smoking • Restaurants with terrace: "Euken" (closed Mon, Tue, open eve only Wed to Sat, open from noon Sun); "Wintergarten" set meal 32-39€, main course 7.50-17€; half board 32€ • Parking; dogs allowed in hotel, not in restaurant • Indoor pool, sauna, solarium, jacuzzi, gym, bicycle hire

135/190 €, Breakfast included (WE: 155/200 €)

AE D VISA MC

Watching the ebb and flow of the tides in Husum harbour

Remember those days? Out of bed at the crack of dawn, only to go to school, sit at your desk and be bombarded with mathematical formulas and German exercises? If your memories of school are just as dull, here's your chance to collect some more postive ones. The former grammar school, built in neo-Gothic style, now provides stylish rooms enhanced by classical elegance and modern comforts. So at last you can get that well-deserved lie-in and enjoy life to the full. You can also relax in the spacious 'wellness-area' or even treat your palate with a visit to one of the two restaurants.

Sights nearby: North Frisia museum & Ludwig Nissen Haus, Theodor Storm Haus

Access: In centre of Husum

12 FRIEDERIKENHOF

Heide Meyer

Langjohrd 15-19
23560 Lübeck-Oberbüssau
Tel. (0451) 80 08 80
Fax (0451) 80088100
mail@friederikenhof.de – www.friederikenhof.de

Open all year • 30 rooms, all non-smoking, 6 with terrace and 1 with disabled access • Restaurant with terrace (closed midday Mon): set meal 16-45€; half board 20€ • Garden, parking; dogs allowed • Sauna, solarium, bicycle hire

90/130 €, Breakfast included
AE D VISA MC

The kindness and efficiency of the Meyer family

Seeing these four brick buildings in typical local style for the first time, you would hardly guess that they only date from 1998, when they were built in this leafy setting on the site of an old farmstead. The comfortable bedroooms are individually furnished and decorated in contemporary country style, with basket-work beds and tasteful fittings creating a welcoming ambience. The restaurant is equally inviting, with sections in styles ranging from rustic to elegant. The culinary offerings are supplemented in the afternoon by coffee and cakes.

Sights nearby: Lübeck Old Town (8 km northeast), Ernst Barlach museum in Ratzeburg (21 km southeast)

Access: 8 km southwest of Lübeck by Kronsforder Landstrassse

13 FORSTHAUS SEEBERGEN

Peter Genke

Seebergen 9-15
22952 Lütjensee
Tel. (04154) 7 92 90
Fax (04154) 70645 – www.forsthaus-seebergen.de

Open all year • 11 rooms • Restaurant with terrace: set dinner 36.50-45.50€ • Garden, parking; dogs allowed

60/90 €, Breakfast included
VISA MC

A meal on the superb waterside terrace

In its idyllic lakeside location, it always seemed a shame that this property was only used as a forestry depot, and so as long ago as 1951 it was decided to establish a restaurant here. It's still here, its interiors ranging in style from rustic to elegant, and following various additions and modifications it is now possible to stay overnight and really appreciate the enchanting ambience. Guests are accommodated in comfortable rooms with some period furnishings and bright, contemporary bathrooms.

Sights nearby: Schloss Ahrensburg (12km west), Butterfly Garden in Friedrichsruh (17km south)

Access: From Exit 6 (Grande) on A 24 by B 404, or from Exit 28 on A 1 via Siek

14 BÄRENKRUG

Familie Sierks

Hamburger Chaussee 10 (B 4)
24113 Molfsee
Tel. (04347) 7 12 00
Fax (04347) 712013 – www.baerenkrug.de

Closed 1-2 Jan, 23-31 Dec • 32 rooms, including 2 with terrace, 1 with disabled access and 14 non-smoking • Restaurant with terrace (open 4pm Mon-Fri, 11am Sat, Sun): set dinner 12.50-42.50€, main course 9.80-28€ • Children's playground, garden, parking; dogs allowed • Sauna, cookery courses

95/125 €, Breakfast included

AE D VISA MC

Relaxing in the garden in the shade of chestnut trees

The symbol of the bear has been the guarantee of traditional hospitality here since 1852, though the property itself is older. The bedrooms in the main building and guesthouse are prettily furnished and decorated in country style, and a number of them also have a fireplace and terrace. The restaurant features local and seasonal specialities and is divided into a number of dining rooms in different styles; it's particularly pleasant to dine in one of the little parlour-like spaces in typical Frisian style, with the wall-tiles so typical of the area.

Sights nearby: Schleswig-Holstein open air museum; Kiel fjord (8 km northeast)

Access: Molfsee/Blumenthal Exit on A 215, then c 5 km further on B 4 towards Kiel

15 **ROMANTIK HOTEL HISTORISCHER KRUG**
Lenka Hansen-Moerck

Grazer Platz 1 (an der B 76)
24988 Oeversee
Tel. (04630) 94 00
Fax (04630) 780 – www.historischer-krug.de

Open all year • 40 rooms, including 5 with balcony and 20 non-smoking • Restaurant with terrace: set meal 27-36€; half board 25€ • Garden, parking; dogs by prior arrangement • Indoor pool, heated jacuzzi, Finnish sauna, Turkish bath, steam bath, solarium, ayurveda beauty farm, bicycle hire, cookery courses

102/168 €, Breakfast included
AE DC VISA MC

The authentic charm and character of this historic local inn

Incredibly, this thatched inn was built way back at the beginning of the 1500s and has been in the family since 1815. You can now choose from a further six houses, all part of an extensive parkland estate which includes a pond, meadows and greenhouses. Some rooms have more in the way of modern comforts and conveniences, but all share the same cosy country style. An unusual highlight is the 'Krugtherme', which has been offering its guests an introduction to Ayurveda treatments and techniques for over two decades.

Sights nearby: Flensburg museum hill (9km north), Glücksburg moated castle (21km northeast)

Access: From Exit 4 on A 7 towards Ostsee/Sörup, then towards Flensburg

16 ROMANTIK HOTEL JAGDHAUS WALDFRIEDEN

Siegmund Baierle

Kieler Straße (B 4)
25451 Quickborn
Tel. (04106) 6 10 20
Fax (04106) 69196 – www.waldfrieden.com

Open all year • 25 rooms, including 1 with balcony and 2 with air conditioning • Restaurant with terrace (closed midday Mon): set lunch 19.50€, set dinner 29-51€; half board 25.50€ • Garden, parking; dogs allowed • Bicycle hire

138/155 €, Breakfast included

AE (D) VISA MC

A morning jog in the forest

This former hunting lodge in the style of a villa with half-timbering and romantic turrets is idyllically located in lovely parkland and still radiates the relaxed atmosphere of the time of its construction in 1902. Both the main building and the guesthouse have rooms furnished and decorated in refined country style, and there's stylishness too where you dine, whether in the restaurant with its open fireplace or in the bright and airy conservatory of the garden building. It's particularly pleasing to sit outside in summer and soak up the atmosphere of the beautiful parkland surroundings.

Sights nearby: Hagenbeck's Zoo, Kunsthalle art gallery in Hamburg (25km south)

Access: Exit 21 on A 7; 3km north of Quickborn on B 4 towards Bad Bramstedt

17 LUNDENBERGSAND

Bernd Peters

Lundenbergweg 3
25813 Simonsberg
Tel. (04841) 8 39 30
Fax (04841) 839350 – www.hotel-lundenbergsand.de

Closed Jan • 18 rooms, including 2 non-smoking • Cafe-restaurant with terrace: set meal 16.50-34€; half board 15€ • Garden, parking; dogs allowed • Sauna, solarium, bicycle hire, guided mudflat walks

85/95 €, Breakfast included
VISA MC

Watching the sun go down over the Wattenmeer

This thatched-roof edifice enjoys an utterly peaceful location right behind the sea-dike. Beyond the dike stretch the mudflats of the Wattenmeer National Park, inviting you to explore their unique ambience and wildlife. The establishment's individually decorated and furnished rooms are given a touch of local colour with names like "Kapitänszimmer" or "Gutsherrnstuv", and there is even a room for newlyweds (bookable by anyone with romantic inclinations!). The tastefully rustic restaurant serves reliable food with emphasis on lamb and fish dishes. You are advised not to overdo things at lunchtime, otherwise you will be unable to appreciate the home-made apple tart at tea-time!

Sights nearby: Theodor Storm house in Husum (7km northeast), Friedrichstadt (16km southeast)

Access: 7km southwest of Husum by B 5

18 FRIESENHOF

Heidrun Bacher

Im Bad 58
25826 St. Peter-Ording
Tel. (04863) 9 68 60
Fax (04863) 968676 – www.friesenhof-stpeterording.de

Open all year • 24 rooms, including 16 with balcony, 1 with disabled access and 15 non-smoking • Parking; dogs allowed • Swimming pool, sauna, solarium, infra-red treatment

140/152 €, Breakfast included
Credit cards not accepted

Summertime breakfasts in the rose garden

A wonderful place for a holiday! Close to the beach, this welcoming brick building offers a variety of types of accommodation, from double rooms to fully equipped apartments with kitchen and balcony. All have the same high quality fittings and furnishings and are outstandingly well kept, while cheerful wood finishes and lovely fabrics create a pleasantly homely atmosphere. If ever bad weather should descend on the coast, the hotel's leisure facilities include a heated swimming pool and a sauna.

Sights nearby: Dünen thermal spa, Westküste park, Eider flood barrier (18km east)

Access: At end of B 202 in St Peter-Bad

19 KAMPHÖRN

Klaus Lorenz

Norderheide 2
25999 Kampen
Tel. (04651) 9 84 50
Fax (04651) 984519 – www.kamphoern.de

Open all year • 12 rooms, all non-smoking • Garden, parking; dogs allowed • Bicycle hire

135/198 €, Breakfast included
Credit cards not accepted

The welcoming sitting room with its open fire and library of books

All its visitors appreciate the individual character and private atmosphere of this thatched brick building on the outskirts of Kampen. The comfortable rooms are bright and cheerful, the most desirable naturally being those with views of the North Sea. The breakfast room also offers a prospect of the waves as well as delicious local seafood specialities like crab and smoked eel, to be savoured at your leisure while perusing the daily paper.

Sights nearby: Red Cliff, Denghoog in Braderup (2km south)

Access: Access by motorail from Niebüll to Westerland (tel: 04651 9950565, www.syltshuttle.de)

20 SEILER HOF

Inken Johannsen

Gurtstig 7
25980 Keitum
Tel. (04651) 9 33 40
Fax (04651) 933444 – www.seilerhofsylt.de

Closed 20 Nov to 15 Dec • 11 rooms • Garden, parking; dogs not allowed • Gym, sauna, jacuzzi, steam bath

145/165 €, Breakfast included
Credit cards not accepted

The Delft tiles in the breakfast room

This 18th century building fits in perfectly with the idyllic thatched holiday homes in Keitum, known as the "green heart" of the island. It too has a roof of thatch, and is surrounded by an attractive garden. The pretty rooms are timelessly furnished in a welcoming country style. You can relax and enjoy yourself regardless of the weather in the sauna with its solarium and jacuzzi. Otherwise picturesque Keitum invites you to explore its lovely avenues and other attractions, ideally on foot.

Sights nearby: St Severin, Morsum cliff

Access: Access by motorail from Niebüll to Westerland (tel: 04651 9950565, www.syltshuttle.de)

21 MÜHLENPARK

Elisabeth Böge-Lübbert

Mühlenstr. 49
25436 Uetersen
Tel. (04122) 9 25 50
Fax (04122) 925510 – www.muehlenpark.de

Open all year • 25 rooms • Restaurant with terrace: set meal 20-30€; half board 10€ • Parking; dogs allowed in hotel, not in restaurant

99/132 €, Breakfast included

AE DC VISA MC

The well-appointed accommodation in the "Villa Mühlenpark"

On the outskirts of Uetersen, this Art Nouveau villa has been extended to include hotel accommodation. The spacious rooms are individually furnished and decorated in a timeless style. The same stylish elegance is carried over into the intimate little restaurant, which features a west-facing terrace where it is pleasant to linger over breakfast when the weather permits.

Sights nearby: Evangelical church, Hamburg marina in Wedel (13km south)

Access: From Exit 15 on A 7 via Tornesch; c 8km, remain on main road

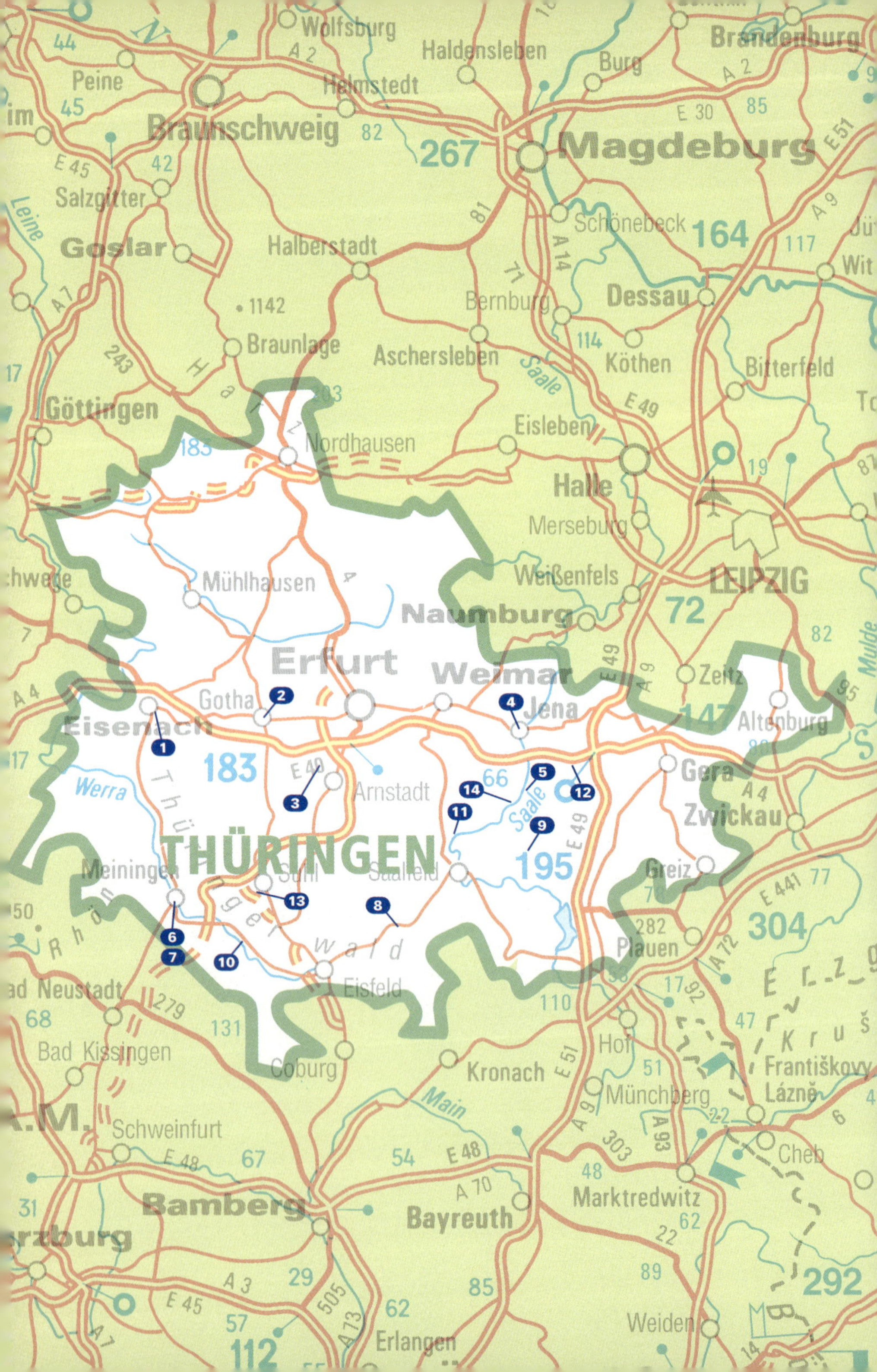

Wolfsburg
Haldensleben
Brandenburg
Peine
Helmstedt
Burg
Braunschweig
Magdeburg
Salzgitter
Schönebeck
Goslar
Halberstadt
Dessau
Bernburg
Braunlage
Aschersleben
Köthen
Bitterfeld
Göttingen
Nordhausen
Eisleben
Halle
Merseburg
Weißenfels
LEIPZIG
Mühlhausen
Naumburg
Erfurt
Weimar
Zeitz
Gotha
Jena
Altenburg
Eisenach
Arnstadt
Gera
Werra
Saale
Zwickau
THÜRINGEN
Meiningen
Suhl
Saalfeld
Greiz
Rhön
Thüringer Wald
Plauen
Eisfeld
Bad Neustadt
Hof
Bad Kissingen
Coburg
Kronach
Main
Münchberg
Františkovy Lázně
Schweinfurt
Cheb
Marktredwitz
Bamberg
Bayreuth
Würzburg
Weiden
Erlangen

Thüringen

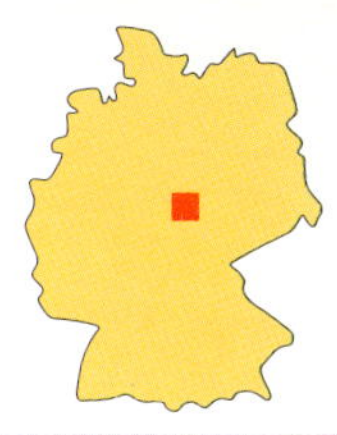

To discover Thuringia's historic towns, follow its ancient East-West highway. First comes Eisenach, overlooked by Wartburg Castle where Luther translated the Bible into German. Next is the regional capital, Erfurt, with the marvellous architecture of its cathedral hill. Finally, the famous statues of Goethe and Schiller keep watch over classical Weimar, where some of the finest chapters in Germany's cultural history were written. The little ducal city is forever associated with the country's first democracy, the short-lived Weimar Republic, as well as with Bauhaus design, but, tragically, it was just outside the town that the Nazis established Buchenwald, one of their most notorious concentration camps. Beyond the cities, you'll find the superb, invigorating countryside of the Thuringian Forest, with its legendary long-distance trail, the Rennsteig, running for over 160 km along its upland crest, and also Oberhof, Germany's most popular winter sports centre north of the Alps. You could hardly leave without tasting Thuringia's great speciality, the deliciously moreish Thüringer Rostbratwurst, a sausage exported worldwide, but of course best enjoyed right here!

1 VILLA ANNA

Susanne Assmann

Fritz-Koch-Str. 12
99817 Eisenach
Tel. (03691) 2 39 50
Fax (03691) 239530
info@hotel-villa-anna.de – www.hotel-villa-anna.de

Closed Christmas • 15 rooms, including 13 non-smoking, 2 with balcony • Dogs allowed • Town tours

72/90 €, Breakfast included (WE: 72 €)

AE VISA MC

The atrium and its little pool

This peacefully located late-19th villa on its sloping site offers comfortable, contemporary accommodation. The spacious bedrooms are furnished and decorated with sure taste, and their stylish bathrooms are spotlessly white. The breakfast room is bright and welcoming, and in fine weather you can breakfast outside. You would hardly know that this was a hotel; the private atmosphere and the comfortable setting are calculated to make you forget that your stay here is only a temporary one.

Sights nearby: Wartburg Castle, Predigerkirche

Access: Follow green hotel-route signs in Eisenach

2 LANDHAUS HOTEL ROMANTIK

Roland Gewalter

Salzgitterstr. 76
99867 Gotha
Tel. (03621) 3 64 90
Fax (03621) 364949 – www.landhaus-hotel-romantik.de

Open all year • 14 rooms, including 5 non-smoking, 1 with balcony and 2 with terrace • Restaurant (eve only; closed Sun): main course 7.50-14.50€ • Garden, parking; dogs by arrangement

77/82 €, Breakfast included (WE: 72/77 €)
AE VISA MC

The "Romantik Suite" with its four-poster bed and big balcony

This family-run establishment is to be found on the eastern edge of the little capital city of the old Duchy of Saxony-Gotha. The charming timber-framed building, partly clad in hung slates, offers lavishly decorated and furnished country-style rooms, much of the decor featuring pretty floral patterns. Brick walls, an open fireplace and exposed timbers help create a welcoming, rustic atmosphere in the restaurant. On fine days you will appreciate the courtyard terrace and the garden with its pool and delightful little bridge.

Sights nearby: Schloss Friedenstein; Marienglas caves (17km southwest)

Access: Towards Erfurt on B 7

3 VESTE WACHSENBURG

Ruth und Georg Wagner

Veste Wachsenburg 91
99310 Holzhausen
Tel. (03628) 7 42 40
Fax (03628) 742461
wachsenburg wagner@t-online.de – www.wachsenburg.com

Open all year • 9 rooms, including 1 non-smoking • Restaurant with terrace (closed Sun eve, Mon from1 Nov to 31 Mar): set lunch 19.50-28€, set dinner 19.50-32€ • Garden, parking; dogs allowed • Exhibitions

80/180 €, Breakfast included
VISA MC

A guided tour of the castle and its museum

Its foundation stone laid in the 10th century, Wachsburg Castle commands panoramic views over the Thuringian Forest. Visible from far away, it is reached by a steep road which climbs up to the top of the cone-shaped height on which it stands. Guests stay in the "Palas", the castle's main living quarters, or in what was once the ladies' boudoir, in rooms in various styles, some with furnishings in rustic oak, others with high-gloss or lustre period pieces. Meals are served in the appropriately historic ambience of the vaulted "Dungeon" or in the romantic courtyard.

Sights nearby: Neues Palais in Arnstadt (5km southeast), Erfurt cathedral (24km northeast)

Access: From Exit 43 on A 4 towards Arnstadt via Mühlberg, or 5km northwest of town if coming from Arnstadt

4 PAPIERMÜHLE

Michael Kanz

Erfurter Str. 102
07743 Jena
Tel. (03641) 4 59 80
Fax (03641) 459845 – www.papiermuehle-jena.de

Open all year • 25 rooms, including 1 with balcony • Restaurant with terrace: set meal 6.50-14€ • Garden, parking; dogs allowed • Brewery tours

67,50/75 €, Breakfast included

AE VISA MC

The venerable linden-tree in the beer garden

Beer was being brewed in the Leutrabach valley as early as 1737, a fact which was taken into account when this establishment was being restored in 1996, so that once again you can enjoy a variety of bottom-fermented, unfiltered beers brewed on the premises. The establishment consists of two brick buildings, the second of which - to the rear - houses a two-storey restaurant with gallery, vats and well-scrubbed tables, full of authentic brewery atmosphere. The bedrooms - in both buildings - are in traditional style with furnishings in dark wood.

Sights nearby: Zeiss planetarium, Göhre town museum

Access: On B 7 towards Erfurt on edge of town

5 ZUM STADTTOR

Hans-Ulrich Förster

Jenaische Str. 24
07768 Kahla
Tel. (036424) 83 80
Fax (036424) 83833 – www.hotel-stadttor.de

Open all year • 13 rooms, including 10 non-smoking • Restaurant with terrace: set meal 11-25€ • Garden, parking; dogs by arrangement • Sauna, bicycle hire, guided walks, wine seminars

65/75 €, Breakfast included

AE VISA

Sitting out in the romantic ambience of the old courtyard

Forming part of the medieval defences of the fascinating little town of Kahla, this timber-framed building of 1468 stands on the site of one of the town gates, remains of which can still be seen in the restaurant and wine cellar.With its exposed stonework and stately timber uprights, the restaurant is full of authentic atmosphere. Some of the individually designed rooms are in rustic style with furnishings in natural wood, while others are more elegant and feature period furnishings.

Sights nearby: Leuchtenburg, Medieval market at Easter and Whitsun, Optics Museum in Jena (17km north)

Access: Exit 53 on A 4; follow green hotel signs in Kahla

6 ERNESTINER HOF

Marion Geis

Ernestinerstr. 9
98617 Meiningen
Tel. (03693) 47 80 53
Fax (03693) 478055 – www.hotel-ernestiner-hof.com

Closed 24-25 Dec • 16 rooms, including 4 with balcony and 4 non-smoking • Cafe (daily 8.30am - 6.30pm) • Garden; dogs allowed

84/94 €, Breakfast included

AE D VISA MC

The bedrooms looking out onto the garden and the "Kavaliershaus"

A small but perfectly formed establishment with an intimate atmosphere. Laid out around a lovely garden are the main buildings with a tasteful traditional cafe and patisserie and the "Kavaliershaus" with its pink gingerbread façade. Breakfast is taken in the welcoming cafe, an enchanting space flooded with light through the glass pyramid in the roofed-in courtyard. The bedrooms are individually designed and feature Italian wood or lacqeured furniture.

Sights nearby: Schloss Elisabethenburg, steam locomotive works

Access: In town centre close to castle

7 ROMANTIK HOTEL SÄCHSISCHER HOF

Peter Henzel

Georgstr. 1
98617 Meiningen
Tel. (03693) 45 70
Fax (03693) 457401 – www.romantikhotels.com/meiningen

Open all year • 40 rooms, including 4 with balcony and 25 non-smoking • Cafe; restaurant with terrace (closed lunchtime and mid to late Jul): main course from 10.50€, set dinner 29.50-39€; half board 18€ • Parking; dogs not allowed • Bicycle hire, cookery courses, cultural events in restaurant

105/195 €, Breakfast included (WE: 110/190 €)

AE, Diners, VISA, MC

Useful help with theatre visits

Built in the early 19th century as a lodging house, then used from 1843 as a post office as well, this establishment is one of the institutions of Thuringia's theatre capital. Crowned heads as well as actors and artists have spent the night here, and you too will appreciate the elegant surroundings. The rooms feature Biedermeier and other period furnishings and their walls are decorated with drawings of theatrical costumes and stage designs.The breakfast room also serves as a cafe, while other meals can be taken in the rustic "Postschenke" with its well-scrubbed tables, or in the stylish wood-panelled "Posthalterei".

Sights nearby: Theatre museum in riding hall, Stadtkirche

Access: On edge of Old Town opposite Englischer Garten

8 SCHIEFERHOF

Lutz Horn

Eisfelder Str. 26
98724 Neuhaus am Rennweg
Tel. (03679) 77 40
Fax (03679) 774100
schieferhof@t-online.de – www.schieferhof.de

Open all year • 38 rooms, including 4 with loggia, 1 with disabled access and 23 non-smoking • Restaurant with terrace: set lunch 23-33.50€, set dinner 23-45€; half board from 13€ • Garden, parking; dogs allowed • Sauna, solarium, cosmetic treatments, massage, bicycle hire, guided walks, climbing tours, creative courses

88/122 €, Breakfast included
AE VISA MC

Water-glass, a speciality of the Thuringian Forest

High in the Thuringian Forest, this establishment attracts active holidaymakers all year round with superb walking along the Rennsteig trail in summer and skiing in winter, both downhill and cross-country. The less energetic can simply relax and enjoy the extensive gardens and magnificent mountain setting of this lovely establishment. Clad in hung slates, the building is impeccably run, with original ideas much in evidence. The comfortable country-style bedrooms feature lovely striped wallpaper and furnishings in native woods. Tasteful colour schemes create a warm and welcoming atmosphere, not least in the attractive restaurant, which is split into several little booths and parlours.

Sights nearby: Morassina visitor mine (6km north), Silbersattel ski arena (11km south)

Access: On B 281 in centre

VILLA ALTENBURG

Haas, Andrea

Straße des Friedens 49
07381 Pössneck
Tel. (03647) 42 20 01
Fax (03647) 422002 – www.villa-altenburg.de

Closed 3-9 Jan • 14 rooms, including 1 with balcony • Restaurant with terrace (eve only Mon-Sat): set lunch (Sun) 15-25€, set dinner 20-30€ • Garden, parking; dogs allowed • Indoor pool, sauna, carriage rides

65/85 €, Breakfast included

VISA MC

The conservatory with its leather couch and an unobstructed view out in summer

In 1928 the local publisher Ludwig Vogel fulfilled his dream of building his own house, and constructed this property high above the town. Based on the famous Krupp villa in Essen (albeit on a smaller scale), the house has seen many changes, but it still retains many original features such as parquet floors, wood panelling and antiques, as well as a period piece of a swimming pool and a lovely park which has lost none of its allure. This is the place to stay if you are looking for something really special.

Sights nearby: Ranis castle (6km south), Franciscan monastery with Saalfeld municipal museum (19km southwest)

Access: From Exit 26 on A 9 towards Saalfeld

10 LANDHOTEL KLOSTERMÜHLE

Christl Kess

Dorfstr. 2
98646 Reurieth-Trostadt
Tel. (036873) 2 46 90
Fax (036873) 246999 – www.landhotel-klostermuehle.de

Open all year • 16 rooms, including 2 non-smoking • Cafe; restaurant with terrace (closed Mon): main course from 14.50€; half board 9€ • Garden, parking; dogs allowed • Exhibitions, organised walks

44/62 €, Breakfast included
Credit cards not accepted

Sitting outside in the charming courtyard

Dating from the 19th century, this lovely, part timber-framed corn-mill in the Werra valley has a completely rebuilt interior. Protected by a preservation order, the external walls and the mill-wheel have been retained, and the overall character of the building has been respected. Inside there are comfortable, contemporary-style rooms, with fine hand-made furnishings in natural wood complemented by a number of antique pieces such as linen chests. Divided into three sections, the restaurant too is a successful blend of old and new, for example in the unusual “Backofenstube” with its old oven, or the “Klosterklause” with its venerable stone walls.

Sights nearby: Vessra monastery with Hennerbergisch museum (5km north), Hildburghausen Old Town (10km southeast)

Access: West of B 89, 1km north of Reurieth

11 ADLER

Herr Heger

Markt 17
07407 Rudolstadt
Tel. (03672) 44 03
Fax (03672) 440444 – www.hotel-adler-rudolstadt.de

Open all year • 40 rooms, including 30 non-smoking • Restaurant with terrace: set meal 6.90-12.60€ • Parking; dogs allowed

80/90 €, Breakfast included (WE: 76/86 €)
VISA MC

Sitting out in front of the hotel and watching the world go by

This venerable hostelry of 1601 stands on the market square in the heart of old Rudolstadt. It's a landmark edifice, with a Baroque portal and scrolled gables topped by double-headed eagles. Inside, accommodation is in elegant, individually furnished and decorated rooms, some with original wood floors, antiques or lovely wrought-iron furniture. Breakfast is taken on the first floor above the restaurant in a beautiful panelled chamber.

Sights nearby: Schloss Heidecksburg, Saalfeld Fairy Grottoes (12 km south)

Access: At junction of B 85 and B 88

12 HAMMERMÜHLE

R. Lennartz

Hammermühlenweg 2
07646 Stadtroda
Tel. (036428) 57 90
Fax (036428) 57990
info@hammermuehle.com – www.hammermuehle.com

Open all year • 28 rooms, including 1 with disabled access and 12 non-smoking • Restaurant with terrace: set lunch 14-33€, set dinner 15-35€; half board 13€ • Garden, parking; dogs allowed • Horse-riding, tennis, bicycle hire, organised walks and longer hikes

80/85 €, Breakfast included
VISA MC

The unusual English clay oven

This lovely, timber-framed mill and farmstead laid out around three sides of a courtyard was first mentioned as long ago as the 15th century. It now provides guests with comfortable country-style accommodation - some of it in the form of maisonettes. There are endless ways of spending your leisure time in the surrounding area, and when you need to recover your strength, the rustic "Scheune" restaurant or the "Mühlenstube" cafe-restaurant and conservatory will supply you with sustenance. Alternatively you can sit outside in the beer garden.

Sights nearby: Leuchtenburg (14 km southwest), Optics museum in Jena (16 km northwest)

Access: Exit 55 on A 4

13 **GOLDENER HIRSCH**
U. Schilling, Frau Höfling

€€ An der Hasel 91-93
98527 Suhl
Tel. (03681) 7 95 90
Fax (03681) 795920 – www.goldener-hirsch-suhl.de

Open all year • 54 rooms, including 27 non-smoking, 2 with disabled access • Restaurant with terrace: main course 7.20-17.90€; half board 16.50€ • Garden, parking; dogs allowed • Tennis, bicycle hire

57/92 €, Breakfast included
VISA MC

The stag's head above the entrance

In the southern part of Suhl not far from the centre, this establishment consists of a historic timber-framed structure of 1616 - the date can be seen over the entrance - and a modern extension in compatible style. The comfortable bedrooms feature country-style furnishings in natural - sometimes coloured - wood. Guests with a romantic turn of mind will be tempted by the room with a four-poster bed. Divided into several sections by timber-framing, the attractively decorated restaurant is a pleasant place to dine.

Sights nearby: Museum of Weaponry, Vehicle museum, Rennsteig garden in Oberhof (15km north)

Access: Exit 20 on A 71; on southern edge of built-up area of Neundorf

14 KAINS HOF

Uta Schroeter

Weißen 19
07407 Uhlstädt-Weißen
Tel. (036742) 6 11 30
Fax (036742) 61011 – www.kains-hof.de

Open all year • 30 rooms, including 4 with balcony and 7 non-smoking • Restaurant with terrace: set dinner 10-15€; half board 10€ • Garden, parking; dogs allowed • Sauna, jacuzzi, massage, bicycle hire, carriage rides, rafting, organised walks

63/78 €, Breakfast included

AE JCB VISA

Rafting on the River Saale

This charming establishment opposite the church in Weissen is a wonderful place to relax. The way to the restaurant and the bedrooms leads through the lovely courtyard full of flowers and plants. The bedrooms themselves feature country-style furnishings in natural wood. On two levels, the rustic restaurant is an inviting and comfortable place, with lots of nice little touches such as "Grandma's canapé" and lace doilies. As soon as the weather permits, the courtyard becomes a beer garden, with the occasional barbecue evening.

Sights nearby: Schloss Heidecksburg in Rudolstadt (8km west), Leuchtenburg castle near Kahla (14km northeast)

Access: 8km east of Rudolstadt by B 88 towards Jena

All of the hotels and inns in this Guide have been chosen for their thoughtful service and charming style, but value for money counts for a lot too. The coin symbol next to an establishment indicates that it offers rooms for no more than €70 per night for two people, not including breakfast.

A really memorable meal can turn a good holiday into a great one. To round off a relaxing day by discovering some of Germany's most enjoyable cuisine, choose one of the hotels and inns from this list, compiled by Michelin's expert inspectors: we found the cuisine particularly good, and hope you will too.

Ready to take on the challenge of a new sport? Feel like a real work-out in the open air? Or maybe its just time to unwind and get in shape. The following establishments will help you let off steam with at least one activity to try: it could be anything from horse-riding, swimming or tennis to a session in the gym or a round of golf. Check the entry for details.

Z

PHOTOGRAPHY

Photographs of the establishments (including cover):

Photography project manager: Alain LEPRINCE
Agence ACSI - A CHACUN SON IMAGE
2, rue Aristide Maillol, 75015 Paris - Tel.: 00 33/(0)1 43 27 90 10
Location photography by: Romain Aix, Lawrence Banahan/ACSI©2004

The following images reproduced by kind permission:
Goldener Löwe: © Goldener Löwe e.K. (interior photograph)
St. Nepomuk: © Hotel St. Nepomuk (interior and exterior photographs)
Parkhotel Wasserburg Anholt: © Parkhotel Wasserburg Anholt (interior and exterior photographs)
Landhaus Berghof: © Mrs. Sonnenschein/Hilbrich & Heseler (interior and exterior photographs)

Regional Introductions:

BADEN-WÜRTTEMBERG : ***Half-timbered houses in Tübingen*** R. Aix, L. Banahan/ACSI

BAVARIA : ***Karlsplatz, Munich*** R. Aix, L. Banahan/ACSI

BERLIN/BRANDENBURG : ***Berlin: the river Spree and the Nikolaiviertel*** R. Aix, L. Banahan/ACSI

HESSEN : ***On the way up to the Niederwald Monument, above Rüdesheim am Rhein*** Rüdesheim am Rhein: Städtisches Verkehrsamt

MECKLENBURG-VORPOMMERN : ***The Old Harbour, Wismar*** W. Ustorp/Wismar, Tourismus Zentrale

NIEDERSACHSEN/BREMEN/HAMBURG : ***The Speicherstadt, Hamburg*** Hamburg Tourismus GmbH

NORDRHEIN-WESTFALEN : ***"Rose Monday" procession in Düsseldorf*** D. Ebels-Klempahn/Düsseldorf Marketing & Tourismus GmbH

RHEINLAND-PFALZ/SAARLAND : ***Bernkastel-Kues and the river Mosel*** R. Aix, L. Banahan/ACSI

SAXONY : ***The Mädlerpassage arcades in the heart of Leipzig*** 2001-2004 DZT/NN

SAXONY-ANHALT : ***Quedlinburg: The Castle Hill and St. Servatius Church*** E. Eichberger/UNESCO-World Heritage in Germany

SCHLESWIG-HOLSTEIN : ***The romantic North Sea island of Sylt*** R. Aix, L. Banahan/ACSI

THÜRINGEN : ***Statue of Goethe und Schiller in front of the German National Theatre in Weimar*** Thüringer Tourismus GmbH

LOWER-PRICED ESTABLISHMENTS : R. Aix, L. Banahan/ACSI

GOURMET ESTABLISHMENTS : R. Aix, L. Banahan/ACSI

ACTIVE BREAKS : Sport und Wellnesshotel Angerhof, St. Englmar

Manufacture Française de pneumatiques Michelin
Société en commandite par actions au capital de 304 000 000 EUR
Place des Carmes-Déchaux, 63 Clermont-Ferrand (France) - R.C.S. Clermont-Fd B 855 200 507
Michelin et Cie, Propriétaires-Editeurs - Dépôt légal Novembre 2004 – ISBN 2-06-710964-2

Printed in France 10-2004/1.1

Typesetting: Maury Malesherbes (France)
Printing and Binding: POLLINA, Luçon - L20134B

Layout: Studio Maogani
4, rue du Fer à Moulin, 75005 Paris – Tél. : (33) 01 47 07 00 06

Published in 2005

YOUR OPINION MATTERS!

To help us constantly improve this guide, please fill in this questionnaire and return to:

Michelin "500 Charming Hotels and Inns in Germany",
Michelin Travel Publications – Marketing Department,
Hannay House 39 Clarendon Road – WATFORD, WD17 1JA – UK

› 1- Have you ever bought other Michelin guides?

Yes ❐ No ❐

If yes, which one(s)?

Red Guide (hotels and restaurants) ❐

Green Guide (tourism) ❐

Other (please specify) ❐

› 2- Did you buy this guide:

For holidays ❐

For short breaks or weekends ❐

For business purposes ❐

As a gift ❐

› 3- Will you be travelling:

In a couple ❐ With family ❐

Alone ❐ With friends ❐

Other ❐

› 4- You are a:

Man ❐ Woman ❐

< 25 years old ❐ 25 – 34 years old ❐

35 – 50 years old ❐ > 50 years old ❐

Profession: ....

› 5-How would you rate the following aspects of the guide?

1 = Very good *2* = Good *3* = Acceptable *4* = Poor *5* = Very poor

	1	*2*	*3*	*4*	*5*
Selection of establishments	❐	❐	❐	❐	❐
Number of establishments	❐	❐	❐	❐	❐
Hotel/Maison d'hôte mix	❐	❐	❐	❐	❐
Prices of rooms	❐	❐	❐	❐	❐
Practical Information (prices, etc.)	❐	❐	❐	❐	❐
Description of the establishment	❐	❐	❐	❐	❐
Photos	❐	❐	❐	❐	❐
General presentation	❐	❐	❐	❐	❐
Distribution of establishments across France	❐	❐	❐	❐	❐
Themed indexes	❐	❐	❐	❐	❐
Cover	❐	❐	❐	❐	❐
Other (please specify)	❐	❐	❐	❐	❐

› 6-Please rate the guide out of 20: / 20

› 7- Which aspects could we improve?

....

> **8**-Was there an establishment you particularly liked or a choice you didn't agree with? Perhaps you have a favourite address of your own that you would like to tell us about? Please send us your remarks and suggestions:

By Gerald Kersh

NOVELS

Jews Without Jehovah
Men Are So Ardent
Night and the City
The Nine Lives of Bill Nelson
They Die with Their Boots Clean
Brain and Ten Fingers
The Dead Look On
Faces in a Dusty Picture
The Weak and the Strong
An Ape, a Dog and a Serpent
Sergeant Nelson of the Guards
The Song of the Flea
The Thousand Deaths of Mr. Small
Prelude to a Certain Midnight
*The Great Wash**
*Fowlers End**
The Implacable Hunter
A Long Cool Day in Hell
The Angel and the Cuckoo
Brock

STORY COLLECTIONS

I Got References
The Horrible Dummy and Other Stories
Clean, Bright and Slightly Oiled
*Neither Man nor Dog: Short Stories**
Sad Road to the Sea
*Clock Without Hands**
The Brighton Monster and Other Stories
The Brazen Bull
Guttersnipe
Men Without Bones
*On an Odd Note**
The Ugly Face of Love and Other Stories
More Than Once Upon a Time
The Hospitality of Miss Tolliver
*Nightshade and Damnations**